City of Rhetoric

City of Rhetoric

Revitalizing the Public Sphere in Metropolitan America

DAVID FLEMING

Cover image: Drawing (aerial view) of North Town Village, Chicago, IL, 2000, by Henry Gould. Reproduced by permission of Holsten Real Estate Development Corporation.

Published by
State University of New York Press, Albany

Printed in the United States of America

For information, contact State University of New York Press, Albany, NY
www.sunypress.edu

Production by Cathleen Collins
Marketing by Anne M. Valentine

Library of Congress Cataloging-in-Publication Data

Fleming, David, 1961–
City of rhetoric : revitalizing the public sphere in metropolitan America / David Fleming.
p. cm.
Includes bibliographical references and index.
ISBN 978-0-7914-7649-9 (hardcover : alk. paper)
ISBN 978-0-7914-7650-5 (pbk. : alk. paper)
1. Urban renewal—Illinois—Chicago. 2. Community development, Urban—Illinois—Chicago. 3. Inner cities—Illinois—Chicago. I. Title.

HT177.C5F54 2009
307.3'4160977311—dc22 2008005523

10 9 8 7 6 5 4 3 2 1

Perhaps the best definition of the city in its higher aspects is to say that it is a place designed to offer the widest facilities for significant conversation.

—Lewis Mumford, *The City in History*

Contents

Illustrations

Tables

Figures

Following page 59

Preface

The book that follows is about the relationship between public discourse and built space in the contemporary United States. It is about how the physical organization of our neighborhoods, cities, and metropolitan areas affects our practices of political expression and debate—the ways we represent our histories to one another, render and negotiate our differences, and determine together our future. It is about how environment influences whom we talk to, what we talk about, and whether or not we value that talking in our hearts and minds. And it is about how those political habits and dispositions, in turn, shape the design of the built world. Using multiple kinds of evidence, I argue that the growing *spatial* stratification of our physical landscape—the decentralization, fragmentation, and polarization of our local geography—is both cause and effect of our increasingly impoverished *political* relations with one another.

This is not, however, a traditional work of social science, meant to test some theory of the world or of human society in it; nor is it an essay in cultural criticism or a brief for a particular ideological program. It is rather a verbal portrait of contemporary civic life in the United States, treating four sites of human habitation within a single metropolitan area—an impoverished African-American central city neighborhood; a well-to-do, mostly white, suburb; a racially and economically mixed "urban village"; and a self-governing, low-income, African-American housing cooperative—as representative scenes of our political relations with one another. It is an attempt to show what the public sphere is really like, from the ground up, for ordinary Americans.

The book is more, though, than a description of some innocent external reality. I try to situate the environments studied here in stories about how they came to be and plans for what they might become. And I try to uncover—behind their facades, under their surfaces—the social meaning that is their simultaneous motivation and result. I attempt, in other words, to crack open the visible world of our local lives and find within it a specifically political rationale. So, where we normally see only bricks and mortar, I look for spaces of dialogue and silence, community and alienation. And where we normally approach such environments as fixed, I treat them here as plastic, made by particular human beings in specific circumstances for concrete purposes and capable therefore of being remade by other human beings in other circumstances for altogether different reasons.

To do this, I bring together three traditions of thought not usually linked: political philosophy, urban design, and rhetorical theory. To my knowledge, this is the first book-length study of modern civic life that connects those three traditions. The linkage is not, however, original to me. For the ancient Greeks, the ways in which a community was governed, the organization of its physical space, and the discursive training it provided its young were matters intricately related and carefully supervised. If what you wanted was a regime in which "the people" (or *demos*) ruled, you needed not only widespread adherence to particular beliefs about equality and freedom—that is, a shared theory of democracy; you also needed a physical setting where you could enact those beliefs, namely, a *polis*; and you needed widely distributed discursive habits—specifically, the routines of verbal argumentation (or *rhetoric*)—in order to reach reasonable decisions together. Democracy for the Greeks, in other words, depended on a close homology among public philosophy, public space, and public discourse.[1]

That world, of course, has passed; and with it, the social, linguistic, and physical relations it both assumed and promoted. But, long after the demise of the polis, people's ideas about politics, their ways of organizing space, and their pedagogies of public discourse remained linked, even when they lacked the language to recognize that linkage or the ability to use it in support of genuine participatory democracy. Take, for example, the period in U.S. history from about 1865 to 1915, when three projects of civic life not usually connected—the professional practice of city planning, the organized reform of municipal government, and the postsecondary teaching of written composition—all emerged at roughly the same time and in basically the same places. Their emergence can be tied to particular historical conditions: the massive urbanization of the United States, as the size and population of the nation's cities swelled from both foreign immigration and internal migration; the heightened diversification of those cities, as residents from different racial, ethnic, religious, economic, and linguistic backgrounds suddenly came into close contact with one another; the rapid industrialization of the period, which saw not only increased capital concentration but also recurring financial panic, labor unrest, and large-scale urban poverty; the ideological conflict produced by the clash of those interests; and the social alienation brought about by the complexity and instability of this new world.[2]

The arts of city planning, municipal governance, and written composition were developed by civic leaders to confront these conditions. Though outwardly distinct, they shared the same technocratic impulse and middle-class professional ethic that were beginning to dominate North American society;[3] and all three sought to use that impulse and apply that ethic to rationalize the new civic order, making it more efficient, transparent, and chaste. They were all three, in their different ways, "professions of improvement,"[4] wedding technical knowledge to moral fervor in the interest of clarifying what was perceived to be an increasingly chaotic society.

And they shared something else as well: an aversion to the city itself—its size, density, and diversity; its fast pace and unchecked growth; its freedom and vitality; its multilingualism and noise; its crime and competition. The three professions manifest this anti-urbanism, of course, in different ways: the new art of city planning, for example, championed physical de-densification and zoning as the ways to bring sunlight, clean air, and reason to the disease and disorder of the modern city. The reform of municipal government, meanwhile, was all about applying nonpartisan problem-solving, technical expertise, and managerial efficiency to practices of political decision-making otherwise dominated by ideological passion, popular participation, and old-world bossism. And the academic discipline of composition-rhetoric was an effort to teach the masses to describe and explain the world, in writing, with clarity, precision, and correctness, as an antidote to the disagreement and excess that characterized public discourse at the time. But however different their tools and methods, and however discrete the realms in which they operated, all three arts rejected characteristically *urban* forms of human contact, based on concentration and variety, and advocated instead scenes of social order and quiet, constituted by sameness rather than difference, organized by separation rather than proximity, and governed by neutral procedures rather than argument, partisanship, and practical reason.

The anti-urbanism they championed was successful in part because it was overdetermined: a function not just of a new public philosophy but also a new way of organizing civic space and a new pedagogy for training the young to speak and write well. But the new order also had an important ally: the fast-growing and increasingly powerful universities of the time, which had begun to privilege research over teaching, graduate and professional training over undergraduate education, disciplinary specialization over common schooling, and individual careerism over the public good. As an institution, the university has perhaps always distanced itself from everyday practical politics,[5] but it was not until the late nineteenth century that North American colleges and universities began to openly turn away from their local communities. The story of Johns Hopkins University and the city of Baltimore during that school's first decade (1876–1886) is instructive here. As Thomas Bender has shown, Johns Hopkins made an explicit attempt at its inception to connect with local, nonacademic intellectuals, reformers, and leaders. But by the early 1880s, under the presidency of Daniel Coit Gilman, scholarship there was moving inexorably in the direction of national disciplines: the Modern Language Association, American

Historical Association, and American Economic Association were all organized during these years by Hopkins professors. The result was a severing of the university's intellectual life from the public culture of its own city.[6]

Of course, antipathy to the city cannot be limited to the Progressive Era, the professional contexts described above, or the modern North American university: as we will see, there is a long streak of anti-urbanism running through the history of the United States. Still, the years discussed above inaugurated a period that turned out to be especially bad for the nation's cities. If industrialization, immigration, and war continued to fuel city life during the first half of the twentieth century, those forces were countered by an aggressive and growing secessionist impulse, as the richest and whitest inhabitants fled the nation's urban centers, leaving them depopulated, devalued, and demoralized. The seceders were not, however, decamping for some agrarian utopia far away; they were settling just outside the city centers but within their regional orbit, where they remained firmly integrated within the various socioeconomic interdependencies of modern urban life. What was happening, in other words, was that American civic space was becoming increasingly *metropolitan* and, in the process, increasingly stratified by race, class, ethnicity, age, and family status.

The result? the unavailability in this country of an everyday politics based on pluralism *and* propinquity, in which individuals different from one another can come together, regularly, through discussion, debate, and negotiation, to supervise what they share. Why? Because, in a world without cities—populous, dense, diverse, open, centered—the exercise of politics turns out to be difficult to stage, even to comprehend. To revive such an activity, we would need first to revive our cities, to design, build, and sustain places where ordinary people can come into daily contact with diverse, free others and learn to collaboratively manage the world they hold in common. But to design and sustain such places, we need the habits and dispositions of politics, of dealing nonviolently with conflict, of managing social differences without either separation or assimilation. The revitalization of civic life is thus a unified project requiring simultaneous changes to the physical world we inhabit, the political practices we use to manage that world, and the pedagogies we employ to acquire those practices.

After all, if we continue to design our landscape so that we need not have contact with people who are different from us, we should not be surprised when the political life that results is impoverished. By the same token, to treat politics as a disembodied procedure, and political education as a matter of providing students with portable skills of personal expression, is to ignore the obligations we have toward the world and the people we share it with.

Both of these trends—thinking of space as apolitical and of politics as ageographical—have been mistakes. I hope the book that follows will help us see those mistakes for what they are and begin to correct them.

ONE

Introduction

Death Corner

Make no little plans.

—Daniel H. Burnham[1]

In June, 1996, when Chicago Mayor Richard M. Daley announced the $1 billion Near North Redevelopment Initiative, the neighborhood he targeted for help—the northwest corner of the city's Near North Side—was one of the most troubled in the city.[2] Just across the river from the downtown Loop, a few blocks west of North Michigan Avenue, and a stone's throw south of Lincoln Park, it was tantalizingly close to the booming Chicago of the 1990s. But proximity to wealth and power had not helped this place much. Dominated by a "notorious" public housing complex called Cabrini Green, it was home to several thousand very poor, mostly female-headed, African-American families, who struggled there amid not only extreme poverty and racial isolation but also near universal unemployment, acute school failure, rampant drug and alcohol abuse, violent crime, and physical blight. Indeed, for most Chicagoans, inured to their city's cold social logic, these families had *caused* the neighborhood's problems; and their removal, clearly foreseen by the mayor's plan, was the first step in its transformation.

In fact, the neighborhood had been troubled long before there was a housing project here. From the start of nonnative settlement in the region, the western half of the north bank of the Chicago River was associated with industrial and other low-rent uses.[3] By the middle of the nineteenth century, it had become the city's main port of entry for European immigrants, its cheap wooden houses and proximity to blue-collar work attracting successive waves of Irish and German workingmen. In time, the Germans prospered and moved farther north; but many of the Irish stayed, putting up brick structures on their lots and moving the old wooden-frame houses to the back to be rented to even poorer immigrants, including, in the 1870s and '80s, large numbers of Swedes.[4] Later, Italians would settle here; and, by 1915, a veritable "Little Sicily" had sprung up along West Division Street.

The eastern half of the north bank, meanwhile, had become the most fashionable address in Chicago. After Potter and Bertha Palmer, the city's real estate king and society queen, moved here in 1882, the center of Chicago wealth gradually shifted from Prairie Avenue on the Near South Side to this northeastern corner of the Near North Side. Soon, the neighborhood had so many mansions it was called the "Gold Coast"; and, by the 1920s, Lake Shore Drive was home to more wealth than any other street in the world, save Fifth Avenue.[5]

Thus it was that in the early decades of the twentieth century the richest and poorest neighborhoods in Chicago were literally within hailing distance of each other. In his 1929 book *The Gold Coast and the Slum*, University of Chicago sociologist Harvey Zorbaugh described the district as a place of extremes: "The Near North Side is an area of high light and shadow, of vivid contrasts—contrasts not only between the old and the new, between the native and the foreign, but between wealth and poverty, vice and respectability, the conventional and the bohemian, luxury and toil" (4). It was a contrast he found unhealthy: "The isolation of the populations crowded together within these few hundred blocks, the superficiality and externality of their contacts, the social distances that separate them . . . the inevitable result is cultural disorganization" (16).

Zorbaugh's "slum"—encompassing the lodging houses along Clark and Wells Streets and south of Chicago Avenue as well as the vast neighborhood of tenement houses stretching from Wells to the North Branch of the Chicago River—had the highest concentration of poverty in the city (5). It was also extremely cosmopolitan, with a half dozen "foreign" colonies existing side by side and "more grades of people" living together than anywhere else in the city (11–12, 140ff). The section from Sedgwick Street west to the river and from Chicago Avenue north to Division, for example, was dominated by Italians and centered on the St. Philip Benizi church at Oak and Cambridge Streets (159ff).[6] Nearby was Jenner School ("our school," the Italians called it), and along West Division Street were Italian grocery stores, markets, cobblers, and macaroni factories. From 1900 to 1916, writes Zorbaugh, the neighborhood was virtually untouched by American customs: it recorded little or no political participation and was controlled largely by the families who lived there (175). What it was best known for, however, was crime: the corner of Oak and Cambridge Streets was the scene of so much violence it was called "Death Corner" (171).[7] Especially worrisome were the high rates of juvenile delinquency here; every boy in Little Sicily, Zorbaugh wrote, was a member of a gang (177).[8]

The other principal subdivision of the Near North slum was the "Negro" section (147ff). African-Americans began trickling up to the "Lower North" from the city's South Side during and right after World War I, when the "Great Migration" of southern blacks put extreme pressure on the city's black belt. The newcomers settled first along Wells and Franklin Streets but then began pushing westward into Little Sicily. More blacks would settle here in the 1920s; by the end of that decade, they would account for a fifth of the neighborhood's population.[9]

Italian parents complained about the presence of black children in neighborhood schools and playgrounds; and some white property owners, Zorbaugh reports, tried to prevent blacks from acquiring property in the area (148).[10] But, on the whole, the coming of blacks to the Italian Near North Side was relatively peaceful: perhaps because the number of blacks was not at first very large or because the two groups were equally destitute or because Italians got along better with blacks than other immigrant groups did.[11] However it transpired, by 1929, a black population of several thousand had settled on the Near North Side, bringing with them their barber shops, pool halls, corner markets, and storefront churches (149).

In the following years, there were few changes in "North Town": neither the population nor the racial composition of the neighborhood underwent any significant alteration, staying around 80 percent white and 20 percent black. But because there was so little construction here during these years—only 221 new housing units were built in the entire city in 1932[12]—the already intolerable housing conditions in the area deteriorated further. In 1939, the *WPA Guide to Illinois* described a neighborhood of "desolate tenements and shacks" inhabited by "Italians and Negroes."[13] And a government study from the time found that, of 683 housing units surveyed here, 50 percent were wooden-framed, most had been built soon after the 1871 fire, 443 had no bath tub, 480 had no hot water, and 550 were heated only by stoves. Forty-three toilets were shared by two families each; for the rest, there were twenty-nine yard toilets and ten under the sidewalks.[14]

The Rise of Cabrini Green

It was here, in 1941, on sixteen acres of cleared slum-land in the heart of Little Sicily, that the Chicago Housing Authority (CHA) began construction of the Frances Cabrini Homes, a federally funded housing project comprised of fofty-five two- and three-story red-brick row houses with 586 units of subsidized housing.[15] The project was named for St. Frances Xavier Cabrini (1850–1917), the first U.S. citizen to be canonized by the Roman Catholic Church and a beloved figure in Little Sicily.[16] When the Cabrini Homes opened in 1942, the

CHA was only five years old, having been created soon after the passage of the 1937 U.S. Housing Act, which provided federal funds to state-chartered municipal corporations for job creation, slum clearance, and housing construction for the poor. An earlier federal program, administered by the Housing Division of the Public Works Administration, had built four housing projects in Chicago in the mid- to late 1930s: three in white neighborhoods and one in the black belt.[17]

The Cabrini row houses were laid out barracks style, the average unit containing four bedrooms and renting for about $30 per month. During construction, which coincided with the entrance of the United States into World War II, the projected tenancy of the Homes was changed from low-income families to war workers and their families.[18] When the war ended, it was changed again, this time to war veterans and their families. In these years, the complex had a racial make-up of 80 percent white and 20 percent black, in keeping with the Neighborhood Composition Rule, which forbade federally funded housing projects from altering the racial character of the neighborhoods where they were placed.[19] According to one resident who lived in the Homes at this time, and was later interviewed by David Whitaker, the proportions were strictly adhered to:

> Now, in order to move into the row houses—it was like, white, black, white, black in every other apartment—and a black individual could not move into the row houses unless a black moved out, or if you were white, a white would have to move out. That's how it worked, but there wasn't no black and white issues at that particular time. We would visit one another, drink coffee together, we had Bible classes together . . . You felt comfortable.[20]

The 80:20 ratio, however, was short-lived. That is because in the years during and right after World War II, the neighborhood around the Cabrini Homes experienced yet another dramatic social transformation. During the 1940s, as part of the *second* "Great Migration" of southern rural blacks to northern cities (again motivated largely by wartime industrial expansion), the black population of the Near North Side tripled, from just over 5,000 to almost 18,000.[21] By the end of the decade, blacks comprised nearly 80 percent of Zorbaugh's old Italian slum.[22]

Despite these changes, from the mid-1940s well into the 1950s, the Lower North was a relatively peaceful place, with a diverse population and thriving small businesses that catered to whites and blacks alike. Here are some residents' memories of that time:

> Down on Hudson Street there was apartment buildings and tenement houses, this was before they tore them down to build the

> high-rises, and they went clean down to Division. There was stores over on Larrabee, like Pioneer Meat Market and Big Frank's and Del Farms, and they had restaurants and everything.[23]

> Oh, I remember Del Farms, and on down Larrabee you had Pioneers and then I think it was Kroger's. We had the A&P up on Clybourn, Greenman's store was at Franklin and Oak, Harry's drug store was on Oak and Larrabee and then the cleaners was right next door to that, and everybody knew everybody in this community.[24]

There were also feasts and parades sponsored by the local Catholic parish, lovingly remembered to this day by some older residents of the row houses.[25]

The number of blacks arriving on the Near North Side, however, kept increasing; and, in the early to mid-1950s, with plentiful new housing now available for whites in the suburbs outside of Chicago, the Italians began leaving in large numbers. Their departure did not, however, ease crowding on the Near North Side because there was so little new construction there, many families doubling and tripling up in tiny apartments.[26] Faced with this situation, the CHA in the late 1950s built the Cabrini Homes Extension: 1,925 units of public housing in fifteen seven-, ten- and nineteen-story red-brick high-rise buildings (the "Reds") on thirty-five acres of land right across the street from the Cabrini row houses. At the time, it was the largest public housing project ever constructed in Chicago.[27] And though these buildings did not age as well as the row houses, they were initially a step up for most of the families in the area.[28]

By 1962, the neighborhood was virtually all black. That year, the CHA opened the William Green Homes: eight fifteen- and sixteen-story exposed-concrete high-rise buildings (the "Whites") comprising 1,096 housing units on nineteen acres across Division Street from the Cabrini Extension and named for a former president of the American Federation of Labor.[29] By now, as shown in table 1.1, the three projects of "Cabrini Green," two of them built under the watchful eyes of Mayor Richard J. Daley, contained more than 3,600 low-income housing units in seventy-eight buildings spread across seventy acres.[30] By the mid-1960s, according to official statistics, 15,000 people lived here, though the actual population was probably well over 20,000.[31]

The die was cast. If the neighborhood had always been, in Zorbaugh's term, a "slum," it earlier possessed redeeming features along with its troubles: racial and ethnic diversity; convenient access to plentiful low-skill jobs; numerous churches, social clubs, and cultural institutions; and a thriving small business community. Although the vast majority of residents were poor, most families (white and black) had at least one person employed outside the home, and there were many lower middle-class families who stayed even when their fortunes rose, wanting to remain close to friends, church, public transportation,

Table 1.1. The Projects of Cabrini Green

Development	*Year Built*	*Acres*	*Units*	*Building Type*	*Cost*
Frances Cabrini Homes	1942	16	586	2–3 story row houses (55 total)	$3.7 million
Cabrini Homes Extension	1958	35	1,925	7- and 10-story mid-rises (12), 19-story high-rises (3) (15 total)	$26 million
William Green Homes	1962	19	1,096	15- and 16-story rises (8 total)	$30 million
Totals	1942–1962	70 acres	3,607 units	78 buildings	$59.7 million

Sources: Devereaux Bowly, Jr., *The Poorhouse: Subsidized Housing in Chicago, 1895–1976* (Carbondale: Southern Illinois University Press, 1978); Chicago Housing Authority, "Cabrini-Green Homes," http://www.thecha.org/housingdev/cabrini_green_homes.html.

and the cultural vibrancy of a large city. By the early 1960s, however, the CHA had become the primary landlord in the area; and poor blacks, the majority of inhabitants. Everyone else fled. Even the St. Philip Benizi church, its parish long since relocated, was torn down in 1965.[32] It was about this time that the urban black family itself began to deteriorate, casualty of a dramatic rise in joblessness, a large increase in welfare dependence, and a sharp decline in two-parent households.[33]

By most accounts, however, the crowning blow for the neighborhood was the rioting that followed the assassination of Martin Luther King Jr. on April 4, 1968.[34] After that, many of the small businesses that had stuck around, some still owned by Italian-Americans, finally left. Whitaker's interviewees are poignant about the impact of the riots on the neighborhood:

> [I]t was real nice until those riots. That's when all them businesses got burnt up. Really and truly, I think the Italians were ready to move out of here anyway, because it was becoming predominantly black, and they were ready to move. But a lot of those businesses up and down Larrabee didn't go 'til then.[35]

> Del Farms grocery store was wrecked and at that time we didn't have a car, so that meant we had to get the bus—we had five children—and we had to get the bus, go up on North Avenue to the grocery store and come back with food on the bus. And the neighborhood looked, it just, it really made you want to cry. . . . [I]t

> gave you a scary feeling. . . . It was like we lost hope. . . . Those stores never came back.[36]

> That's when it got real bad, when they killed Martin Luther King. . . . [T]hey come all down here tearin' up and we had a lot of stores on Oak Street, and they tore all that up, burnt it up and I think they hurt some peoples too, but I stayed inside 'cause I got scared. It started to change right behind that. . . . After that, they never did build it back up.[37]

For the next quarter century, the story of the northwestern corner of the Near North Side was one of almost continual woe.[38]

In the 1970s, the CHA essentially abandoned Cabrini Green and its other projects. A major restructuring of the American economy shifted the nation's focus from manufacturing to services, a change especially harmful to the cities of the northeastern and north central regions. The urban renewal projects of the 1950s and '60s, meanwhile, merely created middle- and high-income buffers *around* places like Chicago's Lower North, shoring up the borders between it and the prospering neighborhoods nearby but doing little to improve conditions inside.[39] Cabrini Green was now largely hidden from the rest of the world and only noticed when the violence there became too horrendous to overlook.

Things got even worse in the 1980s when many of the working- and middle-class blacks who had remained in the central city finally gave up and left, moving into the inner-ring neighborhoods that working-class whites had abandoned (see table 1.2).[40] Vacancy rates at Cabrini Green climbed as high as one-third, making the project less crowded but ultimately more dangerous. Drug and gang problems worsened: in a nine-week period in early 1981, ten residents were murdered, thirty-five were wounded by gunshots, and fifty firearms were seized.[41] That year, Mayor Jane Byrne and her husband moved in for three weeks to dramatize the neighborhood's plight. But the ploy accomplished little: in one half-vacant Cabrini Green building during one month in 1988, there were two murders, six rapes, nine assaults, fifteen robberies, and thirty-one shootings.[42]

By the end of the 1980s, according to long-time observer Edward Marciniak, the neighborhood did not have a single supermarket, department store, movie house, bank, or drug store. What it did have were currency exchanges, vacant lots, and taverns.[43] In the early 1990s, the U.S. Department of Housing and Urban Development (HUD) was referring to Cabrini Green as "severely distressed," a place characterized by extreme poverty, high unemployment, school failure, violent crime, and physical blight.[44] The shooting death, in October 1992, of seven-year-old resident Dantrell Davis, walking to school with his mother, seemed to confirm the label.

Table 1.2. Population of Chicago's Near North Side, 1930–2000

Year	*Total Pop.*	*# Blacks*	*% Blacks*	*% Change*
1930	79,554	4,231	5.3	
1940	76,954	5,158	6.7	+21.9
1950	89,196	17,813	20.0	+245.3
1960	75,509	23,114	30.6	+29.8
1970	70,406	26,090	37.1	+12.9
1980	67,167	22,031	32.8	–15.6
1990	62,842	14,454	23.0	–34.4
2000	72,811	14,023	19.3	–3.0

Sources: Louis Wirth and Margaret Furez, eds., *Local Community Fact Book* (Chicago: Chicago Recreation Commission, 1938); Louis Wirth and Eleanor H. Bernert, eds., *Local Community Fact Book of Chicago* (Chicago: University of Chicago Press, 1949); Philip M. Hauser and Evelyn M. Kitagawa, eds., *Local Community Fact Book for Chicago, 1950* (Chicago: University of Chicago Press, 1953); Evelyn M. Kitagawa and Karl E. Taeuber, eds., *Local Community Fact Book: Chicago Metropolitan Area, 1960* (Chicago: University of Chicago Press, 1963); Chicago Fact Book Consortium, *Local Community Fact Book: Chicago Metropolitan Area: Based on the 1970 and 1980 Censuses* (Chicago: Chicago Review Press, 1984); Chicago Fact Book Consortium, *Local Community Fact Book: Chicago Metropolitan Area, 1990* (Chicago: University of Illinois at Chicago Press, 1995); the Northeastern Illinois Planning Commission, "Census 2000 General Profiles for the 77 Chicago Community Areas," http://www.nipc.org/test/Y2K_SF1_CCA.htm.

Compassionate Gentrification?

It was about this time that something unexpected happened here. The neighborhood began to attract positive attention from outsiders—local and national media, politicians, government bureaucrats, social activists, real estate developers, lawyers, architects, urban designers, and sociologists. In 1993, the CHA announced plans for a $300 million makeover of Cabrini Green, including outright demolition of three buildings and the construction of several hundred new, low-rise, mixed-income housing units in the area—the first such plan for a Chicago public housing project. At the same time, the *Chicago Tribune* announced an international competition to redesign Cabrini Green; more than 300 entries from ten countries were sent in. Meanwhile, real estate developers began buying up land around the project, and prospective homeowners and tenants made inquiries about the area. And, as the first two Cabrini Green buildings were demolished in mid-1995, the residents themselves began organizing proposals for change. Lawyers, social activists, researchers, and others, not only in Chicago but around the country, began paying attention to what was happening in the neighborhood.

Then, in June 1996, Mayor Daley proposed his own transformation, the Near North Redevelopment Initiative (NNRI), which called for tearing down eight high-rises at Cabrini Green, building more than 2,300 new units of mixed-income housing in a 330-acre area around the project, and investing heavily in commercial and public facilities there, including a new shopping center, police station, library, three new schools, and upgraded parks. It was a stunningly ambitious, and expensive, plan.

The biggest project of all, however, was announced in 1999: the Chicago Housing Authority, just months after emerging from four years under federal control, proposed a $1.6 billion "Plan for Transformation" of all public housing in the city, the centerpiece of which was the demolition of every high-rise building in the CHA's stock of family developments, including all twenty-three high rises at Cabrini Green. Some of the units in those buildings, the CHA foresaw, would be replaced with new units in on-site, mixed-income, townhouse communities. Displaced residents who could not get one of those would receive vouchers for use on the private housing market. Cabrini Green was touted as a showcase for the new approach.

There are several potential explanations for this sudden interest in what had been, for years, just another poor black Chicago neighborhood. It is possible that the plight of Cabrini Green had become so bad by the early 1990s that outsiders finally stepped in, out of genuine concern, to help. In support of this theory, many point to the Dantrell Davis shooting as a turning point in the project's history. And it is true that the incident galvanized residents and outsiders as nothing had before.[45] But other observers point to less altruistic reasons for the sudden interest in Cabrini Green at the end of the twentieth century. The 1980s witnessed a massive retreat from the New Deal/Great Society social contract between rich and poor in this country; and, even with a Democrat in the White House, the 1990s saw a continuation of that trend, with more funding cuts from antipoverty initiatives, more government programs privatized, and the public adopting an increasingly stingy attitude toward the poor.[46] By the late 1990s, proposing wholesale demolition, voucherization, and privatization, the federal government seemed to be trying to get out of the public housing business altogether, just as it was shedding its half-century commitment to the welfare program. The country seemed to have entered a "post-entitlement" era in terms of its social consciousness.[47]

Meanwhile, as Cabrini Green was becoming more and more troubled, and the government less and less interested in managing it, the land *under* the project was actually rising in value. By the early 1990s, downtown Chicago had completed its transformation from being the center of an industrial juggernaut to being the hub of a regional service economy, and young white professionals began flocking downtown in search of near-in residences. Their gentrification of the central city, especially the Near North, Near West, and Near South Sides, was encouraged by the city's business and political elite. What the residents of Cabrini Green had long feared seemed to be coming true: they were about to become the victims of a huge land grab.[48]

But regardless of where the interest came from—genuine concern for the city's poor, the retreat of the federal government from its 1949 commitment to provide "a decent home and a suitable living environment for every American family,"[49] the desire of real estate developers, city bureaucrats, and young white professionals to get their hands on valuable central city land—something dramatic was happening at Cabrini Green during the last years of the twentieth century. The neighborhood suddenly seemed almost plastic, as if it could be remade, overnight, in whatever shape was wanted. But what shape *was* wanted? what would the new neighborhood look like? who would live there? what kinds of lives would they lead? how would they relate to one another? and what would happen to those who no longer fit in?

Three Proposals

When I first began visiting Cabrini Green in the spring of 1999, very different answers were being offered to those questions. On one side were real estate developers and city bureaucrats beating a constant drum roll for demolition and redevelopment. On the other side were several thousand poor, black, mostly female-headed families living in the project and fighting to save their community. This was still, after all, their home, a place they had lived and struggled in for several generations. Now, the assistance programs they had relied on were being cut, there was an affordable housing shortage in the city, and the new economy continued to be inaccessible to them. What would happen to these families and the community they had, against all odds, built? The only receptive ears they found were in the federal courts, which in 1996 temporarily halted demolition at Cabrini Green on the grounds that the NNRI would have a disproportionately negative impact on the area's African-American women and children. But when a landmark 1998 consent decree giving project residents a 51 percent stake in the redevelopment of CHA land was voided, the future of the neighborhood was once again clouded in uncertainty.[50]

As 2000 came and went, three proposals were garnering the most attention. One was focused on the public housing families themselves; its goal was to correct a century of residential racial segregation in Chicago by "dispersing" poor inner city blacks into the wider six-county metropolitan area and seeing to it that they would never again be concentrated and isolated, with government support, in urban ghettos. The most progressive version of this proposal used "mobility assistance" to relocate public housing residents from projects like Cabrini Green to the white suburbs of Chicago, especially the job-rich communities of DuPage and northwestern Cook Counties. From the late 1970s to the late 1990s, over 7,000 black families from Chicago's inner city housing projects, including Cabrini Green, used federally funded vouchers, along with assistance from a court-ordered residential integration program, to move to the suburbs, where, researchers claim, they found a "geography of opportunity."

Another proposal was driven less by racial concerns than economic ones and was more concerned with revitalizing the inner city than abandoning it. It allowed some Cabrini Green residents to stay in the neighborhood but brought in large numbers of higher-income residents to live there as well. It called for the redevelopment of Cabrini Green as a low-rise, mixed-income townhouse community on the now-fashionable "New Urbanist" model. In most versions of this approach, about 30 percent of units are reserved for public housing families; the rest are sold or rented at market rate to moderate- and high-income customers, who (it is claimed) will serve as positive role models for the poor who remain and help revitalize the area with their disposable income. The local showcase for this approach is North Town Village, a $70 million development built on seven acres of city-owned land next to Cabrini Green. The Village currently has 281 units of for-sale and rental townhouses, apartments, and condominiums, 30 percent for former public housing residents, 20 percent for the "working poor," and 50 percent for market-rate customers.

A third proposal was as different from the first two as they were from each other. It supported the empowerment of the poor African-American female-headed families living at Cabrini Green, requiring neither their relocation to white suburbs nor the immigration of higher-income residents to the inner city. Instead, it sought to protect and grow the community already in the area. The most compelling version of this proposal was the effort undertaken by one tenant group at the project to convert its building to a resident-owned and -managed housing cooperative. Beginning in 1992, a federally recognized resident management corporation (RMC) took over the fifteen-story, 126-unit building; and, in 2000, this RMC, made up almost entirely of middle-aged African-American women—single mothers and grandmothers—proposed converting the building into a democratically governed, not-for-profit housing co-op, one of the first such proposals in the history of U.S. public housing.

These are three radically different visions of the future of Cabrini Green and its people. They are different in the physical worlds they imagine: in one, single family homes in low-density, automobile-dependent suburbs; in another, a compact, pedestrian-friendly townhouse community; in the third, a densely populated urban high-rise. They are different in the demographic and economic characteristics they assume: in one, a job-rich, mostly white, upper- and middle-class world with a sprinkling of low-income minorities; in another, a lively "urban village" interspersing high-, middle-, and low-income residents, both black and white; in the last, an all-black, working-class housing cooperative. And they are different in the images of civic life they portray: in one, a highly decentralized and fragmented social scene devoted to the private pursuit of wealth and happiness; in another, a diverse but tight-knit community built on close contact, mutual trust, and shared aspirations; in the third, a self-governed collective committed to the social, political, and economic empowerment of its members. They present the current inhabitants of Cabrini Green, in other words, with dramatically different snapshots of the world to come—for themselves, their children, and their children's children.

For these families, the stakes could not be higher. But what happens in this corner of Chicago is of significance, I believe, to us all. The effort to revitalize the neighborhood in and around Cabrini Green may well be the most ambitious remaking of the American metropolitan landscape in half a century. Perhaps nowhere and at no time in our country's history have so many complex and disparate forces—material and ideological, physical and cultural, social and economic, legal and political—collided in such a small space. Perhaps nowhere and at no time have so many different ideas about the good society come into conflict in such concrete and consequential ways. The stories surrounding this neighborhood—its troubled past, its unsettled present, its hesitant future—tell us much about the North American city at the beginning of the twenty-first century: about what has happened to our built world over the last fifty years and how we might build together a new world in the years to come, about the kinds of relations—physical, social, political, economic, cultural—we can imagine and facilitate among ourselves, a people so different from one another and yet so manifestly interdependent.

The Plan of the Book

The book that follows looks at this corner of the North American landscape through a specifically *rhetorical* lens, that is, as first and foremost a scene of social discourse. Now, rhetoric has always firmly embedded language use in social space—especially the space of politics. For the ancient Greeks who first conceptualized it, rhetoric was precisely the skill of inventing and delivering arguments in contexts of public debate and disagreement. In order to manage together their common world, citizens met in assemblies, courtrooms, council chambers, theaters, and other places to hear opposed speeches and pass judgment on the questions put to them. In this way, they governed themselves.[51]

Language so seen was a distinctly *political* way of being; it was not primarily for the Greeks, as it is for us, a way to express their thoughts and feelings; or a means of information exchange; or a form of domination and control. It was rather a social practice of simultaneous separation and connection: it was how equals constituted their union without denying their differences, how they came together and, at the same time, marked their opposition, how they disagreed with one another while maintaining their association. It was how people who lived together managed their conflicts without relinquishing either their freedom or their proximity.

But for language to be this kind of practice, it needed a particular kind of setting: namely, an accessible, diverse, self-governing community, free from both external control (so that members could direct their collective future without interference) and internal domination (so that each member had an equal *say* in that future). It needed a community unified enough that its problems were genuinely shared but diverse enough that the solution to those problems required an airing of disagreement. It needed a community that literally set aside time and space for the public rendering and negotiation of conflicts. It needed, that is, a *polis*—geographically bounded, self-sufficient, and free—the kind of community that Aristotle called *specifically* human, defining "man" as in essence the "political" or city-living animal.[52]

But if language needed the polis, the polis needed language as well. Speaking and writing were how citizens in such a society constituted themselves *as* a community, setting themselves off as a people with a shared history, gods, watering holes, and so on, and protected their freedom by *claiming* that freedom in concrete, everyday social action. Language was how such people participated in their group's decision-making, defending themselves and attacking others, proposing some courses of action and criticizing others, agreeing and disagreeing with one another, asserting their share in governance by enacting that share in public discourse.[53]

With the demise of the polis, however, citizens had fewer opportunities to participate directly in the governance of their own world, and politics became increasingly divorced from the commonplace and everyday. At some point, cities not only lost their power vis-à-vis empires, nations, and states, they essentially dropped out of history itself.[54] Today, "civic" activity in the West takes place largely against the backdrop of extensive representative democracies or virtual societies, defined less by shared space than by shared laws and interests. Two-sided argumentation by ordinary citizens, meanwhile, has lost its centrality; and rhetoricians have come to think of discourse less as an embodied social practice, situated in particular communities, than as a portable skill, comprised of such things as grammar rules, empty text structures, and a vague metadiscourse about clarity and coherence that can supposedly be taught and used independently of both content and context.[55]

As for our cities, it's hard to think of them as places where diverse individuals, free and equal, come together to make binding decisions about their common affairs. Our landscape not only separates us from one another and the world we share; it alienates us from our species-character as human beings.

We are the products of an insistent "privatism," a way of life focused on the individual, his or her family, and their private search for personal happiness.[56] And, therefore, when faced with seemingly intractable social conflicts, the most resourceful among us simply retreat to communities of the like-minded. By dividing up the landscape this way, we have made local politics irrelevant because difference no longer confronts us. What's worse, our children are growing up in communities whose very organization leads them to think of politics as something that occurs, if at all, elsewhere. As far as they can see, people who disagree with one another inhabit different parts of the landscape; as long as everybody stays where they are, conflict need not occur.[57] In sum, as our political and rhetorical theories and pedagogies have become anti-urban; our cities have become antipolitical and antirhetorical.[58]

I try to show here what it means to live in such a world, where politics (the art of living with different others) and rhetoric (the art of rendering and negotiating difference) have been divorced from each other, and both have been torn from their original context, the independent, democratic city. But if I argue for a revival of the old nexus among these three, the vision I propose is not, I hope, merely nostalgic. Despite globalization, despatialization, and sprawl, we still live together in permanent settlements: if anything, we are more enmeshed in our cities—more "political"—than ever, and those cities are more diverse, and more complex, than ever. And thus, despite the troubling nature of what I observe and describe in this book, I try to offer in the end a glimmer of hope. After all, rhetoric and design share a positive orientation toward the world, a creative impulse, a commitment to fashioning practical solutions to common problems. Perhaps bringing them together can help us rethink and rebuild our communities.

The book is divided into three parts. The first part is a theoretical introduction to the whole idea of rhetorical space. It opens in chapter 2 with the problem of citizenship in a world where politics is no longer linked to place, proximity, and the body. I develop there a theory of situated citizenship that I believe can help us better meet our responsibilities to the world and one another. In chapter 3, I examine different sites of such citizenship, including both the nation-state and the neighborhood, two prominent scenes of civic community. I end up, however, proposing the *city*, with its urban districts and metropolitan surroundings, as the ideal space of genuinely political discourse in our society.

Unfortunately, the cities of contemporary North America are not, in general, very promising scenes of public life. We will see in this book how much they suffer politically and rhetorically from the socioeconomic fragmentation, decentralization, and polarization of the United States. The question is, can they be improved? Can they be transformed into sites of authentic civic argumentation? To answer those questions, I turn in part II to a case study of urban design: the ongoing revitalization of the Cabrini Green neighborhood on Chicago's Near North Side. After providing historical background to the formation of the Chicago ghetto in chapter 4, I examine three options for revitalizing this particular neighborhood. Chapter 5 explores the idea that the problem behind inner-city, African-American poverty is the city itself; and the solution, suburban relocation. Chapter 6 considers another theory: that the best hope for Cabrini Green's families is poverty deconcentration, best effected by "importing" higher-income residents to the central city and allowing some of the poor families to stay. Chapter 7, meanwhile, posits a very different idea: that urban African-American poverty is a function of social oppression and political marginalization, and its solution: helping low-income, inner-city blacks chart their own destiny and take control of their own neighborhoods.

On the one hand, all three ideas promise to lessen the fragmentation and polarization of the North American metropolitan landscape. And there are hopeful signs here for the racial and economic integration of the suburbs, the ameliorization of urban poverty, and the physical revitalization of our central cities. But there are also problems. The favored suburbs turn out to be largely closed to economic and racial integration, and Chicago's blacks do not seem to want to move to such places anyway. Meanwhile, the social bracketing behind income mixing, in which residents are supposed to check their race, class, religion, ethnicity, and family status at the door of the new housing developments, turns out to be impractical. Instead, what we see are group characteristics becoming even more salient, blacks losing what little power they had in the central city, and the white upper-classes assuming an undeserved position of moral authority. As for empowerment, the experiment at 1230 North Burling Street comes dangerously close to constituting a racial and economic enclave, predicated as it is on isolation from the mainstream. In the end, the old metropolitan patterns are left unchallenged, even strengthened.

Part III tries to tease out some general lessons from all this. Clearly, places matter; they differ radically from one another; and those differences contribute to social, political, economic, and rhetorical inequality. The idea that we have slipped the bonds of earth, are now independent of place—floating symbolic analysts, mobile information workers—is false. We remain physical creatures, inherently embodied, inextricably situated, resolutely sensitive to proximity; and the weakest and most vulnerable among us remain the most spatially dependent of all. So, in chapter 8, I lay out some broad principles for reflecting responsibly on civic life in contemporary metropolitan North America. First, we need to seriously consider, together, the real condition and role of our bodies in social life, including our manifest needs as physical creatures and our patent vulnerabilities as human beings. And we need, therefore, to make safe and affordable housing a right for all; we need to develop place-based economic policies; and we need to take greater responsibility for the care of our natural and built environments. Second, we need to reimagine politics as taking place in a wide range of sociospatial units so that citizens have a multitude of overlapping, quasi-sovereign communities to participate in, with different units empowered to make different kinds of decisions. Finally, we need to recommit ourselves to open, accessible, diverse, unitary, and empowered *centers* of human settlement: to cities, the urban districts that make them up, and the metropolitan regions that surround them.

But we need to make changes in our rhetorical practices as well—the focus of chapter 9. My overall purpose here, after all, is to better understand the relationship between language and the built world. In the contemporary United States, I believe, our discourse fails to acknowledge our dependence on that world, to recognize the extent to which we are *embodied* actors in our communities. We need a language, therefore, that promotes stability and depth rather than movement and superficiality and that fosters communal attachment rather than self-interest. But there is another problem with our public discourse: its failure to see *conflict* as natural, generative, and good. When faced with conflict, we have tended to believe that we must either separate or assimilate, either avoid difference, turning our back on people unlike us, or purify it, pretending that conflicts are mistakes and that we can live in harmony only if we see the errors of our ways.

We need a third alternative, a practice that acknowledges, even celebrates, conflict but also attempts to resolve that conflict through debate, deliberation, and adjudication. To sustain that practice, however, we need more and better *commonplaces* where people can literally come together to discuss and negotiate their differences, where their freedom and equality can be enacted without either alienation or amalgamation. And we need a public philosophy that says: difference is normal and good; because of it, we must talk to one another; the result of this talking will not always be to our liking, but we will come back the next day to do it all over again.

But here's the rub: to acquire these habits and dispositions, we need settings where they can be practiced, where we can literally see our diversity, where we belong but others belong as well, people who are different from us but with whom we are interdependent precisely because we live together. In other words, we need changes in our *rhetorics* that will help us practice better public problem-solving, and we need changes in our *environments* that will bring us closer together so that such problem-solving is unavoidable.

But let us begin with a bit of political theory.

PART ONE

The Geography of Politics

TWO

The Placelessness of Political Theory

> What once were the experiences of places appear now as floating mental operations.
>
> —Richard Sennett, *The Conscience of the Eye*

The Citizen

At the heart of any democratic polity is the individual citizen—the ordinary man or woman who is, by right, a full and equal member of the polity, who enjoys its benefits and shares in its governance, participates in its decision making, serves in its military, sits on its juries, and obeys its laws (without ever giving up his or her right to complain and dispute). The "public," from this point of view, is nothing more or less than the coming together of such persons.

Now, it might seem that the individual citizen would quickly become lost in the large publics of our time, societies supremely capable of oppressing his or her autonomy; but, in theory at least, it is the *individual's* freedom that remains inalienable in our democracies, his or her rights that are uninfringeable, his or her dignity and worth that are inviolable. A hallmark of modern liberal thought, in fact, is the belief that the citizen is the prior and primary political phenomenon, and community, the secondary, derivative one. The state, by this reasoning, is a creation of the people, not the other way around.

But if the power and autonomy of democratic society is derived from the freedom and equality of its members, where do *their* rights come from? They come, according to a classic formulation, from the character of the species itself, from the essence of a being that is, by nature or God, born free and equal, graced with reason, and possessed of intrinsic worth and dignity.

By a seemingly unassailable logic, then, membership in the modern democracies is said to be maximally open, tied to universal human rights rather than the accidents of biology, ancestry, geography, or culture. In such communities, civic identity is a matter of heart and mind rather than body or status; and citizens know one another, as Martin Luther King Jr. put it nearly forty-five years ago, by the content of their character rather than the color of their skin.

And so we teach citizenship in the United States. According to the *National Standards for Civics and Government*, a 1994 document identifying what American students should know about politics and political institutions, "The identity of an American citizen is defined by shared political values and principles rather than by ethnicity, race, religion, class, language, gender, or national origin."[1] In this country, in other words, we bracket our most fundamental worldly differences when we enter the political arena, our identity there independent of, even transcending, our otherwise divisive particularities. From a world-historical point of view, this is an astounding sentiment but one that most Americans, I believe, would endorse.

If taken as a description of reality, however, the statement is more problematic. For one thing, in its very grammar (its use of the present tense, for example), it hides the struggles that have made such political identity possible. If American citizenship is defined without reference to ethnicity, race, religion, class, language, gender, or national origin, that is a surprisingly recent and still fragile accomplishment, won against traditions of inegalitarianism that are deeply engrained in our history. According to Rogers Smith, "For over 80 percent of U.S. history, American laws declared most people in the world ineligible to become full U.S. citizens, solely because of their race, original nationality, or gender."[2] The fact is that two hundred years ago only white Christian men with property could vote and hold office in most states in this country. The fight to wean ourselves from such a system has been protracted, uneven, and not always inspiring. The U.S. Constitution, in fact, was originally silent on the matter of citizenship; and the current definition allowing that "All persons born or naturalized in the United States . . . are citizens of the United States and the State wherein they reside" was not legally incorporated (as the Fourteenth Amendment) until 1868, after a bloody civil war waged in part over this very question. Operationalized as the right to vote, it would take four more amendments and another century to ensure that citizenship here was not denied on the basis of race (Fifteenth Amendment, 1870), gender (Nineteenth, 1920), failure to pay a poll tax (Twenty-fourth, 1964), or age (Twenty-sixth, 1971).[3]

But even today, membership in the American political community is subject to precisely the kinds of exclusions the *Standards* deny. If race, class, gender, religion, ethnicity, and age can no longer be used to restrict civic rights, national origin in fact remains crucial in determining who is an American, as we saw above with the Fourteenth Amendment.[4] And language turns out to be important since naturalized citizens must demonstrate the ability to speak and read English.[5] Shared political values and principles, meanwhile, though vaunted in the *Standards*, play little role in the actual legal status of U.S. citizens; foreigners, however, must exhibit a commitment to American political principles in order to be naturalized.[6] Finally, when we look at the actual deployment of civic rights, rather than just their definition, we find that political participation in the United States is in fact highly stratified by age, homeownership, education, and other traits.[7] The truth is that cognitive-affective characteristics, like subscribing to certain values and principles, turn out to be less determinative of American civic identity—and ascriptive characteristics like race and class, more—than the *Standards* would have us believe.

Still, we get the point. We want our public realm to be as open, accessible, and inclusive as possible, and political rights and responsibilities to be a function of laws and procedures rather than the attributes and attachments of particular, spatiotemporally situated men and women. We want each citizen to be treated equally, irrespective of worldly status. If there is inequality in *other* realms of society—the family, the market, school, and so forth—we like to think it will go unnoticed in the political arena, where we will confront one another as from behind a "veil of ignorance," without regard to status differentials, disclosing and negotiating our conflicts by unconstrained social discourse and the force of the better argument alone.[8] Thus, no matter how much property a person has—and our system allows astonishing inequality in that regard—each citizen has a strictly equal voice. Race, class, and gender count no more politically than height or left-handedness. As a citizen, in other words, the individual is lifted out of the particularities of his or her earthly position, drained of personal history, family resources, religious faith, and physical attributes, and transformed into a self-contained rational being, floating in a space of neutral laws and abstract procedures to which he or she has (apparently) assented.

But what kind of political life is this? What kind of civic identity is that? Can we really bracket the specific contingencies and circumstances that make us different from one another? We have not done so historically; it is not clear that we can do so now. And perhaps we should not even want to. After all, the bracketing of personal and social attributes in political theory depends on an image of a "degree zero" human being (rational, autonomous, godlike) which turns out, when its promoters are fully candid, to be historically and culturally quite specific, to resemble certain kinds of human beings more than others.[9] To pretend that race, class, and gender are irrelevant, or that one is "blind" to them, is often just a way to favor those who allegedly have no race, class, age, sexual orientation, or gender—that is, white, middle-class, middle-aged, heterosexual men. Despite our common humanity, we are undeniably and inescapably different from one another; and we live in a world where such differences matter, where they are both cause and effect of enormous social inequality. To bracket differences does not in fact lessen their effect; it perpetuates the very inequalities that bracketing was meant to set aside, the claim of neutrality allowing its advocates to pretend that privilege no longer functions when in fact it has now been made implicit and inexplicable and thus more powerful and pernicious.[10]

But we can go further. We are *all* situated human beings with specific attributes; and bracketing may not be good for any of us. We all have bodies, we all grow up speaking certain languages, living in certain places, and occupying certain positions in the world. We are all from somewhere and affiliate with some groups more than others. Our political philosophies should not deny these "irrational" attachments; they are constitutive of who we are, of our very human being. As Rogers Smith has put it, political communities are ultimately *human* creations—"historically shaped collective enterprises created by groups of people to craft richer and freer lives for themselves."[11]

This point has been made eloquently of late by Chantal Mouffe, who argues that liberalism's assumption of an equality based on shared humanity may be useful ethically but is not very helpful politically. For equality to have meaning, she writes, there must be the possibility and risk of inequality; and for citizens to be truly equal with one another, they must partake of a specific commonality not available to everyone.[12] After all, "[i]n the domain of the political, people do not face each other as abstractions but as politically interested and politically determined persons."[13] Democracy is thus inevitably about drawing boundaries around a group of humans who are equal to one another but superior, at least in certain respects, to outsiders.

So, against liberalism's dream of a humanity that transcends difference, self-interest, and exclusion, democracy requires a specific, situated *people*, an "us" set against a "them." These remarks are unpleasant to liberal ears, but they are probably inescapable.[14] A community in which the individual citizen is unencumbered by history, geography, family, and desire is neither possible nor desirable. Theories of citizenship must reference, therefore, not just universal human rights but particular human contexts. The *National Standards* are revealing in this sense: despite the disembodied civic identity posited above, from which ethnicity, race, religion, class, language, gender, and national origin have been drained, the *Standards* define politics itself as always involving groups of people,[15] civic life as inextricably tied to community, and the citizen as a member of that community.

But what groups are we talking about here? what kind of community? membership in what? In the legal tradition, there are two principal ways to define citizenship in *specific* terms, often referred to by the Latin shorthand *jus sanguinis* (right of blood) and *jus soli* (right of place). We usually count as progress the gradual weakening of the first definition, which privileges characteristics like race and ancestry. But we are also uneasy about the second, in which all who are born or reside in a certain place are accorded political rights there. And for good reason: *jus soli* seems insufficiently cognitive to us, insufficiently principled. After all, politics should be about people not territory; civic life, about allegiance to law not land; civic activity, about reason not property. Defining citizenship in terms of geography sounds too much like a blind devotion to fatherland. Why should our political rights be limited to the state or country where we were born or currently reside? And why should we lack rights in a community just because we weren't born there or our bodies don't physically reside there now? Today, with porous borders, worldwide media, and the ability to travel and communicate quickly across vast distances, many people think of themselves not as members of a single polity but as "citizen pilgrims,"[16] "cosmopolites"[17] who claim general political rights and powers across the globe.

Locality retains its hold on us, however; and place remains a powerful basis for civic lives. For one thing, defining politics in spatial terms reminds us of our embeddedness in, and dependence on, the natural and built worlds, our inherently human *being*. It reminds us that politics is at bottom about securing food, water, shelter, rest, and protection in environments that have limited resources and manifest inhospitalities. It reminds us of what comes first, of priorities and preliminaries, of our inexorable and unalterable physical needs, which, despite technological developments, have not fundamentally changed in millennia. We remain, after all, terrestrial animals, living neither in the air nor the trees, neither underground nor in the water. If our social, economic, and cultural relations have changed dramatically across time, our bodies have not. As a species we are still roughly the same size we were thousands of years ago. We are still bilaterally symmetrical. We can still walk about the same distance without tiring; our very young and very old are still largely immobile; we still need clothes and shelter, good water and clean air.[18] A politics based on this embodied experience, a politics which pays close attention to the environments in which we live, work, and love, is thus a decidedly *human* politics.

What's more, the body is something that we share with one another. It connects us in need and desire, suffering and joy, aches, pains, and raptures. *Pace* liberalism, what we most obviously have in common is not some god-like reason but this experience, at once mundane and extraordinary, of being *grounded* in the physical world. Obviously, our bodies are also sites of difference—of gender, race, age, and so on—but we remain biologically more alike than different; and the resulting connection provides a more open framework for community than history or ancestry, religion or class. Our living together in space creates a "fortuitous association"[19] that may in the end be stronger and more lasting than any other. Humans are exquisitely attuned, after all, to proximity, to what is close by, both in terms of people and things.[20] Architect and urban designer Daniel Solomon describes this as our love of nearness, the sixth sense we have of the world around us, the connection "between our consciousness and the context of our lives."[21] On this view, democracy is more than anything about sharing space with one another.

But place is not just the scene, empty and neutral, of our experiences, the backdrop for our accidental communities. It is the medium with which we positively organize our social lives, the material with which we give form to our communities. Space is plastic, and we can mold it to our purposes, putting us in contact with, but keeping us from tripping over, one another, allowing us to come together yet remain distinct. Like Hannah Arendt's table, built space is ideally located *between* those who share it, relating and separating them at the same time.[22]

The Places of Political Theory

Unfortunately, rather than helping us understand and improve the world we share, contemporary political philosophers and civic educators have been seduced, I believe, by the promises of despatialization, by the image of a human *being* for whom natural and built environments are unimportant. Of course, there is nothing new in this: religion, philosophy, science, and other projects given to abstraction and transcendence have been globalizing thought for centuries. But there is a placelessness to contemporary political theory, I believe, that seems especially oblivious to the local geography of our lives, that consistently portrays the citizen as a disembodied rights-bearer, a roving cosmopolite, an itinerant consumer, a migrant worker.

Some of this can be explained, of course, by the changing conditions of residence, work, and play in our time, changes that have allowed us to think that we are less dependent on place than we once were, that physical proximity is no longer relevant, that cities have become obsolete, that new modes of transportation and communication have accomplished "an awesome technological destruction of distance,"[23] that the "new" economy, driven by these changes but motivating them as well, has "delocalized" human life, making us less attached to and less dependent on place than ever before. The evidence for these changes has been summarized elsewhere: corporations dispersed across the globe, their components linked by high-speed communication and transportation networks; a dramatic rise in the mobility of capital, with international trade increasingly comprised of financial services and investment funds rather than raw materials and agricultural goods; and labor astonishingly mobile as well, with jobs relocating overnight from one place to another, crossing borders previously thought to be impermeable.[24] It is not for nothing, Richard Sennett has written, that the fastest-growing sector of the U.S. economy is temporary work and that graduates of business schools are now urged to work on the outside rather than the inside of organizations, to avoid becoming too entangled in local politics, to eschew long-term attachments to place and company. One imagines the worker of today as a kind of floating subcontractor: flexible, inventive, oriented to ideas rather than things, traveling from airport to airport with a phone on his belt, a computer on her lap.[25]

But the ways we conceptualize, discuss, and teach politics are not fully explained by simple reference to economic, technological, and other material forces. For the rest of this chapter, then, I want to see how our political philosophies approach space. I begin by discussing two prevalent traditions of modern political thought: republicanism and liberalism.[26]

Republicanism

Republicans (with a lower case "r") celebrate the active involvement of ordinary citizens in the self-governance of their own communities, claiming a strong connection between such participation and the health of the group in general. For republicans, politics is not just something one does occasionally or a practice delegated to others (representatives or experts): it is perhaps the most important part of our everyday human lives.

The key historical moment for republicans remains classical antiquity, and in particular the direct democracy of golden-age Athens (and, to a lesser extent, the early Roman republic and the communes of the Italian Renaissance). Republicans thus tend to evince nostalgia for relatively small, independent, self-governing, and self-sufficient human communities, founded and maintained by selfless citizens zealously guarding their own and their fellows' freedom through physical combat and public displays of verbal eloquence, practical wisdom, and communal spirit.

Republicanism therefore rests on a demanding image of civic life; its ethical basis, "the ancient ideal of the *homo politicus* . . . who affirms his being and his virtue by the medium of political action."[27] In the Italian communes, for example, at least according to John Pocock, politics was an art of face-to-face verbal decision-making, and human life was viewed "in terms of participation in particular actions and decisions, in particular political relationships between particular men."[28] In republicanism, "the development of the individual towards self-fulfillment is possible only when the individual acts as a citizen, that is, as a conscious and autonomous participant in an autonomous decision-taking political community, the polis or republic."[29]

The problem with republicanism, of course, is that politics can become *too* demanding, too consuming, with insufficient protection for the freedom of those community members for whom other *non*political ends are also or even more valuable.[30] In addition, republicans' focus on the common good, and on the individual's selfless sacrifice to it, can be stifling, leaving little room for difference or anonymity. One way to rephrase all of this is to say that, in republican approaches to public life, politics often becomes too "thick," requiring unwavering assent to the community's canon of heroes, sentiments, places, and texts. This is what Habermas refers to as republicanism's "ethical overload."[31]

Liberalism

A liberal approach to public life, by contrast, is one that privileges individual rights above all else—including the right not to be involved in politics. The only common good is the right of each to pursue his or her own good; and the purpose of public life is to ensure that this right is protected. To facilitate that project, the group needs not so much constant participation by all in public life, or even common assent to particular beliefs and values, as it does laws, procedures, and institutions that guarantee fairness and dictate as little as possible in the way of substance. Liberals therefore show less interest in qualities of character among citizens than republicans do; in fact, they sometimes seem to want to "citizen-proof" the state so that it does not depend on the virtues of particular individuals.[32]

If the key historical moment for republicans is classical antiquity, for liberals it is the transatlantic Enlightenment (that is, eighteenth- and nineteenth-century Britain, France, Germany, and the United States, with their democratic revolutions and universal declarations of human rights). According to Habermas, the key development here was the emergence of a "civil society" between the state, on the one hand, and the world of private inequalities, on the other. Once the latter was bracketed so that arguments could be adjudicated irrespective of the personal status of the arguer, the "reason" of rational discussion could effectively supervise and counteract the otherwise uncontested power of the state.[33]

Civil society was thus the private sphere's buffer against the state, and protecting the private sphere became a key project of liberals. From this point of view, individual happiness is best supported and protected not through participation in the public *agon* but by involvement in family, church, and other nonpolitical realms. The freedom pursued by liberals is thus mainly freedom from the state; and the public sphere is in consequence a relatively narrow (though crucial) space tasked with confronting the state in the name of protecting individual rights.[34]

If the dangers of republican life are mainly dangers of excess—too much politics, too many politicians—for liberals, the danger is the opposite: too little politics and too few politicians. Liberalism often fails in fact to generate enough participation by ordinary citizens in self-government to prevent a "soft despotism" of professional politicians (or "representatives") and administrators.[35] We might rephrase all this by saying that, in liberal approaches to public life, politics often becomes too "thin." If republicans can be accused of ethical overload, liberals can be criticized for their seeming ethical apathy.

Despite these differences, however, both ideologies claim to be democratic and to support self-governing communities constituted by their members' freedom and equality; both place a premium on debate as the mechanism of that self-government; and both recognize the role of a healthy *public*—a "coming-together of equals"—in countering tyranny.

But where and when does this public occur? How does it show up in concrete, everyday life? Republicans often assume a temporal attitude toward the *res publica*. Hannah Arendt's positive assessment of the polis was largely based, for example, on the opportunities it afforded citizens to live out their lives in public contest, which not only steered the state but offered glory to its members. Similarly, John Pocock, writing about Renaissance Italy, connected the rise of republicanism there to the advent of a new way of viewing time, particularized and secular.[36]

But more powerfully undergirding republicanism, I believe, has been a spatial image: the relatively small, self-governing community *where* citizenship is played out and to which it is dedicated. For republicans, genuine freedom and equality can only be achieved in a community that is human-scaled, in a place where we know our fellow citizens and they know us, a space of face-to-face interpersonal action, where the very streets have meaning. It is thus nearly impossible to imagine republicanism without at some point calling up particular public scenes: Greek city-states, Italian republics, Swiss cantons, New England townships. Republicanism is fundamentally, I would argue, a geographical conception of political life.

Liberalism is also clearly beholden to a spatial order. But its geography, unlike that of republicanism, is mainly private. The citizen in liberalism becomes fully human not, as Arendt and Pocock would have it, when he or she is in the public arena but rather when he or she is at home, on the job, or in church, pursuing his or her interests, taking care of his or her family, praying to his or her God. The other key spaces of liberalism—the marketplace, for example, and the civil society of coffee shops and union halls—are in some sense an extension of the private realm because, like it, they need protection from the state.

Despite this topography, however, liberalism is predominantly, I believe, a politics of time. A state in which people are mostly left alone is best achieved by the thinnest kind of political life imaginable: namely, a shared set of procedures for resolving conflicts and protecting individual freedoms. And because liberal polities typically refuse in principle to impose one set of substantive beliefs on all, liberalism is at bottom concerned mainly with fairness.[37] It lacks both the partiality and the social content required of republicanism. In this regard, liberalism can be seen as essentially ageographical.

In fact, it has become commonplace to interpret the advent of modernity as entailing an ideological shift away from a predominantly spatial (republican) and toward a predominantly temporal (liberal) mode of politics, a shift, that is, from territory to consent. Foucault, for example, pointed (in a 1982 interview) to that moment in the late eighteenth to early nineteenth centuries when Napoleon realized that the state was no longer just a matter of space; it was now also about society, something with a complex and independent reality of its own, a reality that would turn out to be far harder to govern than mere land.[38] In other words, if Western democratic thought begins with the small face-to-face community, governed by individuals who know one another's character, it proceeds toward the large, print-mediated society, governed by neutral procedure and impersonal law. Though nostalgia for the former paradigm persists, the main direction of political philosophy in Western history has been toward the latter. There is thus, we might say, a clear preference in modern public philosophies for processual entities.

That is, until recently, when a reconfiguration of the "sociospatial dialectic"[39] occurred.

The Postmodern Public

As we saw above, Foucault identified the late eighteenth and early nineteenth centuries as the time when politicians realized that the state was no longer simply *territory*; it was also a *society* and thus as much a temporal as a geographic entity. Sometime during the twentieth century, however, the pendulum swung back again. In a 1967 lecture, Foucault claimed that:

> [If t]he great obsession of the nineteenth century was history . . . [t]he present epoch will perhaps be above all the epoch of space. We are in the epoch of simultaneity, . . . the epoch of juxtaposition, the epoch of the near and far, of the side-by-side, of the dispersed. We are at a moment, I believe, when our experience of the world is less that of a long life developing through time than that of a network that connects points and intersects with its own skein.[40]

Certainly, there were signs of this shift earlier in the century, in, for example, Saussure's rejection of historical—in favor of synchronic—linguistics; but the change only became obvious after mid-century, with what Soja has called the "spatial turn" in social theory. By the end of the 1970s, David Gross was writing in *Telos* that "spatialization has now become our basic modality for organizing and structuring the world." And in 1984, Frederic Jameson famously proclaimed that "our daily life, our psychic experience, our cultural languages are today dominated by categories of space rather than categories of time." More recently, Susan S. Friedman has discerned a new and central role for space in contemporary feminism.[41] Clearly, something is theoretically afoot, something that I believe is especially welcome at a time when the dominant discourses are so intent on obscuring the role of space in our lives, telling us that distance is irrelevant, space is conquered, proximity is unimportant.[42]

But what is the nature of the space we now inhabit? If the world of republicanism was the human-scaled community of face-to-face interaction, a space best imaged by the open public square or town commons; and the world of liberalism was largely ageographical, a society of laws and procedures rather than things; what is the space of postmodernism? The answer, I believe, is surprisingly obvious. And it involves a geographics not of location but of interconnection, whose key spatial image, evident already in Foucault's 1967 lecture and now so frequently indexed that it has become a cliché, is the *network*, with its intricately connected and relationally constituted nodes and links: an open, decentralized, imminently flexible structure with interchangeable parts, built to facilitate movement, association, and change.

We do not need a precise date for this shift—the invention of the microchip in 1959, the Kennedy assassination in 1963, or the 1972 demolition of the Pruitt-Igoe public housing complex in St. Louis—to agree that sometime in the last half of the twentieth century, the culture and economy of the West underwent a large-scale shift, and a new era began: the postindustrial society, transnational capitalism, the post-Fordist economy, or the New World Order.[43] In the academy, theoretical projects like poststructuralism, postcolonialism, and postmodernism have both responded to and influenced this shift and have led to a genuine change in our intellectual universe. As theorists and teachers, we have moved away from cultural models based on top-down planning, teleological development, and unified method and toward models of discontinuity, juxtaposition, and hybridization.

These theories have been helpful in our understanding of at least three key spatial features of the cultural moment (I take these loosely from Friedman's *Mappings*). First, there is *globalization*, the way any point in the network seems to be connected to all the others, the way transnational organizations and permeable borders now facilitate the rapid deployment of capital, labor, information, and products across space. Our location in such a world is decidedly interstitial, known more by what we are connected to than by where we actually are. Thus, in the humanities, we talk now about subjects between spaces, crossing boundaries, inside contact zones.[44] The second spatial feature illuminated by the new theories is *diaspora*, the large-scale movements and demographic changes of postindustrial life: the intense hyperactivity, fluidity, and ephemerality of our times. Thus, in the contemporary humanities, there has been substantial interest in such things as migration, nomadism, and tourism.

Finally, there is *multipositionality*, Friedman's word for the way identity is now radically fragmented and overdetermined at the same time, best understood not in essential terms but as something emerging at the intersection of multiple, overlapping, and often contradictory systems of stratification. What all this engenders is a culture of pronounced heterogeneity.

So, the postmodern "spatial turn" has *not* meant a simple revival of republicanism after the liberal hegemony of modernity. Neither of the ideologies presented above fits the new order because, for all of their differences, they both posited unitary, hierarchical, and stable publics, while postmodernism has been all about pluralism, decentralization, and instability. From this point of view, contemporary public life is inherently "multiform and fluid," characterized by a profusion of "counterpublics," each confronting official power with a variety of "vernacular" tactics.[45] In other words, if we define "the public" as a "coming-together of equals," we now need to imagine "comings-together" that are more transitory and unconventional, set in a world that is both more fractured and more interconnected, than publics of the past.

All of this makes sense. Both republicanism and liberalism were tied to systems of exclusion, enslavement, and violence and based on models of "publicity" that are no longer acceptable: republicanism, with its subordination of the individual to the community; liberalism, with its dream of an "unencumbered self"[46] whose rights are set over against the community. In rejecting these, we also reject the old notions of political space and time on which they were based, and we commit ourselves to crafting an alternative political ecology.

But what would that new ecology look and feel like in human terms? Here, I believe, contemporary theory has not been much help. According to the new geographics, we are now everywhere and nowhere at once: in between, on the border, restlessly traveling, migrating in and out of virtual communities, living out our fragmented lives in a space of events, a flow of bits. Sometimes it seems that, for all the talk of spatialization, postmodernism has only taken the liberal preoccupation with time and turbo-charged it: space has finally, we might say, become absorbed into history, and human life, reduced to activity. Sometimes, the situation seems downright frightening, as with Foucault's "heterotopias" (the prison, brothel, and clinic), Jameson's "hyperspace" (his Westin Bonaventure Hotel in Los Angeles is so confusing our bodies can no longer even navigate it), or Davis's "fortress" communities, walled off and armed against a hostile world but ironically providing no peace to those inside.[47]

For all the talk of locality, embodiment, and position, in other words, the new cultural geographies have had little to say about place that can help us actually live in *this* world. Recent work in the field of rhetoric and composition, for example, seems to go out of its way to deny traditional places their role in politics: we have Rosa Eberly's call for a "processual" account of public discourse, in which community is seen less as a thing-in-space than a construction-in-time; Carolyn Miller's proposal that we no longer see "the public" as an empirical social structure but as "the framework for an event: for debate, discussion, dialogue, dispute"; and Susan Wells's claim that, although we still imagine linguistic interaction occurring in a unitary public space, "with secure and discernible borders," our actual encounters with civic space are discontinuous and fragmented, and public speech is therefore best seen as "a performance in *time*, located at specific historical junctures, temporary and unstable" (emphasis added).[48]

But it is German philosopher Jürgen Habermas who has most tellingly tried to locate the elusive "placeless place" of postliberalism.[49] Rejecting as a basis for our political decisions both the concrete lifeworld of particular communities (as in republicanism) and the transsubjective abstractions of universal law (as in liberalism), Habermas puts faith in reasoned discourse itself, thus radically decentering and despatializing politics. Whatever its virtues, though, the proposal shares with the ideas cited above, I believe, a profound topophobia.

Postmodern political theory, in other words, has failed to provide us with reliable *ground* on which to build ordinary political life. What is worse, we can no longer even imagine the possibility of forming stable, situated publics together. Where the ancient Greeks could literally use their eyes to see their culture's values, we cannot. As Richard Sennett has put it:

> [W]ere modern architects asked to design spaces that better promote democracy, they would lay down their pens; there is no modern design equivalent to the ancient assembly. . . . As materials for culture, the stones of the modern city seem badly laid by planners and architects, in that the shopping mall, the parking lot, the apartment house elevator do not suggest in their form the complexities of how people might live. What once were the experiences of places appear now as floating mental operations.[50]

For all the help the new theories have provided in thinking about such things as globalization and diaspora, in other words, they have not been very helpful in actually placing the everyday lives of most people, who are, I would argue, surprisingly situated, local, even territorial creatures. In the words of Eric Oliver, "Citizens do not float about in civic ether but live in distinctive social and institutional contexts, contexts that are important determinants of their behavior."[51]

Theories of multipositionality and migration, I fear, have only taught us to ignore the environments around us, the depletion of the world's natural resources, the devastation of the landscape, the privatization of built space. Our mobility has not made place unimportant; it has in fact accelerated and expanded the ability of some to accumulate power and left others literally and figuratively homeless. The problem is that we can no longer even see this happening. The placelessness of contemporary thinking has blinded us to the fragmentation, degradation, and polarization of the spaces around us, both natural and built. And it has also allowed us, I would argue, to ignore one another and the world we hold in common.

The Persistence of Space

Places matter! And the way we know this is that we routinely make discriminations among them: we know which are better and which are worse, which are ours and which are someone else's. And this is true even on a global scale: despite the apparent geographic neutrality of the new world economy, characterized by nothing so much as the increased mobility of jobs, capital, goods, and people, some places are flourishing, while others are not. Production itself may be dispersed, but different kinds of production are increasingly concentrated, so that some parts of the globe have become home to predominantly low-wage, low-skill manufacturing and tourism labor, others to mainly high-wage, high-skill information and service work, and others to not much of anything at all. As Saskia Sassen has put it, the new world order is best characterized geographically as combining *dispersal* of economic activity with *concentration* of command and control functions in such places as export zones, offshore banking centers, high-tech districts, and so-called global cities like New York, London, and Tokyo. The result is an intensification, not a relaxation, of the age-old spatial division between places that have and those that have not, a division that predates the electronic era but has deepened during it. As Manuel Castells describes it, the postmodern landscape is comprised of "valuable" spaces that are increasingly linked together and "devalued" spaces that are more and more isolated and separated both from each other and from the valuable spaces.[52]

From a national, rather than a global point of view, meanwhile, we can see that some locations in the United States are capitalizing on the economic transformations of our time—places like Boulder, Raleigh-Durham, Austin, and Washington, DC, variously labeled "creative centers," "ideopolises," or "latte towns"[53]—while others are stagnant or declining.

The spatial manifestations of this disparity at the metropolitan level can also be readily observed. Myron Orfield's cluster analysis of the twenty-five largest U.S. metropolitan areas shows huge disparities in the local resources of our civic landscape.[54] Within any single urbanized region, Orfield writes, one finds a proliferation of independent municipalities with dramatically different tax bases, expenditure needs, population densities, housing stock, minority populations, poverty rates, office space, and growth. If we take, for instance, the large metropolitan areas of the upper Midwest (Milwaukee, Chicago, Detroit, Cleveland, etc.), we see similar patterns in the configuration of social space. Downtown is now focused primarily on financial services, government, and legal work. Enmeshed within and right around downtown are high-end cultural-entertainment complexes and recently gentrified urban neighborhoods, both targeting the young professionals who work in the central city and the tourists (from the local suburbs as well as farther away) who come to visit it. Next comes a ring of increasingly distressed minority neighborhoods, which have suffered dramatically under the service economy. Usually right beyond them lies a ring of working-class, white neighborhoods, their populations graying and economies stagnating. Farther out, of course, are the suburbs, but that word masks enormous variety, most importantly between those communities that have the largest and most expensive houses, the highest-end retail centers, and the most office space and those that have little or none of these. Finally, far out from the urban center are older, at-risk satellite cities—now home to many of the low-skill workers serving the favored suburbs—and, beyond them, increasingly resource-strapped and depopulated rural areas.

It is a landscape in which residential areas are separate from commercial ones, single-family from multifamily housing, rental from for-sale properties, and people of one social group from those of all others. Young affluent white families with children, for example, live in one part of the metropolitan area, older white couples without children in another, the very old in yet a third. Lower- and middle-class whites live over here, professional singles over there, blacks in that direction, Hispanics in this.[55] And these groups are only growing farther apart, with the upper classes increasingly wealthy, the working and middle classes increasingly stressed, and the disparity between them growing.[56]

As for genuinely common ground, there is little or none. What is most distinctive about the contemporary United States is in fact the coexistence of extraordinary private affluence with astonishing public squalor.[57] As new houses in the United States have grown larger and larger, a threefold increase in just fifty years,[58] they are increasingly set in a landscape whose most vibrant social spaces are private shopping centers and megasize churches. Meanwhile, poor, middle-class, elderly, young, and minority residents face a growing affordable housing shortage and an increasingly severe housing burden in their budgets.[59]

New technologies have *not* made place irrelevant in our lives or fundamentally altered our embeddedness in the physical world. If anything, they have made place more important. Despite our fractured subjectivity, our insistently networked existence, and our hybrid culture, the ground under our feet remains surprisingly important to us and desperately in need of our care. I am not sure that the new theories of cultural geography have grasped that fact.

Take migration. It is true that many of us move about a great deal these days, either by choice or necessity, and that our society is marked by relatively high levels of mobility. And yet, according to recent demographic data, most Americans are actually quite fixed. In 2000, the share of the U.S. population moving from one home to another during the course of a year was 16 percent, the lowest point since the end of World War II.[60] True, there is a great deal of mobility in the highest and lowest socioeconomic strata;[61] but the dream of most people is not migration—it is to improve their lives in the places where they already live.

I think the feeling is widespread: despite the hyperactivity, interconnectivity, and fluidity of our era, most people want more than anything to inhabit communities where they can flourish. Richard Sennett has written that one of the unintended consequences of modern capitalism—with its flexibility, temporariness, impatience, uncertainty, and absence of deeply rooted trust and commitment—is that it has strengthened the value of place for people, has aroused in them a longing for scenes of attachment and depth to make up for the superficiality of their jobs.[62]

None of this is to deny the force of globalization and interconnectivity in our lives or to pretend that there are not problems with place-based thinking. But we need to remind ourselves that globalization, migration, and multipositionality do not exhaust the contemporary spatial experience. Still prominent in our social imaginary are literal *places* where we come together, as citizens, to manage the world we hold in common: middle grounds—accessible, open, attractive—where we all belong but are not under threat of assimilation, where we retain our freedom and equality but still connect, where we oppose, contend, and argue but still share, where we are human without denying the humanity of others.

Commonplaces

We need social spaces, in other words, that are open to hybridity, pluralism, and mobility but still allow us to make a livable world for ourselves, where we can disclose our differences to one another but also solve our shared problems, where we can encounter conflict and opposition but still feel that we belong and matter. We need, that is, *commonplaces* that can link us to one another and the earth but where we remain free and unique as individuals.

The political life I have been working toward in this chapter, in other words, requires place even as it can't be reduced to it. If a public is at bottom a coming together of individuals who share a world and a relation of equality that allows them to manage that world in freedom, it requires spaces where, as Arendt put it, we can meet without falling over one another; and it requires borders that define who we are, that constitute our equality by setting limits to it.[63] Postmodern political philosophies, I believe, have failed to provide this kind of public for us.

Even in an era of multiculturalism, hybridity, and multipositionality, that is, we still need spaces that are (1) *grounded*, real and reliable, that reflect our literally embodied existence even as they respond to our intellectual, ideological, and emotional needs; (2) *unitary*, that we can all feel we belong to, that can function as centers of social expression and exchange; and (3) *official*, that we know we are all bound to, where our differences are not just aired and tolerated but are also actually, practically, resolved, however provisionally and partially.

I will be treading here, in other words, a familiar landscape: the old territorial publics, defined and constituted by simple copresence in space, whether that space is a building, neighborhood, city, state, nation, or the globe itself. Such publics are what Frug calls "fortuitous associations"; what Williamson, Imbroscio, and Alperovitz refer to as "geographically demarcated communities in which a diverse array of citizens join together in self-governance"; what Young defines as social groups based not on mutual identification but on simply living together in space, the "solidarity" of a people who "are all affected by and relate to the geographical and atmospheric environment, and the structural consequences of the fact that they all move in and around this region in distinct and relatively uncoordinated paths and local interactions."[64]

It is to such publics that I now turn.

THREE

A New Civic Map for Our Time

> Ten persons is too small for a polis; but a hundred thousand is too large. The right number is probably somewhere in between.
>
> —Aristotle, *Nicomachean Ethics*[1]

In the previous chapter, I argued that, because of our bodies, because of the force of proximity in our lives, because of the plasticity and vulnerability of the physical world, *place* deserves a more prominent role in our theories of civic identity and interaction. Although our contemporary political landscape is increasingly fragmented and polarized, and our public philosophies seduced by the promises of mobility, multipositionality, and globalization, we are still, after all, situated beings; and we need, more than ever, publics that are grounded, unitary, and official—defined, at least in part, by simple copresence in space.

Such publics obviously vary dramatically not only in location but also in size, shape, density, diversity, and power. They can be as small and homogeneous as condo associations or as large and diverse as the globe itself. The question for us is: does this kind of variation matter to political and rhetorical theory? do different kinds of territorial publics encourage different kinds of social and discursive life? do they require different civic skills and dispositions? The answer we have tended to give to these questions, I believe, is *no*: it is important to situate our civic selves somewhere, but it does not really matter where. Democracy is democracy, whether it occurs in a PTO meeting, a jury room, the op-ed page of a local newspaper, an Internet discussion list, the street, a national legislature, or a forum in the global civil sphere. Insofar as social theory draws any distinction at all between small and large groups, wrote Mancur Olson forty years ago, "it is apparently with respect to the scale of the functions they perform, not the extent they succeed in performing these functions or their capacity to attract members. It assumes that small and large groups differ in degree, but not in kind."[2] "Think globally, act locally" is a watchword for this attitude: it does not matter where you are a citizen; just be one.

But communities differ radically from one another in political terms; and, as citizens, we experience those differences acutely. Territorial publics can be distinguished by how much we know about and are familiar with them; the extent to which we have affinity for and derive emotional sustenance from them; how likely we are to have a voice and be heard in them; how open they are to our differences and conflicts; the extent to which they are independent of other publics; and how effectively they solve their own problems. Given such differences, it is surprising that the "one size fits all" theory of democracy has survived as long as it has.

This variety of publics is significant rhetorically. In large, diverse societies, ruled by professional politicians and powerful interests, managed by technical experts, and supervised by the mass media, the issues of public debate are huge, complex, and attention-grabbing; conflicts are stark and heated; and considerable resources are available to deal with them. But as lively and effective as all this is, it can seem remote from the point of view of the individual citizen, who is usually little more than a spectator of it. Smaller publics, on the other hand, like neighborhoods or villages, often do a better job of encouraging and rewarding direct involvement by ordinary individuals in communal self-determination. But they usually lack the conflict that stimulates political discourse to begin with; and they are often too small to exercise control over the issues that concern members the most.

What does all this mean for civic education and, in particular, for the *rhetorical* training we provide our future citizens? In this chapter, I try to answer that question by looking at various "scenes" of democracy and the different educational projects they sponsor.

The Nation-State

The dominant scene of political education in the United States for more than a century now has been the nation-state. This is perhaps unsurprising given that the nation has been the dominant geopolitical force on earth during most of the modern period, more important than both smaller entities like the city and larger ones like the international alliance. The *National Standards for Civics and Government* make it clear that, when one looks at civic education and political socialization in the United States, the most important political community of which citizens are members is the nation: it issues our passports, guarantees our rights, is home to our political parties and locus of our most cherished political principles.[3] The classic studies of civic activity by Sidney Verba and his colleagues also reveal the extent to which democratic participation for us is more often than not a *national* phenomenon: voting in elections, following debates on TV and in newspapers, understanding political history and institutions, attending to campaigns and interest groups—these are usually seen in specifically national terms.[4] Similarly, "politics" in school is usually national politics, a matter of presidential elections, congressional debates, Supreme Court decisions, and large protest movements.

Still, rhetoric's ancient association with smaller, city-size communities, as well as the United States' strong federalist tradition, particularly its highly decentralized educational system, make it at least plausible that a localist tradition in political education would have developed here. That has not in general been the case. By the end of the nineteenth century, I would argue, the teaching of writing and speaking in this country, and ipso facto the teaching of *public* writing and speaking, was almost entirely driven by the national political scene.

Rhetorical education is crucial for nation-states because they need shared discursive processes, artifacts, and curricula to constitute and maintain themselves as cultural and material entities.[5] But the flip side is also true: rhetorical education, at least in this country, and at least over the last century, has depended on the nation-state for its very existence. My own field of composition-rhetoric has been for nearly 150 years now literally sponsored by the United States, including its federal government, which through its policies and resources has helped shape the postsecondary writing course—the most required course in American higher education[6] and one that is still largely unique to the United States—and the student population it serves.[7] The course has returned the favor: the "scene" of writing underlying it is usually the nation itself, a situation that has determined much about *what* "writing" in the North American composition classroom is, *where* it occurs, *who* does it, *how* they go about it, and *why*.

One place where all this can be discerned is the textbooks used to teach writing here. As a discipline, composition has been unusually dependent on textbooks because for so long it lacked a graduate curriculum; teachers therefore taught themselves (and perpetuated) the discipline through the textbooks they used.[8] And, because of the centralized nature of the publishing industry in this country, with the same textbooks used nearly everywhere, composition was largely the same wherever it was taught, a sameness that was, I would argue, specifically American.

A quick glance at some representative textbooks will reveal the national scene that lies behind writing instruction in this country.[9] Diana Hacker's *Writer's Reference*, for example, the best-selling college textbook of any kind in the United States, draws on a specifically North American tradition in the teaching of writing.[10] The language used here (e.g., "clustering," "thesis statements," "global revision") is unique to the world of U.S. "composition" and used across this country, in remarkably consistent ways, in an astonishingly wide variety of educational contexts. Writing itself, meanwhile, is presented as an abstract process of planning, drafting, and revising, a process that does not change in its essence over either space or time, though its underlying ideology is arguably biased toward the interests of the modern North American *bourgeoisie*.[11] The material used in this process, meanwhile, is "standard" English (though it should probably be labeled, and in some textbooks is, "standard edited American English"); writers for whom English is a second language are ghettoized in their own separate chapter.[12] Documentation styles, a key feature of academic writing in U.S. colleges and universities, are all American, the big four sponsored by the Modern Language Association, the American Psychological Association, the American Historical Association (via the *Chicago Manual of Style*), and the Council of Biology Editors—all U.S.-based organizations. Curiously, despite this obvious national setting, nowhere in Hacker's text is mention ever made that the subject of the book is writing *in the United States* and its target audience, student-writers *in the United States*. According to its title, this is a "writer's" reference—no further specification is needed, an elision that obscures for teachers and students alike the geopolitical particularity of the writing taught here.

We see something similar in Annette Rottenberg's *Elements of Argument*, the all-time best-selling argument textbook in the United States.[13] *Elements* is also clearly geared toward writing in standard edited American English and contains a similarly abstract, and peculiarly American, technical apparatus.[14] Sample arguments are nearly all written by Americans; and the issues for debate are mostly "American" issues: affirmative action, shopping malls, gun control, legalizing drugs, jury reform, animal rights, human cloning, women in the military, euthanasia, sexual harassment, the death penalty, sex and violence in popular culture, and so forth. Participation in public discourse, from the point of view of *Elements*, is participation in *national* public discourse, which means here reading about current events in the mass media for the purpose of becoming better informed about those events, increasing one's critical purchase on them through argument analysis, and developing one's own opinions, in writing, about them.

We could do a similar analysis of Rise Axelrod and Charles Cooper's best-selling *St. Martin's Guide to Writing* or of any of the essay anthologies meant to prompt and inspire student writing, like *The Presence of Others*, *Rereading America*, or *Patterns for College Writing*.[15] What almost all these books share is a set of pedagogical, theoretical, and ideological assumptions that can be tied, I believe, to a specifically national history and that operate with specifically national scope; and what they all work toward is a specifically national set of discourse habits and dispositions. All this makes Janet Emig's name for the five paragraph essay so beloved of American teachers—"the fifty star theme"—highly apt.[16]

So, what's wrong with all that? The discipline of composition-rhetoric has probably done more than is generally recognized to help build an American social, political, and cultural community, assist individuals (native and otherwise) to enter the American mainstream, help form a distinctly American character, and maintain and perpetuate specifically American discourse practices. Certainly there has been some good in all that. My point here is that the nationalization of composition instruction in this country has not been an innocent project; for good or ill, it has defined "writing" in some ways rather than others and served some groups more than others. The notion that teachers in the field are teaching writing in an unaffiliated and decontextualized sense, as some kind of general skill or process, is simply false: in American composition pedagogy, the "public" of public discourse is the United States itself.

How has this national scene of writing instruction influenced students' habits of and attitudes toward language? How has it shaped their ways of reading, writing, speaking, and debating, as well as their ideas about where such things take place, how they unfold, who participates in them, and what their potential and actual effects are? For one thing, it has encouraged them, I believe, to see democracy as unfolding primarily on large canvases, where ordinary individuals like themselves participate, if at all, indirectly, and where most decision making is conducted by professional politicians and technocrats, who are motivated by special interests and supervised by the mass media. The role of individual citizens in such politics is almost entirely, therefore, spectatorial.

Nancy Fraser has called this kind of polity a "weak public," whose deliberative practice consists mainly in opinion formation. The decision making usually associated with sovereign political bodies, groups that Fraser calls "strong publics," is here inaccessible to most citizens.[17] In a writing class based on such a "weak" public, the student-citizen is rarely an actual political problem-solver—she is at best someone who helps choose the problem-solvers and is, at worse, a mere onlooker of others' problem-solving. She may be a reader, perhaps a voter, hopefully a critical thinker, occasionally a writer of letters to the editor or a joiner of campaigns. But she is almost never a *citizen* in Aristotle's sense of one who shares in judgment and office.[18]

Even opponents of this paradigm often replicate its problems when they craft alternative images of public life. In her 1997 article "Encouraging Civic Participation Among First-Year Writing Students," for example, Elizabeth Ervin criticizes classrooms where students do little more than read magazine articles in anthologies such as *America Now* or *Our Times* and then talk and write about the current issues treated therein. Such classrooms promote, she says, a "voyeuristic" view of politics. What she wants instead is for the writing class to promote actual civic action outside of the classroom. Unfortunately, Ervin fails to realize that what maintains this voyeuristic view of politics is not anything particular teachers or anthology editors do but the very scene against which politics, in this paradigm, occurs. And, because her alternative model for the teaching of public discourse does not fundamentally abandon that scene, the pedagogy she advocates ends up mimicking, I believe, the model she criticizes.[19]

Regarding a unit in *Our Times* concerning acquaintance rape, for example, Ervin wonders why the editors of the book limit its use to encouraging in-class discussion and essay-writing:

> What if *Our Times* had suggested that students write an essay designed to raise campus or local awareness about the issue, and then publish their writing for a relevant audience? Students might be inspired to give a presentation to residents of their dorm, and then leave their essay in a dorm lounge or library. They might want to revise the essay into an open letter for the campus newspaper in which they assessed the problem from the perspective of students and proposed policies that could help publicize or eliminate it. They might become a leader of a local "Take Back the Night" march. (389)

Other forms of civic participation that Ervin mentions include voting; joining or volunteering one's time for an organization like Greenpeace; participating in a political campaign; lobbying City Council for wheelchair accessibility in public buildings; writing a letter to a congressperson; talking back to a mall preacher; running for office. Like the activities mentioned above to combat date rape, these are all worthwhile behaviors; but their setting, I would argue, is still a representative democracy; the public that students join is still a "weak" public oriented primarily to opinion formation; and the purpose of participating in such a public is still largely expressive, only rather than just writing essays, there are now meetings to attend, letters to compose, and protests to join, all for the purpose of "taking a stand."

Admittedly, this is not a passive view of politics, and for that reason, Ervin's approach has merit. In fact, she often uses "activism" as a synonym for the kind of civic participation she tries to encourage here. But it is a politics, I believe, in which the citizen can only *influence* other decision-makers, rarely is one herself. Government is still remote and other; the issues are still ideologically stark; and politics is still something you do primarily by choice, not because you are asked or required to, because it is part of your everyday social responsibility, or because the flourishing of your local world depends on it; but because you feel strongly about some issue, and, as a result of that overflow of emotion, your voice literally rises.

There's an exception to all this in the article, and it's the one instance in the piece where Ervin relates unalloyed success in engendering civic participation in her students. One Saturday, her students all load into a van and drive to a neighboring town to help with a local history project. There, they spend the day going through Town Council records in order to write, together, a thirty-year time line of the place. It turns out to be a complex and messy project, but it works. The students are faced with genuine "political" issues and a real purpose for discoursing about them; they have a real audience for their work; and they are dependent on one another to complete it. But Ervin seems unsure how to translate that experience into a full-blown theory of public discourse and political education, and she fails to recognize that what is different about the project from both the voyeuristic curriculum she criticizes and the activist pedagogy she favors is the *scene* of the public that her students join, if only for a day.

The Neighborhood

What we need, in other words, is a different kind of context for the teaching of public discourse: a smaller democracy, where ordinary individuals can engage, in person, in public judgment and decision-making, where politics can be the everyday literal enactment of every citizen's freedom and equality, where a world of social cooperation but also of differentiation and resolution—a world beyond work, family, religion, and play—can be accessible to all. The favored model for this kind of social world remains, as it was for Plato, the compact, face-to-face social group based on likeness, affinity, and proximity—what we often call "community." The spatial exemplar of such sociality for most people remains the small town, rural village, or tight-knit (sub)urban neighborhood. If there is an antithesis to the anonymous, remote nation, it is this; and if there is a stark alternative to the spectatorial politics of citizens in a national public, it is the participatory politics available here.[20]

One of the best modern treatments of the small public occurs in the final chapter of Hannah Arendt's *On Revolution*, which tells the story of the local democratic councils that have periodically sprung up in modern history whenever imperial or national power structures have collapsed.[21] Arendt calls them the "lost treasure" of the revolutionary tradition. Arising in urban neighborhoods, rural districts, and workplaces, they were scaled for direct participation by ordinary humans in the public affairs that concerned them. Arendt recounts the "natural" dispersal of political power into such local councils that occurred in, among other places, France in 1789 and 1871, Russia in 1905 and 1917, and Hungary in 1956. In each case, small groups of ordinary citizens claimed power to rule themselves through discussion, argument, and decision making. They were thus publics of genuine freedom and action. They were also, typically, nonpartisan (for Arendt, party democracy is inextricably linked to the nation-state), even as they were exclusively political (i.e., they typically did *not* absorb economics and other aspects of social life). In addition, councils usually joined up with other councils to form a federal system, one built, however, from the bottom up rather than the other way around.

For Arendt, this kind of democracy is necessarily local, not only because its impetus is typically a coming together of neighbors but also because the political freedom it enacts can only take place in person, in a physical union with finite boundaries.[22] Freedom for Arendt is possible only among equals, and equality—to be more than an abstract piety—has limits; it requires a realm of nonequality to which it is constantly, constitutively, opposed.[23] We are equal, in other words, only when we enact that equality ourselves, when we are actually *being* equal with our fellow citizens. Equality, and thus freedom, is meaningless if it is not exercised.[24]

Unfortunately, writes Arendt, in every case where council democracy has emerged, it has been crushed by threatened elites. In the French Revolution, for example, "[a]n enormous appetite for debate, for instruction, for mutual enlightenment, and exchange of opinion . . . developed in the sections and societies; and when, by fiat from above, the people in the sections were made only to listen to party speeches and to obey, they simply ceased to show up."[25] The enemies of the council system, from this point of view, are the nation-state, the party system, and the principle of representation through which both operate.

In the United States, the most eloquent advocate of the council system, as Arendt shows, was Jefferson.[26] For him, the national, state, and even county governments of the new United States were simply too large and unwieldy for direct participation by ordinary citizens. The glory of the old New England townships, he realized (perhaps too late), was that they permitted citizens to participate directly in public business. The new federal Constitution, by contrast, gave power to the citizens but failed to give them opportunities to actually *act* as citizens. Only the representatives could express, discuss, and decide; only they exercised truly public freedom. Jefferson's solution to this problem, proposed in a series of letters that he wrote to friends after his retirement from politics in 1809, was to divide the counties of each state into wards, "little republics" of about 100 citizens each that would make the government a living presence in the midst of the people. The idea, as Jefferson described it, was not to increase the power of "the many" but to strengthen the power of "every one"—at least every white male landowner. The wards were thus public spaces where the individual's freedom could appear, where each citizen could share in public power and experience public freedom.[27]

Jefferson knew that his proposal was a recipe for instability, but he believed that was the price to pay for freedom and equality. The American struggle for independence, after all, was a revolution, and the problem with the government established by that revolution was that it made future revolutions nearly impossible. Others have also bemoaned the absence of local, direct democratic institutions in the U.S. federal system. For Lewis Mumford, as for Jefferson and Arendt, the founders' failure to incorporate townships and town meetings into the U.S. constitution—their provision of public space only for the representatives of the people but not for the people themselves—was a "tragic oversight" that permanently located power in the national and state governments and abandoned local ones.[28]

If we have lost the possibility of ward-size, nonpartisan, direct democracy in this country, at least in the way that Arendt describes it, the twentieth century did see the apotheosis in design terms of a space of social union that borrowed unapologetically from both the language of personal citizenship with which Jefferson described his "little republics" and the language of community with which countless others have described their ideal sociospatial environment. That space is the *neighborhood.*

Though similar to "community" in its warm connotations, "neighborhood" can be defined much more precisely. Indeed, according to Douglas Kelbaugh, the neighborhood unit has served roughly the same purposes and had roughly the same dimensions across a remarkably broad spectrum of places, cultures, and times.[29] In simplest terms, it is a subdivision of the city, scaled to the practical, physical, social, and emotional needs of ordinary human beings. Traditionally, it is the area that urban residents can comfortably walk in doing their daily chores, a space big enough to meet their basic needs (buying groceries, stopping by the bank, going to the post office, having a drink at a bar, etc.) but small enough that they still feel it is theirs. This has typically been pegged at about a half mile squared or a circle with a half-mile diameter, the distance that the ordinary human being can walk in, say, fifteen to twenty minutes. At about 160 acres, the unit corresponds to the old "quarter-section" of the North American surveying tradition, being one-quarter of a 640 acre "section" of the classic six-square-mile "township."[30]

If the size of the neighborhood is relatively uniform, its population has varied dramatically depending on density of settlement. It can range anywhere from less than 1,000 inhabitants to more than 20,000 (that is, from less than 10 persons per acre to more than 100). In its prototypical manifestation, however, it contains about 5,000 residents (30 per acre or so), most of them from middle-class nuclear families, since the North American neighborhood is traditionally residential and defined less in terms of self-sufficiency or pedestrian scale than by its focus on the elementary school, the catchment area of which it is sometimes identified with.[31]

But where did *that* come from? Although it is clear that both ancient and medieval cities were divided into neighborhood-like units,[32] the great theorists of the residential neighborhood have been mostly modern and mostly American; and the emergence of the neighborhood unit as a planning tool can be seen as a reaction to the alienation, disease, and turmoil that accompanied urbanization in this country.[33] As Banerjee and Baer describe it, neighborhood-based design of the late nineteenth and early twentieth century may not have been explicitly *anti*-urban, but it was definitely an attempt to *humanize* the new cities of the industrial United States. Such design was supported by research that extolled the role of primary group associations, especially the family, in child development;[34] and it accompanied the concurrent rise of universal free public education in this country. As we will see below, the neighborhood was also tied to a desire to counter the growing heterogeneity, complexity, and intermingling of city life by segregating urban functions and groups and making each part of the city more homogeneous, and the whole more "rational."

But the remarkable uniformity, persistence, and influence of the neighborhood idea in both the social landscape and the cultural imagination of North America has another history. As the key unit of urban design, town planning, and residential development in this country, the neighborhood was essentially invented in one fell swoop by an American planner named Clarence Perry in the 1929 *Regional Plan of New York*.[35] Perry thought of the neighborhood as a unit meant to be repeated like a cell throughout an entire urban area. It had four basic features: it was centered on an elementary school; about 10 percent of its area was devoted to parks and playgrounds; small stores were to be located at important points (especially on the periphery); and it was designed to be pedestrian-friendly. Perry's neighborhood was roughly circular, with a radius of one-fourth of a mile and a total area of about 160 acres. At its center was open space for institutional uses, and on its boundaries were arterial streets to handle traffic, diverting cars away from the neighborhood itself. Most important of all, Perry's neighborhood was family-based, and the family imagined was the nuclear, middle-class, white family.[36]

By the late 1940s, Perry's neighborhood had been adopted by the American Public Health Association and thenceforth became a ubiquitous feature in North American town, urban, and residential development. If some of its features have had to be adapted to today's socioeconomic conditions, namely, the scarcity of cheap land for large-scale residential development and the decreasing demographic importance of the nuclear family, the *idea* of the "neighborhood" and its association with the good life persists. Perhaps the most eloquent proponents of neighborhood-based design in contemporary American planning are the New Urbanists, planners like Andres Duany and Elizabeth Plater-Zyberk, whose Traditional Neighborhood Development model builds explicitly on Perry's work.[37]

But how does the neighborhood function as a political unit? In the *Laws*, Plato famously stipulated that the ideal polis has a population of 5,040, the figure you get when you multiply together the first seven numbers.[38] Though apparently random, the figure seems to accord almost perfectly with the population of a Perry-style neighborhood. But Plato was counting *citizens*: for him, freeborn, native, adult males; the total population of his polis (including women, children, slaves, and foreigners) would have been more like 50,000,[39] far larger than most neighborhoods today. Five to ten thousand *citizens* was also the size of Hippodamus's ideal city[40] and conforms as well to Aristotle's rule that in a polis, everyone (i.e., all citizens) should be able to gather in one place and hear a speaker[41] (10,000 seems to be a kind of natural upper limit here[42]). The number is also very close to the quorum of the Athenian Assembly during the fifth and fourth centuries, BCE—roughly 6,000 individuals.[43]

With the *modern* neighborhood, however, we are talking about a *total* population of 5,000–10,000. For the Greeks, this would have been too small for an independent polis; but for us, it is a size that has acquired a kind of social magic. Christopher Alexander and his colleagues, for example, have proposed that the community of 7,000 be the central unit in human political life; in groups larger than 10,000, they argue, individuals have no direct connection with their local officials and representatives and thus no effective voice.[44] In spatial terms, their community of 7,000 would be spread over about 75 acres, the area that can be walked in ten minutes or so; its density would therefore approach 100 persons per acre. Importantly, Alexander and his colleagues imagine these communities having the power to initiate, decide, and execute their own affairs (schools, welfare, police, streets, etc.). And they recommend that each one have a political "center of gravity," a visible and accessible place where residents can feel at home and where they can talk directly to the person in charge.

This is not just armchair political philosophy. There is some evidence that modern communities of 5,000–10,000 total population are uniquely effective at encouraging and supporting high levels of civic involvement. In their 1973 book *Democracy and Size*, still a leading work on this topic, Robert Dahl and Edward Tufte report a study from Denmark that found that political participation and effectiveness there were best achieved in densely settled communities with populations under 8,000.[45] In such places, the authors argue, people are more likely to be members of organizations and to know their local representatives, two variables associated with high levels of political discussion and participation. More recently, Eric Oliver has found that small political units, whether urban, suburban, or rural, are associated with more effective mobilization of citizens by their neighbors and higher levels of interest in local affairs. For most civic acts, writes Oliver, the smaller the unit, the higher the level of civic involvement.[46]

Even the U.S. Census Bureau recognizes the importance of the 5,000-member unit. For the past 100 years, the "census tract" has been defined in neighborhood-based terms:

> Census tracts are small, relatively permanent statistical subdivisions of a county . . . delineated for most metropolitan areas (MA's) and

> other densely populated counties by local census statistical areas committees following Census Bureau guidelines. . . . Census tracts usually have between 2,500 and 8,000 persons [the target population being about 4,000] and, when first delineated, are designed to be homogeneous with respect to population characteristics, economic status, and living conditions.[47]

When first developed at the turn of the twentieth century, in fact, the census tract was about one quarter of a square mile, or 160 acres, in size—the area of the modern "neighborhood."

Neighborhood-based design has not been without critics, however, as Banerjee and Baer remind us: it has been accused of preoccupation with the physical aspects of the good community—like distance from edge to center and interlacement of streets—when social homogeneity turns out to be the feature people seem most attracted to. It has been described as inappropriate for *urban* planning since its model is more like a rural village. It has been criticized for subscribing to ethnocentric assumptions about the good life (in, for example, the primacy it accords the nuclear family). And it has been charged with anachronism and even irrelevance—research consistently shows, for example, that the behavior of most adults in our society is not limited by neighborhood boundaries in any meaningful way.[48]

The criticism that concerns me most here, however, is political. Despite research cited above showing higher levels of civic participation in smaller communities, a neighborhood-size polis (with a total population of 5,000–10,000 at American-style densities of ten to thirty units per acre) may be too small to be truly self-sufficient (and thus independent), to support genuine individual freedom, and to be able to actually solve the kinds of problems that people care most about. But the most compelling political criticism of the Anglo-American residential neighborhood unit, I believe, is that it tends, in both theory and practice, to be too homogeneous to generate the conflict needed for genuine political engagement. The composition of the traditional American neighborhood—its small size, isolation from the rest of the city, bias toward the detached single family dwelling and thus toward low-density settlement, functional segregation, and demographic homogeneity—inhibits meaningful public argument by making sure that there is very little to argue about. Again, there is empirical evidence to support this claim. Oliver's research shows that economically homogeneous communities, whether uniformly affluent or poor, exhibit strongly depressed civic participation rates, regardless of their size. The highest level of political activity, he found, takes place in the most economically *diverse* places,[49] apparently because the conflict stimulated by heterogeneity increases civic participation among residents. And since residential neighborhoods in the United States are intensely segregated by race, class, age, familial status, ethnicity, and so on, there is good reason to believe that they may not, after all, be very promising scenes for vibrant and meaningful civic life and education.

In fact, the single biggest impetus for neighborhood-based design in the United States may well be our fear of difference; and the smallness, low-density, privatism, and mono-functionality of American suburbs may be, at bottom, about placating that fear. We have tended, in other words, to define our ideal socio-spatial environment as a "community," to construe that in terms of harmony,[50] and to imagine it, physically, along the lines of the suburban neighborhood. The ideal civic scene in our minds is thus the most homogeneous.

This dark side of neighborhood-based civic life can be seen in the rise of residential community associations (RCAs) in American culture and politics. Probably the fastest growing form of grassroots democracy in the United States, RCAs are legally defined organizations that unite contiguous property-owners. The most important kind of RCAs are common interest developments (CIDs), which include condominium associations, housing cooperatives, and homeowner associations.[51] According to Evan McKenzie, a housing development is considered a CID if it has three features: common ownership of shared facilities (like pools, clubhouses, and yards), mandatory membership in a nonprofit community association, and a requirement to live under private laws. In 1999, there were 231,000 such developments in the United States, up from just 500 in 1965. As for RCAs in general, more than 50 million Americans now live in them, about 15 percent of all U.S. homes and 50 percent of all new homes in major metropolitan areas, especially in Florida, California, Arizona, and Texas.[52]

Most RCAs are small, about 150 units or so, and well-organized; and they provide, in theory at least, valuable opportunities for direct participation in local political affairs. In fact, some have argued that RCAs are the most responsive form of democracy found in America today and the most significant political movement in our society.[53] From a rhetorical perspective, they would seem to be promising contexts for the development of discursive habits. The ability of RCAs to foster civic virtue, however, has recently come under question.[54] For one thing, rather than encouraging citizen activity, they seem more often to depress it, generating a culture of *non*-participation,[55] their very privatism, exclusionary tactics, and social segregation making them more like schools of selfishness than democracy. They are also typically run like businesses, with developers sometimes using them to build quasi-private states run *without* politics.[56] And when people do participate in RCAs, it is more often out of a desire to protect property values than a recognition of social interdependence or responsibility.[57] Civic engagement thus occurs for the narrowest of reasons, with detrimental consequences for the public at large; RCA-based arguments are already being used, for example, to exempt residents from having to pay local taxes.[58] *Pace* Robert Putnam, this kind of voluntary association, rather than promoting civic virtue, allows its members to further their interests at the exclusion of others.[59]

Thus, whatever increased opportunities RCAs provide for political voice in our society, they come with a high social cost. In the words of Theodore Roszak, "A city whose sense of politics never gets beyond selfish defensiveness, and an obsessive concern for property values, is a sick city."[60]

The Dilemma

We face, then, a dilemma. Small democracies promote and rely on direct participation by ordinary citizens in public life, strong feelings of belonging, and a shared sense of the common good; but they typically lack the conflict that generates debate to begin with as well as the resources and independence needed to solve members' most significant problems. Large democracies, on the other hand, have sovereignty, power, and diversity, but they present few opportunities for "strong" participation by ordinary citizens. I am not the first to point out this dilemma. Here, for example, is Iris Marion Young:

> On the one hand, self-determination, cultural specificity, participation, and accountability seem best realized in relatively small political units. On the other hand, values of taking into account the needs and interests of differently situated others with whom local affinity groups dwell are best realized in political units wide in scope, comprising at least broad metropolitan regions. Is there any way out of this dilemma that can balance local self-determination with a region-wide acknowledgement of the legitimate interests of others?[61]

Eric Oliver writes of a similar quandary: local governments need to be small to be accessible to the maximum number of citizens; but they need to be representatively diverse in order to encompass the predominant social conflicts of a geographical area and not give any group monopolistic control over government.[62] And Patricia Roberts-Miller has described a related problem: the more a public sphere becomes democratized, the less it is able to sponsor "rational-critical argument," wide participation and deep ratiocination being, apparently, mutually exclusive: "If the discourse group is very large, and everyone is to have a chance to contribute, then people can speak only very briefly, and only once." Take the Internet: as newsgroups become increasingly inclusive, they also become less deliberative. To counteract that, large groups often splinter into smaller ones, which are able to sponsor more meaningful participation but tend to be less heterogeneous and therefore more like enclaves.[63]

Thirty years ago, Dahl and Tufte helpfully divided this dilemma into two separate ones:

> First, the *effectiveness of the citizen* who is in concord with the preponderant majority of other citizens in his unit may well be maximized, as Rousseau thought, when the unit is small and homogeneous. The politics of homogeneity serve this citizen best. Yet in such a unit the effectiveness of the dissenting citizen is minimized by his difficulty in finding an ally, and by the weakness of political competition. The politics of diversity in the larger, more heterogeneous unit may serve the dissenting citizen best. And yet the same citizen may sometimes be in concord, sometimes in dissent.
>
> Second, and most important, the goal of maximizing citizen effectiveness on matters that are highly important to him can and does conflict with the effort to maximize the *capacity of the system* (and hence ultimately, though in a different sense, the citizen's effectiveness) for dealing with these matters. In the extreme case, a citizen could be maximally effective in a system of minimal capacity for dealing with major issues (e.g., international violence) or minimally effective in a system of maximal capacity for dealing with major issues.[64]

In other words, as we increase the capacity of the political system to handle critical problems (and some problems, clearly, are *trans*national in scope), we decrease the effectiveness and power of the individual citizen, making it harder for him or her to "acquire the sense and the reality of moral responsibility and political effectiveness."[65] But when we increase the civic capacity of individual citizens, we decrease the power of the system as a whole.

Aristotle made a similar argument more than two millennia ago. For the best polis, he wrote, 10 citizens is too small, and 100,000, too large.[66] The former cannot be truly "political" because such a group would not be self-sufficient, that is, independent of other groups. Besides, a community the size of a household or village—made up of "fellows of the same milk," as Aristotle memorably put it—is by definition "*pre*political," since it is ruled not by rational discussion and debate but by fiat of the eldest males.[67] The large public, meanwhile, also cannot be truly "political" because it cannot be governed well—citizens need to know one another in order to rule themselves for anything other than mere survival.[68] The best polis, Aristotle implied, is somewhere between the household or village, on the one hand, and the nation or empire, on the other, characterized by neither pure identity nor pure difference. It is composed of a multitude of dissimilars in which each takes his turn at governing and is devoted to making himself, his fellows, and his polis more just and noble.[69] So, to the question, should citizens in the polis share everything or nothing, Aristotle's answer was: neither. Referring to Plato's vision of a community that is "all one," he wrote:

> As the city becomes more and more of a unity, it will cease to exist. For a city is in its nature a certain multitude and not a single individual. A city is made up not only of many humans but of humans who differ in kind. No city comes into existence from those who are all alike. . . . As a city progresses towards unity, it would be like reducing a many-voiced harmony to unison.[70]

Aristotle's good polis arises, therefore, precisely when individuals from *different* families and villages form a single self-sufficient community, one which does not require that the differences of its members be obliterated or transcended.[71]

What we are looking for, then, is a space *between* community and society,[72] one capable of sponsoring relations different from both the intimate bond of family and friends and the mutual suspicion of strangers, a setting which is true to human diversity but still allows for "commonality" and "solidarity."[73] Carolyn Miller expresses the double nature of this space well: "Because there are many citizens, there are differences; because there is one polis, they must confront those differences."[74] This is also, I believe, the kind of scene we need for the development of good *rhetorical* habits and dispositions, which improve as the relevant group gets small enough to allow for genuine participation by ordinary members but which require for stimulation the conflicts and disagreements of large groups.

City, District, and Metropolis

Can the *city* solve this dilemma? Can it fill the gap between the small and large public? between the compact, face-to-face, familiar but homogeneous *neighborhood* and the extensive, print-mediated, diverse but distant *nation*? between the community of belonging and the society of autonomous individuals? Might it constitute the form of "publicity" we have been looking for: "strong enough to institute a 'demos' but compatible with pluralism"?[75] Can it sponsor "difference without exclusion,"[76] generating affinity and allowing for direct participation by ordinary people in the decision-making that affects them but still accommodating variety of beliefs and having the resources to actually solve the most serious problems its inhabitants face? Can it be a place "of unification without homogenization . . . where society's members might come together without forfeiting their multiple social identities . . . [a place] of commonality and connection that [does] not pulverize differences"?[77] Can the city, that is, mediate the apparently incompatible political virtues of *accessibility* and *diversity*?

I believe it can. But first, we need a definition. In an oft-cited 1938 article in the *American Journal of Sociology*, University of Chicago sociologist Louis Wirth defined the city as "a relatively large, dense, and permanent settlement of socially heterogeneous individuals."[78] By this he meant, I believe, that the city is, first, a well-delimited physical *place*, a ground for its inhabitants' embodied lives, of a size big enough to provide for their needs and wants but small enough to still feel like it is their's. Second, those inhabitants are *many*, a multitude or plurality of individuals, most of whom do not know one another, not being related by ties of kinship, friendship, or formal responsibility. Third, despite the lack of such ties, residents of a city are cognizant of *sharing* space, of living together, of having concrete relations with one another, being always, potentially, in one another's way and yet also intricately interdependent. And, finally, the city is a place of *difference*, where residents are aware of their constant potential for conflict.

Now, we have seen that, historically, it was the cities (*poleis*) of the Greek classical era—and the public spheres they supported (assembly grounds, council chambers, courtrooms, theaters, marketplaces, etc.)—that first motivated a specifically *rhetorical* self-consciousness. These were communities built by and productive of argument.[79] But we need not confine ourselves to the past to see the city as important for those interested in human politics, social discourse, and public education. Today, the city is an increasingly important setting of human rhetorical activity. Half the world's population now resides in cities, and that proportion is growing rapidly.[80] And cities have increased in economic importance as well, partly because of increasingly decentralized national governance and liberalized world trade.[81] More to the point of this book, the city has begun to permeate our thinking about, and teaching of, writing, speaking, and critical thinking. The rise of "comp studies" in the 1960s and '70s, for example, can be tied, I would argue, to the post–World War II metropolitanization of the United States.[82]

But the main reason for privileging the city in civic education, I believe, is that the city remains the place where the possibility of negotiating our differences within a context of commonality is most alive. Richard Dagger has described that possibility this way:

> [O]ther forms of political association, such as province, nation-state, and empire, are too large and too remote from the everyday lives of their inhabitants to inspire the kind of interest and effort that citizenship (in the ethical sense) demands. The city is more accessible to its residents than these larger bodies, more closely tied to its residents' interests, and more likely to promote the sense of

> community usually associated with effective citizenship. Yet it is also large enough and sufficiently diverse in its composition to offer what the village cannot—a truly political environment.[83]

Dagger has not been alone in wanting the city to be the "true home of citizenship."[84] Unfortunately, our cities today are both too small and too large to serve this function well. They are too small in the sense that they are typically powerless vis-à-vis states and the nation; and they often fragment our landscape along socioeconomic lines. At the same time, they are typically too large for the kinds of personal involvement in politics advocated in this book.

So, we need two additional units, one bigger and one smaller than the city, to complete our new map of political geography. Those units are the metropolitan area and the urban district.

A "metropolis" I define, following the U.S. Census Bureau, as any geographical area comprising a large population nucleus (i.e., 50,000 or more inhabitants) together with all adjacent communities "that have a high degree of social and economic integration" with that nucleus—in other words, a central city and its suburbs.[85] There are, says the federal government, more than 250 such places in this country, ranging in size from the huge Los Angeles, New York City, and Chicago metropolitan areas, with their millions of inhabitants, to the tiny Enid (Oklahoma) metropolitan area, with only 57,000. Eighty percent of the U.S. population now lives here.[86]

Perhaps *this* should be the key public sphere between community and society. Although political life in this country is usually played out at either the supra- or submetropolitan levels—in the nation, states, and counties that make up our federal system or the townships, municipalities, neighborhoods, and other jurisdictions into which our local landscape is divided—metropolitan areas may be the most crucial scenes of everyday civic life in our world. As Iris Marion Young has written recently: they are united by climate, vegetation, topography, and waterways; they are connected by high-density economic processes and movements, including labor and consumer markets; they are even the area spanned by a strong radio signal.[87]

Further, regardless of their more local affiliations, people typically treat the metropolis in which they reside as a single place. They wake up in one part of it, go to work in another, shop in a third, and visit friends in a fourth without ever thinking that they have left town. They drive across multiple municipal boundaries to reach "their" airport; go downtown to see "their" sports team; and move from one school district to another without also changing their job, church, or dentist. If it is true, as Gerald Frug has written, that the modern North American metropolis is intensely fractured along lines of race, class, and ethnicity, and that there are places where we do not go because we do not "belong" there,[88] it is also true that many of us move freely across multiple submetropolitan boundaries in our everyday lives and think little of it.[89]

But even absent this internal mobility, the metropolis can be seen as a unitary "public" because (and to the extent that) what its residents do in one part affects people in other parts.[90] Take, for example, the purchase of a new house in a suburban development zoned for detached single family dwellings on large lots. This may seem like a purely private, and narrowly local, act with few public consequences. But because the very form of the development mandates the use of private automobiles for nearly all the transportation needs of the people who live there, and because those residents are among the most mobile in the metropolis, this act contributes in a real way to increased traffic and air pollution at the metropolitan level. In other words, although a suburban community may retain exclusive right to the benefits it derives from its advantages over neighboring communities (e.g., its ability to generate very high revenue from relatively low property tax rates), it often shares its negative byproducts (e.g., air pollution) with the whole region. The appropriate ground on which to "publicize" and govern such acts, therefore, would be the metropolis—that is, if fairness were an important criterion for decision-making in our world. As Iris Marion Young has put it, "The scope of a polity . . . ought to coincide with the scope of the obligations of justice which people have in relation to one another because their lives are intertwined in social, economic, and communicative relations that tie their lives."[91]

To imagine the metropolitan sphere as an important, even primary, public in our social lives is thus to imagine living in an inclusive, rather than exclusive, polis; it is to think about our everyday private acts as having public consequences of a far-reaching sort; it is to believe that a community need not be homogeneous or harmonious to be "good" and that we can make reasonable political decisions together by appealing to something other than self-interest. It is to imagine our lives as intertwined with the lives of people very different from us, people with whom we share a world and the responsibility of caring for it. And it is, finally, to match the boundaries of our political world with the geography of our everyday lives. Clearly, there are other ways that we inhabit and share the earth, and, admittedly, the metropolis does not currently play a prominent role in our social and political consciousness—in most places, it has no legal status whatsoever. Nonetheless, it is one of the key ways in which we organize our everyday physical relations with one another and with nature.

Unfortunately, the metropolis, while more capable of supporting a "strong public" than the nation-state, is still too large for the broad and deep political participation we have been seeking here. We need something big for dissent, anonymity, and power, but not so big that we lose the openness, contact, and mutuality of "community." And that leads us to our final sociospatial unit, the one that turns out, in my opinion, to be *rhetorically* the most interesting of all.

If, as we saw above, 10,000 citizens is the upper limit for a direct, face-to-face political assembly,[92] the number of people who can gather together in space and time, render their diversity, and still be "one," what size *total* population would that correspond to—that is, if we placed no significant restrictions on citizenship except age?[93] Well, let us assume that of our total population, about one-third will be under eighteen years old, and another one-sixth or so will be infirm, institutionalized, transitory, or otherwise unavailable for politics. Together, that would take care of about half the total population ($^1/_3 + ^1/_6 = ^1/_2$). Of the remaining half, all adults capable of regular political action, the majority might reasonably be expected to directly and substantively participate in the deliberative politics of their local community, in one way or another, at one time or another, about once a year. A goal in fact might be to have one person per household participate actively in the sovereign decision-making of his or her polis at least once a year (through attendance at a meeting, service on a committee, etc.). This seems to me a good balance between an excessively direct democracy, in which politics is pretty much all anyone does, and a representative system in which a tiny elite governs, and the rest do virtually nothing.

Let's say, then, that about one-fourth to one-fifth of those community members capable of participation (that is, one-eighth to one-tenth of the total population) can be expected, at any given time, to participate in the direct self-governance of their local public, for example, by attendance at an assembly meeting.[94] If such attendance were targeted at 5,000 to 10,000, and that were to represent one-tenth of the total population of the polis (or one-fifth of those members capable of active participation), then the relevant size of the political unit itself would be about 50,000 to 100,000 inhabitants. This is a "public," I believe, in which ordinary members have a reasonable chance to directly participate in binding, effective, political decision-making, a public that can mediate the apparently conflicting sociopolitical criteria of accessibility and diversity.

To that end, I propose here the *urban district* of around 50,000–100,000 people, subunit of a larger metropolis or region, as a neglected but potentially powerful scene of politics and rhetoric in our lives, a category around which we might organize civic projects of importance to us. Such a district would be characterized by relatively circumscribed territory and a measure of geographical-cultural identity, a social setting small enough that individual residents feel they belong to it and have a reasonable chance to be seen and heard in it, but large enough to allow for a measure of both diversity and power. It would be a place where there is disagreement among residents about public issues and where that disagreement matters, where people belong but where others different from them belong as well, a place that is their's but not their's alone.

The unit is not my invention. The concept of the urban district of around 50,000–100,000 inhabitants was developed by two scholars working independently of each other in the 1960s: the urbanologist Jane Jacobs, who introduced the term in her 1961 book *The Death and Life of Great American Cities* as a mediating space between the humane but politically powerless street "neighborhood" and the powerful but overlarge "city-as-a-whole" (her districts, modeled on Greenwich Village in New York City, were around 100,000 in population),[95] and the political philosopher Robert Dahl, who argued in a 1967 paper that the city of 50,000–100,000 population (a political space between the village and the state) was the optimum-size unit for a democratic system, "powerful enough, autonomous enough, and small enough to permit, and in the right circumstances to encourage, a body of citizens to participate actively and rationally in shaping and forming vital aspects of their lives in common."[96]

If the size of the classic American residential neighborhood is one-quarter of a square mile (160 acres) and its total population, about 5,000–10,000 (about 30–60 persons, or 10–30 units, per acre), the district described here would be about ten times that, or about 1.5 square miles (1,600 acres) in area and about 50,000–100,000 in population. This is clearly an abstraction, but there are concrete approximations of it in the real world: Chicago's seventy-seven "community areas" of about 75,000 each, of which the Near North Side is one; New York's fifty-nine "community districts" of about 125,000 each,[97] even Paris's twenty *arrondissements*, which vary from under 20,000 to over 200,000 in population.[98] The urban district need not, however, be so prototypically "urban": my own city of Madison, Wisconsin, with about 200,000 total population, could be easily subdivided into four districts, each with about 50,000 residents, centered on a high school, and composed of about ten neighborhoods of 5,000 residents each, centered on an elementary school.

If the urban district has not been especially prominent in recent sociological or political theory, it still occasionally shows up. Anthropologist Roger Sanjek, for example, draws on Jacobs's "district" in his 1998 study of the Elmhurst-Corona section of Queens, *The Future of Us All*. And political scientist Eric Oliver has resurrected Dahl's medium-size city in his own empirical work. As we saw above, Oliver's research supports the claim that civic participation in this country (as measured by such things as voting in local elections and attending community board meetings) increases as city size decreases, even when the smaller city is a unit within a large metropolitan area; Oliver finds that smaller-size political entities, whether urban or rural, are associated with more effective mobilization of citizens by their neighbors and higher levels of interest in local affairs. But Oliver also found that, when the economic segregation of the American social landscape is included in the analysis, diversity becomes an important variable, with political participation lowest in cities that are economically homogeneous (whether rich or poor). Diverse, middle-income cities, Oliver reasons, generate high levels of conflict, which, in turn, stimulate political interest and involvement. When we combine these two findings, we are back, I believe, in Dahl's optimum-size democratic unit, cities (or parts thereof) "small enough to facilitate civic participation but large enough to generate meaningful political discourse."[99]

Unfortunately, the district of 50,000–100,000 has not been a prominent category in American politics or design.[100] It is completely ignored, for example, by Christopher Alexander and his colleagues, whose otherwise comprehensive book jumps literally from the major city of 500,000 to the community or town of 7,000.[101] In fact, most cities are *not* formally subdivided by district. Nor, to my knowledge, has the "district" *ever* appeared in rhetorical theory and education, although it corresponds almost exactly to the most famous rhetorical scene in history—golden-age Athens, which, according to Hansen (and *contra* persistent claims that it was a small, homogeneous, face-to-face society[102]), had a *citizen* population between 30,000–60,000—and although it is roughly the size of the feeder area for the American high school, where rhetorical education in our culture has traditionally begun.

So, we have ended up in the *city*, with its metropolitan surroundings and internal districts, as a neglected but potentially important scene of human politics and civic education. My point here is not to say that public life should now be exclusively located here but to add these new units to our mix and grant them appropriate rights and powers. Clearly, we all participate in geographically defined political groups of varying shapes and sizes, from neighborhood associations to nation-states and beyond. My goal is to remind us—who have too often, I believe, treated politics in general and democracy in particular in excessively uniform ways—of the enormous variety of political environments in which we live and interact and to suggest how these environments might require, support, and engender very different kinds of political habits and dispositions. We need multiple scenes in which to act politically, from neighborhoods and regions to nations and the globe. But we should also be careful that, in our civic practices, philosophies, and pedagogies, we do not neglect these crucial middle spheres.

But it is time now to leave the realm of theory and look at the actual neighborhoods, urban districts, cities, and metropolitan areas in which we live. What are they like as rhetorical scenes? Are they places in which ordinary people can come together without fear of assimilation? in which individuals have a chance of being heard in public concerning matters on which there is disagreement? And, if our urban districts, cities, and metropolises are not now such places, can they be redesigned in that direction?

PART TWO

Designing the Twenty-first Century Public Sphere

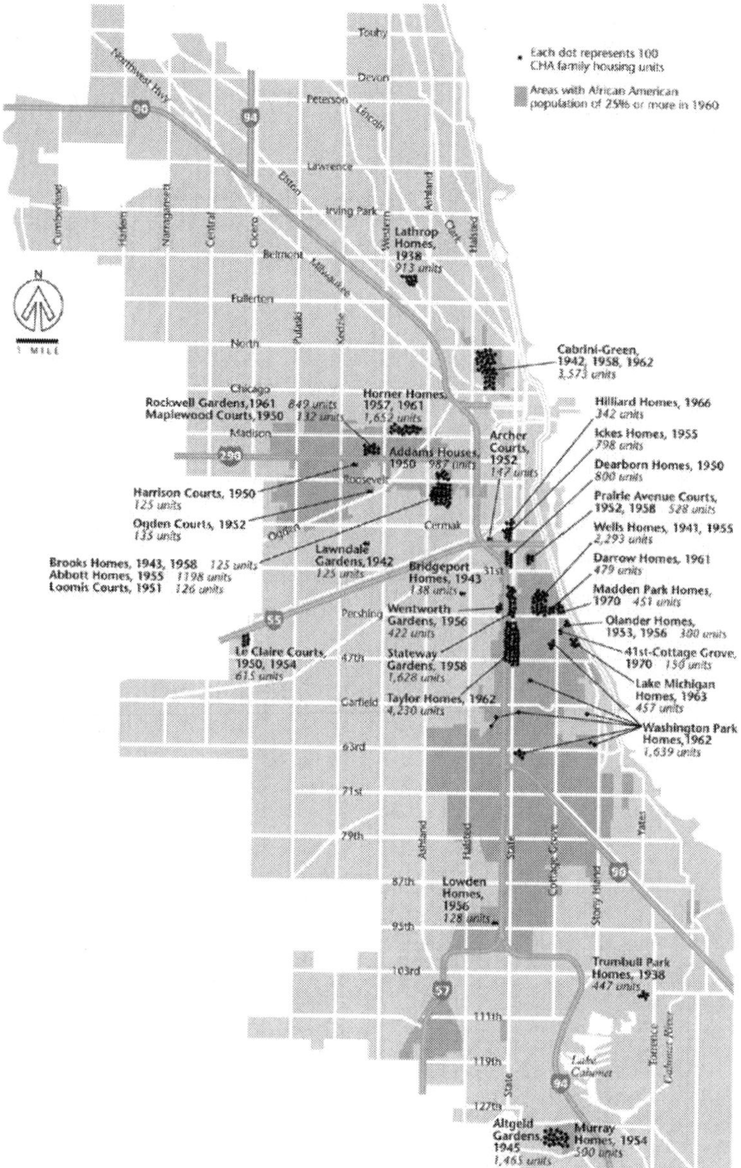

Figure 1. Map of Chicago Housing Authority Family Projects, 1985

Source: James R. Grossman, Ann Durkin Keating, and Janice L. Reiff, eds., *The Encyclopedia of Chicago* (Chicago: University of Chicago Press, 2004), 137. Map by Dennis McClendon. Copyright held by Newberry Library, Chicago, IL. Reproduced by permission of Newberry Library.

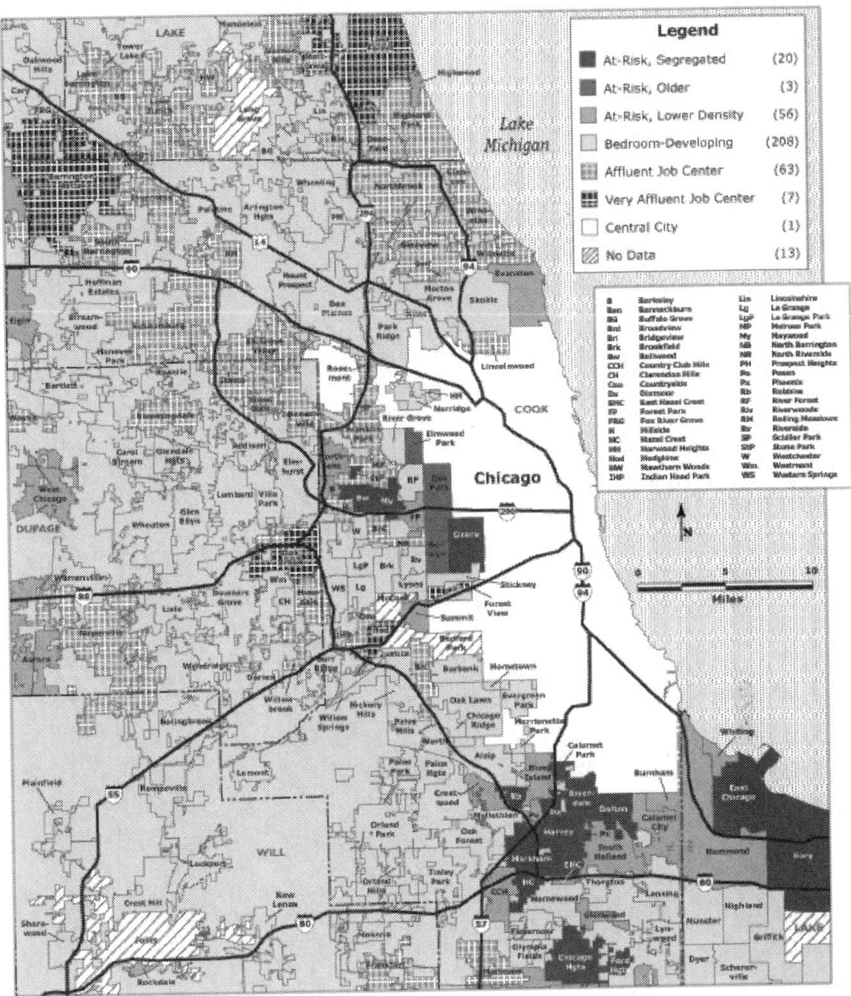

Figure 2. Map of Chicago Region (Central Area): Community Classification, 2002

Source: Myron Orfield, *American Metropolitics: The New Suburban Reality* (Washington, DC: Brookings Institution Press, 2002), Map 2–3 (following p. 48). Map copyright held by the Metropolitan Area Research Corporation (now Ameregis), Minneapolis, MN. Adapted for this use by and reproduced with the permission of Ameregis.

Figure 3. Drawing (aerial view) of North Town Village, Chicago, IL, 2000

Source: Holsten Real Estate Development Corporation, Chicago, IL. Drawing by Henry Gould. Reproduced by permission of Holsten Real Estate Development Corporation.

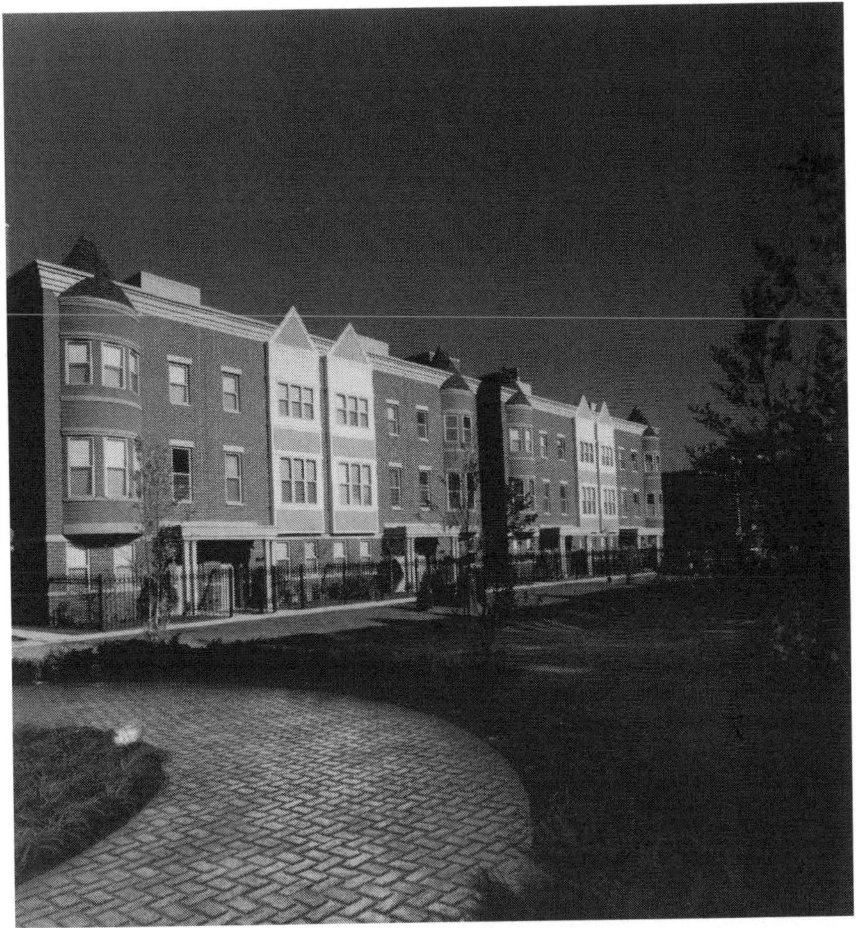

Figure 4. Photograph (street level) of North Town Village, Chicago, IL, 2002

Source: Holsten Real Estate Development Corporation, Chicago, IL. Reproduced by permission of Holsten Real Estate Development Corporation.

Figure 5. Photograph of 1230 North Burling Street, Chicago, IL, 2000

FOUR

Ghetto

Chicago, 1995

Why they make us live in one corner of the city?

—Richard Wright, *Native Son*

If, as W. E. B. Du Bois predicted, the problem of the twentieth century was the problem of the color line,[1] then nowhere was that line more literal than in Chicago, which remains to this day one of the most segregated cities in North America. The arrangement is not innocent, either in cause or effect. The concentration, confinement, and isolation of Chicago blacks was consciously intended and methodically achieved, by whites, through both private and public means; and it has functioned not just to keep whites and blacks apart in that city but to leave blacks with the worst housing in the worst neighborhoods, the worst jobs, the worst schools, and the worst government services.

And Chicago is only an egregious example of a pattern evident across the United States and throughout its history: the socioeconomic subjugation of African-Americans, which has changed over time but has not fundamentally ceased. The extreme spatial manifestation of that subjugation is, of course, the *ghetto*, defined by the 1968 Kerner Commission as "an area within a city characterized by poverty and acute social disorganization and inhabited by members of a racial or ethnic group under conditions of involuntary segregation."[2] Chicago provides perhaps the prime example of an American ghetto.

But what makes the Chicago ghetto an especially compelling story is its recurrent juxtaposition of oppression with opportunity, confinement with freedom, disaster with hope. For much of the twentieth century, it was, at one and the same time, a scene of both despair and promise. This paradox was best expressed half a century ago by the novelist Richard Wright, who wrote in 1945 that blacks had come to Chicago "to seek freedom":

> And there in that great iron city, that impersonal, mechanical city, amid the steam, the smoke, the snowy winds, the blistering suns; there in that self-conscious city, that city so deadly dramatic and stimulating, we caught whispers of the meanings that life could have, and we were pushed and pounded by facts much too big for us. . . . Chicago is the city from which the most incisive and radical Negro thought has come; there is an open and raw beauty about [it] that seems either to kill or endow one with the spirit of life.[3]

The white response to black Chicago has been similarly conflicted. The city provides the classic case of American racial residential segregation; but it is also the foremost American city for urban renewal and subsidized housing, and it is today a leader in both mobility and mixed-income redevelopment programs. In addition, it has been home for over a century now to some of the most important research in the world on urban life: "For Chicago, with its famously divided segments, its infamous segregation, and its stark inequality, is not only the quintessential American city of extremes. It is also the city in and through which scholars founded and developed the American approach to urban studies."[4]

The city also provides the backdrop for a set of events probably unique in world history: a single people suffering through three economic revolutions in less than a hundred years. The story of blacks in Chicago is the story of a people moving, literally, from an agricultural to an industrial to a service economy—and from a rural to an urban to a metropolitan geography—all within a century. At each step along the way, they were both indispensable and ill-served. Promised forty acres and a mule after the Civil War, southern blacks got only tenant farming and debt peonage. Moving to the urban north in the years before, between, and after the two World Wars, blacks in industrial-era Chicago were left with the domestic service and then the nonunion factory and slaughterhouse jobs that white immigrants would not take. Later, still in the central city after most of the whites had left, Chicago's blacks suffered from the "spatial mismatch" of the new economy, in which the low-skill jobs they needed moved to the suburbs and the sunbelt. In other words, in the agricultural economy, blacks were landless; in the industrial economy, unorganized; and in the service economy, underemployed. In each case, they were the last invited to the table and the only ones still there when the feast had moved on.

In this chapter, I tell the story of blacks in Chicago from the city's founding until today. It is in the main a story of ghetto formation and collapse. I rely in large part on the remarkable historical trilogy of Allan Spear's *Black Chicago: The Making of a Negro Ghetto, 1890–1920*, St. Clair Drake and Horace R. Cayton's *Black Metropolis: A Study of Negro Life in a Northern City*, and Arnold Hirsch's *Making the Second Ghetto: Race and Housing in Chicago,*

1940–1960. I supplement those with other sources that fill in the gaps and bring us up to the present.

The First Ghetto

The first permanent nonnative settler in what would become Chicago was, in fact, a free black man. Jean Baptiste Point Du Sable was the son of a slave woman from Santo Domingo (now Haiti) and a French merchant. Born around 1745, he was raised and educated a Catholic. In 1779, at the age of thirty-four, he traveled as a trader and explorer up the Mississippi River to the Great Lakes region, where he settled on the shore of Lake Michigan, at the mouth (and on the north bank) of the Chicago River, just east of today's Michigan Avenue Bridge. On this site, Du Sable established a trading post, dealing in furs and grains, and a homestead that was the site of the first marriage, first election, and first court in the region. Du Sable was a skilled carpenter, cooper, miller, and distiller; he was also a husband and father, marrying a Native American woman and raising two children with her.[5]

Sometime in the late 1790s, Du Sable sold his Chicago homestead and left with his family, apparently for St. Louis.[6] A few years later, in 1803, the U.S. Army began construction of Fort Dearborn on the south bank of the Chicago River, and the next few decades in the settlement's life were dominated by the upper Midwest fur trade and the protection given to it by the U.S. military. But even without Du Sable, Chicago in the first quarter of the nineteenth century was home to extraordinary sociocultural diversity; it was a place where free blacks, mulattoes, Native Americans, "half-breeds," and English- and French-speaking whites mingled freely and amicably.[7] Donald Miller has described the settlement this way:

> At various times there were Frenchmen in the village who had fought with Napoleon at Jena and Waterloo, Yankees who had been with Andrew Jackson at New Orleans, and Indians . . . who had fought alongside the legendary Tecumseh. . . . At the Sauganash and its neighboring hotels, men and women of every color and class were welcome; and whisky, song, and dance were the great democratizers.[8]

By 1830, the settlement along the Chicago River was large enough, and promising enough, to be platted; and in 1833, it was incorporated as a town, with a population of 400 living on a square mile around the Chicago River. Then, in 1836, work began on the Illinois and Michigan Canal, which would eventually link the Chicago and Desplaines Rivers and, through them, Lake

Michigan and the Mississippi River. The canal was the major impetus for the town's rapid growth during the 1830s. By 1837, when Chicago was incorporated as a city, it had a population of 4,200, a tenfold increase in just four years, and occupied ten square miles of land from North Avenue to Cermak Road and Lake Michigan to Wood Street.

In the 1840s, according to St. Clair Drake and Horace Cayton, there was already a small community of free blacks living in Chicago, probably numbering in the hundreds.[9] The city had become by then a stop on the Underground Railroad to Canada, though many of the slaves who traveled that route ended up staying. No doubt they experienced the discrimination typical of northern cities at the time, but they were at least free and could participate in the city's economic growth.[10] By the 1870s, Chicago was home to a black population of around 3,000, most of them interspersed with whites, though something of a black neighborhood had begun to form along the east bank of the south branch of the Chicago River, between Harrison and Sixteenth Streets (39).[11]

This neighborhood was spared destruction in the Great Fire of 1871; but after suffering through a smaller fire in 1874, many in the black community relocated farther south to a narrow strip of land between Wentworth and State from Twenty-second to Thirty-first Streets (47). The South Side of Chicago, where the new "black belt" was located, was the fastest growing part of the city in the years between "the fire and the fair" (the World's Columbian Exposition of 1893). And it was home to a wide range of groups. To the west was the working-class Irish neighborhood of Bridgeport. To the East were German Jewish and "native" white middle-class neighborhoods. Due north was the Levee, the city's red-light district. And to the northeast was Prairie Avenue, where the wealthiest families in Chicago lived in stone townhouses on tree-lined boulevards. In other words, the black belt was hemmed in on nearly all sides, with room to expand only southward.[12] By 1893, many of the 15,000 blacks living in the city were concentrated here, the seeds of a ghetto to come (Drake and Cayton, 47; Spear, 11–12).

During this time, Chicago was growing at a spectacular rate, both economically and demographically. It became a center of manufacturing, meatpacking, and retail; and it was soon the most important transportation hub on the continent.[13] It was also becoming famous for *building*: in the decades after the Great Fire, modern architecture was essentially invented here.[14] The city was a center of labor agitation as well, especially in the vast immigrant neighborhoods on the West Side.[15] Blacks were largely uninvolved in this unrest because of their inferior position in the job market.[16] Although they were used as "scabs" in the 1904 stockyard and 1905 teamsters strikes, they were discharged once the strikes ended, an experience that left a legacy of distrust between blacks and ethnic whites in the city (Spear, 36–41).

In general, though, black-white relations were not a major source of tension in the city. In 1900, the black community in Chicago was still quite small and not truly ghettoized. According to Spear, fourteen of thirty-five wards in the city had a negro population of at least 1 percent, and in only two wards were blacks more than 10 percent of the population. About a quarter of the city's blacks were contained in truly black neighborhoods, while 30 percent lived in neighborhoods that were more than 95 percent white (Spear, 14). As late as 1910, blacks in Chicago were actually *less* segregated from "native" whites than were Italians (15).

Still, their numbers and concentration were increasing. Between 1880–1910, many educated southern blacks, the so-called talented tenth, migrated to the north, fleeing Jim Crow (Drake and Cayton, 53).[17] The black belt on the South Side became home to most, and it consequently expanded, shifting its center south to Thirty-first and State Streets. Thirty percent of Chicago's blacks now lived in predominantly black sections of the city, and over 60 percent in areas with more than 20 percent blacks. Although no census tract in the city was more than 61 percent black, and most had at least some blacks (Spear, 17), the black population was gradually becoming confined to a small number of areas, where housing conditions were among the worst in the city.

Meanwhile, hostility against blacks was increasing. In 1908, the residents of Hyde Park organized an "Improvement Club" to keep blacks confined to certain districts, promote the hiring of white janitors for the neighborhood's buildings, petition the city for racially separate schools, and blacklist real estate firms that allowed blacks to move into white neighborhoods (Spear, 22).[18] Overall, however, blacks in Chicago in the early years of the twentieth century were left to themselves. And, with the help of a growing middle class, a black elite began to envision a self-sufficient "city within the city" on the South Side (Drake and Cayton, 396), a "black metropolis" (Spear, 91) with its own churches, hospitals, YMCAs, women's clubs, settlement houses, social and fraternal organizations, banks, real estate firms, newspapers, and factories.

The Great Migration

But no one was prepared for what happened in the years during and immediately after World War I, when the racial landscape of Chicago changed forever. In one of the major social transformations in American history, southern blacks moved north in huge numbers. In Chicago alone, the black population more than doubled (a 148 percent increase) between 1910 and 1920, most of it during the so-called Great Migration of 1916–1919, when 50,000 new blacks arrived in the city (Spear, 129–46). There were several causes for this mass migration. With the outbreak of war, American industry expanded rapidly, but foreign immigration to the United States (and the cheap labor it supplied) had been virtually shut off overnight. Northern labor agents, therefore, had to look elsewhere for war workers. Meanwhile, because of the low price of cotton, the flooding of 1915–16, and the boll weevil plight, farmers in the South were turning to food crops and livestock, which required less labor than cotton. Another crucial factor in the black exodus was the "pull" exerted by Robert Abbott's *Chicago Defender*, the most important black newspaper in the city and the most widely read black newspaper in the South. In May, 1917, Abbott launched the *Defender*'s "Great Northern Drive" to convince southern blacks to flee "Egypt" and come up to the "Promised Land" (Spear, 135).

The Great Migration of 1916–19 was different from the migrations of the 1880s and '90s. It was more sudden, involved larger numbers, and drew more attention. And it involved migrants who were, for the most part, poorer and less well-educated than before; they were also more likely to come from the lower rather than the upper south, fully one-third of the Great Migration originating in Mississippi and Alabama (Spear, 138–45; Drake and Cayton, 58–64).

Fortunately, the job market for blacks in Chicago expanded significantly, with factory jobs opening up at Swift, Armour, Pullman, International Harvester, and other companies. In 1910, 51 percent of black men in Chicago worked in domestic service; by 1920, only 28 percent did.[19] But if there was some improvement in the employment situation, there was little in the residential sphere. The Great Migration created a new impetus for concentration, most of the migrants heading straight from the terminus of the Illinois Central Railroad at Twelfth Street and Michigan Avenue to the black neighborhoods on the South Side. By 1920, 35 percent of blacks in Chicago lived in census tracts that were over 75 percent black, and half lived in predominantly black areas.[20] The black belt, in other words, was converting from a mixed to an exclusively black population: its density increased sharply; its area consolidated, extending now from Twenty-sixth to Fifty-first Streets and from Wentworth to Cottage Grove Avenue (Spear, 222); and its center continued to march southward, stopping now at Thirty-fifth and State Streets. Eighty-five percent of Chicago's blacks lived here.[21]

Whites living nearby began to grow nervous. Before the Great Migration, with no real competition between them for jobs or houses, blacks experienced only sporadic violence from whites in Chicago. During the Great Migration, however, overcrowding in the black belt threatened nearby white neighborhoods, especially those of working-class Irish and Poles to the west and middle-class whites to the south and east. In 1917, alarmed at what they saw as an overflowing black belt, white property owner associations on the South Side began to focus on "protecting" their neighborhoods from "racial succession," the process whereby a residential area moves from dominance by one race to another. And working-class "athletic clubs," like those in the Irish neighborhoods west of the black belt, began openly assaulting blacks on the street.

Meanwhile, the Chicago public schools were becoming more segregated: before World War I, only two or three schools in the city were predominantly black; by 1920, eleven were (Spear 203–4).[22] Public parks, beaches, and playgrounds were also sources of conflict: Irish and Polish gangs, for example, terrorized blacks who tried to use the Armour Square recreation center (Spear, 206). The real point of hostility, however, was residential incursions, especially east of Cottage Grove Avenue and south of Fifty-first Street. In 1918, the Kenwood and Hyde Park Property Owners Association announced its intention to "keep Hyde Park white" (Spear, 210). But blacks continued to move in. The result? Between 1917 and 1921, 58 homes or businesses in the black belt were bombed (Drake and Cayton, 178; Spear, 211).

In the "Red Summer" of 1919, with the national economy moving into a recession, tensions escalated dramatically. That year, the athletic clubs were especially active along the western boundary of the black belt and in Washington Park.[23] On the night of June 21, two blacks were killed; and on Sunday, July 27, a black youth named Eugene Williams was killed by a gang of whites at the Twenty-ninth Street public beach. When the police refused to make any arrests, blacks rioted. Later that night, whites retaliated, assaulting 38 blacks and killing two. On Monday night, July 28, 20 people were killed and hundreds injured. The violence continued on Tuesday. Finally on Wednesday, July 30, the state militia were called in, and the violence waned. By the end, 38 people were dead, and 537 injured, black and white (Spear, 216).[24]

The 1919 riots changed everything. It was a turning point for race relations in Chicago, "destroy[ing] whatever hope remained for a peacefully integrated city" (Spear, 221).[25] Although a state Commission on Race Relations issued a report condemning forced residential segregation in the city and criticizing living conditions in the black belt (Drake and Cayton, 69ff), there were few signs of interracial cooperation. Police and prosecutors targeted blacks for arrest and trial; whites clamored for stricter segregation; more bombings occurred; and, in 1921, the Chicago Real Estate Board voted unanimously to expel any member "who sells a Negro property in a block where there are only white owners" (Drake and Cayton, 179).

The most important result of the 1919 riots, however, was the adoption by Chicago whites of the "most potent weapon yet devised" for defending the residential color line: racially restrictive real estate covenants (Spear, 221). These were contractual agreements among property owners (and their heirs) stipulating that blacks could not own, occupy, or lease any covered property and taking effect when some specified percentage of owners in a neighborhood—typically 75 percent—had signed on; the agreements usually lasted twenty years.[26] If the covenant was violated, the transgressor (that is, the white property owner who had sold or rented to a black) could be sued by any other party to the agreement. The covenant, then, was not just a deed restriction; it was a guarantee of collective action and an enormously effective way to exclude blacks from entire areas of the city.[27] During the 1920s, racially restrictive real estate covenants became widespread in Chicago: by some counts, three-quarters of all property in the city were bound by them (Drake and Cayton, 184).[28]

Through such means, blacks in Chicago were confined by the mid-1920s to a bona fide *ghetto* with sharply drawn boundaries: Twenty-second Street to the north, Cottage Grove Avenue to the east, Fifty-fifth Street to the south, and Wentworth Avenue to the west. When the flow of southern blacks resumed after the 1919 recession and riots, the population of the ghetto expanded again, doubling between 1920 and 1930. With their community now hemmed in on all sides with a new ferocity, blacks had no choice but to densify; at one point, there were 90,000 people per square mile in the black belt (compared with 20,000 in adjacent white neighborhoods).[29] The congestion took its toll: a 1923 study found that only 14 percent of the buildings in the Federal Street slum were in good repair (Spear, 148). To add insult to injury, blacks paid more for rent than whites because of the housing shortage in their part of the city (Spear, 23–24).[30]

Bronzeville

For all that, the 1920s and '30s were years of relative prosperity for blacks in Chicago.[31] In 1928, the South Side elected the first black representative to the U.S. Congress since 1901. And from 1930–45, the area called "Bronzeville," whose center kept moving south until it settled on Forty-seventh Street and South Parkway, was the heart of black America. For newcomers, many of them former tenant farmers from the deep South, this was truly a promised land:

> Here were colored policemen, firemen, aldermen, and precinct captains, state Representatives, doctors, lawyers, and teachers. Colored children were attending the public schools and the city's junior colleges. There were fine churches in the Negro areas, and beautiful boulevards. . . . Negroes were making money in the steel mills, stockyards, and garment factories, in the hotels and kitchens, on the railroads, and in a hundred other spots. . . . What did it matter if white men snubbed black men socially? Negroes were building an attractive home life and "society" of their own.[32]

The promise of Bronzeville was still evident as late as the 1940s, when a new migration of rural southern blacks flowed into Chicago and transformed it yet again. As Lemann describes it:

> [N]early a generation after the fading of the Harlem Renaissance, the South Side had become the capital of black America. It was (and still is) the largest contiguous settlement of African-Americans.

> It was home to the heavyweight boxing champion of the world (and the most famous black man in America), Joe Louis; the only black member of Congress, William Dawson; the most prominent black newspaper, the *Defender*; the largest black congregation, J. H. Jackson's Olivet Baptist Church; the greatest black singer, Mahalia Jackson; and a host of lesser-known prosperous people whose presence was proof that Chicago was a city where a black person could be somebody. . . . By the 1940s Chicago had supplanted Harlem as the center of black nationalism in the United States. . . . The South Side had half a dozen shopping districts (Forty-seventh Street was the grandest), containing department stores, banks, nightclubs, movie houses, and such nationally known black institutions as the Regal Theater, the Savoy Ballroom, and the Hotel Grand. It had several wide boulevards lined with substantial homes . . . a spacious public park and a beach along Lake Michigan.[33]

It was a place that also exhibited all the features of social organization—including "a sense of community, positive neighborhood identification, and explicit norms and sanctions against aberrant behavior."[34] Vertically integrated, with lower-, middle-, and upper-class black families all living in the same neighborhood, Bronzeville benefited from the stability that its less distressed families provided the others.[35]

Unfortunately, overcrowding was taking its toll. From 1930–1945, there was little residential construction in Chicago, although an additional 100,000 blacks arrived during this period. The number of dwellings built in the city dropped from 18,837 in 1929 to 221 in 1932; by 1935, there was a shortage of 61,000 homes in the city, with the black belt suffering the worst.[36] According to a 1938 study, two-thirds of private housing units occupied by blacks lacked complete facilities of central heating, gas, electricity, unshared kitchen, and private bath.[37] At the national level, "housers" like Catherine Bauer began to argue for a U.S. housing policy that would include both slum clearance and new construction. In 1933, President Roosevelt created the Housing Division of the Public Works Administration (PWA); and in 1936, the nation's first federally funded public housing project, Techwood Homes, opened in Atlanta. The PWA, essentially a jobs program, would build three projects in Chicago, all in 1938: two for whites (Lathrop Homes on the North Side, Trumbull Park on the Far South), and a third with a 6 percent set-aside for blacks (Jane Addams Homes on the Near West Side). These were the first government subsidized housing projects in the city.[38]

Then, despite fierce resistance from the nation's real estate and construction lobbies, which saw subsidized housing as "socialistic," the 1937 Housing Act was passed, designed to create jobs, facilitate slum clearance, and provide "decent, safe, and sanitary dwellings" for the poor. The Act created the U.S. Housing Authority, forerunner to the Department of Housing and Urban Development (HUD), transferred responsibility for construction to local agencies, and placed income ceilings on tenancy.[39] Soon after, the Chicago Housing Authority (CHA) was incorporated by state statute as a municipal, not-for-profit corporation with commissioners appointed by the city's mayor. Its first executive secretary, Elizabeth Wood,[40] conceived of its mission as providing temporary housing for working people; early tenants were thus "complete" families not on aid (i.e., the "deserving" poor). And, because of the Neighborhood Composition Rule,[41] Chicago's earliest projects reflected the demographic proportions of the areas where they were built. In 1941, the CHA's first project built exclusively for blacks, the Ida B. Wells Homes, opened on the South Side, with 18,000 families applying for 1,662 units. Unfortunately, it did little to relieve the housing shortage, displacing sixteen more families than it housed.[42]

The new program was thus a solution to neither the housing shortage in Bronzeville nor the racial segregation of Chicago's residential patterns. With the black belt already severely overcrowded, and the threat of violence from neighbors growing, the situation on the South Side in the early 1940s was ripe for trouble. All that was needed was a wave of new immigration, like that of 1916–1919. And that is precisely what came in the years after World War II, when the black population of Chicago nearly quadrupled in less than twenty years.

The Second Ghetto

From 1945 to 1970, the *second* great migration of blacks from the rural south to the urban north occurred, propelled mainly by the economic boom of World War II (especially in the industrial north) but also by the 1944 invention of the mechanized cotton picker in the south.[43] Taking into account all south-to-north and rural-to-urban movement of blacks in the postwar years, it was the greatest mass migration in the country's history. In Chicago, as table 4.1 shows, the percentage growth in the black population from 1940–1960 was not as steep as it was from 1890–1930; but in absolute numbers, the increase was astounding. Chicago had 278,000 blacks in 1940 (8.2 percent of the city's total population); in 1960, there were 813,000 (20 percent of the total population). At one point, more than 2,000 blacks were arriving *every week*;[44] and, by 1980, blacks made up nearly 40 percent of the city's population. Probably few other large cities in the history of the world have experienced such a huge demographic transformation in such a short period of time.

The immediate concern right after the end of World War II, however, was housing war veterans.[45] The response was slow, especially from the government;

Table 4.1. Blacks in Chicago, 1850–2000

	Black Population	*% of Total*	*% Change from Prev. Decade*
1850	323	1.1	—
1860	955	0.9	+196.0
1870	3,691	1.2	+286.0
1880	6,480	1.1	+75.0
1890	14,271	1.3	+120.0
1900	30,150	1.9	+111.3
1910	44,103	2.0	+46.3
1920	109,458	4.1	+148.2
1930	233,903	6.9	+113.7
1940	277,731	8.2	+18.7
1950	492,265	13.6	+77.2
1960	812,637	22.9	+65.1
1970	1,103,000	32.7	+35.7
1980	1,197,000	39.8	+8.5
1990	1,087,711	39.1	–9.1
2000	1,065,009	36.8	–2.1

Sources: Arnold R. Hirsch, *Making the Second Ghetto: Race and Housing in Chicago, 1940–1960* (Cambridge: Cambridge University Press, 1983), 17; Allan H. Spear, *Black Chicago: The Making of a Negro Ghetto, 1890–1920* (Chicago: University of Chicago Pressm, 1967), 12; 2000 U.S. Census data, http://www.census.gov/.

but eventually private enterprise kicked in, and the nation began building again. Between 1945–60, an unprecedented building boom took place in the country's suburbs, making possible a massive exodus of middle-class whites from cities like Chicago. Several factors help account for this exodus, including federal support for the new thirty-year fully amortized mortgage loan, the postwar baby boom, the development of mass building techniques, government funding of road and highway construction, the general prosperity of the country during these years, and whites' outright fear and hatred of blacks, who were now firmly associated in their minds with urban life.[46] In the Chicago metropolitan area during these years, 688,000 new homes were built, three-quarters of them single family dwellings in the suburbs. During 1950–56 alone, more than 270,000 whites moved out of the city; and Chicago's share of the metropolitan area's population fell rapidly.[47]

Meanwhile, with new blacks from the South pouring in, middle- and upper-class white families moving out, and the increasing use of "blockbusting" techniques by real estate agents, white neighborhoods on the periphery of the black belt succumbed to rapid "racial succession."[48] The South Side ghetto expanded east into the Oakland-Kenwood and Hyde Park areas and west into Englewood, its center shifting southward one more time, from Forty-seventh to

Sixty-Third Street and South Parkway. The black enclaves on the Near North and Near West Sides grew dramatically. This expansion of black Chicago in the years after World War II has been termed by Arnold Hirsch "the making of the second ghetto."[49] As for the response of Chicago whites to this phenomenon, Hirsch identifies three: violence, urban renewal, and public housing. Let us look at these in turn.

Violence

In 1946, the Chicago Housing Authority, which had always made sure that its projects did not upset the city's racial geography, temporarily set aside the Neighborhood Composition Rule to house returning black veterans in "white" projects.[50] The result? In December of that year, a race riot broke out at Airport Homes when a black family moved in. The next year, in August, another riot erupted, this one at Fernwood Park. For the next five to seven years, there was almost constant violence on the fringes of the black belt and at mixed public and private housing facilities: at Park Manor and Englewood in 1949, for example, and in Cicero and Trumbull Park in 1951–53. Hirsch refers to these years as a period of "chronic urban guerrilla warfare" (41). Most of the incidents involved white demonstrators who threatened individual blacks or the whites willing to sell or rent to them. Unlike earlier Chicago race riots, however, the post–World War II events displayed fewer ideological overtones, no real incursions of whites into black neighborhoods looking for victims, and less indiscriminate violence. Instead, these were focused attacks on black families moving into "white" neighborhoods. According to Hirsch, the police were notoriously inactive, inefficient, and biased during these riots (95). And the mass media were largely silent. Compared to the 1919 riots before and the 1968 turbulence to come, the violence of these years was, to use Hirsch's word, "hidden" (63).

Who were the demonstrators at Fernwood, Englewood, and Cicero? They were neither outsiders nor out-of-control youths, the two explanations most often given by local whites. Arrest records, analyzed by Hirsch, show clearly that most of the agitators lived within a few blocks of the house or building targeted. Their average age was close to thirty, and 20 percent were women (74). We also know, Hirsch claims, that most of those arrested were working-class ethnic Catholics: Irish, Czech, Polish, and Italian (78). Hirsch's portrait reveals a population economically unable to move to the suburbs themselves and resentful of becoming a "buffer" between inner-city blacks and better-off suburban whites (78). These were immigrant families who had only recently begun to be perceived by mainstream America as "white" themselves, people especially attached to the American dream of owning a house with a bit of land around it. The violence they directed at blacks, Hirsch argues, was a sign of their own economic and cultural anxiety. That made it no less effective, unfortunately.

Urban Renewal

Meanwhile, another group of Chicago whites—this time Loop businessmen and South Side professionals—began formulating their own plans for dealing with the black ghetto. Their tack would be very different from the physical intimidation used by working-class ethnic whites in Trumbull Park and Cicero. Executives from the downtown department store Marshall Field's and others associated with the Metropolitan Housing and Planning Council, concerned about the decline of State Street and the decentralization of shopping that was taking place in the postwar metropolitan area, formulated a plan to clear the black slums then encircling the Loop, revitalize central Chicago, and re-attract a "solvent" population downtown (Hirsch, 101).

Other groups were more focused on the health of the South Side's "white" institutions. In 1945, executives from Michael Reese Hospital (at the time, the largest privately endowed hospital in the country with a $10,000,000 investment in its South Side location), the Illinois Institute of Technology (whose development plans included large chunks of historic Bronzeville), and other establishments (e.g., the Illinois Central Railroad) formed the South Side Planning Board to "protect" their properties and employees. Another group, even farther south, with backing from the University of Chicago, began working to ensure the "health" of the Hyde Park–Kenwood neighborhood. The common plan that these groups arrived at was for public agencies to obtain "slum" land through purchase or condemnation, write down its cost, and then sell it to private developers who would build residential properties for middle and upper-class customers (Hirsch, 104). Their efforts, in many ways, marked the beginnings of large-scale, government-funded "urban renewal" not only in Chicago but in the United States as a whole.

In June, 1947, these white professionals and businessmen got their wish when the state legislature in Springfield passed the Blighted Areas Redevelopment and Relocation Act, which provided authority and funds to clear Chicago's slums and relocate the poor (Hirsch, 107). One of the first projects funded through the Act was the Lake Meadows apartment complex on the Near South Side (Hirsch, 115). With state and city funding, "slum" land along South Parkway from Thirty-first to Thirty-fifth Streets was condemned, purchased by the city, and then sold at a discount to the New York Life Insurance Company, which from 1952–60 built there ten high-rise apartment buildings, an office building, and a shopping center. When it was finished, the complex included 2,033 apartments (replacing 3,416 housing units originally on the site), renting for three times the preclearance levels.[51] New York Life not only got the cleared land at reduced cost (with assemblage, purchase, clearance, and write-down essentially paid by taxpayers); it also got tax concessions of its own. And then, in 1969, it sold the whole thing for $28 million.[52]

As Hirsch describes it, the Lake Meadows project demonstrated that the city, against all logic, was willing to actually cut the supply of low-income housing on the South Side by declaring whole blocks blighted, tearing down buildings, and making the land available to developers for a profit and to middle- and upper-class whites for close-in residences. As for displaced blacks, they were then left to fend for themselves in a racially discriminatory environment with no new affordable housing in the area.[53] In all, the 1947 urban renewal projects on the Near South Side displaced nearly 26,000 families.[54] The CHA consequently gave up on its original mission of providing affordable housing for the city's poor and became in essence a public arm of real estate developers, helping free up land for private businesses by clearing "slums" and relocating their residents further into the ghetto (Hirsch, 122).[55]

Of course, there were financial gains for the city; substandard buildings were demolished;[56] and urban blight was kept from moving in certain directions.[57] But the overall result was to protect private interests, either by attracting high-end customers back to the city or setting up middle- and upper-class enclaves on the fringes of the ghetto to act as buffers between blacks and "white" institutions like department stores, hospitals, and universities. Meanwhile, because the public housing needed to shelter displaced residents could not be built either in the renewal zone (that was now for higher-income residents) or outside of the ghetto (because of ethnic white resistance), it was built where poor blacks were already concentrated: "Thus urban renewal programs frequently only shifted the problems of blight, crime, and instability from areas adjacent to elite white neighborhoods to locations deeper inside the black ghetto."[58] In addition, public housing now had to accommodate the residents of both the neighborhoods razed for urban renewal and the slums cleared for public housing. In the end, urban renewal destroyed more housing than it replaced. Nationwide, between 1949 and 1967, 400,000 buildings were demolished and 1.4 million persons displaced. The primary beneficiaries? private developers, middle-class urban residents, and "white" institutions.[59]

Public Housing

The participation of the Chicago Housing Authority in the making of the "second ghetto" deserves special attention of its own. The early years of the CHA, from its inception in 1937 until 1949 or so were not entirely lamentable. The agency built solid low-rise projects (like the Cabrini Row Houses), maintained them well, and took care in tenant selection, focusing on working families in temporary economic trouble. CHA buildings substituted air and light for the unhealthy fire traps of tenement houses and two- and three-flat wooden buildings; and, in fact, many were quite attractive and even deemed progressive by architects and social workers across the country. If, in the early years, the CHA did little to either integrate racial residential patterns or increase the actual number of low-income housing units in the city, at least it did not make things worse. Condit argues that CHA's period of "civic enlightenment" culminated in the years 1948–51, when projects were placed where housing was most needed, suitable land existed, and a balanced racial composition was maintained. Some of the 1948 sites, writes Condit, reveal the highest architectural, functional, and social standards of the entire CHA stock.[60]

Eventually, however, and especially after 1951, CHA site selection, tenant assignment, and building design policies began to actually further the segregation, containment, and isolation of blacks in central Chicago. Of course, as Michael Schill and Susan Wachter have argued,[61] two of the biggest problems were written into the 1937 Housing Act itself: the stipulation that federally funded housing be built only in municipalities that asked for it; and the statute limiting public housing to the poor, that is, families making less than 80 percent of area median income. The first feature allowed prosperous communities to opt out of subsidized housing; the second concentrated the poor, leaving the neighborhoods including and surrounding public housing projects without the middle- and working-class families who had traditionally provided the central city with stability, political power, and moral supervision.[62]

But to the two problems described above, Chicago added a deadly third: overt racism. As part of the negotiations over the 1947 Illinois Redevelopment Acts, and just a few months after the violent protests against integration at Airport Homes and Fernwood, the state legislature, in an unprecedented move, ceded to the Chicago City Council authority over public housing site selection (in all other cities, the public housing authority is a state-chartered entity independent of local politics). As a consequence of this legislation, Chicago aldermen from white neighborhoods essentially had veto power over CHA decisions.[63] The 1949–50 fight over CHA sites, the subject of Meyerson and Banfield's classic study, *Race, Politics, and Housing*, demonstrated that the rules of the game had changed.[64] Promising "a decent home and a suitable living environment for every American family,"[65] the U.S. Housing Act of 1949, modeled on the Illinois Redevelopment Act of 1947, provided funding for a massive urban renewal effort in the nation's cities, including 800,000 new public housing units, more for Chicago than for any other city in the country. In July of that year, Elizabeth Wood's CHA, with the support of its chairman, Robert Taylor, announced plans for seven new sites, many on vacant land in outlying (i.e., white) areas. But, in February, 1950, after intense debate, only two of those sites, both in black slums, were approved by the Chicago City Council. The CHA then told the council to come up with its own sites. It did: later that year, a subcommittee of the council proposed 12,500 new units of public housing in Chicago, 10,500 of them in black slums (for black tenants), and 2,000 in white neighborhoods (for white tenants) (Hirsch, 226).

In the end, the subcommittee approved eight sites in the black belt (including the two already approved) and seven smaller projects on vacant land in white neighborhoods. In August, the full council approved the plan. Among the projects that came out of the 1949 Act were the Harold Ickes Homes, the Ida B. Wells Extension, the Grace Abbott Homes, the Henry Horner Homes, the Cabrini Extension, and the Brooks Extension. All were in the middle of preexisting black neighborhoods, and none significantly increased the supply of low-income housing there. In fact, because of the demolition required to build these projects, Chicago was left, after all of the 1949-funded projects were built, with a net increase of only forty-seven units (Hirsch, 226).

The new projects were very different in design from the old row houses and garden apartments of the 1930s and '40s. They were mostly "gallery-style" high-rises: eight or more stories with exposed hallways and elevator shafts.[66] And they were placed on "superblocks" rather than the old Chicago grid, their high towers overlooking acres of empty land and housing hundreds of poor families with children. The design of the buildings was so bad that a federal judge in the late 1960s forbade the CHA from ever building such complexes again.[67]

What was the result of all this? If the authority's earlier role had been mainly to reinforce and occasionally clarify the city's racial boundaries, after 1950, the CHA positively contributed to the social and economic isolation of the black ghetto. As Hirsch puts it, the CHA's policies amounted to governmental institutionalization of the ghetto. It was for these reasons that, in November, 1950, Robert Taylor resigned as chairman of the CHA board. Elizabeth Wood stayed on as executive secretary for another three years; but in 1953, after the CHA voted to integrate public housing in Chicago, the mayor and city council had had enough of her as well. In 1954, she was finally deposed and the CHA's integration program canceled.

The next year, 1955, Richard J. Daley began his two-decade reign as mayor, and the CHA, with another infusion of federal funds, proposed eleven new sites for city council approval, six in white areas and five in black. Unsurprisingly, the only ones approved were those located in the city's black belt, along State Street, Cottage Grove Avenue, and South Parkway, most between Thirty-eighth and Sixty-third Streets. If the CHA had begun its postwar building boom after the 1949–50 fight, in 1955 it kicked into high gear, initiating a massive demolition and construction campaign in the black ghetto and eventually depositing there a sea of high-rise elevator buildings in huge superblocks, with exposed concrete frames and open-air galleries on each floor. Within a decade, 15,591 low-income housing units would be built in the city, all but 696 in high rises, virtually all in black neighborhoods on the South, Near West, and Near North Sides (see figure 1).[68] Of thirty-three family housing projects approved between 1950 and the mid-1960s, only one was in an area less than 84 percent black. The few projects built in white areas were mostly for the elderly (Hirsch, 242–43).

Most impressive of all was the solid corridor, four miles long, of high-density, government-sponsored, racially segregated public housing along State Street from Twenty-second to Fifty-first Streets, culminating in the Robert Taylor Homes, the largest public housing project in the world: 4,312 units of low-income housing in twenty-eight identical sixteen-story buildings on ninety-five acres, housing 27,000 residents, all poor, virtually all black, nearly all in large families, with 20,000 children and (officially) only 2,600 men.[69] It was, wrote Condit, "a vast urban disaster . . . one of the worst tragedies that architects have created . . . a physical and moral wasteland."[70]

So, if the first Chicago ghetto was achieved mostly by "private" means (restrictive real estate covenants, threats of physical violence, etc.), the second was sanctioned and supported by local, state, and national governments (Hirsch, 9). Whether it was police inactivity during the race riots of 1946–53, city and state cooperation in the postwar urban renewal schemes, or federal support of discriminatory housing policies, the government did not merely acquiesce to residential segregation in Chicago, it gave it a permanence never before seen (Hirsch, 254).[71]

By the mid-1960s, the southern migrations to Chicago had slowed, most of the boundary disputes between whites and blacks had been settled, and the CHA essentially stopped building. Physically speaking, the ghetto was complete. In less than a century, nearly 1,000,000 blacks had been concentrated, contained, and isolated in a huge ghetto ringing downtown; and Chicago had become the most segregated city in the United States.[72] This segregation, I hope to have shown, did not come about accidentally; it was an *achievement*, the product of hard work by the city's whites: neighborhood residents, policemen, real estate agents, bankers, judges, business leaders, and politicians—with immense help from local, state, and federal agencies.

Disaster

For all that, the 1960s started off reasonably well. D. Bradford Hunt has shown how the initial tenants of the Robert Taylor Homes, for example, were predominantly working-class families with "low but not impoverished incomes."[73] In 1963, just one year after it opened, two-thirds of families were still headed by two parents. Roughly half received no government assistance at all, with a third relying on the federal Aid to Dependent Children (ADC) program (Hunt, 108)[74] and the rest on other forms of assistance, such as Social Security.[75] Their median income, adjusted to 1984 values, was $12,700, about half of Chicago's median at the time (Hunt, 108). Now we see those high rises as huge mistakes; but in 1962, they appeared clean, light, airy, and safe, each apartment with its own kitchen and plenty of bedrooms for children.[76]

But something happened around 1966 or 1967, and for the next seven years or so, the Taylor complex suffered astonishing social and physical deterioration.[77] According to Hunt, the percentage of working-class families in the project fell from 50 percent to 10 percent; reliance on ADC increased from 36 percent to 83 percent; and median family income plunged from $14,000 per year to $5,000 (in 1984 dollars) (Hunt, 108–9). Sudhir Venkatesh reports similar statistics: from 1964 to 1970, the proportion of household heads at Robert Taylor under thirty years old increased from 33 to 55 percent, and there were fewer two-parent families (from 60 percent in 1964 to 18 percent in 1973).[78] By the end of the 1960s, Taylor was home to a mostly young, unemployed population.

The project was not alone. Starting sometime in the mid-1960s, conditions in America's inner cities began to deteriorate dramatically, though the decline was especially dramatic in the large cities of the northeast and north central regions, where the ghettos grew larger, blacker, poorer, and less dense. As Paul Jargowsky has shown, looking at U.S. metropolitan area census tracts with more than 40 percent poverty population, there was huge growth in the nation's high-poverty landscape between the 1970 and 1990 censuses:

- the physical size of high-poverty urban areas more than doubled, from 1,177 to 2,726 census tracts;
- the total number of people living in high-poverty urban neighborhoods nearly doubled, from 4.1 to 8 million, up 92 percent (vs. 28 percent population growth in metro area as a whole);
- the number of poor people in such areas nearly doubled, from 1.9 to 3.7 million, up 98 percent (vs. 37 percent increase in metro poor in general);
- the proportion of African Americans in such places increased 70 percent, from 2.4 to 4.2 million (about 50 percent of the high poverty population);[79]
- the concentration of the poor increased, the proportion living in high poverty neighborhoods rising from 12 percent to 18 percent, 26 percent to 34 percent for blacks; and finally,

- the number of people living in these neighborhoods declined, suggesting that, as the ghetto was growing larger and poorer, it was also becoming more sparsely populated.[80]

John Kasarda has found similar rates of change for the same period.[81]

What was going on in inner-city black neighborhoods during these years? First, the adult men were increasingly jobless. The unemployment rate for black male teens, for example, rose from 22.5 percent in 1966 to 39 percent in 1974 without a corresponding rise in school enrollment.[82] In the three community areas at the heart of Chicago's South Side black belt, the proportion of males working fell from 64 percent in 1960 to 37 percent in 1990.[83] Second, the families in such places were increasingly headed by single females. Female-headed families accounted for 30 percent of the black poor in 1959, 35 percent in 1965, 61 percent in 1973, and 74 percent in 1984.[84] Meanwhile, the percentage of black children born out of wedlock rose from 17 percent to 50 percent between 1966 and 1980.[85] In 1970, 50 percent of all black births in Chicago were to unmarried women; in 1983, the figure was 75 percent.[86] Third, income in these families was increasingly derived from federal aid. The national welfare rolls grew from 3 to 11 million between 1960 and 1972.[87] In 1964, 29 percent of single mothers were on welfare; in 1972, 63 percent were.[88] Fourth, the children in these families were increasingly dropping out of school; by the early 1990s, nearly half of inner-city blacks were leaving high school before finishing.[89] And fifth, crime and incarceration in these places was increasing at a horrifying rate. The arrest rate for black males thirteen to thirty-nine years old rose by 49 percent between 1966 and 1974;[90] in Chicago alone, the number of murders rose from 195 in 1965 to 970 in 1974, the majority of perpetrators and victims alike black.[91]

And yet, when compared to the "halcyon days" of the 1920s and '30s, the Chicago inner city of the late 1960s was no more racially segregated and no more poor.[92] Making the situation even more puzzling, while the ghetto was becoming increasingly disorganized, the income of black married couples nationwide was approaching parity with white couples, the birth rate for blacks actually dropped below that of whites,[93] and national rates of poverty and racial segregation were either stagnant or declining.[94] So why did Chicago's public housing projects deteriorate so sharply and rapidly at the end of the 1960s and beginning of the 1970s? Was it, as is often claimed, due to the policies of the federal public housing program (namely, the exclusion of middle-class families by law and of working-class families by the rule that fixed rent at 25 percent of resident income, thus penalizing families whose incomes increased)? Hunt discounts this explanation locally, though he suggests that it may have had some effect nationwide (109). He believes that the deterioration can be explained by several factors. First, by the time Robert Taylor and other Daley-era projects were built in the early 1960s, at the peak of the public housing construction boom in Chicago, the CHA had relaxed its screening standards, mainly because of the sheer number of spaces that now needed to be filled (109).[95] For this reason, high numbers of "problem" tenants began to plague CHA developments. Second, the agency's mounting budget problems led to lax maintenance and management, even as welfare reform expanded the housing rolls (110). Third, the sheer number of children at Robert Taylor—20,000 total, three for every adult in the project, almost the reverse of the average Chicago neighborhood—turned out to be a recipe for disaster: there were simply too many kids and not enough adults to supervise them (111).[96] Fourth, local employment opportunities for African Americans in central Chicago diminished dramatically in the late 1960s and early 1970s, as the stockyards and steel mills closed (110). Fifth, and perhaps most importantly for Hunt, massive white flight from central Chicago in the 1950s and '60s finally eased the long-standing housing crunch in the city's black belt and made a great deal of affordable, close-in housing available to working- and middle-class blacks. Before the mid- to late 1960s, the CHA could count on these families for its own projects because of the housing shortage in the black belt (110).

We have before us, then, a number of specific, mostly local, factors that might account for the dramatic deterioration of Chicago's ghetto neighborhoods in the late 1960s and early 1970s. But what about causes that are metropolitan, regional, national, or even global in character? The most obvious of these is *racism*. According to Massey and Denton, "[R]acial residential segregation is the principal structural feature of American society responsible for the perpetuation of urban poverty and . . . racial inequality in the United States."[97] Alone among ethnic groups, blacks have never become spatially free in this country (Spear, 26, 229). As Drake and Cayton put it fifty years ago, the pattern of immigrant residence in the United States since the mid-nineteenth century has been for previously excluded groups to secure a toehold in low-rent areas and then, one or more generations later, to move to somewhat more prosperous but still segregated areas and from there to gradual absorption into the general population. Blacks have followed the pattern's first two steps, though unevenly; they have never made it to the third (17). According to Joe Darden:

> For other minority groups, socioeconomic mobility leads to significantly reduced levels of residential segregation and ultimately to greater assimilation. For blacks, socioeconomic mobility is no guarantee of freedom of spatial mobility—that is, freedom to move into the residential area of one's choice subject only to ability to pay . . . Census data have shown that, given the same occupation, education, and income, most blacks and whites still do not live in the same neighborhoods.[98]

Other ethnic groups never experienced this level of social isolation in the United States, and what ghettos they had were always temporary. The highest recorded level of social isolation for a European immigrant group in the United States was Italians in Milwaukee in 1910 at 56 percent. By 1970, at the end of the postwar black migrations to the urban north, the *lowest* level of spatial isolation for blacks in the United States was 56 percent in San Francisco. Chicago's rate by then was 90 *percent*.[99] As Massey and Denton put it in 1993

> [N]o group in the history of the United States has ever experienced the sustained high level of residential segregation that has been imposed on blacks in large American cities for the past fifty years. . . . Not only is the depth of black segregation unprecedented and utterly unique compared with that of other groups, but it shows little signs of change with the passage of time or improvements in socioeconomic status.[100]

The poverty and social disorganization of places like Robert Taylor is a function, according to this theory, of the historic subjugation of blacks in this country.

But it may well be macroeconomic forces, combined with historic racism, that is the real culprit here.[101] The period we are examining, from the late 1960s to the mid-1970s, witnessed a shift in the American economy from a goods-producing to an information processing base and a sharp decline in jobs that did not require a college education, especially for men.[102] What low-skill, low-education, manufacturing jobs survived relocated from the northern cities to the suburbs, sunbelt, and other countries. Thus, while suburban Cook and DuPage Counties gained 60 percent of the new jobs created in the Chicago metropolitan area after 1970, the city itself lost 326,000 manufacturing jobs between 1967 and 1987, 60 percent of the manufacturing sector there.[103]

Take North Lawndale on the West Side, which, during the 1950s completed "one of the most rapid and complete ethnoracial transition processes in U.S. urban history," turning over from 90 percent white (mostly Russian Jewish) to 90 percent black in a single decade.[104] Along with that demographic shift, the neighborhood suffered from a mass exodus of small businesses, which accelerated exponentially after the 1968 King riots. By 1970, the neighborhood had lost 75 percent of its preriot businesses.[105] But the next economic transformation was even more brutal. In the late 1960s, the International Harvester factory, located in North Lawndale for generations, and employing 14,000 workers, closed; in 1973, the world headquarters of Sears (employing 10,000), also a Lawndale fixture, moved to the Loop; in 1984, the giant Hawthorne plant of General Electric (with 43,000 workers at its height) shut down; and in 1987, the United States Post Office bulk mail facility (3,000) relocated.[106] Between 1970 and 1990, half of the population of North Lawndale migrated out.[107] In 1986, this community of 66,000 had one bank, one supermarket, forty-eight lottery agents, fifty currency exchanges, and ninety-nine liquor stores or bars.[108]

Nationally, these macroeconomic shifts hurt workers at the low end of the labor market worse than those higher up—from 1969 to 1989, the percentage of low-skilled workers who dropped out of the job market doubled while their real wages decreased by a third.[109] But the changes were especially harmful to blacks in the urban north, who had come to rely on central-city manufacturing jobs with low education requirements. Unsurprisingly, as we saw above, when those jobs left or disappeared after the mid-1960s, there was a sharp increase in the jobless rate for young urban black men. In 1974, the percentage of inner-city black men aged 19–28 working in manufacturing or construction was 57 percent; in 1987, it was down to 31 percent. No other male ethnic group experienced such a steep decline in employment.[110]

There were devastating "concentration effects"[111] on the low-income, inner-city blacks who remained in the ghetto after the black middle class fled in the 1970s and '80s.[112] To illustrate this phenomenon, Wilson takes eight Chicago community areas (all at least 90 percent black) that had poverty rates above 30 percent in 1970 and in which the poverty rate increased from 1970 to 1980 (six moved to above 40 percent, one to 61 percent).[113] In all of those areas, the actual number of poor people stayed about the same, but the areas together had a 42 percent net population *loss* during the decade (i.e., 151,000 blacks left these community areas).[114] The increasing poverty rate of these neighborhoods was no doubt caused in part by the increasing joblessness of their residents; but, clearly, it was also caused by the outmigration of higher-income blacks. This abandonment of the ghetto was, in some cases, spectacular: from 1960 to 1990, for example, the population of Woodlawn on the South Side declined from 80,000 to 24,473.[115]

In Wilson's theory, the ghettos thus lost the "social buffer"[116] of the working and middle classes, and children growing up there were increasingly unlikely to interact with people who held "mainstream" values of work and behavior. The difference between growing up poor white and poor black in the 1980s (or between growing up poor in Bronzeville in the 1940s and poor there in the 1980s) was thus primarily *ecological*: in the latter cases, you were not only poor, unemployed, and unenrolled in school, you were surrounded on nearly every side by neighbors who were equally poor, unemployed, and unenrolled in school. It was this unrelenting concentration of poverty, says Wilson, that made living in these communities so awful.[117]

Jargowsky's study confirms all this. In his analysis, the factors contributing to increasing neighborhood poverty among urban blacks from 1970 to 1990 include the decline in union jobs in northern cities, the deconcentration of employment, the rise of income inequality among blacks, the lingering effects of historic racial segregation, and the differential outmigration of blacks from ghettos.[118] But the main causes of ghetto expansion and deterioration in these years, especially in the northeast and north central regions, were the decline in mean metropolitan income, the rise in metropolitan-wide income inequality, and the process of neighborhood sorting (the way neighborhoods become distinguished from one another along primarily economic and racial lines).[119] Ghetto poverty, that is, is almost entirely a function of income generation and neighborhood differentiation *at the metropolitan level*, processes that work against poor minority communities.[120] This explanation argues against both of the mainstream accounts of persistent black urban poverty: government largesse and the "culture of poverty," with its self-perpetuating mechanisms and social isolation.

Two events in the early to mid-1980s added dramatically to the woes of Chicago's poor urban black neighborhoods. The first was the massive cuts in federally funded social programs during the Reagan era. The peak year for federal spending on public housing, when seen in real dollars, was 1974; from that time on, funding has declined, despite progressively worsening housing conditions in the inner city. During Reagan's two terms, for example, HUD's funding was reduced 76 percent.[121] The second was the growing level of black-on-black violence in ghettos, spurred on by the emergence of large, entrepreneurial, "supergangs," the lingering effects of the massive incarceration of black male youths from the 1970s on, and the devastating presence of crack cocaine. By 1987, writes Sudhir Venkatesh, Robert Taylor was "out of control."[122]

In Chicago, as crime in the housing projects became endemic, vacancy rates shot up. The total population of CHA's family developments dropped from 137,000 in 1970 to 76,000 in 1992, though there was no reduction in the actual number of units. The projects were simply being abandoned, a process that is especially pernicious in a low-income neighborhood.[123] Critics of the CHA referred to the phenomenon as "de facto demolition."[124] By 1995, the agency was so chronically "underperforming," that it was literally taken over by HUD.

So, to summarize the story we've been telling: first, racism confined and concentrated Chicago blacks in inner-city ghettos (a process that was largely complete by the early 1960s); then, after 1965, macroeconomic changes resulted in increased joblessness in those neighborhoods; in the 1970s and '80s, middle-class blacks fled, leaving unemployed inner-city residents without the social buffer that higher-income families provided; finally, during the Reagan years, the government itself withdrew.

The Ghetto as Public Sphere

By the mid-1990s, the Chicago ghetto had become a scene of extreme poverty, chronic joblessness, violent crime, school failure, family breakdown, alcohol and drug abuse, and physical blight. What Nicholas Lemann said about the

Robert Taylor Homes at this time could have been said about any number of Chicago ghetto neighborhoods: it was probably the worst place in the world to raise a family.[125]

But what were these places like as scenes of public discourse? of political decision-making and civic activity? What were they like as environments for bringing diverse individuals together, in freedom and equality, to discuss shared problems and manage a common world? Obviously, the residents of places like Robert Taylor face numerous *individual* obstacles to civic participation. An unemployed, single, teenaged mother can be forgiven for devoting most of her time and energy to trying to keep her family safe, housed, and well-fed, and thus for not participating much in local public decision-making. Even if she had the time to engage in such activity, she would probably lack the resources needed to do so effectively and efficiently.

But over and above these individual obstacles to civic life, I believe, there are *ecological* attributes of these neighborhoods that prevent the individuals who live in them from building strong publics together. First, an environment of uniformly poor, black, female-headed families isolates and stigmatizes those families and leaves them without mainstream contact. Of course, all of this is just another way of saying that such places are *ghettos*, where a disparaged group is concentrated, contained, and isolated form the rest of society. As Massey and Denton put it:

> Typical inhabitants of one of these ghettos are not only unlikely to come into contact with whites within the particular neighborhood where they live; even if they traveled to the adjacent neighborhood they would still be unlikely to see a white face; and if they went to the next neighborhood beyond that, no whites would be there either. People growing up in such an environment have little direct experience with the culture, norms, and behaviors of the rest of American society and few social contacts with members of other racial groups. Ironically, within a large, diverse, and highly mobile post-industrial society such as the United States, blacks living in the heart of the ghetto are among the most isolated people on earth.[126]

Such isolation was dramatically depicted by a 1985 Philadelphia study in which blacks there were shown to have remarkably homogeneous friendship networks, something directly related, the researchers argued, to their residential concentration.[127]

Chicago's ghetto is no different. White people are largely absent in the three best-known accounts of public housing in Chicago, all from the 1990s: Alex Kotlowitz's *There Are No Children Here* (about life in the Henry Horner

Homes), Nicholas Lemann's *The Promised Land* (in part, about a family in the Robert Taylor Homes), and LeAlan Jones and Lloyd Newman's *Our America* (about the Ida B. Wells Homes). "A white person in the project," says Lemann of the period, "was an extremely rare sight, except on television. 'People didn't talk about white people,' [Taylor resident] Robert Haynes says. 'You couldn't *conceive* of what they'd do except put you in jail. . . . White people weren't an issue.' "[128] Further evidence for racial isolation in the inner city is provided by a 1991 study of Chicago's poorest neighborhoods, which found that blacks there had extremely narrow geographic horizons, many informants from the South Side never having been to the Loop, a large number never having left the immediate confines of their neighborhood, and a significant percentage leaving the neighborhood for the first time only as adults.[129] The social, economic, and psychological results of such isolation are devastating. As Darden puts it, "Segregated housing leads to segregation in other areas of life—schooling, religion, recreation, and employment, for example. Housing segregation is related to inequality and subordination; it limits the options for social mobility by consigning the segregated group to inferior life chances."[130]

So, we have a low-status group segregated from others, isolated from the wider world, cut off from power, its members placed on a life trajectory that promises only increased inequality and thus increased segregation. In addition to the obvious social and psychological problems with such a system, it is clearly not conducive to a healthy public life. Research suggests, for example, that homogeneity depresses political participation rates,[131] the very lack of diversity at a place like Cabrini Green preventing it from sponsoring a healthy public sphere.[132]

But even if the residents of such a community had the time and resources for public debate, and the community had the diversity to call it forth, there are no physical spaces here where such language might be safely aired. That is because a distinctive feature of the Chicago ghetto is the "terrorization" of its public spaces. In surveys and interviews with public housing residents about their neighborhoods, nothing is more prominent than the fear of public space in the projects—and no public spaces are more fearsome than those right around the residents' own apartments, especially the hallways, elevators, stairwells, lobbies, and laundry rooms inside their own buildings and the playgrounds, parking lots, and fields outside. Rubinowitz and Rosenbaum, for example, found that public places in the projects—elevators, lobbies, and playgrounds—were the most unsafe there;[133] and a Metropolitan Planning Council study found that nearly 100 percent of murders in Chicago public housing projects occurred in public common spaces: lobbies, elevators, stairs, laundry rooms, and parking lots, half the respondents claiming that the elevators in particular were unsafe even during the day.[134] To be "in public" in a place like this, in other words, is to be at risk for one's life.

The streets around these spaces, unfortunately, are no better. Street life in the typical Chicago public housing project is dehumanized in at least three ways: First, the "superblock" system of many Chicago complexes, in which multistory elevator buildings are set back from the street in a Corbusian "tower in a park" arrangement, makes it difficult for parents, especially on the upper floors, to look after their children below, creates acres of "no man's land" throughout the complex, and prevents adequate surveillance by residents.[135] Second, the commercial abandonment of these neighborhoods has left the streets sterile and depressing, with only the occasional liquor store or lottery agent.[136] And, third, the abandonment of the old rectangular street grid in these neighborhoods makes them confusing.[137] The original grid of North Town, for example, was lost when Cabrini Green was built; the complex consists now mostly of barracks style low-rises lined up in a sunken pit or randomly sited high-rises surrounded by massive fields and parking lots. There are no through streets, disorienting dead ends, and huge swaths of empty space. In fact, a 1991 report complained about confusing circulation patterns in Cabrini Green and recommended that the old Chicago grid be reasserted to make the neighborhood safer and more comprehensible.[138] And a 1997 revitalization proposal claimed that the maze-like layout of Cabrini Extension North violates almost every principle of "defensible space" and called for a clearer demarcation of public, semipublic, and private space in the project, eliminating the no man's land and establishing new, healthier relations between housing and the street.[139]

Finally, from a rhetorical perspective, the ghetto silences its inhabitants. Because of the high rates of criminal activity, people here mind their own business and raise their children to do the same. The cardinal rule is not to mess in other people's affairs. Kotlowitz's account of Chicago's Henry Horner Homes in the 1980s is perhaps the most dramatic account of this code of silence: half the residents then had no phone; many parents would not let their children go outside to play; people did not call 911 for fear of being labeled a snitch; and even after the police set up a special hotline and promised confidentiality, only twenty-one calls were made during the whole of 1986. One little boy in the book tells his mother, "I have no friends, just associates."[140] It is a frightening snapshot of the pervasive and palpable mistrust that the projects breed.

FIVE

Suburbia

Schaumburg, Illinois

> We can solve a housing problem, or we can try to solve a racial problem. But we cannot combine the two.
>
> —William Levitt[1]

In the Summer of 1966, a group of Chicago public housing residents, with the help of the American Civil Liberties Union and its lead local attorney, Alexander Polikoff, sued the Chicago Housing Authority (CHA) and the U.S. Department of Housing and Urban Development (HUD), alleging that the racially discriminatory policies of Chicago's federally funded public housing program had violated their constitutional right to equal protection under the law. The first named plaintiff in the lawsuit, Dorothy Gautreaux, was a community organizer and activist; and the lawsuits that she and her fellow residents filed (*Gautreaux v. CHA*; *Gautreaux v. Romney*), as well as the relief program that resulted, have ever since been known by her name.[2]

The plaintiffs claimed that, between 1954 and 1966, 99 percent of the CHA's 10,256 new family units were placed in black neighborhoods for black residents and that the few projects located in white neighborhoods were 100 percent white (Rubinowitz and Rosenbaum, 23). This amounted, they argued, to government support for the concentration and segregation of blacks in urban ghettos. Two and a half years later, in February 1969, U.S. District Court Judge Richard Austin agreed, holding that the CHA had violated residents' constitutional rights in its site selection and tenant assignment policies (24). In July of that year, Austin adopted the plaintiffs' own relief plan, ruling that the first 700 units of new public housing in Chicago, and 75 percent of units after that, had to be built in white neighborhoods (25).[3] It was the earliest and still one of the only instances of court-mandated residential racial integration in this country.

Unfortunately, no timetable was announced, no target numbers set, and no existing projects forced to change (25). And, because the Gautreaux order used a supply-side approach, mandating the actual building of new units in white areas, there was fierce community resistance to it (28). Consequently, the CHA simply stopped constructing new family public housing in Chicago, although before the lawsuits it had been planning to build 10,000 more units (27).[4] Mayor Daley was apparently especially dismissive of Gautreaux because it pitted two of his constituencies, inner-city blacks and ethnic whites, against one another (29).

In 1979, faced with a recalcitrant CHA, the Gautreaux court removed the requirement that the first 700 units be built in white areas and changed the ratio of units in white versus black areas from three-to-one to one-to-one (31). Still, the CHA dragged its feet. In 1987, with only several hundred "scattered-site" units built in almost twenty years, Judge Marvin Aspen (whose court inherited the Gautreaux case) appointed a "receiver," the Habitat Corporation, to build public housing in Chicago. By 1997, it had built 1,846 units in three-quarters of Chicago's community areas (1,161 in white neighborhoods, 685 in black ones) (33); but community obstacles remained (34), and concerns have since been raised about Habitat's designation of Latino neighborhoods as "white" (35).[5]

It was the Gautreaux plaintiffs' lawsuit against HUD, however, that produced the best-known residential integration program in U.S. history. In 1970, after ruling for the plaintiffs in their case against the CHA, Judge Austin dismissed the case against HUD; but in 1971, the U.S. Court of Appeals reversed that decision, arguing that the federal agency had continued to fund the CHA even though it knew about its racially discriminatory policies. As remedy for HUD's role in the city's practices, the plaintiffs proposed a metropolitan-wide residential desegregation program, arguing that the number of families involved—over 40,000—and the economic and educational remedy they deserved required a larger relocation area than just the central city (36). When Austin rejected this plan in 1973, he was again reversed by the U.S. Court of Appeals; and in 1976, the U.S. Supreme Court, in *Hills v. Gautreaux*, affirmed metropolitan-wide relief (37).[6]

Soon after, the Gautreaux Assisted Housing Program began.[7] Unlike the effort described above, it used a demand-side strategy, giving families rent vouchers to pay for private housing anywhere they could find it. The real key to the program, however, was the "mobility assistance" provided to families by the Leadership Council for Metropolitan Open Communities (LCMOC), a fair housing organization set up in 1966 during Martin Luther King Jr.'s Chicago campaign (41–43).[8] The LCMOC counseled families, recruited landlords, and worked with local housing agencies in the six-county area to ensure successful moves. The Gautreaux program operated until 1998, when it reached its goal of assisting 7,100 families, 75 percent of whom had relocated to the white suburbs of Chicago (39–40).

Over the course of twenty-two years, this program spread low-income black families among several million mostly white suburbanites in more than 100 communities across an area larger than Delaware (45). Despite its slow pace (about 30–40 families per month), wide dispersal, and relatively small numbers—all to avoid visibility and stigma (46–48)—the Gautreaux program became by far the nation's largest, longest-running, and best-known residential integration effort (and the paradigm for current "mobility" programs) (49). The positive effects reported by its participants have been touted as evidence against theories of "inherent deviance" in black families and for the overriding influence of environment on individual and family success (82).

From the point of view of Gautreaux, the best hope for residents of Cabrini Green and places like it is to leave the central city and settle where there is less crime, better schools, and more jobs. After all, according to Nicholas Lemann, "The impressive record of black success in America's cities since the 1960s has been almost entirely bound up with leaving the ghettos rather than improving them."[9] That is because the problems of the black urban poor are largely ecological: "[Y]ou cannot disentangle the objective conditions of a place like East New York," writes James Traub, "from the habits and values of [its residents]. The most effective solution . . . is to move families out of the ghetto environment altogether."[10] Or, as Owen Fiss puts it: "the only remedy that has any meaningful chance of success recognizes the ghetto itself as a structure of subordination and seeks to provide those who live within its walls what earlier generations secured for themselves—an opportunity to leave."[11]

Fortunately, a governmental mechanism for mobility, the federal Housing Choice Voucher Program, has been in place for decades. This program, usually known as "Section 8,"[12] instead of providing poor families with subsidized rental *units* in poor-only public housing projects, gives them federally funded rent *certificates* redeemable wherever they can find suitable housing in the private market. HUD describes Section 8 this way:

> The housing choice voucher program is the federal government's major program for assisting very low-income families, the elderly, and the disabled to afford decent, safe, and sanitary housing in the private market. Since housing assistance is provided on behalf of the family or individual, participants are able to find their own housing, including single-family homes, townhouses and apartments. The participant is free to choose any housing that meets the requirements of the program and is not limited to units located in subsidized housing projects.[13]

More than 2 million families are currently assisted through this program.[14] It works this way: once enrolled, the voucher holder must find his or her own housing unit and reach an agreement with its landlord or owner—who is under no obligation to participate. If the landlord/owner agrees to accept the voucher, the local public housing authority (PHA) inspects the unit for quality and rent reasonableness. Once the lease is signed, the voucher holder pays 30 percent of his or her family's monthly adjusted gross income directly to the owner; the PHA, using federal funds, then pays the difference between that and a locally devised payment standard for rent (based on a HUD-determined "fair market rent" for that size unit in that area[15]).

Ideally, housing voucher programs get the government out of the construction business, support private providers, give poor families greater choice in housing type and location, as well as flexibility to change housing when their needs change, mix those families in with "working" families (providing them with positive role models and improving government and commercial services in their area), and spread poverty more equitably across a metropolitan area. They are also, some argue, less expensive than the building and maintenance of "hard" units.[16] Section 8 has many backers these days,[17] the federal government being the biggest of all: it is the only federal housing program for the poor that has grown with the nation's population over the last twenty years, while there has been virtually no new building of old-style public housing in years.[18]

Unfortunately, there are problems with Section 8. The program is woefully underfunded: the Chicago-based Lawyers Committee for Better Housing claimed in 2002, for example, that there were 500,000 Section 8 eligible families in that city alone, though only 41,000 actually received vouchers.[19] And the program has done nothing to increase the *supply* of low-cost housing in this country—the federal Millennial Housing Commission reported in 2002 that the country had a shortage of 1.8 million units for extremely low income renters (those with income below 30 percent of the area median).[20] Another problem with Section 8 is the reluctance of landlords to accept subsidized tenants.[21] But perhaps most troubling of all is evidence that, at least in the Chicago area, public housing residents are using vouchers to simply move from one economically and racially segregated part of the city to another: in a 1998 article in the *Chicago Reporter*, Brian Rogal claimed that 80 percent of former CHA families with Section 8 certificates had moved to census tracts that were more than 90 percent black and that almost 70 percent had moved to areas with a per capita income below $10,000.[22] Other data show that such trends have continued.[23]

For vouchers to be the answer to racial and economic segregation in Chicago, then, they would need to help public housing residents move further out than other black neighborhoods in the city or black suburbs nearby. Many antipoverty advocates in Chicago, in fact, have their eyes fixed on the white suburbs north and west of the city, especially those in the job-rich "golden corridor" of northwest Cook County. It is these places that are often showcased in success stories about Section 8, stories that portray the relocation of inner-city blacks to white suburbs in almost biblical terms—as the "exodus," "escape," or "diaspora"[24] of poor blacks from the "reservation"[25] of the inner city to "the promised land" of the suburbs.[26]

So, for our first option in reimagining the civic world of central Chicago, let us head out to suburbia, the current center of North American residence, employment, retail, politics, and religion, and the place where inner city families have been promised security, good schools, and jobs.

Suburbia

Liberals, academics, urban designers, and others are often accused of harboring thinly veiled disdain for suburbia.[27] Readers who have stuck with me this far will not be surprised that I am a committed "urbanist"; but in the next few pages I want to think through this issue as patiently and fairly as I can. I'll begin with a definition.

In geographical terms, says the U.S. Census Bureau, a "suburb" is any place beyond the boundaries of a "central city" (a population center of at least 50,000 people) but still within the "urbanized," or relatively dense, economically and socially interconnected "metropolitan area" that surrounds that city.[28] Thus, political scientist Eric Oliver defines the suburb geopolitically, as any small or medium-size municipality that is not legally part of a central city but is still within a densely populated metropolitan area.[29]

This is helpful, though it seems to miss something important from the word's valence as typically understood: a place not just outside a large city but between city and country and constituted in part by its simultaneous distance from the former (though it remains close enough to take advantage of urban amenities) and attraction to the latter (though it shies away from both agriculture and true wildness). As Mary Sies has put it, the suburban ideal is based on the paradoxical welding of pastoralism (with its anti-urban, romantic impulse) and technocracy (with its demands for security, cleanliness, efficiency, and homogeneity).[30]

If we move in a bit closer, however, we see not so much a place on a map as a set of recurring components and functions. These are listed differently by different observers, though there is substantial agreement on the main ones, especially when we think of the paradigmatic postwar North American suburb. So, to take Kenneth T. Jackson's oft-quoted list of attributes, the suburb is a residential district, settled at relatively low density, comprised of detached single family dwellings, each on a relatively large lot with an ornamental front yard and a recreational back one.[31] If we update this list to include some of the more recent nonresidential components of the suburb, we would have to add shopping centers surrounded by ample free parking, low- and medium-rise office buildings in landscaped parks, also with ample free parking, civic institutions like post offices (again, with ample free parking), all connected by often curvilinear streets.[32] Most of these features remind us of the extent to which suburbia is a function of the automobile, which many observers see as the key cultural force in its development.[33]

But we still seem to be skirting the thing about suburbia that both its celebrants and detractors alike dwell on most: its character as a particular kind of *community*. From this point of view, the suburb is the prototypical backdrop for middle- and upper-middle class North American (white) families, whose primary civic concerns are protection of property values, freedom from crime, and good schooling for their children. It is, in other words, the environmental manifestation of what we have been calling American "privatism"—with its focus on the individual, his or her family, and their search for personal happiness, "community" intended primarily to keep the peace among these people and create a setting for their prosperity.[34] This ideology can be seen in relatively benign terms, for example, in Downs's description of the "suburban vision" as ownership of a single-family dwelling with a yard, unlimited use of the automobile, employment in a low-rise workplace in a parklike setting, citizenship in a small community with a responsive local government, and no poverty.[35] Or it can be viewed in more political terms: Martinson, an apologist, writes that suburbanites dislike centralized government; while Schneider, a critic, says that they simultaneously distrust government *and* demand good schools, low crime, well-maintained streets and highways, clean air, and a well-regulated health delivery system.[36] We can also, of course, put the suburban ideology in more starkly repressive terms: the suburb is a place *where there are no city-dwellers*, who, from this point of view, are racially and ethnically "other": foreign, hypersexed, poor, sick, elderly, and so on.[37]

Of course, these three definitions of suburbia, the geographical, architectural, and sociological, are intertwined: peripheral location (1) makes low-density housing (2) possible, while the fear of urban heterogeneity (3) makes it attractive. As Dolores Hayden has put it, suburbia is the physical expression of the middle-class desire for living in a detached house (2) with like-minded neighbors (3) in a quasi-pastoral setting (1).[38]

The picture just painted, unfortunately, masks enormous diversity among suburbs and also risks treating suburbia itself as a kind of natural, even inevitable, form, independent of the specific historical forces that produced it. Jackson and others have helped us understand how suburbs came to be and how different they are from one another.[39] But no one has done more of late to point out "the myth of the suburban monolith" than Myron Orfield.[40] As I mentioned in chapter 2, his cluster analysis of the twenty-five largest U.S. metropolitan areas groups suburban communities according to several measures relating to both their fiscal characteristics (primarily tax capacity and expenditures) and sociopolitical environment (e.g., poverty rate, population density, housing age, growth characteristics, and personal wealth). The analysis suggests at least six broad types of suburban communities in the contemporary United States.[41] First, there are three kinds of "at-risk" communities, those under significant fiscal or social stress, which he labels (1) at-risk segregated suburbs, like Yonkers, New York, with low tax capacity, high municipal costs, and high concentrations of minority children in the public schools; (2) at-risk older communities, like Brookline, Massachusetts, with low poverty rates but also low tax capacity and slow growth; and (3) at-risk low-density satellite communities, like Elgin, Illinois, with higher-than-average poverty rates and growth but low tax capacity. There are also (4) bedroom-developing communities, which are fast-growing, low-density settlements with low minority and poverty rates but which have modest fiscal resources. And, finally, there are two kinds of communities that have both high-end housing and large amounts of desirable office and commercial space and which are thus under little stress from either low tax capacity or high costs: (5) affluent and (6) very affluent job centers, like Irvine, California, and Needham, Massachusetts. Given this diversity, writes Orfield, we should be wary of any blanket use of the word "suburb."[42]

And yet, the term is still meaningful. For one thing, people often use it to describe their own communities. As we will see below, the official Web site of Schaumburg, Illinois uses "suburb" or one of its derivatives five times on its opening page.[43] And, as the *New York Times* reported in 1999, politicians frequently use the word "suburban" as shorthand for affluent, well-educated, family-oriented, mostly white voters deeply attuned to political debates surrounding such domestic issues as taxes and education.[44] The word is also meaningful from an international perspective to refer to a quasi-distinctly North American phenomenon. It can be used, that is, to refer to the characteristically single-use, low-density, automobile-dependent, residential neighborhoods of the United States, with their detached single-family homes and relatively spacious yards. Finally, "suburbia" is still a useful category for comparison with other broadly construed metropolitan scenes like the urban ghetto. In this regard, Downs's thirty-year-old comparison between "suburbs" and "central cities" still makes sense:

1. suburbs in general contain lower proportions of low- and moderate-income households;
2. they have more new housing units;
3. they have higher rates of homeownership;
4. both rental and owner-occupied housing is more expensive there;
5. housing markets are more stable (with lower turnover and less frequent transitions);

6. the number and percentage of nonwhite residents is lower;
7. population densities are lower;
8. median age is lower (there are fewer old persons and more children);
9. suburban governments typically provide a narrower range of public services and spend less on them per resident, though they often spend more for education; and finally,
10. crime rates in general are lower in suburbs than in central cities.[45]

Let us look more closely at suburban Chicago.

Chicagoland: Decentralization, Fragmentation, and Polarization

The current social and physical landscape of the Chicago metropolitan area is, in many ways, a product of the restructuring of the world economy during the latter half of the twentieth century. One sees there the results of both massive deindustrialization, that is, the dramatic decline of the manufacturing sector and rise of service firms and low-wage service jobs, and profound globalization, the simultaneous worldwide decentralization of production and centralization of control and administration.[46] The Chicago metropolitan area, then, looks like other U.S. metropolitan areas with its well-developed downtown, complete with office space and cultural facilities for the work and play of information workers, while an equally well-developed suburban landscape serves their residence and child-rearing needs.[47] Meanwhile, the neighborhoods in between—the inner-city ghettos and inner-ring suburbs in particular—have deteriorated, sometimes badly. These structural and spatial transformations, as we noted earlier, have been accompanied by growing inequality in personal income and wealth. And all of this has proceeded with the unabashed support of local, state, and national governments.[48]

What the Chicago metropolitan area provides, in other words, is an example of what may be the single most important change in American society during the past half century: the simultaneous decentralization, fragmentation, and polarization of the civic landscape.[49] By decentralization, I mean the way middle- and upper-income whites moved first their homes and then their stores, churches, and jobs out of the central cities and into the outlying regions around those cities, a process that can be traced back quite far but which really accelerated only after World War II. The result is the low-density settlement pattern of our metropolitan areas.[50] By fragmentation, I mean the way this social space has been balkanized into thousands of small and medium-size communities, most of them legally autonomous and socioeconomically isolated from the others.[51]

Finally, by polarization, I mean the way these communities have developed unevenly, some becoming prosperous and others, stagnant or distressed.[52]

It is the polarization, of course, that makes all of this so worrisome. The first two trends would be of less concern if they were not accompanied by so much inequity. And that inequity would not be quite so disturbing if decentralization and fragmentation did not so powerfully fuel it,[53] leading to ever-increasing inequity and hence even greater demands for decentralization and fragmentation. That is, in a society in which people increasingly live in metropolitan areas organized in an increasingly dispersed and balkanized fashion, the communities that are well-situated with respect to such things as household income, employment opportunities, low crime rates, and good schools will, because their environment is so clearly attractive, only increase their advantage over those communities not so well-situated, whose lack of such things dooms them to ever greater distress precisely because they are so unattractive. Place has become, therefore, both marker and maker of massive and growing inequality in our society.

Let us look more closely at these phenomena. First, decentralization: from 1920 to 2000, Chicago's share of the total six-county metropolitan population declined from 75 percent to 36 percent (for the 2000 numbers, see table 5.1).[54] The city's share of metropolitan retail sales declined similarly: from 78 percent in 1929 to 40 percent in 1972.[55] Nearly all of the decline in industrial employment in the Chicago metropolitan area during the last twenty years, meanwhile, was in the city, even as most of the growth in service jobs was in the suburbs. The overall historical result has been a massive shift in employment out of Chicago and toward the suburbs. During the 1980s, for example, the city lost some 91,000 jobs, while the region as a whole gained 424,000, the most rapid growth occurring in DuPage, Cook, and Lake Counties, all overwhelmingly white and prosperous even before this shift.[56]

Table 5.1. Population Figures for the Six-County Chicago Metropolitan Region (2000)

County	*Total Pop.*	*% White*	*# Black*	*% Black*
Cook	5,376,741	56.3	1,405,361	26.1
City of Chicago	*2,896,016*	*42.0*	*1,065,009*	*36.8*
DuPage	904,161	84.0	27,600	3.1
Kane	404,119	79.3	23,279	5.8
Lake	644,356	80.1	44,741	6.9
McHenry	260,077	93.9	1,523	0.6
Will	502,266	81.8	52,509	10.5
Total	8,091,720	NA	1,555,013	19.2

Source: 2000 U.S. Census data, http://www.census.gov/.

Accompanying this decentralization of people and business in the Chicago area has been astounding political balkanization. The Chicago metropolitan area is comprised of six counties, 113 townships, and 270 municipalities, each relatively independent of the others.[57] This fragmentation has allowed many of Chicago's suburbs to legally wall themselves off both from each other and the central city.[58]

Which brings us to polarization. Some of the communities in this metropolitan region are affluent, and increasingly so; others are stressed, and becoming more so. As the *Chicago 2020* report convincingly demonstrated, income segregation is increasing, both in the city and the region as a whole.[59] To get a better view of this, let us divide the area, as Orfield does, into the following seven geopolitical categories (see figure 2):

1. the central city (Chicago proper—itself, of course, intensely segregated along lines of race, class, age, land use, etc.);
2. declining, segregated, inner-ring suburbs like Cicero and Robbins;
3. at-risk, older suburbs: high-density and low-poverty but also with low tax capacity and slow growth, like Oak Park and Evanston;
4. stressed, middle-class, lower-density outer suburbs (or satellite cities) like Elgin, Joliet, and Aurora;
5. upper-middle-class but low-revenue, "bedroom-developing" suburbs like Streamwood, Wheaton, and Arlington Heights;
6. affluent northern and western suburbs like Schaumburg, Naperville, and Winnetka; and
7. *very* affluent job centers like Lake Forest and Oak Brook.[60]

There are not only wide differences among these communities in median income and personal wealth but also in revenue generating capacity. According to Orfield, most of the disparity can be accounted for by the unequal distribution of high-end housing and office space and the effects of that distribution on tax revenues. In 1994, for example, an at-risk predominantly black suburb like Maywood, Illinois, needed to levy taxes of $4,672 per year on a $100,000 house in order to support local school spending of $3,350 per pupil; while the affluent suburb of Kenilworth, Illinois, *in the same metropolitan area*, had a tax rate of only $2,688 per year on a $100,000 house but, because housing values were so much higher there, could raise enough money to spend over *$10,000* per pupil.[61] To put this another way: in the 1990s, there was a 33-to-1 disparity in tax base among the 241 school districts in the Chicago region.[62]

This inequity only breeds more inequity. Let us compare just the relatively stagnant inner suburbs (categories 2 and 3 above) and the thriving north and western suburbs (categories 6 and 7), each with around 20–25 percent of the total Chicago metropolitan population.[63] In 1990, the former had a median household income of $37,288, down 1.8 percent from 1980, while the latter averaged $54,106, up 9.7 percent. In the inner suburbs, 10.4 percent of children lived in poverty, a gain of 12.4 percent in the 1980s, while in the northwest suburbs, only 2.7 percent did, a 30 percent decrease. In the inner suburbs, 17.5 percent of households were headed by females, up 30 percent in a decade, while only 8.6 percent of households in the northwest suburbs were female-headed, up 3 percent. In the inner suburbs, 30.7 percent of students in grades 1–4 were non-Asian minorities; in the northwest suburbs, the figure was 5.3 percent. In 1990, 95 percent of schoolchildren in mostly black East Chicago Heights were eligible for free or reduced lunches; in white Naperville, the figure was 0.2 percent.[64]

More recent figures show these disparities continuing to grow. Table 5.2, using Census 2002 data, compares two Chicago suburbs, one thriving, one troubled, on four criteria.[65] Much of this inequity, it should be said, is supported by laws and policies, such as class-based zoning, that amount to a government-sponsored social partition of the metropolitan landscape.[66]

There is a racial component to all this as well. The best recent study of residential racial segregation in Chicago's suburbs comes from Mike Leachman and his colleagues.[67] Their study begins by comparing the current racial landscape of Chicagoland with that of 1968, the year of the U.S. Fair Housing Act. Not surprisingly, the authors find progress (1–3). Blacks in the region have benefited from the 1969 and 1976 *Gautreaux* rulings, the 1977 Community Reinvestment Act, and the Fair Housing Amendments Act of 1988 (8–12). The real estate industry is more sensitive to racial issues (12–13); there are now stable communities in the region that appear to be comfortably multiracial (e.g., Oak Park, Evanston) (13);[68] and minorities are now found in concentrations greater than 5 percent in many suburbs (14). Between 1980 and 1990, 74 percent of 117 municipalities in the area showed an increase in the number of blacks (14).[69]

But the statistics reveal some disturbing trends as well. The number of communities with more than 30 percent blacks actually grew, and the greatest black population increases in the suburbs were in municipalities with already

Table 5.2. Comparing Two Chicagoland Suburbs in 2000

Suburb	*Median Income*	*Median Home Value*	*Adults with BA/BS*	*Poverty Rate*
Kenilworth	$200,000	$972,000	89%	0%
Ford Heights	$17,500	$42,300	4%	49%

Source: David Mendell, "The Boom Decade: Census Data Show Chicago Area Rode Wave of Economic Prosperity in '90s," *Chicago Tribune*, May 15, 2002.

high numbers of blacks (14–15).[70] Thus, while it appears that minorities have more housing opportunities, they tend to move to areas of high minority concentration. Faced with such trends, Americans often blame class differences rather than racial discrimination. So, Leachman and his colleagues used an empirical test, derived from the work of John Kain, that allowed them to gauge the validity of this explanation (17–18). They identified the percentage of blacks in each income category in the entire metropolitan area; then, they identified the number of households in each category for each municipality and allocated the number of black households expected to reside in each municipality based solely on income; finally, they summed over all categories to arrive at the predicted number of blacks for each municipality. Using this method, they compared the predicted and actual racial composition of 117 municipalities in the Chicago metropolitan area for both 1980 and 1990 (18–19).

What they found in an overwhelming number of municipalities in both years is that African-American households were significantly *under*represented *even after controlling for income* (see table 5.3). The number of such municipalities decreased slightly between 1980 and 1990; but the number of municipalities in which the percentage of black households was *over*represented actually increased, suggesting that many places in the region are actually *resegregating*, that is, moving rather quickly from predominantly white to predominantly black populations (18).

Why are people still segregated by race in the Chicago area? The authors posit three reasons (22–29). First, and most obviously, is continued racial discrimination (22–23). This can be both blatant (there were 107 hate crimes reported in the Chicago suburbs in 1996) and subtle (discrimination even against middle- and upper-class blacks in the housing market remains common) (22–23).[71] The lingering effects of past discrimination are also still felt: for example, 61 percent of all black households have no savings or financial assets (23).

The second reason for continued racial residential segregation in the Chicago area is the lack of rental and/or affordable housing (23–27). In many suburbs, land costs are simply too high.[72] Suburban zoning and tax policies also

Table 5.3. Actual versus Predicted Black Households in Chicago Area, 1980–1990

	1980	*1990*
# municipalities more than 5% *below* predicted value	102	92
# municipalities within 5% predicted value	9	12
# municipalities more than 5% *above* predicted value	6	13

Source: Mike Leachman, Phil Nyden, Bill Peterman, and Darnell Coleman, *Black, White and Shades of Brown: Fair Housing and Economic Opportunity in the Chicago Region* (Chicago: Leadership Council for Metropolitan Open Communities, 1998), Appendix B, table 4.

discourage the construction of multi-family and affordable housing.[73] The result is that most of the affordable housing in the Chicago suburbs is in those communities with the weakest economies (30–34). In fact, there appears to be an inverse relationship between affordable housing and economic opportunity (33). The suburbs account for 49 percent of the region's affordable homes and 23 percent of its affordable rental units, but only 29 percent of those homes and 23 percent of those rental units were in municipalities with healthy job growth.[74] Race is implicated in this equation as well: municipalities with sizable African-American populations are typically those experiencing job loss or stagnation. In 1990, for example, 86 percent of all African-American households in the region were living in municipalities that experienced job losses or stagnation since 1980 (34–35), significantly higher than what one would expect if race were not a factor in residence patterns. Further, the communities which are experiencing the greatest increase in black population are overwhelmingly job poor.[75]

Besides racial discrimination and the lack of affordable housing, the region remains racially segregated because of differences in people's investment decisions (27–29). Blacks and whites, Leachman and his colleagues claim, consider dramatically different factors when buying or renting a place to live. For blacks, to live among other blacks is to avoid white hostility and prejudice and to have the support structures of the African-American community (27). But in making that choice, blacks pay a price, literally: the value of homes in such neighborhoods is lower than in white ones, and the communities are generally less healthy economically (28). One researcher found that, in 1990, houses owned by blacks were worth about half the value of houses owned by whites, and their value was declining (28). Whites, on the other hand, do not have to choose between "house" and "home." The social concerns that whites consider—good schools, proximity to work, safety—are generally compatible with their financial interests, and vice versa (28–29).[76]

We should look at how these trends have played out in a single suburb. Now, I might have chosen here a lower- or middle-class black suburb on Chicago's South Side (e.g., Robbins), since clearly many Section 8 holders from the city are moving in that direction. But this kind of *re*segregation is precisely what progressive housing advocates are against, so it would not make sense to look there for a solution to the problems of the ghetto. Nor would we want to look at a relatively diverse, high-density suburb like Evanston or Oak Park for the simple reason that such places are atypical in the metropolitan region as a whole. Equally unsatisfactory would be a working-class white suburb like Berwyn or Cicero, still largely off-limits to blacks—ditto for a place that is *too* affluent, like Lake Forest or Winnetka. We need a suburb that offers economic and educational opportunities but is still, on its face at least, a viable alternative for lower-income black families. I have chosen Schaumburg, Illinois, because there is some evidence that it is the kind of place targeted by programs like Gautreaux: a "golden corridor" suburb, job-rich but neither blatantly racist nor exceptionally affluent. It shares many of the suburban characteristics described above—white, well-to-do, automobile-dependent—but also has a high percentage of office and retail space.[77] It is in many ways an alluring model for the twenty-first century city.

Schaumburg, Illinois

According to its own Web site, the Village of Schaumburg, Illinois, is the "pre-eminent community in the Chicago metropolitan area's thriving northwest suburbs."[78] It is located twenty-six miles from downtown Chicago at the convergence of three key transportation arteries: Interstate 90 (the Northwest Tollway); Interstate 290 (Illinois 53); and the O'Hare Expressway. The village was incorporated in 1956 and has grown since that time at a breathtaking rate: from just 130 residents on two square miles to 77,000 residents on almost twenty square miles.[79]

Schaumburg was settled by Germans in the nineteenth century, and German remained the first language in many homes until the 1950s and was still being used at the town's oldest church in 1970.[80] A 1900 brochure described Schaumburg as "the model community of Cook County": its people were prompt in the payment of their taxes and supportive of their churches and schools. The village had the best roads in the area and no need for a jail. Through most of the first half of the twentieth century, it had less than 100 residents.

Two events changed that: first, the expansion of nearby O'Hare airport in 1955 and, second, the building of the Northwest Tollway in 1956. In response to these pressures, the village incorporated. Then, in 1959, Alfred Campanelli, who would go on to build nearly 7,000 homes here, began construction of Weathersfield, the first large residential subdivision in the village. But, while its similarly situated neighbors (e.g., Arlington Heights, Barrington Hills) restricted development in their villages to single-family homes, Schaumburg, as its Web site says, "had the foresight" to encourage a mix of development types. The village's 1961 comprehensive plan, for example, earmarked portions of the community for both multifamily housing and intensive business development. So, in 1967, the International Village Apartment Complex opened; and in 1968, Motorola began building its world headquarters on the Northwest Tollway (it now employs 7,000 people there). With the opening in 1970 of Interstate 290 on the village's eastern boundary, the town was poised for the biggest plum of all: the opening in 1971 of Woodfield Mall, at the time the largest indoor shopping mall in the world.[81] Throughout the 1970s, the village continued to grow rapidly (see table 5.4), with development now including corporate office buildings, warehouses, and hotels. By the 1980s, with vacant land running

Table 5.4. Population of Schaumburg, IL, 1956–2000

Year	*Population*	*Percent Increase*	*Persons per HH*	*Housing Units*	*Number Black*	*Number Asian*	*Number Hispanic*	*Median Income*
1956	130	NA	NA	NA	NA	NA	NA	NA
1960	986	658.5	NA	286	NA	NA	NA	NA
1970	18,730	1,799.6	3.30	5,013	NA	NA	NA	$12,063
1980	53,305	184.6	2.73	21,514	645 (1.21%)	1,573 (2.95%)	986 (1.85%)	$26,273
1990	68,586	28.7	2.48	29,499	1,487 (2.17%)	4,414 (6.44%)	1,649 (2.40%)	$47,029
2000	75,386	9.9	2.36	33,093	2,526 (3.35%)	10,697 (14.19%)	3,988 (5.29%)	$60,941

Source: Village of Schaumburg, "Demographics," http://www.ci.schaumburg.il.us/vos.nsf/schaumburg/MFRK-5U4MCK.

out, the village's growth rate slowed, although the 1990s witnessed significant development of commercial space.

Today, according to village figures, Schaumburg has more than 3,400 businesses employing over 78,800 people.[82] It has 10.2 million sq. ft. of commercial space, including sixty-five shopping centers. Retail sales in 1998 generated taxes of $24.6 million for the village, second only to Chicago in the state of Illinois. The village also has 11.1 million square feet of office space in fifteen major complexes and 12.2 million square feet of industrial space in 9 industrial parks. Not surprisingly, Schaumburg boasts "a strong fiscal posture." It levies no municipal property tax, with most government services funded by the local sales tax, which makes up 63 percent of the village's general revenues.[83] Per capita sales tax revenues in 1994 were $331.47 ($24.4 million divided by the total population of 73,745). The main tax levied against citizens is $3.35 per $100 of assessed property valuation for School District 54. In 1993, per capita assessed valuation in the village was $27,034 (compared to the metropolitan average of $8,106).

On its Web site, Schaumburg claims to be a "comfortable" place to live, raise a family, and relax.[84] In addition to abundant shopping, there are 231 restaurants and several parks. The school system, the village claims, is one of the best in the nation; and, in 1995, the library had a circulation of 2.2 million items, the second largest in Illinois. But Schaumburg is not a typical suburb; it is an example of a very particular, distinctly North American, kind of suburb: an *edge city*. Edge cities are, in the words of Joel Garreau, intensely planned, job-rich, low-density communities, usually sited along interstate highways, with large portions of their land given over to office space (in technical terms, any suburb with more than 5 million square feet of office space and more jobs than bedrooms is an edge city).[85] Bob Thall, a Chicago photographer who has written about such places, has called Schaumburg the best example of an "edge city" in the nation.[86] Lockwood, too, calls it one of the largest and most successful edge cities.[87] The village was in fact host to the national Edge City Conference in 2001, with Garreau as the keynote speaker.[88]

But not everyone uses the phrase "edge city" as a compliment. Thall notes that, in Schaumburg, "there are virtually no places where a stranger has the right to walk around with a camera on his or her shoulder or set up a tripod" (15). There is little clearly marked public space in the village; almost everything turns out to be private property. As for social diversity, there are some minorities but compared to the city, very few (17). Thall finds in Schaumburg few old people, few people of color, few poor people, few new immigrants. "It's difficult not to see these new places as symptoms of, and contributors to, the increasing social polarization in the United States" (17).

Much of Schaumburg's business and commerce, meanwhile, is under the control of national corporations and large chain retailers; and local franchises show little architectural accommodation to their location. For Thall, most of the residences are bland-looking. Whereas, in the city, every empty storefront is the "husk of some small business tragedy" (17), a unique story worth telling, everything in Schaumburg is new. Things seem safer, but also boring:

> The lack of trees, the cheap standardized construction, the ceaseless flow of cars, the acres of blacktop and concrete, and the unwalkable distances across open, flat land would leave me with an overwhelming and chilling sense of desolation. (18)

For Thall, a city is partly designed, but it is mostly "an accommodation to existing circumstances, the passage of time, economic constraints, political antagonisms, infrastructure decay, and the changing social environment" (20). Places like Schaumburg, by contrast, begin with a clean slate, a clear purpose, and financial power. These are not always good things.

A series of events in the late 1990s can be seen as an admission on the part of village leaders that Thall was right about their town. At the time, Schaumburg had no real town center; in the words of one reporter, it "has no core."[89] So, the village literally built one from scratch.[90] In 1995, it purchased a twenty-nine-acre site at its traditional crossroads and began selling parcels to private businesses. The center turned out to be mainly a parking lot, but it did include a large new public library and a fifty-five-foot clock tower, in addition to a large grocery store and several shops. According to the mayor, the center gave people in the village a place to gather, to bump into one another. For Lockwood, it suggested only a deep hunger for community.[91]

But the real attraction of Schaumburg from Chicago's point of view is its jobs. For the executives whose offices are located there—close to their homes, their children's schools, and the restaurants and stores they frequent—Schaumburg works well. It is less satisfactory, however, for the service employees who commute there everyday from Chicago. Here is a description of a similar geographical mismatch as it plays out in the parking lots of Atlanta's suburban Perimeter Center at 5:00 p.m. every workday:

> Executives and professional get into their Cadillacs and BMWs for the relatively easy drive home or a visit to one of the nearby "formula" restaurants for a drink. At the same time, many black employees are walking through the parking lots—Perimeter Center has few sidewalks—on their way to the bus stops, which are little more than a pole with a bus sign on top, planted on a flat, grassy spot that usually turns into mud when it rains. Atlanta's working-class black sections are south of downtown, fifteen to twenty miles

> from Perimeter Center, but the roads and bus lines to them don't follow a straight line. With one or maybe two transfers, many bus passengers endure a one-to-two hour ride twice a day.[92]

But what if the low-wage workers from the inner city could actually move to the suburbs, living as well as working there? As it turns out, Schaumburg is precisely the kind of place targeted by mobility programs like Gautreaux; let us look, then, at its recent history with low-income blacks.

Although the village has experienced phenomenal growth since the 1950s, going from 130 to 75,386 residents in less than fifty years, it remains a remarkably homogeneous community. Schaumburg is proud of this fact; on its Web site, village leaders describe their residents as "more racially homogeneous" and "better educated" than those in the region as a whole.[93] The population is also described as having a larger concentration of twenty-one- to forty-four-year-olds and "a large, middle class work force." There are also fewer old people (though there has been steady growth in this group since 1970, from 2 percent to 11 percent). And, says the Web site, Schaumburg is a "family oriented community," with most adults married.

It is at this point in the Web site that the village admits to a growing minority population, now nearly 10 percent, the largest subgroup being Asians (Hispanics come next, and, finally, blacks, who accounted for only 3.4 percent of the population in 2000[94]). Despite this growth, the village is still "much more homogeneous than the entire Chicago metropolitan region"—"though, interestingly," the Web site adds, there are "more Asians than in the region as a whole."

If we return briefly to Leachman et al.'s study of racial residential segregation in the Chicago suburbs, it is clear that the number of blacks in Schaumburg is far below what it should be if the metropolitan area were stratified only by class (see table 5.5). Including in this analysis data from 2000, we see growth in the black proportion of only about 1 percent per decade.[95]

As for housing, the most common type in Schaumburg remains the single-family detached dwelling.[96] In the 1970s, when multifamily housing

Table 5.5. Actual versus Predicted Black Households in Schaumburg, IL, 1980–1990

	Total HH	*Pred. Black HH*	*Actual Black HH*
1980	19,528	14.6%	1.4%
1990	27,542	14.2%	2.3%

Source: Mike Leachman, Phil Nyden, Bill Peterman, and Darnell Coleman, *Black, White and Shades of Brown: Fair Housing and Economic Opportunity in the Chicago Region* (Chicago: Leadership Council for Metropolitan Open Communities, 1998), Appendix B, tables 8 and 9.

represented only 8.5 percent of the housing stock, there was a push to build more rental apartments here, but many of those have since been converted to owner-occupied townhouses and condos.[97] And, although one-third of the housing stock in Schaumburg is rental, the village admits (or warns?) on its Web site that "it is still not an easy proposition for people of moderate income to live in the Village."[98] According to Leachman and his colleagues, in 1990, only 3.7 percent of Schaumburg's owner-occupied homes and 3.4 percent of its rental units were affordable for people making less than 80 percent of the area median income. The rental figure is low even by suburban standards: only 8 of 172 communities in the metropolitan area had a smaller percentage of affordable rental units; and Schaumburg ranked last among communities with more than 10,000 population.[99]

My own investigation into Schaumburg's use of federal Community Development Block Grant (CDBG) funds reveals the village's reluctance to make room for low-income families. The CDBG was the first block grant in the nation's history, devised as part of Nixon's "New Federalism" initiative to devolve federal power back to states and municipalities.[100] The program was enacted in 1974 via the U.S. Housing and Community Development Act, which consolidated seven programs for urban development (including Urban Renewal and Model Cities) into a single "block" of funds allocated by formula to states and cities for implementing activities "to develop viable urban communities by providing decent housing and suitable living environments, and by expanding economic opportunities, principally for persons of low and moderate income."[101] Under program rules, CDBG-funded projects must benefit low- and moderate-income persons, prevent or eliminate slums or blight, or meet other urgent community development needs.[102] CDBG grantees[103] are allowed to develop their own programs and funding priorities but must give "maximum feasible priority to activities which benefit low- and moderate-income persons."[104] Appropriate activities include property acquisition, relocation and demolition, building rehabilitation, and construction of public facilities, such as streets, sewer facilities, and so forth.[105]

In Schaumburg's *Consolidated Plan* for fiscal years 2000–2005, the village admitted that it was not especially active on the low-income housing front: it had very low vacancy rates, many rental units were being converted to owner-occupied units, and the housing stock was mostly new and in excellent shape.[106] Nor did the village "currently have any public housing projects nor does it expect to develop any in the future"; instead, its "long-term housing goals center on integrating subsidized and non-subsidized housing."[107] But the details provided do not bear out even this modest goal. According to the village's own documents, the only government-subsidized housing units in Schaumburg are in (1) an apartment complex that sets aside 20 percent of its 768 units for low- and moderate-income residents paying no more than

30 percent of their income, some using Section 8 certificates;[108] (2) another complex (financed, in part, through HUD's Section 236 program), which was in the process of converting to luxury apartments and would no longer accept Section 8 certificates; (3) two complexes with subsidized units for the elderly, one of them with a two-year wait; and (4) four apartment complexes which, in 1985–86 used mortgage revenue bonds from the village in exchange for setting aside 20 percent of their units (a total of 241) for low and moderate income tenants (two have since paid off their bonds and will no longer have the set-aside, leaving only 115 units).[109] By my count, in 1999, Schaumburg had only 268 nonelderly subsidized housing units (less than 1 percent of total households in the village[110]); the number of Section 8 households administered by the city, meanwhile, was only 223.[111] Nowhere does the village discuss how it might raise these numbers or even claim that as a goal.[112]

But what is so startling about all this is that the village receives, every year, nearly half a million dollars of CDBG funds from the federal government specifically for housing and community development for the poor. During fiscal years 2000–2002, for example, Schaumburg was reimbursed $430,907 through the CDBG for the repaving of Hartung Road, a street on the far northern edge of the village (7).[113] Now what could that have to do with community development for the poor? According to Schaumburg officials, the road is located in a "CDBG eligible area," that is, an area in which 51 percent of residents are low or moderate income.[114] Having driven on this road and noticing that one apartment complex on it rented two bedroom apartments in 1999 for $1,230 per month, I assume that Schaumburg is using a loophole here that allows funding of projects in neighborhoods where the proportion of low and moderate income families is "within the highest quartile of all areas in the municipality."[115]

The Village may not be doing anything illegal or deceptive here; it is, after all, only taking advantage of 1960s era federal largesse. But given the dire need for housing assistance in the Chicago area, these half million dollars spent on a mostly middle-class, predominantly white suburban neighborhood does not appear to be a responsible use of taxpayer money meant to help urban communities deal with poverty.[116] The village is receiving federal funds intended to help revitalize low-income urban neighborhoods; but Schaumburg is not urban, has very few low-income residents, no slums or blight, has stated explicitly that it does not want public housing in its midst, and apparently has no plans to increase the number of subsidized housing units there. It is using federal money to repave a road that winds by several apartment complexes on the edge of town, in one of which, as far as I can tell, 20 percent of the residents are low or moderate income. It would be hard to claim that in return for that money, Schaumburg is furthering fair housing goals, trying to increase its non-Asian minority population, supporting affordable housing, or helping in *any* way to share the social costs of poverty and unemployment in the Chicago metropolitan region, an area from which it has benefited enormously.

The story of Schaumburg and Chicago is similar to the one Kenneth Jackson tells about Darien and New Canaan, Connecticut, and Newark, New Jersey. The first two achieved their success, he claims, by excluding everything they did not want from their borders:

> They zoned out industry, raised minimum lot requirements for new houses, refused public housing, restricted their schools and even their beaches to the wealthy and the comfortable, and discriminated against minorities. For those self-centered decisions [they] have been rewarded. . . . Newark, by contrast, encouraged industry, welcomed minorities, provided for entry-level housing, integrated its schools, and constructed public housing. For its pains, it became one of America's poorest and least attractive cities.[117]

The Village of Schaumburg would, no doubt, like to tell a story about itself that focuses on its humble beginnings and careful development once interstate highways were thrown in its path, a story about self-determination and foresight. The town motto, after all, is "Progress through Thoughtful Planning."[118] But what has Schaumburg been planned *for*? What has it been thoughtful *about*? To Chicagoans, it would appear that the village has been planned around the protection of private property for middle- and upper-middle-class white families. It would even appear, especially when one looks at Schaumburg's resistance to subsidized housing and its apparent indifference to segregation, that the town was planned, at bottom, out of fear of Chicago itself, as a way for its families to avoid contact with citydwellers even as they took advantage of the city itself.

If so, the plan worked; Schaumburg today is a place without the "problem" of poverty and the "trouble" of color. And *that* is why the village's new Town Center is so artificial: there is no public life here for the simple reason that there is no conflict to call it forth.

The Gautreaux Program

The fact is, though, that some low-income blacks from Chicago's public housing projects are finding their way to places like Schaumburg. Let us return, then, to the Gautreaux Assisted Housing Program described above, the program that was meant to correct HUD's long-standing support of racially discriminatory housing policies in Chicago by forcing it to provide eligible Chicago families with "mobility assistance" to find and pay for housing in the suburbs.

One of the best things about the Gautreaux program, according to Leonard Rubinowitz and James Rosenbaum, who have written an extensive evaluation of it, was that it not only helped move low-income families out of the concentrated poverty of inner-city public housing projects and racially integrate the suburbs; it also offered researchers an opportunity to study the effects of geography on family success.[119] Were the problems associated with the Chicago ghetto caused by the people who lived there? Or were they a function of the ghetto itself? Gautreaux seemed to offer a chance to answer those questions. How? Because, of the 6,000 families who participated in the relocation program over a twenty-year period, two-thirds (4,000) moved to the suburbs, and one-third (2,000) moved to other locations within the city, usually places with a higher percentage of blacks and a lower median income than the suburbs, though with lower concentrations of poverty than in the projects (68). Because families in the two groups (the authors call them "suburban movers" and "city movers") were similar and because they were assigned in a quasi-random way, a kind of natural experiment resulted.

Rubinowitz and Rosenbaum compared the two groups with each other, the suburban movers before and after their move, and both groups over time. In addition, comparisons were made with a control group: families who stayed in public housing (75). All families in the study—suburban movers, city movers, and those who stayed in the projects—were black, low-income, female-headed, public housing families from inner-city Chicago (77), although the Gautreaux families were screened for three attributes—having four or fewer children, a good record of rent payment and a regular source of income, and positive housekeeping inspections—that made them somewhat different from the control group (80). In 1982, the researchers interviewed 114 suburban movers and 48 city movers; and in 1989 they conducted follow-up interviews with 68 of the original suburban families and 39 of the city ones (76).

Before we get to their findings, however, let us look at some of the general problems and successes associated with this landmark program. Although, in 1976, when the program began, the demand for suburban relocation among public housing residents was low, by the 1980s, the phone-in application system for Gautreaux was taking 17,000 calls yearly (53–55). According to Rubinowitz and Rosenbaum, families were interested in the program because of the "pull" of suburban schools, jobs, and safety. In addition, the continuing deterioration of the Chicago inner city during the 1980s, the growing shortage of affordable housing, and the continuing cutbacks in welfare also prompted residents to call. The counseling and mobility assistance associated with Gautreaux were also attractive (54–57). Still, although all 40,000 public housing families in Chicago were eligible, only about 2,000 registered each year, and, of these, only about

300–400 actually used the program to move out of their public housing units (67, also 212, n. 83).

Supply was a bigger challenge for the program, especially since participation was voluntary, both for municipalities, which are not required to set up a public housing agency, and for landlords, who are under no obligation to accept renters with Section 8 certificates (57ff). This unwillingness of towns and landlords to participate in Gautreaux was clearly, at times, due to the race, class, gender, family composition, and inner-city origin of residents (60). Other supply problems included the generally tight rental market in the Chicago metropolitan area and the paucity of suitable units. The southern and southwestern suburbs had the best supply of affordable rental housing in the region, but they also had large numbers of blacks, so that moving families there would defeat the whole purpose of the program (58).

Is there any evidence that Gautreaux families ended up in Schaumburg? Specific information regarding where families settled is not provided, but Schaumburg was clearly the *kind* of place targeted. According to Rubinowitz and Rosenbaum, the initial goals of the program called for most of the suburban units to be in DuPage and northwest Cook County (40, 51), and the authors later assert that "the most common destination . . . was northwest Cook County" (68, 212, n. 86). In 1977, Schaumburg had actually sought in court *not* to participate in the program because, it claimed, it already had subsidized housing in its midst. But the excuse was disallowed, and the village was forced to take some of the families (62, 211, n. 72). The number of such families was never large, however: if, as program records indicate, 4,000 families were scattered over more than 100 suburbs during the twenty years of the program, and if that distribution was even, only about two families per year would have ended up there (64). My guess is that Schaumburg, a center of low-wage retail work, took more, though probably not much more given the almost imperceptible increase in the number of blacks there during the 1980s.

What did the researchers find out about the families who moved to places like Schaumburg? First, not surprisingly, the suburbs turned out to be far safer than the city (83–102). Inner-city Chicago, as we have seen, can be a frighteningly dangerous place. Its rate of violent crime during the 1980s, when most of this research was conducted, was among the highest in the country. In 1980, the residents of Robert Taylor Homes, 1 percent of the city's population, accounted for 10 percent of its murders, assaults, and rapes (83). Women in the Gautreaux study, the authors write, were subjected in the inner city to a constant barrage of criminal acts, suffered from feelings of helplessness and distrust, and experienced chronic fear and anxiety (84–5). "I was afraid of everything," one told the researchers (89). Crime also tore at the social fabric of the community, weakening contacts and controls, and promoting passivity and isolation (91).[120] In the suburbs, on the other hand, gangs were no longer a threat, and there was more peace and quiet (93ff). There was still danger (especially racial harassment) (96ff) but usually little physical violence (99). As one mother noted, "my mind is at ease out here; the children are softer" (101).

Second, suburban relocation did not seem to isolate former public housing families, as had been feared; the movers reported the same levels of social interaction and friendliness from neighbors as low-income black families elsewhere (103–126). This surprised Rubinowitz and Rosenbaum, since research has shown isolation effects both among black families in distressed inner-city neighborhoods, who suffer from lack of contact with mainstream society, and among low-income blacks in middle-income white settings, who must deal with the suspicion and fear of their new neighbors. Thus there was an expectation that suburban movers would experience depressed social interaction in the suburbs (103–105). The reality was more complex: suburban movers reported more interactions with their neighbors than did the city movers, yet they described their new neighbors as less friendly (105–106). They also reported more negative incidents, though these declined with time (106). Some reported a sense of community in the suburbs that was lacking in the city (107–110); others detected a congenial yet distant social environment, focused on the nuclear family (110–111). Suburban children, meanwhile, reported the same number of friends as city-moving children but more outside play (117).

Third, the children who relocated to the suburbs appeared to benefit from the greater resources of the schools there (127–160), which were newer, safer, better looking, and cleaner; they had better playgrounds, newer textbooks, more computers, and better extracurricular programs (130). Class sizes were smaller, and the students were, in general, better behaved (131–133). Parents also found higher academic standards in the suburbs—in many cases, a grade level higher than the schools the children had attended before (134). This meant, of course, that there was more schoolwork and that it was more challenging, but the suburban teachers were more helpful and encouraging (135). The mothers especially liked the better and more regular school-parent communication (143–147). The suburban children, meanwhile, reported better attendance, slightly fewer behavioral problems, and slightly declining or maintained grades (a positive sign given the higher standards) (153–156). And they reported significantly better athletic performance in the suburbs than the city, which had a positive impact on their grades (158).

Finally, the suburban moving children reported higher levels of employment, school completion, and enrollment in higher education than those who stayed in the city (161–172). There is thus some support here for the so-called spurred achievement thesis and against notions of permanent disadvantage among low-income blacks (161–162). In the suburbs, the relocated children had a lower dropout rate and a higher rate of enrollment in college-track courses

(164–165). Later on, more were enrolled in college (165). As for employment, more suburban children worked, made more money, and had better jobs with benefits than children who stayed in the city (166–167). The new environment, write Rubinowitz and Rosenbaum, seemed to have stimulated youth motivation among these families (168).

The Gautreaux experiment, therefore, offered support for the idea that there is a "geography of opportunity" in this country, that the places in which people live affect their life outcomes (1–16, 173–190), and that the suburbs are better places to raise a family than the inner city. They provide freedom from crime, an accepting social environment, better schools, and access to more and better jobs. The suburbs do not deserve all the credit here: the women in the study, Rubinowitz and Rosenbaum write, showed enormous persistence, courage, and strength of will (189). And their experiences were complex and not all positive, as we will soon see. But, in general, according to these researchers, Gautreaux supports the idea that, "[I]n changing their environment, these families improved their lives" (176).

Many antipoverty workers are now touting programs, like Gautreaux, that promise to "open up" the suburbs to the urban poor.[121] The success of Gautreaux prompted, for example, the federally funded Moving to Opportunity (MTO) project, authorized by the 1992 Housing and Community Development Act, which appropriated $70 million for 1,300 Section 8 housing certificates and mobility assistance to help low-income families with children residing in large-city public housing projects move to areas with lower concentrations of poverty.[122] In March, 1994, five sites were selected for the project: Baltimore, Boston, Chicago, Los Angeles, and New York. Like Gautreaux, a research component was attached to the project: subjects at each site would be randomly assigned to one of three groups: (1) an experimental group to be provided with Section 8 vouchers restricted for use in low poverty census tracts as well as counseling assistance to find suitable units; (2) a Section 8 control group, with geographically unrestricted housing vouchers but no special counseling; and (3) an in-place control group which would continue to receive project-based assistance in high-poverty areas. From 1994 to 1998, about 4,600 families were recruited for the program; about 1,700 families across the five cities found units and moved to the suburbs.

Preliminary results seem to confirm the positive effects of suburban relocation found with Gautreaux. In Boston, Los Angeles, and New York City, families in the experimental group were living in neighborhoods with significantly lower rates of poverty, welfare receipt, and female headship, and higher rates of employment, education, and managerial and professional jobs.[123] And there were large positive effects for safety, health, and behavior: suburban movers across all MTO sites reported increased security and reduced victimization and exposure to violence; and there were reports of improved physical and mental health.[124] In New York City, for example, suburban-moving mothers reported decreased depression and anxiety; and their children reported increased feelings of happiness.[125] In Boston, there were also decreases in injuries among children and a decline in childhood asthma.[126] In Chicago, mothers in the experimental group reported higher levels of safety, cleaner environments with less public drug and alcohol use, fewer unemployed people walking around, and less crime and violence overall.[127] In addition, boys aged eight to fourteen in Boston reported fewer behavior problems in the suburbs than the city, and suburban subjects reported fewer arrests for violent crimes.[128] Finally, Baltimore children from the experimental group showed a slower rate of decline in test scores and improved reading scores when compared with children who stayed in the city.[129]

But as positive as some of these effects are, the studies also reveal a dark side to the suburbs, one especially worrisome to those committed to improving the public sphere in our metropolitan areas. Though in all cases the researchers forthrightly admitted negative outcomes, they have tended to downplay them, presenting suburban relocation as, on balance, a good thing for inner-city blacks. Take MTO's indices of economic self-sufficiency: there was a drop in welfare use among suburban movers in Baltimore but none in Boston or New York, and there were few significant employment effects in any of the studies.[130] Perhaps more troubling were the education results. In Baltimore, rates of grade retention and placement in special education actually increased among the suburban moving children; and effects on older children were similarly mixed: suburban moving teenagers reported higher rates of grade retention, expulsion, and dropping out than those who stayed in the city.[131]

There were also mixed results from these studies regarding the geography of social capital. The Chicago MTO study, for example, showed no effects for either "feeling at home" or social interaction in moving to the suburbs.[132] In Boston, Los Angeles, and New York City, despite indications of higher neighborhood quality, there were few significant positive effects for social life at the individual level; and when there were significant differences, those in the experimental (suburban-moving) groups almost always fared worse.[133] Girls in the Boston experimental and Section 8 groups, for example, were less likely to have a friend in the neighborhood than those in the control group; Section 8 adults in Los Angeles were less likely to attend church than those who remained in the projects; adults in the New York City experimental group were less likely to volunteer and less involved at school than those in the control group; and Section 8 children there were less likely to participate in student government than those in the inner city.[134]

Similar findings were reported by Rubinowitz and Rosenbaum in the Gautreaux research. In fact, despite their obvious attempt to give the project a favorable evaluation, the researchers concluded that nearly *everything* about suburban relocation was mixed, ambiguous, and complex. For example, despite less physical violence and fear in the suburbs, there were numerous incidents of verbal mistreatment: harassing letters, car chases, racial slurs, thrown rocks, violent threats, name-calling, and eviction petitions (96–102; 118–120).[135] As for social interactions, neighbors were less friendly in the suburbs, and residents reported "distant" relationships, race-based social rejection, and "silent" racism: for example, suburban parents sometimes refused to let their children play with children who had grown up in public housing (110–123). Finally, the Gautreaux record on schooling was not all positive: placement in special education, for example, was significantly higher among suburban-moving children than those in the city (19 percent vs. 7 percent) (137–141), and there were reports of mistreatment in suburban schools from teachers and peers alike: verbal disrespect, humiliation, and isolation on buses and at lunch (though most of these declined with time) (149–153).[136]

In addition, the Gautreaux results seem unreliable given the flawed nature of the study. As we saw, participants did not represent a true sample of public housing families, since heads of large families and families with large debts and/or bad housekeeping records were not eligible (80).[137] In addition, many suburbs were excluded from the study, including those with a history of "intractable racism"[138] and those with average rent too far above Section 8 ceilings (46, 57–65). Ironically, then, the most prejudiced and affluent suburbs were excluded from a project whose very goal was to *integrate* Chicagoland.

The program's effects were also limited by its reluctance to call attention to itself (9, 28, 47, 62–65); as I have already noted, it sent only a few black families to each municipality each year both to avoid pushing places past a "tipping point" of black presence (sometimes pegged at about 7 percent of population) and to keep the program low-key.[139] In other words, success for the Gautreaux program was predicated on the assumption that raising black numbers in the suburbs would only succeed if blacks remained invisible there. If biblical metaphors have been common when describing suburban relocation from the point of view of relocatees (Gautreaux promised an "exodus" to the "promised land"), a very different vocabulary is used when the project is described from the point of view of the suburbs (blacks are to be "scatter[ed]," "sprinkle[d]," "dilute[d]" across the region).[140] As Owen Fiss put it in his own proposal for massive relocation of ghetto residents to the suburbs, "The approach I envision entails moving few enough ghetto residents into each middle- or upper-class neighborhood that the prior residents remain."[141]

Finally, even if we allow some success for mobility assistance, is this remedy commensurate with the disaster it was designed to correct? Is 4,000 families relocated to more than 100 suburbs over the course of twenty years

(200 families a year spread across a region half the size of New Jersey) just compensation for a hundred years of intense ghettoization that destroyed the lives of hundreds of thousands of black Chicagoans?[142]

Expanding the program, meanwhile, would only make it unpopular—on this point, program designers are right. Whites in Chicago continue to make it clear that they do not want to live next door to public housing residents.[143] Further, most public housing residents in the city apparently do not want to move to the suburbs; there is, for example, a general distrust and dislike of the Section 8 program. One Cabrini Green resident told a community activist, "When I worked as a case manager, I told people not to take the [Section 8] certificates because they were placing people out in the suburbs away from transportation and jobs."[144] The late Wardell Yotaghan put it this way: "[P]eople want to remain in the same area where they and their families have lived for years."[145] In Ronit Bezalel's documentary film *Voices of Cabrini*, one of the subjects interviewed describes suburban relocation as "tantamount to taking someone and dropping them on a desert island."[146] In light of all this, Fiss's claim that "with the prospect of a subsidy, most will leave" is simply untrue.[147]

The Suburbs as Public Sphere

What, in the end, can we say about suburban relocation? The first thing is that the variety of people's goals, as well as the diversity of their experiences in trying to achieve those goals, deserves our respect. For some former residents of Chicago public housing projects, the suburbs may well be the promised land: they may find there decent jobs; good schools; safety; and peace of mind. These are qualities not to be sneered at. And, though it is in my opinion less likely, some low-income blacks may even find community in places like Schaumburg, may come to feel that they belong there, that they want to and can be involved in the self-determination of such a place. With all that in mind, suburban relocation should be a live option for residents of Chicago's public housing projects. We should be committed to opening up the suburbs—*all* the suburbs—to people from every race, class, age, ethnicity, religion, familial status, and so on; to increasing the number of housing vouchers (and improving mobility assistance) to help families leave distressed neighborhoods; to enhancing public transportation and child care options for low-income suburban families; to more equitably distributing resources across the metropolitan area; to helping make our society more integrated in every way.

At the same time, we should be wary of aggressively pursuing suburban relocation to the detriment of urban revitalization efforts like those described below in chapters 6 and 7. I mentioned above some reasons to be skeptical of the praise being lavished on Gautreaux-type mobility programs. But there are at least two other reasons why I believe we should resist putting too many of our community development eggs in the suburban basket. First, for suburban relocation to actually put a dent in the problem of urban poverty and joblessness, we would need to bring much more of the city out to the suburbs than the Gautreaux program ever did. But moving too much of the city to the suburbs is antithetical to the whole idea of suburbia, the tendency of which is insistently centrifugal. Making the suburbs too much like the city, in other words, would only result in the suburbs sprouting suburbs of their own, the fragmentation, decentralization, and polarization of the landscape only accelerating and expanding.

From this perspective, suburbia is not so much a place as an impulse, a verb rather than a noun, a manifestation of our unending quest to go farther out, to build bigger houses on cheaper land, to surround ourselves with fewer and fewer people but ensure that they are more and more like us, to be ever closer to "nature" and yet, by roads and cables, always within reach of higher and higher levels of consumption and lower and lower rates of taxation. From this point of view, suburbia is about our "resistance to heterogeneity and desire to remain apart."[148] It is this anxiety about pluralism, this fear of conflict, this unease about *politics*, that Gans found in Levittown forty years ago and that more recent scholars continue to find in suburbia.[149] Its very geography is both cause and effect of a secessionist impulse.[150]

Second, the suburbs may be, by their very form, unfavorable to public life. They are chaotic,[151] incapable of being mentally mapped,[152] vertiginous,[153] and centerless.[154] They abandon the rectilinear grid of the city and replace it with disorienting curvilinear streets.[155] Their scale is awkward (things are too far away from one another), their land use is rigid (too much segregation of functions), their density is socially unsatisfactory (too little unplanned contact among individuals), and what public spaces they have are few and far between.[156] All this is especially harmful for the very young, teenagers, the very old, low-income families, and minority residents; but I think it is bad for all of us.

In sum, as a healthy public sphere, the typical North American suburb does not and probably cannot work. By its very design, this "collective attempt to live a private life"[157] is *a*political and may even be, in essence, *anti*political. Take Schaumburg, which, since 1974, has been ruled by a council-manager form of government with a president and six member Board of Trustees, each member elected at large by a non-partisan ballot, the whole group then selecting and overseeing a professional manager supported by divisions and departments: accounting, planning, streets, fire, police, and so on, as well as various advisory boards and committees. This is no polis; it is a private corporation designed to protect property values and keep taxes in check.

Let us turn around and head back into the city.

SIX

The New Urbanism

North Town Village

Right smack dab in the middle of town
I've found a paradise that's trouble proof.

—"Up On the Roof," by Gerry Goffin and Carole King

At 11:00 a.m. on a sunny June day in the Summer of 2000, several dozen new townhouses were put up for sale at North Town Village, a private real estate development on seven acres of formerly city-owned land on North Halsted Street in Chicago. The $70 million project would eventually contain 261 housing units: both for-sale and rental, in a variety of townhouse, rowhouse, apartment, and condominium configurations; but, for now, just the townhouses were on the market. And the market loved them. Before the sales trailer closed that day, 47 were sold, some for close to half a million dollars; by the end of the week, the number was almost 100. In August, the *Chicago Tribune* called it the hottest-selling residential development in the city.[1]

It is not hard to see why: North Town Village was shaping up to be an attractive, high-quality community designed on the model of the "urban village": compact, low-rise, mixed-use, moderate-density, pedestrian-friendly—a traditional city neighborhood with red-brick townhouses, six- and eight-flat walk-ups, gridded blocks, and prominent public spaces. But there was one thing about the development that made its success somewhat surprising: it was located next door to the "infamous" Cabrini Green public housing project on the city's Near North Side, just yards away from one of the sixteen-story high-rises in the dilapidated and dangerous Green Homes. The shadow of public housing fell, literally and figuratively, across North Town Village. And yet it did not seem to have repelled buyers at all.

Redevelopment had been inching toward Cabrini Green for years, from River North below, Lincoln Park above, the Gold Coast and Old Town to the East. But never had so much new housing been built at such high prices so close to the project. And not just close; the owners of North Town Village townhouses would literally be sharing their community with former residents of Cabrini Green. The city sold the land to a private developer on the condition that 30 percent of housing units developed there (79 total) would be reserved for former Cabrini families, their rent paid by the Chicago Housing Authority (CHA); another 20 percent (52 units) would be set aside for moderate income residents, their rent or mortgage subsidized by affordable housing funds; the rest (130 units) would be sold or rented at market value. The request for proposals (RFP) that the city issued for the property further required that these different type units—public housing, affordable, and market-rate—"be dispersed evenly throughout the . . . parcel with no visible distinctions from the outside."[2] As the local newspapers and even the television program *60 Minutes II* pointed out after the development broke ground, what this meant was that young, professional, childless, white couples, paying close to half a million dollars for their townhouses, would be living next door to former public housing residents, mostly unemployed black women with children, paying virtually nothing for identical units.[3] Given the history of residential patterns in Chicago, *that* was unusual.

But it was becoming less unusual. In the Fall of 2002, the developer of North Town Village was chosen to revitalize a huge section of Cabrini Green itself: twenty acres of CHA-owned land right in the heart of this fast-changing neighborhood, across one street from a new shopping center, across another street from a new police station, and next door to a new elementary school and a rehabilitated Seward Park. For that project, the eight buildings of Cabrini Extension North, long considered among the worst in the complex, would be demolished (five were already down), and a mixed-income townhouse community of 700 units would be built—three times the size of North Town Village—with about 200 units reserved for former residents of Cabrini Green.[4]

Meanwhile, the CHA has issued a $600 million RFP for the revitalization of the ABLA housing project on the Near West Side (eventually to contain 3,000 mixed-income units); a $300 million RFP for the revitalization of Madden Park/Ida B. Wells in Bronzeville (another 3,000 mixed-income units); and a $300 million RFP for the redevelopment of Stateway Gardens (1,300 mixed-income units), which, it is hoped, will anchor redevelopment of the four-mile State Street public housing corridor on the South Side.[5] And in other cities across the country—Boston, New York, Atlanta, Charlotte, Cleveland, Seattle, Miami—mixed-income developments are rising on the former sites of public housing projects.

Clearly, the country has not given up on the inner city. And that is good news since, as we saw in the previous chapter, suburban relocation is not a viable solution for the problem of urban poverty. Places like Schaumburg, Illinois, will never allow the influx of poor minorities required to create a fair dispersal of poverty and race across their metropolitan areas. And, besides, public housing residents apparently do not want to leave the central city, do not want to abandon their family, friends, and neighborhood to live among potentially hostile whites in automobile-dependent suburbs. In this chapter, then, we will look at a second idea for rethinking metropolitan America: the mixed-income, urban townhouse community.

Sources for the Urban Village

If naturally occurring, socioeconomically diverse neighborhoods were common in the early history of North American cities,[6] intentionally "mixed" neighborhoods—where lower- and higher-income residents are placed side-by-side through some kind of government or philanthropic intervention—have been rarer. Wendy Sarkissian has traced precursors for "social mixing" in nineteenth-century British town planning.[7] But the idea of integration was broached in the United States, too: in 1955, for example, U.S. public housing officials were warning the CHA about its plans to concentrate low-income families in very large developments;[8] and in the early 1960s, Jane Jacobs was extolling the benefits of Greenwich Village–style mixed communities, in which a variety of income groups live in close proximity to one another.[9]

By the late 1960s, however, whatever demands there were for residential integration in this country were couched almost exclusively in *racial* terms.[10] It would be another two decades before the idea of the *economically* diverse "urban village" would begin to attract attention. But once it did, it quickly monopolized discussions about reviving inner cities. Today, with the success of the federal government's HOPE VI program, mixed-income developments are practically the only way to talk about public housing anymore. All across the country, projects are being demolished, residents displaced, and new mixed-income developments built in their place. What accounts for the rather sudden and nearly hegemonic turn to this idea?

Let's begin with the facts. As we saw in chapter 4, during the 1970s and '80s, many inner-city public housing projects in this country became virtually uninhabitable.[11] Some of this distress could be attributed to neglectful public housing authorities, rising urban joblessness, and other contextual factors. But deterioration could also be traced to the way the federal housing program was set up in the first place.[12] As Wilson and others have argued, policies that isolated low-income families from the rest of society left them without models of mainstream behavior and fated their communities to rapid destabilization.[13] The situation was exacerbated when the housing projects were large, as in Chicago: whole neighborhoods became unrelentingly poor. Some kind of poverty "deconcentration" seemed necessary.

The courts agreed. Even if the 1969 *Gautreaux* ruling did not explicitly ban government-sponsored class-based residential segregation, and even if it mandated no changes to existing projects, it clearly changed the rules for public housing in Chicago. By forbidding any *further* concentration of poor blacks in large, high-rise projects in predominantly black, mostly poor neighborhoods, the courts cast a pall on all *existing* projects. Alexander Polikoff, still the plaintiffs' attorney in the *Gautreaux* case after more than thirty years, continues to insist that *all* the projects be dismantled and their inhabitants dispersed throughout the metropolitan area.[14]

Unfortunately, by the late-1990s, both of the Gautreaux remedies—the scattered site initiative and the mobility project—had run their stipulated courses. And the growing Section 8 program was, in many people's view, simply reconcentrating former public housing residents in new "horizontal ghettos," often far from the old black belt. The suburbs, meanwhile, as we saw in chapter 5, were not exactly welcoming them with open arms. And no one in either Chicago or Washington relished the prospect of putting thousands of poor families out on the street, though clearly that has happened in some cases.[15] The residents themselves, meanwhile, have been moderately successful in a spate of lawsuits (at, e.g., Cabrini Green, Henry Horner, and ABLA), in which they have complained about the racially discriminatory impact of large-scale displacement from the central city, despite the conflict with *Gautreaux*, in which they objected to being concentrated there in the first place.[16] The only apparent alternative—given the illegality of continued governmental concentration and the unfeasibility of metropolitan-wide dispersal—is to deconcentrate the poverty in existing projects by bringing in higher-income residents.

Recent federal legislation has made such redevelopment feasible. In 1995, Congress suspended and then later repealed the old "one-for-one" replacement rule that had, for years, required no net loss of public housing units during redevelopment.[17] With that rule gone, it is now legally possible to tear down a public housing project and build in its place a community with a drastically reduced population of very low income residents.[18] Then, in a dramatic reversal of half a century of federal public housing policy, the U.S. Congress began to explicitly allow income-mixing in public housing projects; recently, it has actually *required* "poverty deconcentration" in new projects.[19] Next, in 1996, as a result of the 1992 report of the National Commission on Severely Distressed Public Housing (NCSDPH), HUD established a "viability test" for all large public housing developments with a vacancy rate of 10 percent or more, which required public housing authorities (PHAs) to convert all units in such developments to Section 8 vouchers if conversion was cheaper than physical rehabilitation.[20] In Chicago, twelve developments totaling nearly 18,000 units, including all of the city's gallery high-rises, failed the test; and the city seemed therefore compelled to demolish them.[21]

Fortunately, since 1992, the federal HOPE VI program (another result of the NCSDPH) has made more than $6 billion available to PHAs for demolition and revitalization of family housing, with the latter specifically predicated on the mixed-income model.[22] And, in Chicago, the Gautreaux court, the main legal force behind metropolitan-wide residential racial integration there, began to allow construction of new public housing units in predominantly black areas (that is, on and around current CHA sites like Cabrini Green) as long as the new units are part of a plan for the economic revitalization of the area, which, it is hoped, will also produce racial integration.[23] Federal, state, and local governments, meanwhile, have begun to pursue innovative public-private redevelopment partnerships, such as the use of tax increment financing.[24]

Finally, by the mid-1990s, the Chicago Housing Authority, with a big push from Mayor Richard M. Daley, began thinking big again, after nearly thirty years of foot-dragging, neglect, and corruption. Although there had been in the past both rumors of and explicit recommendations for large-scale demolition of Chicago's housing projects (see, e.g., the 1988 Harold Washington[25] and 1993 City Club[26] reports), these had always been met with the obvious counterarguments: large-scale demolition involved too much resident displacement, was too costly, would not pass judicial scrutiny, and so on. By the mid- to late 1990s, however, the city was talking seriously for the first time about demolition and revitalization; and when the CHA was returned to local control in 1999, it promptly unveiled a $1.5 billion plan to demolish every gallery-style family public housing high-rise in the city while promising not to displace any lease-compliant residents.[27]

By this point, there were on both the local and national stage well-publicized success stories about the conversion of troubled housing projects into mixed-income communities, most notably Harbor Point in Boston, Techwood Homes in Atlanta, and the CHA's own Lake Parc Place.[28] There were also, throughout the 1980s and 1990s, energetic local and national leaders advocating the mixed-income model, most notably Bill Clinton's first HUD secretary, former San Antonio mayor Henry Cisneros.[29] Developments in urban architecture and design also supported the idea of the low-rise, mixed-income community. In the 1970s, for example, Oscar Newman had made a persuasive case against the modernist high-rises of the 1950s and 1960s and for what he called "defensible space."[30] But it was the "New Urbanism" of the 1980s and '90s that most persuasively heralded a new (or, rather, old) kind of inner-city neighborhood, the "urban village": compact, low-rise, mixed-use, moderate- to high-density, pedestrian-oriented, with prominent public spaces and gridded blocks integrated into the rest of city. The idea was pushed vigorously by both HUD and the CHA as well as the New Urbanists themselves.[31]

An additional force converging on the idea of the mixed-income urban village was a literal and metaphoric "return to the city" by a country that had largely spurned urbanity after World War II. Gentrification, immigration, a reawakened business attraction to the inner city,[32] and various high-profile revitalization projects in cities across the country (represented in Chicago most spectacularly by the revival of the Loop[33]) were resulting in a modest, though noticeable, revivification of America's urban landscape.[34] In the case of Chicago, the 2000 Census recorded the first population increase in that city in half a century.[35] (Of course, for some, this reclamation of the inner city was less an innocent return by young urban professionals or third wave immigrants than an attempt by corporations and private developers, with full governmental support, to make a profit from publicly owned central city land.[36])

For these reasons, federal subsidized housing policy has come to embrace mixed-income redevelopment. Let us see how the idea has played out in one neighborhood.

Renewal on the Near North Side

As we saw in chapter 1, the area in and around the Cabrini Green public housing project on Chicago's Near North Side was, by the mid-1990s, a troubled place indeed, characterized by extreme poverty, racial isolation, near universal unemployment, school failure, rampant drug and alcohol abuse, violent crime, and physical blight.[37] Of course, Cabrini Green was not the Robert Taylor Homes: it was too near a thriving downtown where young and upwardly mobile workers now wanted to live. When the Lincoln Park and North Michigan Avenue areas gentrified in the late 1970s and early '80s, it was impossible for the "yuppies" not to look west of Wells and south of North Avenue and wonder: shouldn't *that* be ours too?[38]

Sure enough, development began to creep toward the project. A new theater district emerged on Halsted Street, the New City YMCA opened on North Avenue, a Crate & Barrel was built nearby, and the old Marshall Field Garden Apartments were rehabilitated and renamed.[39] In the late 1980s and early 1990s, developers were buying parcels throughout the district in expectation of a boom. And, by 1986, pressure began to mount on Cabrini Green itself:[40] there were rumors of a secret $100 million buy-out of the whole complex.[41]

It was about this time that the Near North Development Corporation (NNDC), a community group dating from the 1960s, began to pursue a "nativist" plan for redevelopment. In 1990, the NNDC, through its North Town Redevelopment Advisory Council (NTRAC), published the *North Town Community Redevelopment Plan*, which envisioned a "safe, drug-free neighborhood" on the Near North Side. According to the plan, the area's diverse population was an asset, and the city should maintain its economic, social, and racial integration.

The group's fourteen "community goals" included the building of a Town Center, the provision of new parks and community institutions, and the installation of better circulation patterns around and through the Cabrini Green site. But housing was the top priority, and the group's key recommendation was to add 2,500 units of mixed income housing to the area's supply through a large-scale, public-private redevelopment effort. What is most distinctive about this plan, though, is how unambiguously and forcefully it argues that North Town belongs as much to its public housing residents as it does to anybody else. *All* Cabrini Green residents who want, the report asserted, should be able to stay in the neighborhood after revitalization. Twenty years later, it remains the only major proposal that ever made, and clearly meant, that recommendation.[42]

Unfortunately, the NTRAC proposal did not generate much interest or publicity; and the neighborhood itself continued to deteriorate through the early 1990s. During those years, violent crime rates at CHA family projects soared,[43] and vacancies skyrocketed.[44] The CHA responded with more neglect. Despite the commercial activity all around it, the area right around Cabrini Green saw little improvement. It would take the murder of a little boy for the city, and the nation, to focus on Chicago's Near North Side ghetto.

On the morning of October 13, 1992, while walking to school with his mother, seven-year-old Dantrell Davis, who lived in one of the high-rises at Cabrini, was shot and killed by a sniper.[45] The man who fired the gun from the tenth-floor window of a vacant apartment in a nearby building, thirty-three-year-old Anthony Garrett, later claimed he had been aiming his assault rifle at a group of rival gang members on the ground below. Garrett himself had spent almost half a lifetime committing crimes in Cabrini Green. But Dantrell Davis's short life had been troubled as well. Born to a fifteen-year-old single woman whose uncle, the *Chicago Tribune* would later report, ran a Chicago street gang from prison, Dantrell had been diagnosed with behavioral problems and was in a special education class at his school, where, between September 1991, and March 1992, he accumulated more than twenty absences. In the early morning hours of March 31, 1992, just six months before the shooting that killed him, Dantrell was found in his apartment, alone, over a quarter of his body burned from a fire. His mother was later charged with child neglect, but when she agreed to attend parenting classes, those charges were dropped. Meanwhile, Dantrell's father, twenty-seven-year-old Kelvin Davis, died in September 1992, from a drug overdose.

But the tragedies that year were not confined to the Davis family. In the summer of 1992, sniping from vacant apartments at Cabrini Green had become so bad that more than 150 residents, attending a public meeting at a local church, demanded that the city and the CHA do something to protect the people there. That meeting came on the heels of the July 23 sniping death of fifteen-year-old Laquanda Edwards, who had been shot in the back of the head at Larrabee and Hobbie Streets while on the way to the store for milk.[46]

Almost immediately after the Dantrell Davis killing, the talk in Chicago's newspapers was of demolition, the usual white response to a crisis in the city's black ghetto.[47] But there was also mobilization of a different order. As we saw in chapter 1, the *Chicago Tribune* announced an international competition to redesign Cabrini Green, eventually eliciting more than 300 entries from ten countries.[48] And the Chicago Housing Authority began its own plans to rehabilitate the project.[49] Under the direction of its chairman, real estate developer Vince Lane, who had had success with the mixed-income model at Lake Parc Place,[50] the CHA submitted the first of a contentious series of proposals for redeveloping Cabrini Green.[51]

The 1993 CHA plan called for a 10-year, $350 million make-over of the project. Phase 1 would cost $120 million and be focused on half of Cabrini Extension North, a nine-acre parcel near Division Street.[52] It would use $50 million of federal HOPE VI funds to demolish three of the worst buildings at the project (two were already vacant) and renovate a fourth. In all, Phase 1 of Lane's plan contemplated the demolition of 660–690 units at Cabrini Green. And, since the one-for-one replacement rule had not yet been repealed, the CHA would be legally required to replace all of them. This it planned to do by building 300–330 new units on the nine-acre Cabrini North site and in the immediate vicinity for a mixed tenancy of working-class families (with incomes under 80 percent of area median income [a.m.i.]) and very low income families (with incomes under 30 percent a.m.i.);[53] 190 "hard units" would then be scattered across the metropolitan area and 167 Section 8 vouchers provided for use wherever the holders could find housing.

With the completion of both phases of the plan, the CHA foresaw about 1,200 new housing units in the area, 75 percent of which would be for "working-" or moderate-income residents and 25 percent for very low income families.[54] At the time, it was the most radical plan for remaking a Chicago public housing development in decades. Some residents, as well as the local U.S. congressperson, however, worried that the plan involved too much displacement of Cabrini residents;[55] and that summer, the proposal was turned down by HUD.[56] A slightly reworked effort, however, won a $50 million HOPE VI grant late that year,[57] and the CHA began making plans for demolition on the Phase 1 site. Meanwhile, other efforts by Lane in the area were beginning to bear fruit. In 1994, ground was broken at Orchard Park, a private development of fifty-four townhouses on Clybourn Avenue, thirteen of which were reserved for former Cabrini Green families, the first government-supported effort to turn the Lower North into a mixed-income community with both low and high-income residents.[58]

Private developers were indeed busy in the neighborhood. If, between 1991 and 1995, there was only $4.1 million in construction activity here,[59] in 1996–67, that number jumped to $45 million.[60] The biggest player was Dan McLean of MCL properties, who had purchased, among other parcels, both the ten-acre "Oscar Mayer" site (at Goethe, Scott, Sedgwick, and Well Streets) and the five-acre CHA playing fields on Division. By the mid-1990s, he was hard at work on a $50 million residential project called Old Town Village, consisting of 150 condos, townhouses, and single-family homes, and had plans for a shopping center on the old playing fields.[61] Both Old Town Village and McLean's Mohawk North development[62] would include public housing units, agreements apparently extracted by the local alderman, Walter Burnett.

The CHA, meanwhile, suffered the first of what would be many setbacks in the revitalization of Cabrini Green. In June 1995, just as the first two demolitions were underway at the HOPE VI site, Lane was ousted from his position at the CHA, which had been taken over by the federal government due to alleged mismanagement. New director Joseph Shuldiner shelved the HOPE VI plan and, in October, issued a new Request for Proposals for Cabrini Green, based on the $50 million HOPE VI funds now in CHA's bank account.[63] This RFP elicited ten plans of widely varying scope and shape. The largest was from McLean: a massive $1 billion public-private initiative involving the demolition of twenty-one of twenty-three Cabrini Green high-rises over five years and the building of 1,620 new units, 450 of them public-housing eligible (about 28 percent of total units), on 40 acres (including the entire twenty-acre Cabrini Extension North site). It also envisioned a new public library, rapid transit station, and a 150,000-square-foot shopping center for the neighborhood.[64]

A screening committee reviewed the proposals in January 1996, and rejected all of them, though the McLean proposal had by then made its mark in government corridors and with the media. Shuldiner argued that the revitalization needed more than the nine acres of the HOPE VI Phase 1 site and more incentives for market-rate housing. His request was answered in June, when Mayor Daley proposed a compromise between the old Lane plan—resident-friendly but modest—and the recent McLean proposal—ambitious but disruptive. This was, as we have already seen, the Near North Redevelopment Initiative (NNRI): a $1 billion, ten-year, public-private plan to build a mixed-income community in the area, with new housing scattered across 70 acres of a 330-acre redevelopment district. The initiative would use all 20 acres of the Cabrini Extension North site plus 50 acres of city- and privately owned land, much of the latter held by McLean. The Mayor also promised substantial investment in the area's infrastructure: two new schools, new and upgraded parks, a new library and police station, as well as help with a privately developed Town Center, including a grocery store employing 200 area residents.[65]

According to the mayor's proposal, all eight buildings of Cabrini Extension North (comprising 1,324 units) would be demolished. The remaining fifteen high-rises (the rest of the "reds" and all of the "whites") and all of the row houses would be rehabilitated. As with the NTRAC and Vince Lane plans before it, the neighborhood would then be converted into a mixed-income community, but the mix would be quite different from the earlier proposals, both of which integrated the "very low income" residents of Cabrini Green with the so-called working poor. Of the 2,000–2,300 units to be built in the mayor's plan, 50 percent would be sold or rented at market rate (for residents with incomes above 120 percent a.m.i.); 20 percent would be "affordable" (for moderate-income residents at 80–120 percent a.m.i.); and 30 percent would be for public housing eligible residents (see table 6.1). But the proposed economic transformation of the area would be even more dramatic than those numbers suggest, since only half of the public housing units would be for "very low-income" families, those at 0–50 percent a.m.i., like virtually all Cabrini Green tenants; the other half would be reserved for the "working poor," with incomes between 50–80 percent a.m.i. Thus, of the original 1,324 very low income units on the site (over one-third of which were vacant in 1995), only 350 would be replaced at that income level, some of which would be off-site. The end result would be a 74 percent reduction in the number of very low-income housing units in the area—during one of the worst affordable housing shortages in city history.[66]

About all this, the residents were furious; and they were angry as well that, although they had been involved in both the NTRAC and original HOPE VI plans, they were shut out of the Mayor's NNRI; as the *Chicago Tribune* reported, not a single public housing resident was on the dais when Daley announced it.[67] After a more inclusive December 1996, charrette, however, the Mayor upped the number of new units to 2,600 by adding more public housing units. But the plan still contemplated a massive loss of very low-income housing in the area, even as it foresaw huge profits for private developers (estimated at more than $100 million).[68]

In October 1996, the Cabrini Green Local Advisory Council (LAC) sued the CHA to halt redevelopment at the complex, alleging that the NNRI would have a racially discriminatory impact on the neighborhood's African-American women and children; and in December, a federal judge enjoined further demolition.[69] In March 1997, the LAC added the city to its lawsuit as it unveiled its own Lane-like proposal for the revitalization of Cabrini Green.[70] Although public-private development on non-CHA land in the area proceeded, redevelopment at Cabrini Green itself ground to a halt. It wasn't until July 1998, after almost two years of bitter negotiations, that the Cabrini Green LAC, the city, and the CHA finally signed a consent decree concerning the HOPE VI project. In it, the LAC agreed to demolition of the remaining

Table 6.1. Chicago's Near North Redevelopment Initiative

Purpose	*Area*	*Public Facilities*	*Commercial Facilities*	*New Housing*	*Cost*
To create a thriving community in a once-troubled neighborhood	330 acres on the Near North Side, bounded by North Avenue, Wells Street, Chicago Avenue, and the North Branch of the Chicago River	Two new elementary schools, one new high school, new police station, new public library, upgraded parks, etc.	New Town Center with grocery store, coffee shop, etc.	2,300–2,600 units in 16 separate developments totaling 65 acres, at a density of about 40 units per acre, with the following income mix: • 50% *market rate*, for residents with incomes above 120% a.m.i. (c. 1,200 units), • 20% *affordable*, for residents at 80–120% a.m.i. (c. 500 units, with half reserved for former public housing tenants below 80% a.m.i.), and • 30% *public housing* eligible, for residents below 80% a.m.i. (c. 700 units, with half reserved for families with a member working 30 hours per week)	$700 million—$1 billion in public-private funds, including TIF revenues

Source: City of Chicago, *Draft Near North Redevelopment Initiative* (June 1996, with updates in February and December 1997 and January 1998).

six buildings in the NNRI plan (the rest of Cabrini Extension North); and the CHA agreed to build at least 895 public housing eligible units within the NNRI site, 700 of which would be for displaced and current Cabrini Green families earning below 30 percent a.m.i., while the remaining 195 units would be for families with incomes at or below 40 percent a.m.i., a significant increase from the mayor's plan.

But there was a breathtaking new twist in the consent decree. The Cabrini Green LAC—the political organization representing the residents themselves—was to be cogeneral partner in all development of CHA land in the neighborhood, with a 51 percent controlling interest in the project. For the first time since the federal public housing program began in the 1930s, low-income residents were being granted a determinative role in the shaping of their own communities; they would, in effect, be landowners.[71]

Immediately, there were protests; the *Chicago Tribune*, for example, came out against the consent decree.[72] More damaging was the complaint made by the Habitat Corporation, CHA's court-appointed receiver for all new development, which asked that the decree be halted because it had been left out of negotiations to which it had a mandated role; it also argued that the 51 percent interest granted to the residents would make it nearly impossible to find a willing private developer for the project. The judge agreed, at least with the first charge; the consent decree was voided; and the players headed back to the negotiating table.[73]

After another two years of bitter discussion, a second consent decree, approved by all parties, was signed on August 30, 2000.[74] Under it, a Working Group, comprised of representatives of the LAC, the CHA, the city, the *Gautreaux* plaintiff (Alexander Polikoff), the Habitat Corporation, and HUD (sitting in as an observer), was now in charge of all rehabilitation and revitalization on CHA land in the area. As with the first decree, the LAC agreed to the demolition of the remaining six buildings on the HOPE VI site, and the CHA agreed to build 700 new public housing eligible units in the NNRI area (still a net loss of 624 very low-income units), with no minimum income requirement and rent fixed at 30 percent of family income, half to be reserved for families with one member working at least thirty hours per week.[75] In addition, the city agreed to reserve 270 of the "affordable" units for families making less than 80 percent a.m.i. For all subsidized units, current and displaced Cabrini Green families would have priority. Meanwhile, the income mix of new units on all city or CHA land would be 50 percent market rate, 20 percent affordable, and 30 percent public housing. Finally, any RFP for development on the CHA land required that the LAC be cogeneral partner with a financial stake *up to* 50 percent.[76]

In October 2001, nearly a decade after the killing of Dantrell Davis, the city issued an RFP for the redevelopment of Cabrini Extension North, the cornerstone of the NNRI.[77] On these 18.4 acres, where eight "notorious" high-rise buildings once housed over a thousand very low-income families, a low-rise mixed income townhouse community will be built. There will be about 635–700 total units, with income groups mixed at the now-familiar proportions of 50 percent market rate, 20 percent affordable, and 30 percent public housing. The goal of the project is to create a "quality residential neighborhood"—safe, stable, economically diverse, and physically cohesive, integrated into the fabric of the surrounding community. In the Fall of 2002, the developer for the project was named, and work commenced in 2003.[78]

Of course, there was still much to be done on the Near North Side. Two-thirds of Cabrini Green was untouched by any revitalization plan. There was nothing in the consent decree about Cabrini Extension South (the seven remaining "red" high rises), nothing about the Green Homes (the eight "white" high-rises), and nothing about the row houses. But, by 2002, the NNRI was in full swing, with numerous sites under development or in preparation. One of those was North Town Village.

The Case of North Town Village

On January 31, 1998, the City of Chicago issued an RFP for the purchase and redevelopment of a seven-acre parcel of city-owned land on Halsted Street, just North of Division and next to the William Green Homes.[79] Until the plans for the Cabrini Extension North site were unveiled at the end of 2001, this was the largest development site in the mayor's NNRI. The city contemplated there a relatively high-density, low-, and medium-rise, mixed-income residential community. Later called North Town Village but at this point referred to only as "Halsted North," it will be the focus of the rest of this chapter.

Like other NNRI projects, the Halsted North project was part of the city's effort to revitalize the Cabrini Green neighborhood "by utilizing its natural strengths" (3), including its prime location and proximity to transportation. The central feature of the project, however, was income mixing, meant to "knit together the vacant and disparate elements" of the neighborhood into a viable community (3). There would be three economic categories in the development, "dispersed evenly throughout the . . . parcel with no visible distinctions from the outside" (5). Fifty percent of the units would be rented or sold at market rate—that is, at whatever price the developer could get for them (1). Thirty percent would be reserved for public housing eligible families (those with incomes less than 80 percent of a.m.i.) and made available to the CHA through sale or lease for at least forty years (5).[80] And 20 percent of the units would be "affordable" to persons making no more than either 120 percent of a.m.i. (for-sale) or 80 percent a.m.i. (rental), with affordability based on the resident spending no more than 30 percent of family income on housing (7).[81]

As for the actual design of the development, the Halsted North RFP reminded prospective respondents about the NNRI's goal of reinforcing and strengthening the "physical, economic, and social aspects of this complete community" (8). And it encouraged proposals that would try to restore the "traditional urban fabric" (9) of the Near North Side, helping to make it a compact, pedestrian-friendly, mixed-use, and secure urban neighborhood. "Mixing" was the key word throughout, not just in terms of income groups but also in terms of building scale, housing type, and population density. Developers were encouraged to break down the existing "superblock" of the site into more conventional blocks linked by a network of city streets, each with two travel lanes, two parking lanes, sidewalks, trees, and landscaped curbs (9).[82]

The RFP also recommended that developers meet the needs of a variety of residents—for example, in the number of bedrooms provided (10)[83]—and suggested that most units have direct access to the street to "promote daily interaction among residents and encourage their collective stewardship of the neighborhood" (10). And it recommended that the design "incorporate elements of a traditional downtown Chicago neighborhood": internal streets lined with rowhouse-scaled buildings and major streets lined with larger buildings of "a more urban character" (10). Lower-density housing would consist mainly of 1–3 unit row houses, 3–4 stories high, using a traditional Chicago architectural vocabulary: brick facades, masonry trim, frequent cornices, and large windows—all to create a sense of human scale and variety, maximize the number of front doors,[84] provide for different "street walls," and make good use of special features like porches, bay windows, gables, dormers, and balconies (11).[85]

The higher density housing, by contrast, would include elevator buildings of 4–6 stories, with studio to three bedroom apartments or condos, also using brick facades, masonry trim, arches, cornices, and large windows (11). Developers were encouraged to be contemporary but convey "the dignity and scale" of turn-of-the-century Chicago landmarks: consistent vertical rhythms marked by recessed window openings, facade elements, and diverse roof forms to create "a rich silhouette against the sky" (12). The city was clearly contemplating here a community whose nontraditional population would be housed in very traditional looking buildings.

One of the firms that responded, in March 1998, to the Halsted North RFP was the Holsten Real Estate Development Corporation (hereafter, "Holsten"), a small firm founded and still run by Peter Holsten that has been rehabilitating, building, and managing affordable housing in Chicago since 1975. With its main office right across the street from Cabrini Green, Holsten was familiar with the neighborhood and, in its proposal, played up its history with the local community and its desire to help current and prospective residents achieve their "vision of a beautiful, safe, and affordable community."[86]

Holsten's overall goals for the property, it claimed, were to have all persons of all income levels living next door to one another; to work with current Cabrini Green residents concerning their needs; to find "common ground" under all the residents in the development; and to give them the chance to help manage their own community (Development Team Approach, 1). But the firm admitted that the key to the project's success was to attract market rate customers (cover letter, 1). And the way to do that was, first, to build high-quality housing—beautiful, practical, and long-lasting (Proposed Use and Concept, 1)[87]—and, second, to ensure that the poorer residents met the behavioral standards of the wealthier ones without being stigmatized by them (Development Team Qualification, 1). While unabashedly catering to the desires of the wealthy, in other words, the developer promised "respect for all persons in all walks of life . . . to avoid a class system and two tiers of expectations" (Development Team Qualification, 1). The tension between these two principles—between meeting the aesthetic, functional, and behavioral standards of the market-rate customers while treating the poor with dignity and respect—is evident throughout the proposal and is, I would argue, the fundamental tension in all mixed-income housing plans. Holsten admitted in its proposal, for example, that its market-rate units would be targeted to single individuals and childless couples in their thirties. Hopefully, the firm argued, those residents would stay in the area permanently; but for now, the idea was to offer them more space than comparably priced units in Old Town or Lincoln Park, space that could be turned later into additional bedrooms for an expanding family (Proposed Use and Concept, 2).

As for the actual development, the plan emphasized three features: beauty, long-term survival, and practicality (Proposed Use and Concept, 1). The goal was to create a neighborhood that would endure market cycles, continue to be desirable well into the future, and be exemplary in both construction and style. It was a plan, the firm asserted, that could serve as a model for the Cabrini redevelopment as a whole.

Here is how it worked: cars and pedestrians coming into Halsted North would enter a new Evergreen Street through a two-story arch; they would then proceed to a forty-two-foot wide landscaped Circle with benches (see figure 3). Ground-floor rooms in the surrounding buildings would be devoted to retail and community purposes. The actual housing units, meanwhile, would be in "stacked duplexes" with coach houses in the rear, townhouses, and apartment/condo mid-rises on the corners. Other features of the design included perimeter fencing, a greenway path to the nearby YMCA and Stanton Park, and potential retail space at three locations. All this ground-level activity would, Holsten argued, enhance security: with so many common spaces, outside decks, and separate doorways, there would be "eyes" everywhere and activity day and night (Proposed Use and Concept, 1–7).

Buildings in the proposal included a six-story, sixty-two-unit rental mid-rise, with one and two bedroom units, all public housing; an eight-story, seventy-two-unit condo mid-rise, with one and two bedroom units, mostly market-rate with some subsidized units; three- and four-story stacked duplexes, with both rental and for-sale units (one to four bedrooms), for all income types; coach houses for all income types, rental and for-sale; and three-story townhouses (three to four bedrooms), all owned, also for all income types. The design of the development would thus provide integration among low-, middle-, and higher-income residents and between homeowners and renters (Overall Unit Counts).[88]

The proposal foresaw 281 total housing units at Halsted North. Market rate customers would have 144 of those, all one and two bedroom; all for sale, except the coach houses, which could be rented; all owner-occupied (again, except the coach houses), with the condo mid-rise governed by a condominium agreement; and all tied to a master homeowners association. Other than those stipulations, "MARKET HOUSEHOLDS HAVE NO OTHER RESTRICTIONS" (Homeowner Deed Restrictions, 1, emphasis in original). Eighty-one units, meanwhile, would be for current and former Cabrini Green residents, with incomes less than 80 percent a.m.i., and rent limited to 30 percent of household income. These units would be owned by the CHA, which would have to pay condo and other fees for their upkeep (Homeowner Deed Restrictions, 1–2). A high proportion of these units would contain three, four, and five bedrooms. Finally, there would be 56 "affordable" units (all numbers from Overall Unit Counts and Detailed Unit Mix).

The majority of total units, Holsten proposed, would be for-sale (172 vs. 109) to ensure the community's long-term stability and help persuade initial customers to buy. Seventy-five percent of these units would be reserved for market-rate customers (Detailed Unit Mix, 1).[89] As for the rental units, all prospective tenants would have to provide information regarding their employment, income, and renting and credit history; and they would have to take a drug test (Management Plan, 4). Holsten would handle maintenance, rent collection, evictions, and tenant-management relations; and it would hire a liaison to work with local social service agencies (Management Plan, 5–7). Meanwhile, renters and owners alike would have to attend a half-day "community seminar," which would describe the goals of the development, subvert myths about public housing, offer conflict resolution tips, and conclude with a tour of Cabrini Green (Screening Criteria and Pre-approval Community Seminar). Renters would also have to attend monthly tenant meetings at least three times a year (Screening Criteria).

Holsten claimed that it could build the project for $63 million: $2.5 million for the land, $51 million for construction (at about $180,000 per unit), including streets, sewer, landscaping, contractor overhead, and profit, and $9 million in fees for architects, attorneys, brokers, and so forth. Funds would come, the firm proposed, from a variety of public and private sources: city-issued tax-exempt bonds, federal CDBG funds, city tax increment financing (TIF) funds, federal Low Income Housing Tax Credits (LIHTC),[90] CHA purchase of for-sale units and development subsidies, federal and state grants, construction loans, and developer equity. Repayment of loans and bonds would come from the sale of market units, rental income, TIF revenues, equity payments from LIHTC, and CHA's operating subsidies (Budget and Financing Plan).

The biggest challenge facing the development, Holsten admitted, was not, however, design, construction, marketing, or financing, but rather confronting the endemic social segregation of Chicago's residential patterns (Management Plan, 1). Thus, the firm imagined not just a set of attractive and long-lasting physical structures but a social environment oriented to healthy contact among its diverse individuals. This goal would be achieved through a combination of "natural" and "staged" human interactions. The "natural" interactions, Holsten argued, would come from the residents simply living side-by-side in low-rise structures (Management Plan, 1–2). The Circle on Evergreen Street, for example, would promote socializing, as would the common backyards, grounds, and parks. Contact would also occur, Holsten argued, on the street, since the project was designed to be pedestrian-friendly (Proposed Use and Concept, 1–7).

But simply putting residents side by side, Holsten wrote, would not be enough to promote *community* among them (Management Plan, 2).[91] The proposal thus included some innovative ideas for building social trust at Halsted North. There would be, for example, dedicated space for resident meetings, probably on the ground floor of the buildings surrounding the Circle on Evergreen Street (Proposed Use and Concept, 2–3). These meetings, called "staged" interactions in the proposal, would include the preapproval seminars and monthly resident gatherings as well as meetings about community service and other projects. Even the tenant grievance procedure was designed to encourage participation in the care of the community. The hope behind all this was that the formal events, which would initially bring residents together, would eventually spark more informal interactions among them (Management Plan, 2).[92]

Another important outcome of these "staged" interactions, according to Holsten, was a community covenant that would set standards concerning safety, cleanliness, behavior, and mutual respect at the development. This covenant was to be initiated by the public housing residents: the developer would record their "wish list" for the community, giving them "first say" in the document and letting them know that community standards were not meant to favor one group over another. They would be asked, for example, what they thought the different income groups should be called. Later, the developer would meet with the higher-income residents, sensitive to the risks they had undertaken in moving to the development. The two sets of expectations would then be synthesized into a single covenant binding on the whole community (Management Plan, 2–3).

But by far the most important and distinctive "staged" interaction in Holsten's plan for Halsted North was an innovative program of "storytelling" that would be proposed to the community once it was up and running (cover letter, 2; Management Plan, 3; Community Building Storytelling Project, *passim*). The idea was to bring residents together to discover what they had in common; telling stories about their lives and dreams, hopes and fears, would help them establish mutual trust, welcome new members, and provide a forum for discussing issues and problems. I will have more to say about the Storytelling Project below.

In June 1998, in reply to questions from the city, Holsten submitted a revised proposal with a reduced request for public funds.[93] There was also now a greater mix of income groups within each building, more open space, a taller rental mid-rise with more market-rate residents, a decrease in the overall unit count, and more affordable and public housing units in the condo mid-rise. The revised count is broken down in table 6.2.

Table 6.2. North Town Village: Breakdown of Units

	Building Type	*Market-Rate Units*	*Affordable Units*	*Public Housing Units*	TOTALS
Rental	7-story mid-rise	29	32	27	88
	6-flats	4	2	6	12
	8-flats	4	6	6	16
For Sale	3-story townhomes	44	0	16	60
	condo townhomes	13	5	6	24
	duplexes	6	2	4	12
	coach houses	6	0	3	9
	12-unit condo bldg	8	0	4	12
	3–4-story condo bldgs	16	5	7	28
TOTALS		130	52	79	**261**

Source: Holsten Real Estate Development Corporation, *Proposal for Redevelopment of Halsted North Community* (Chicago: March 30, 1998).

In July 1998, Holsten and MCL Properties were named finalists for the project;[94] and, in September, Holsten was selected by the city to be the developer.[95] Construction began almost immediately; and, two years later, the first for-sale units went on the market (see figure 4). The development was officially opened by Mayor Daley, who had already begun touting it as a model for the transformation of public housing in the city.[96] North Town Village would later win the 2000 *Chicago Sun-Times* Mixed-Income Housing Award, the governor's Illinois Tomorrow award, a YMCA 2000 Business Leadership Award, and the 2004 Outstanding For-Profit Real Estate Project from the Chicago Neighborhood Development Awards.[97] In Spring 2001, the first tenants moved in; and, in Fall 2002, the Village was showcased nationally on *60 Minutes II*.[98]

North Town Village as a Public Sphere

From a rhetorical point of view, the main tension in the Holsten proposal, practically foreordained by the city's RFP, is between community and difference, harmony and conflict. The latter term in these binaries is easy enough to see, and certainly there is more discussion of diversity here than in the projects we encountered in chapters 4 and 5. North Town Village incorporates a variety of housing types, unit sizes, and architectural styles. It accommodates a diversity of households, from single individuals to childless couples to small and large families, abled and disabled persons, young and old residents. It provides for both private and public space, commercial venues, and even a versatility of transportation methods (residents can walk, bike, drive, take the bus, the "el," etc.). Most importantly, it includes a diversity of income groups, symbolized by the much-noted young white professional childless couple moving into a half-million dollar townhouse next to a single black mother with three children and no job paying essentially nothing for an identical unit. The proposal notes with pride, for example, that, just among its renters, income would range from below $6,000 to above $60,000 per year, a tenfold difference (Development Team Qualification, 2). As one reporter wrote about another mixed-income housing project nearby: "This isn't the very poor moving next to working poor or even middle-class neighbors"; it is unemployed public housing residents paying $3 a month moving next door to people who have plunked down hundreds of thousands of dollars.[99]

And yet, the overriding tone of both the city's RFP and Holsten's winning proposal is unity, harmony, and integration. Halsted North, its sponsors say, is not about socioeconomic difference but about *community*, about building bridges among formerly separated people. Despite the plurality of inhabitants, in other words, North Town Village is meant to be a single thing. The city requested developers, after all, to design a neighborhood with a "compact and identifiable character" (9), a singular presence that would "knit" residents together (3) into a cohesive whole. It is this unity that is appealed to time and again in Holsten's proposal. The firm writes repeatedly, for example, about how *all* people, regardless of background or income category, want to live in "an attractive, affordable, and safe community" (cover letter, 1). And it envisages a development united around a common name, encircled by a fence, distinguished from the rest of the neighborhood by the arch over Evergreen Street, and integrated through consistent architecture and landscaping (Proposed Use and Concept, 1–7). As we will see below, the impulse toward unity is especially prominent in the Storytelling Project that Holsten proposed for social interactions at the development.

Thus, rather than *difference*, what is really celebrated here is *mixture*: "HALSTED NORTH IS FOR PEOPLE WHO WANT TO GAIN THE BENEFITS OF AN ECONOMICALLY INTEGRATED COMMUNITY" (Proposed Use and Concept, 7, emphasis in original). The whole development, after all, is modeled on an image of interspersal, the taking of pregrouped individuals and mixing them with one another so that they are no longer grouped. The goal, of course, is laudatory: to prevent the segregation that we described (mostly in racial terms) in chapters 4 and 5. At North Town Village, individuals from different income groups would be evenly distributed throughout the complex so that a market-rate resident would be located next to a moderate-income one, who would live beside a public housing family, which would live next to a market-rate one, and so on (Development Team Approach, 1).

Integration, however, goes beyond simple interspersal here. In Holsten's plan, all residents are treated equally: selection criteria for rental units are uniformly applied, and no one is *not* shown or rented an apartment because of race, color, sex, familial status, and so on (Development Team Qualification, 1; Management Plan, 1–7). And the point is not just copresence and equal treatment: it is hoped that the design and government of the development will encourage actual interactions among these diverse individuals (Management Plan, 1–2).

The residents of the community are also, claims Holsten, intricately and insistently connected to the rest of the Near North Side. The Halsted North complex would not be an isolated island of poverty like the public housing projects it replaced. This vision would be achieved in part by the abandonment of the superblock layout and the reintroduction of the Chicago grid (Proposed Use and Concept, 1–7).[100] It would also be achieved, as Holsten argued in its June 1998 *Reply* to the City, by the "integration" of North Town Village with its immediate neighbors: most importantly, the New City YMCA, Stanton Park, and Cabrini Green itself. Connections would also be made to the various social and political institutions in the district, including the Cabrini Green LAC, the

CARE Center, the Mohawk North Homeowners Association, the Moody Bible Institute, the Near North Development Corporation, and so forth (7–9).[101]

Finally, integration is even used as a way to talk about the role of housing in individual flourishing: in the original *Proposal*, Holsten clearly imagined building on the site of Halsted North not just a set of physical structures but a new context for healthy human *lives*—thus, the importance there of helping the public housing residents become more financially independent (Management Plan, 8).[102] In sum, the community is designed to be a place where residents from different backgrounds are brought together and treated equally, their differences rendered invisible and their common hopes and dreams highlighted.

And yet a closer reading of both the city's RFP and Holsten's winning proposal, as well as reports from mixed-income developments elsewhere, reveals some of the problems created by this overriding focus on integration and harmony. Although the planners of this and similar communities talk repeatedly about diversity, at every step of the way they betray a profound anxiety about it and a desire to tame and neutralize it.

First, despite all the talk here of equality, interspersal, and unity, these plans are clearly biased, I would argue, toward the interests of high-income residents: those with the money, mobility, and the agency to choose where they will live in the metropolitan area. If the innovative element here is the incorporation of low- and moderate-income housing, the overall design is clearly driven by the goal of attracting high-end buyers and renters, a goal that often conflicts with the desire for equity and justice that supposedly motivated the projects to begin with. In the end, it is the market-rate customers who are honored and empowered, while the poor—*as* poor, as racially different, as unemployed, as parents—are disregarded and made invisible. "This place will be run," Peter Holsten told me in an interview, "as a market-rate community that just happens to have public housing residents."[103] In other words, while the needs, desires, expectations, and values of the wealthy are endorsed, those of the poor are diluted or erased. And if the impetus for the building of North Town Village comes from a genuine impulse to integrate the Near North Side and treat all its residents equally, the effect of its design is to tame and silence difference and to affirm a status quo in which poor, black, inner city families are denied a place to stand *as a people* and participate in a free and open public.

For example, in the discourses surrounding the Cabrini Green redevelopment, the rich are consistently described as choice-makers, autonomous agents with the power to determine how they will inhabit the city. The poor, on the other hand, are a preexisting environmental condition, a feature of the neighborhood that comes with the territory. Why, for example, does Holsten place so much emphasis on the beauty and long-term survival of Halsted North's buildings? on constructing a community that is both attractive and well-built? on structures that will age well, endure market cycles, and continue to be desirable places to live? Because, the *Proposal* says, "market households have choices other than to live in a mixed income environment" (Proposed Use and Concept, 1). The whole design of North Town Village is based on the deliberative agency of the rich. As the *Proposal* puts it, market-rate residents are "taking a chance" on the inner city (Management Plan, 3), and they deserve a good deal, as well as amenities like extra bedrooms that can be used as home offices (Proposed Use and Concept, 2).[104] In an interview with the *Chicago Sun-Times*, Peter Holsten argued that mixed-income housing had to be carefully sited and planned: "Otherwise, you never get the people who can choose to live wherever they want."[105] (Of course, the desire to attract market-rate customers is one reason these places are so expensive to build.[106])

The poor on the other hand are without options, lucky to be in the development, winners of a metaphoric lottery that has allowed them to stay in the neighborhood despite the fact that they can't afford it any more. As one reporter described the situation, mixed-income developments are "an extraordinary opportunity for the former Cabrini families and, so far, a good deal for the homeowners, who knew they'd have poor neighbors but couldn't pass up the financial opportunity of homes made cheaper by the city assembling the land."[107] Later in the same article, one of the homebuyers says of her $500,000 home in a mixed-income development: "We thought this was a lot of house for the money."[108] The former Cabrini Green residents, meanwhile, see living in the development as a way to literally keep their children alive.

There is every indication that Holsten is genuinely committed to building and maintaining affordable housing in Chicago and is sensitive to the experiences and needs of its neighbors at Cabrini Green. But the Halsted North project as proposed does not allow those experiences and needs to coalesce in the way that they do for the rich, who are empowered as a group by the agency that their money gives them. The problem is not unique to North Town Village. In their report on the Harbor Point mixed-income redevelopment in Boston, Breitbart and Pader note how the black women who suffered the most and worked the hardest on that site were consistently erased in stories about it, in which middle-aged white developers and upper-middle class young white couples were celebrated as "conquerors" of a wild landscape, bravely investing in the inner city and transforming it through their "pioneering spirit."[109]

This bias toward the wealthy also shows up in discussions concerning resident relations at North Town Village. According to Holsten's *Proposal*, Cabrini Green families will be assured, for example, that "community standards" will not favor one group over another and that nondiscriminatory language will be sought to refer to the different income groups (Management Plan, 2–3). But there are subtle indications here that behavioral expectations at Halsted

North are class-based. For all the talk of interspersal, integration, and equality, Holsten admits that its first contact with prospective tenants will be to divide them into income groups (Management Plan, 4) and that the success of the development will depend on the lower-income groups meeting the standards of the highest (Development Team Qualification, 1).

In fact, mixed-income developments are often justified on the grounds that contact with middle- and upper-class individuals improves the character of the poor,[110] those with full-time jobs possessing standards of behavior that lower-class individuals need to emulate in order to lift themselves out of poverty.[111] The most eloquent advocate of this view, as we have seen, is William Julius Wilson, who has argued that when middle- and working-class black families fled the ghettos in the 1970s and '80s, the poor who stayed behind were left without mainstream "role models" to "keep alive the perception that education is meaningful, that steady employment is a viable alternative to welfare, and that family stability is the norm, not the exception."[112] Unfortunately, evidence from studies that have tested this theory has been mixed (see below); and, as far as I have been able to determine, no developer, politician, or government bureaucrat has yet suggested, as Wendy Sarkissian does in her history of the idea of "social mix" in town planning, that "the mixed community is an educational two-way street; it is, if anything, the middle class which is most in need of education."[113]

In other words, the poor blacks who have lived and suffered on the Near North Side for half a century consistently get the short end of the stick in its "revitalization." First, they are told that their homes are "blighted"; then, those homes are demolished, and they are relocated elsewhere: in another dilapidated unit at Cabrini Green, a flat in one of Chicago's many "horizontal ghettos," an apartment in a faraway suburb. If they are lucky, some will be allowed to stay in the neighborhood in a new mixed-income townhouse community dominated by young white childless professional couples. But in the process, they will have lost their homes, their friends, family, and old neighbors, their numerical dominance in the neighborhood, even their political representation through CHA's old Local Advisory Councils.[114] And all this will happen without any real input from them.[115] In the end, North Town Village is, like Gautreaux, about the disintegration of a community and the dispersal of its members into a hostile city.

Adding insult to injury, those who do remain and move into places like North Town Village will get a new apartment but often little else in terms of the help they need to get back on their feet. All this is taking place despite the fact that three of the key goals of HOPE VI, Salama reminds us in his study of the program, are to deconcentrate the poverty of public housing projects while avoiding massive displacement of residents, provide opportunities for social and economic redevelopment as well as physical rebuilding, and involve residents in the planning and implementation of revitalization.[116] Schubert and Thresher's study of income-mixing concluded that inner-city renewal projects needed to focus more on *neighborhood* revitalization and not simply provision of new housing.[117] And recent evaluations of the HOPE VI program have complained about the program's neglect of the low-income residents it was designed to support: funded projects, these evaluations have concluded, have involved too much displacement of current residents, have not moved quickly enough to find new housing for those residents, have been too driven by profit-seeking for developers, have not sufficiently targeted the housing needs of low-income persons, have not incorporated enough resident participation, and have in general been too costly, resulting in less money for other low income and affordable housing efforts.[118]

But what may be most troubling of all are doubts about whether socioeconomic integration, and especially the "uplifting" of the poor through interclass contact, can *ever* come about in a place like North Town Village. The evidence on the social effects of mixed-income communities is in fact mixed. Brophy and Smith report a general failure of mixed-income developments to generate interclass social interaction; Schwartz and Tajbakhsh argue that there is a lack of evidence concerning social effects in such developments; studies by Popkin and her colleagues and Von Hoffman express similar skepticism about mixed income housing; and Sandra Newman found conflicting results from income mixing in neighborhood effects studies.[119]

Take Chicago's own Lake Parc Place (50 percent very low-income, 50 percent low income). As Schill argues, the project was much safer, cleaner, and more stable than the public housing complex it replaced. But there was less success in role model socialization.[120] Status differentials and hierarchies among the income groups persisted and even worsened; residents themselves often distinguished between "working" and "non-working" tenants, and middle-income residents consistently attributed laziness and messiness to the poor. Places like Lake Parc Place, in other words, may actually *increase* group distance. Rosenbaum and his colleagues also looked at Lake Parc Place and found that interclass tension at the complex seemed to decrease only among close income and racial groups. In all, the development was a success, but there was little evidence of effects on social interaction, role modeling, and even economic development.[121]

Similarly, Mayer and Jencks, Brooks-Gunn et al., Luttmer, and Ellen and Turner all argue that the relationship between neighborhood characteristics and outcomes is highly contingent (for example, low-income blacks and whites are affected differently by the same environment).[122] Poor black teenaged boys, for example, may actually fare *worse* when surrounded by middle- or upper-income white adults than they would in an all-black, all-poor environment. One study, for example, found that the number of affluent, high-occupational-status and two-parent families in a neighborhood did positively affect youth behavior there, but the effect was greater for white, affluent teenagers than for poor black ones.[123] It is possible that Wilson's vertical integration thesis only holds true *within* racial groups and that mixed-race vertical integration could in fact be harmful, at least in a society with a long history of racial oppression. A recent study from Harvard, meanwhile, found that having neighbors with higher incomes was associated with lower levels of self-reported happiness for *all* groups; people are apparently happiest when surrounded by others like—or below—them in socioeconomic status.[124]

In other words, physically interspersing individuals from different backgrounds may not automatically produce harmonious and flourishing neighborhoods, ones where diverse individuals establish mutual trust and even learn from one another. The outside of the units at North Town Village might be the same, but the people inside are still different. And it is not just that these differences cannot be erased; they might actually become more polarizing precisely because of the interspersal. People are different in more than just their income category. The market-rate residents, for example, are not just richer: they are also whiter, younger, better educated, better employed, and have fewer children.[125] At Harbor Point in Boston, for example, problems arose because children were concentrated in the buildings where the low-income renters live. And, as mostly white, childless, professional couples in their thirties, market-rate customers are less committed to staying in the area for the long haul. Market-rate tenants at Harbor Point, for example, have shown higher turnover rates than lower-income residents.[126] Even Holsten admits, in its *Proposal*, that the real challenge at North Town Village will be to keep the market-rate couples in the development after they start having children (Proposed Use and Concept, 2). And in the *60 Minutes II* show on North Town Village, it was revealing that the market-rate residents shown were a young, white, childless, professional couple, while the public housing residents shown were all single-parent black families with multiple children.[127] North Town Village is clearly about more than income mixing, and yet there is no language for talking about difference in any way other than income and for talking about social interaction in any way other than interspersal.

As Bennett argues, the external indistinguishability criterion at places like North Town Village—the idea that social distinctions should be invisible—will probably fail.[128] Income differences are often a proxy for other differences that are very visible indeed: race, gender, familial status, even education and employment. If one's income cannot be determined by merely looking at the outside of the apartment, these other things often turn out to be discernible as soon as someone walks out the door. If those who are different in income from you are also different in skin color, age, number of children, and so on, this may create only resentment. Yet these visible differences are almost completely elided from discussions of mixed-income urban revitalization efforts. Race, for example, is never mentioned—not once—in either the city's RFP or the Holsten proposal for the Halsted North parcel.

The worst thing to do in a place like North Town Village, in other words, is pretend that diverse individuals will get along just because they are living next door to one another. As we have seen, the whole ideology of mixed-income communities is based on this goal: a reporter for the *Chicago Tribune*, writing about the new neighborhoods, talks of the challenge of different classes living "in harmony"; in the same piece, Dan McLean says the goal of Mohawk North is to show that different people can live "in harmony."[129] And in a piece in the Chicago *Sun-Times*, residents in the new communities are encouraged to think, not "there's a public housing resident" but "there goes my neighbor."[130]

And here arises another problem with the idea of mixing: even if it could work, what would be the result? a homogenization that would be a loss for all of us. In *A Pattern Language*, Christopher Alexander and his colleagues criticize the whole idea of residential interspersal, what Herbert Gans long ago referred to as a "balanced community."[131] They compare three ways in which people can be distributed throughout a city:

> 1. In the heterogeneous city, people are mixed together, irrespective of their lifestyle or culture. This seems rich. Actually it dampens all significant variety, arrests most of the possibilities for differentiation, and encourages conformity. It tends to reduce all life styles to a common denominator. What appears heterogeneous turns out to be homogeneous and dull.
>
> 2. In a city made up of ghettos, people have the support of the most basic and banal forms of differentiation—race or economic status. The ghettos are still homogeneous internally, and do not allow a significant variety of life styles to emerge. People in the ghetto are usually forced to live there, isolated from the rest of society, unable to evolve their way of life, and often intolerant of ways of life different from their own.
>
> 3. In a city made up of a large number of subcultures relatively small in size, each occupying an identifiable place and separated from other subcultures by a boundary of nonresidential land, new ways of life can develop. People can choose the kind of subculture they wish to live in, and can still experience many ways of life different from their own. Since each environment fosters mutual support and a strong sense of shared values, individuals can grow.[132]

It is this last pattern, which they call "a mosaic of subcultures," that Alexander and his colleagues advocate and which they see as preferable to either interspersal or ghettoization.

Similarly, Iris Marion Young has argued against the idea of a "transparency of subjects to one another," the dream of mutual understanding that characterizes all forms of communitarianism: "In this ideal, each understands the other and recognizes the other in the same way that they understand themselves, and all recognize that the others understand them as they understand themselves."[133] The reality is that any such attempt at "pure copresence" is, in the end, assimilation, the absorption of all into "mainstream" society, a process brought about by the dominant group's fear of conflict and its desire for nondisruption of the status quo.[134]

This impulse toward harmony at North Town Village is nowhere more apparent than in "The Storytelling Project" put forward by Holsten as a way to facilitate social interactions at the development (Management Plan, 3). According to a proposal from the group contracted to run the Project and included in Holsten's *Proposal* to the city, "storytelling" is about "providing opportunities for people to come together and . . . discover what they have in common."[135] When those commonalities are discovered, participants move toward "unity." Through storytelling, in other words, residents air their fears and dreams, build relationships, and develop the ground on which "common-unity" can grow (1).

Healthy community life, according to the proposal, needs structured social gatherings where people can learn about each other and develop mutual trust (2). The two main purposes of "ritualized storytelling" are thus, first, to "strengthen relationships and build community" and, second, to "help clarify and resolve issues that confront and divide people" (3). But why stories? Through stories, the proposal states, we pass on what is "deepest and dearest" to us. Stories shape who we are and what we will become, teach us how to behave, and provide us with heroes. The Storytelling Project is thus about community-building, not urban design. And community develops when people are provided safe spaces to give voice to their experiences: their histories, hopes, fears, and visions (3). The goal, then, is *unity*. And this is different from organized struggle; it is more permanent (4). Storytelling is thus oriented toward instilling values: "to hear, understand, and respect my story is to hear, understand, and respect me" (5).

What kind of stories would be elicited at North Town Village, according to the contractor? For Cabrini Green residents, the stories would be about their lives at the project and "their dreams of a better future for their children and grandchildren," their desire "to stay in a place called home and build a better community" (1); for the working-class families, the stories would concern their desire to live close to work and to where they used to live; for the middle- and upper-income people, the stories would be about their desire "to raise their children and live in a diverse community" (1); and, finally, for the developers, the stories would concern their dreams of making a difference in people's lives "by creating a community of diverse people living and working together in a unified and respectful environment" (1).

The Storytelling Project thus represents an alternative to the rhetoric of exclusion and separation we saw in suburbia; but the ideal of harmony appealed to here has its own problems—as do all such projects based on celebrations of "community."[136]

In sum, North Town Village is based on a thoughtful plan, is an attractive place to live, and has so far been astoundingly successful. But, the net effect of it and similar developments in the area, I believe, will be the displacement of thousands of current Cabrini Green residents,[137] continued silence about race in discussions of metropolitan design in the Chicago area, a bias toward the rich in inner-city neighborhood development projects, and the persistence of the notion that public housing residents cannot make it without higher-income people living around them. In the new Lower North, the rich will have the numbers; their standards will be endorsed; their agency affirmed; and, given their mobility and resources, their risk in all this will be low.

But perhaps worst of all, North Town Village is based on a an unrealistic dream of social harmony. In the end, it seems as afraid of conflict as the communities we saw in chapter 5. If the suburbs have avoided conflict through zoning and other strategies that wall out difference, North Town Village cannot do that. So it deals with conflict by degrouping, interspersing, and individualizing urban residents, thus not so much building community among diverse peoples as simply trying to absorb all of them into the private economy.

SEVEN

Home

1230 North Burling Street

Freedom, wherever it existed as a tangible reality, has always been spatially limited.

—Hannah Arendt, *On Revolution*

The proposals we have looked at so far—suburban relocation and mixed-income redevelopment—treat the residents of Chicago's public housing projects as *problems* to be solved by others, wards of society incapable of building and sustaining their own communities and needing the material and moral resources of middle- and upper-class (white) neighbors. They imply that poor blacks can only participate in viable publics from positions of subordination and in proportions and configurations that prevent their exerting power as a group: in the suburbs, they should be invisible or nearly so; in the central city, not more than 30 percent of the population and interspersed with others. The projects examined in chapters 5 and 6, in other words, are about scattering black residents so thinly across the metropolitan region that they are never in a position to politically coalesce.[1]

But what would happen if the low-income African-American families of Cabrini Green were allowed to create and pursue their *own* designs for the neighborhood? What future would *they* imagine for the Near North Side? What kind of community would *they* build there? Characterized by others as abnormal, their homes as disorganized, their communities as hellish, how would Chicago's public housing residents represent themselves and their world? How would they become subjects of their own destiny, architects of their own future?

Portions of this chapter were originally published in "Subjects of the Inner City: Writing the People of Cabrini-Green" in *Towards a Rhetoric of Everyday Life: New Directions in Research on Writing, Text, and Discourse*, edited by Martin Nystrand and John Duffy (Madison, WI: University of Wisconsin Press, 2003): 207–244; reprinted by permission.

In the pages that follow, I try to give voice to the residents' own plans for the revitalization of Cabrini Green. Unfortunately, the discourses surrounding and constituting these plans have had to compete against the vastly more powerful discourses of government bureaucrats, local and national politicians, real estate developers, academic researchers, and editorial writers, discourses which have consistently denied the residents of Chicago's public housing projects basic rights of self-determination in communities they have lived and struggled in for decades. So, before considering our third option for urban revitalization in Chicago, I look at the ways in which discourses about public housing in this country bar its residents from even thinking about, let alone developing, their own plans for redevelopment.

Cabrini Green and Its People as Seen by Others

The language used to describe the residents of inner-city public housing in the United States has historically served to deny them status as full-fledged citizens of their own communities.[2] It has done this by representing them, first, as people who are different from (and less than) the rest of us—as poor, dependent, and troubled. Second, it has depicted their neighborhoods as chaotic and disordered. And, third, it has denied residents any long-term claim to those very neighborhoods. What has taken place, in other words, is a pathologizing of public housing residents and their world and a denial of their rights to territorial control and communal self-determination. The effect of such representations has been to strengthen and propagate the belief that the families of Cabrini Green can legitimately be displaced from their own neighborhoods, their homes demolished, and their communities made over as gentrified "urban villages," in which, if they have a presence at all, it is a minority one.

Let us begin with the first of these representations, that of the people themselves. In most discourses about them, the residents of Chicago's public housing projects are known first and foremost as *poor*, that is, as having less money than others. In fact, as we have seen, in order even to be eligible for federally funded public housing in this country, a person must have an income below 80 percent of area median income.[3] This restriction of public housing in the United States to the poor came about largely because, in the debates leading up to the passage of the U.S. Housing Act of 1937, the National Association of Home Builders, the U.S. Savings and Loan League, and the National Association of Real Estate Boards waged a relentless and ultimately successful campaign to ensure that government-owned housing in this country would be unavailable to the middle class and therefore compete as little as possible with the private real estate market.[4] From the beginning, in other words, the federal government supported, rather than checked, the economic segregation of the U.S. population. And it did so through language that, even today, equates "public" housing with poverty: according to the U.S. Housing Act of 1937, "[t]he term 'public housing' means low-income housing."[5]

What are the effects of this discursive pauperization? Most obviously, it reduces the people who are victims of it, portraying them through a single feature and impeding other and fuller descriptions of them. In a study of representations of public housing in the late 1990s, for example, I found that race was almost never used in public discussions about Chicago public housing, although project residents were overwhelmingly African-American.[6] Their membership in a historically subjugated racial minority was mentioned with regularity only in the federal courts, since one of the few recourses public housing tenants have had at their disposal has been the ability to sue government officials on the basis of constitutionally prohibited racial discrimination.[7] Of course, *any* linguistic reduction of a human being—any taking of a full and complex individual and turning him or her into a type—is dangerous. As we will see below, in representing themselves, public housing residents consistently ask to be seen and treated not as poor, black, or anything else, but as full and normal human beings.

Another effect of defining individuals exclusively by their economic class is to stigmatize those who end up in the bottom group. To be "poor," in other words, is not just to be a member of one or another economically defined group; it is to be a member of a specifically disparaged one. Alvin Schorr has called policies that provide benefits and services only to the poor "exceptionalist" because they deal with individuals defined as exceptions, those who earn *below* others, who have *failed* a means test, who have *less* than the norm.[8] Such policies construct aid recipients as "shamefully different and needy"; and, unfortunately, he writes, it is an easy step to go from disparaging a class of individuals to isolating them in one part of a city, consigning them to live "in a mean and . . . angry world, closed off from the rest of the citizenry."[9]

Distinguishing one another by class also contributes to social fragmentation. "Public" housing in this country, after all, was never about building a genuinely public sphere, one open and accessible to all; it was about protecting the private interests of a few and consigning the most desperate to a ghetto. Writing of the post-1949 housing debate and its obsession with class and race, Meyerson and Banfield claimed that "[i]n almost no city was a public housing program developed as part of a long-range plan for all types of housing or as part of a . . . comprehensive plan for the growth and development of the community."[10] To enact such a plan, we would have to "mainstream" our social programs better than we currently do, meeting the needs of "those who may be poor without asking them to perceive themselves as poor."[11]

The use of relative income as a way to identify people also deflects attention away from the material reality of poverty. The indexing of a person's income to the area median may tell us how that person stands economically in relation to others in his or her community; but it obscures what it is like to have insufficient money in our society, to be unable to afford adequate nutritious food, for example.[12] It also deflects attention away from the cost of housing, since most families with below average income cannot afford safe, decent housing in this country without incurring a prohibitive burden on their budget.[13] Median income figures also say nothing about work since it is possible to work full time in this country and still be "poor."[14]

We also saw in chapter 6 how the discourses of public housing consistently disempower the poor—characterizing them as lacking options and therefore lucky to be able to stay in a revitalized central city—and represent the wealthy as people with choices and agency, people "who can choose to live wherever they want."[15] In the dominant discourses surrounding the revitalization of the Near North Side, in other words, the people of Cabrini Green are repeatedly diminished, dehumanized, and disempowered.

But what about the places where they live? The language here is also reductive, stigmatizing, and unrelentingly hyperbolic. "Hellish high-rises" is how both the *Chicago Tribune*, in a 1998 editorial against the Cabrini Green consent degree, and *Tribune* architecture critic Blair Kamin, in a 1997 piece on Cabrini Green in *Architectural Record*, describe the projects.[16] (Unsurprisingly, the people who live there are equally infernal. As one South Shore resident said about the relocation of public housing residents, "It is as if the gates of Hell . . . opened and these people were let out. I had to ask again, where did these people come from? And, lo, I was told they came from the projects, the CHA. And as they tear down more projects, we can expect more of these people to be relocated in our neighborhoods."[17])

But other ways to describe the places are just as pejorative. Probably the single most frequently used word to describe Cabrini Green is "notorious,"[18] but other descriptors are equally negative: one observer called the project "a Corbusian nightmare . . . where gunslingers and crack ghouls overrun anonymous corridors, stalking enemies and innocents alike."[19] After the 1992 killing of Dantrell Davis, some began to call the open area where he was murdered a "killing field,"[20] and Rybczynski compared the project to Sarajevo in the mid-1990s.[21] This kind of language has a long history: a 1968 presidential commission wrote of Chicago's public housing that the "child caught in such a social environment is living almost in a concentration camp from which he has little chance of escape."[22]

The projects have been described as "warehouses for the poor," brick towers built on treeless stretches of land, "isolated fortresses in a neighborhood mired in crime, joblessness, and dependence."[23] Another frequently used epithet is *-ridden*, as in crime- or drug-ridden, apparently meaning "overwhelmed by" or "burdened with." Marciniak says Cabrini Green is "*riddled* with drugs, gangs, crime, and poverty" (emphasis added).[24]

Kotlowitz paints an especially dramatic picture of the projects, a place where young children live amid unceasing violence and chaos. The language here is memorably concrete:

> Sometimes at Henry Horner you can almost smell the arrival of death. It is the odor of foot-deep pools of water that, formed from draining fire hydrants, become fetid in the summer sun. It is the stink of urine puddles in the stairwell corners and of soiled diapers dumped in the grass. It is the stench of a maggot-infested cat carcass lying in a vacant apartment and the rotting food in the overturned trash bins.[25]

Lemann's picture of the Robert Taylor Homes is no prettier:

> The entrance to 5135 [South Federal St.] is bleak and forbidding. Most of the time it is littered with empty bottles and piles of uncollected garbage. Gang symbols are spray-painted all over the lobby. The open plaza on the State Street side is barren of greenery. The elevators, stripped of their emergency-stop buttons, are jerky and unreliable. . . . All the access points to the building—the elevator cabs, the stairwells, and the hallways—reek of urine and cheap wine. Gang members regularly shoot out the lights in the breezeways and stairwells, so coming home to 5135 after dark is a terrifying experience.[26]

As we have seen, HUD's word for all this is "distressed," a project that

> requires major redesign or demolition; is occupied predominantly by families with children who are in a severe state of distress, characterized by such factors as high rates of unemployment, teenage pregnancy, single-parent households, long-term dependency on public assistance and minimal educational achievement; is in a location for recurrent vandalism and criminal activity; and cannot remedy these elements through assistance under other programs.[27]

The ghetto is thus described by outsiders in predominantly *privative* terms, as a place of lack and disorder: "a repository of concentrated unruliness, deviance, anomie and atomization, replete with behaviors said to offend common precepts of morality and propriety."[28] This kind of unrelentingly negative language, of course, gives permission for dramatic solutions, for "sweeping" by police[29] and "bulldozing" by developers.

To add insult to injury, the residents of public housing projects are denied any long-term rights to these places, no matter how long they live there, how much they suffer, or how hard they work to establish viable communities in the projects. For many conservatives, public housing is by definition temporary, a steppingstone, not a destination.[30] Here, for example, is Ed Marciniak, writing in *Commonweal* in 1996:

> Not long ago, I attended a national housing conference where a featured panelist was a woman introduced as a longtime resident of public housing. She herself noted, matter-of-factly, that she had lived in public housing for forty-five years. For me, that admission was mind-blowing. Even more startling, however, was the realization that her remark had not caused even a ripple of surprise among the subsidized-housing professionals in the audience. Nonchalantly, they had come to accept public housing's way of life as a given, for which they felt no personal responsibility.[31]

The CHA itself is heavily invested in this particular narrative:

> The Chicago Housing Authority (CHA) was organized in 1937 to provide temporary housing for those people whose incomes were insufficient to obtain "decent, safe and sanitary dwellings" in the private market. Over time, the notion of "temporary" housing became lost, and generations of low-income families came to depend upon this government safety net as a permanent way of life. From there, life in public housing degenerated into warehouses for the poor, plagued by crime and welfare dependency.[32]

But why then did the CHA name its Near North Side complexes the Frances Cabrini *Homes*, the William Green *Homes*? And why are officials surprised, then, when residents themselves look at their projects as *home*? As Carol Steele, former president of the Cabrini Green Row House Tenant Management Council and cofounder of the Coalition to Protect Public Housing, has said, "Public housing is just like any other apartment or housing. Home is where your heart is."[33]

The debate in Chicago about whether a unit in the projects should be seen as a "home" or a "way station" emerged most explicitly in the aftermath of two events that seemed to give inordinate control over public housing complexes to residents, one in 1995, when the Henry Horner consent decree allowed Annex residents to vote on whether their building would be demolished or rehabilitated; the other in 1998, when a Cabrini Green consent decree gave residents there a historic 51 percent interest in the redevelopment of their project. As for the first, the *Chicago Sun-Times* stated in an editorial on Christmas day, 1995, that the vote by Annex residents to stay put had "belie[d] the original purpose of public housing: a way station for poor people." For too many families for too long, the paper continued, "public housing is claimed as a place to stay forever." These are, after all, buildings "built with taxpayer dollars and owned by the government."[34] As for the second, the *Chicago Tribune* editorialized on August 3, 1998: "Never before has anyone taken it into his head to cede the prerogatives of ownership to renters, as the CHA would do under this stupendously ill-advised deal. . . . The very valuable land on which Cabrini-Green sits belongs to the people of the United States of America. They are the owners; the CHA is their agent, charged with managing the project in their best interests."[35] The two most important newspapers in Chicago were thus arguing *against* the development of long-term communal ties by low-income central city African-Americans in their own neighborhoods.

Given these depictions, and the extraordinary power they have exerted on North American public opinion regarding low-income urban blacks, there would appear to be only one real option for housing projects like Cabrini Green: to demolish them, wipe the slate clean, raze the neighborhoods to the ground and start all over, preferably with a whole new population. There is, as we will soon see, a disturbing and deeply ironic thread of violence in these discourses, a pervasive appeal to dynamiting, bulldozing, toppling, and so on. This can be seen as early as the 1949–1950 fight over CHA sites; according to Meyerson and Banfield, "[T]here were many prominent people, including aldermen and commissioners of the Authority itself, who took pride in wiping out slum neighborhoods and replacing them with clean and spacious projects. 'It had always been an aspiration of the Board to clear slums,' one of the commissioners later explained."[36] But in the late 1990s, this celebration of clearance and demolition seemed to have reached a fever pitch. Here are just a few examples of articles about public housing projects appearing between 1995 and 1998 that open with images of demolition:

> From the living-room couch of his small, spotless apartment, Foster Harris looks forward to the day a wrecking ball will demolish the dilapidated Chicago tenement where he and his wife reared a dozen children over 30 years. The demolition, expected to begin soon at the Henry Horner Housing Project, represents the first step in a major new federal strategy to replace America's vertical tenements with low-rise, mixed-income communities. Mr. Harris has few regrets about the obliteration of his home.[37]

> Imagine leveling whole blocks of decaying, crime-ridden slums in one great sweep, and building in their stead modern apartments with plenty of light and fresh air and high-rise views. Think about replacing crowded streets and decrepit playgrounds with paths for

pedestrians and bicycles, winding between wide lawns. Picture that, and in 30 years or so you'll have re-created . . . Cabrini-Green, the notorious Chicago housing project, eight of whose 23 buildings are to be demolished in what the city administration hails as a great step forward in public housing. . . . It's always exciting when high-rise housing projects are demolished, because the very factor that made them fail in their purpose—their isolation amid desolate patches of lawn—means they can be safely imploded with explosives.[38]

Twenty-five years after explosives brought down three of the high-rises at the Pruitt-Igoe housing project in St. Louis and shattered the Modernist credo that good design could effect the good society, the curtain is about to rise on a new social housing drama in Chicago, and it will be watched anxiously nationwide. . . . Redevelopment could transform the notorious Cabrini-Green public housing complex—a three-quarter mile-long stretch of high-rises populated almost exclusively by the poorest of the poor—into a neighborhood with a mix of uses and income groups, seamlessly rejoined to the rest of the city.[39]

The wrecking ball slammed into the 16-story high rise in the bright morning sun in Chicago. A building in Robert Taylor Homes, part of the four-mile stretch of the most densely concentrated public housing in the nation was coming down. All around the country, the massive, often roach-infested, graffiti-covered buildings are being knocked down, or in some cases blown up, a testament to what many are calling a public housing policy that has failed.[40]

The wrecking-ball is swinging in Chicago. The city's housing authority has demolished ten high-rise public-housing buildings, including one in the notorious Robert Taylor Homes, and has plans to demolish nearly 20 more. It is not merely toppling buildings; it is striking at half a century of flawed housing policy.[41]

Little more than a year ago, wrecker balls and dynamite began razing Cabrini Green, the infamous crime-ridden public housing facility in South Chicago [*sic*]. Today, many of the hideous high-rises are gone; nearly all have been cleared of their residents. And just down the street, in an area where drug dealers and gangs recently ruled, buyers are snapping up new homes at the rate of nearly seven a month for as much as $600,000 a pop.[42]

> In the space of 24 seconds on Saturday, decades of misbegotten public policy are supposed to be obliterated when dynamite levels four yellow-brick high-rises along the South Side lakefront. The image of the Chicago Housing Authority buildings tumbling to the ground—one of the most dramatic implosions of public housing in American history—is meant to symbolize a dramatic departure from the days when the city's poorest black residents were concentrated in a few blighted areas.[43]

> Verdell Wade will let out a sigh of relief Saturday morning when the four Chicago Housing Authority high-rises that for 35 years have towered over her home, blotting out the sun, are reduced to rubble in the city's first public housing implosion. "I will be very happy to see them down—I didn't know if I would live to see it happen," Wade said.[44]

Perhaps no one has been a stauncher advocate of demolition than Alexander Polikoff, the ACLU lawyer who pled the Gautreaux case thirty years ago and is still the lead counsel for its plaintiffs. In a 1993 paper, he patiently considered alternatives to demolition—empowering the residents to manage their own buildings, rehabilitating the high-rises and bringing in higher-income working families to "deconcentrate" the poor, and so on—but found them all inadequate to the problems of the ghetto, particularly the problems caused by high-rise, inner-city, public housing complexes like Robert Taylor, Henry Horner, and Cabrini Green. The only viable (in fact, according to Polikoff, the only *legal*) solution to such problems, he has said again and again, is to tear the buildings down and scatter their residents throughout the metropolitan area. "In the appropriate circumstances, where rebuilding high-rises is costly and conditions are 'inhumane,' demolition should be encouraged as an opportunity to rid ourselves of past mistakes and do better by residents."[45] Later, Polikoff talks of "eliminating" the long shadow of dysfunctional inner-city high-rises.[46]

In a 1996 HUD report, meanwhile, Secretary Henry Cisneros reported almost gleefully on the progress of demolition in the mid-1990s: "Prior to this Administration, legislative impediments and preservation of the status quo led to approximately 1,600 units of public housing torn down per year. The Clinton administration will tear down an unprecedented 24,000 units of bad public housing. That 4-year pace betters the 20,000 units demolished in all of the last ten years combined."[47]

Blair Kamin, architecture critic of the *Chicago Tribune*, is one of the few who has been publicly concerned about these demolition stories, which he sees as part of "the American fantasy of wiping the slate clean and starting anew."[48] Sudhir Venkatesh as well writes of the way in which the media seem to endorse the view that the projects are breeding grounds for social pathologies that require aggressive forms of eradication: "Armed with the popular appeal of 'urban renewal,' the remedy becomes obvious: destroy the high-rise structures and you destroy the cause of the pathology. What could be simpler?"[49] But no one has argued more eloquently against demolition than the residents themselves, who consistently vote to rehabilitate their buildings rather than tear them down, even when the government promises scattered-site housing or vouchers for living anywhere in the city.[50]

Cabrini Green and Its People as Seen by Its Residents

Let us turn, then, to how Chicago's public housing residents represent *themselves* and their neighborhoods when they speak and write about such topics. Not surprisingly, what they say turns out to be very different from what outsiders say: rather than troubled, abnormal individuals living at others' mercy in disorganized environments, they are full human beings with the desire and competence to establish deep and permanent ties with others and build safe and vital communities, who have in fact already done so against enormous odds, who live in neighborhoods that exhibit the same impulse to order that all neighborhoods exhibit, neighborhoods to which they have, therefore, a legitimate, long-term claim.

First and foremost, when they speak and write about their lives and neighborhood, the residents of Chicago's public housing projects remind us that they are, after all, human beings. Barbara Moore, president of a tenant board at Robert Taylor, once said, in a 1999 interview:

> Public housing residents are considered the lowest scum on earth. At the mere mention of Robert Taylor people get scared and hold their purses. It is wrong to stereotype, not everyone is on drugs, not every girl is pregnant or prostituting. Not all guys are carrying guns or stealing. We have college graduates come from this area also. People should not prejudge us, there is good and bad everywhere. . . . We want to be thought of as human beings. We are not the worst of people. We are people.[51]

Similarly, Cabrini Green residents refuse outsiders' characterizations of them "as gang-bangers, welfare-dependent, . . . drug abusers, hopeless people, uneducated, and not caring about their homes" and assert that their neighborhood "is a lot more like the average Chicago neighborhood than you might think."[52] Charles Coats, former resident of Robert Taylor, for example, resents the suggestion that public housing families need training in order to live in middle-class neighborhoods: we do not "need help being people."[53]

Residents should have a voice, then, in policies and programs that affect them, especially since they are also fully competent *rhetorical* agents, that is, speakers and writers of substance and power. In a newsletter for a local civic organization, for example, they write of the need "to speak for ourselves" about issues affecting them: "These voices are often not heard in community planning and decision making."[54] And in a letter inviting community leaders to a public meeting, Cabrini Green residents write that the redevelopment of the project is "our" endeavor, based on *our* vision, *our* history, *our* plans, *our* achievements, and *our* struggles: "Only the residents," they claim, "can fully inform developers and planners about the achievements and struggles experienced in creating community at Cabrini and convey how they intend to continue strengthening the neighborhood. . . . [W]e are capable of speaking on our own behalf."[55]

But a resident-centered view of Cabrini Green must involve more than just a different picture of its inhabitants. It needs as well a redescription of their neighborhood, one that, unlike the accounts sampled above, depicts this corner of the Near North Side as a bona fide *home* to thousands of families, a place where generations of mothers, fathers, sisters, and brothers have lived, loved, worked, studied, suffered, celebrated, and died,[56] and where, against enormous odds, they have built full and meaningful human lives, complete with family, friends, churches, businesses, schools, clubs, and so forth. From this point of view, the ghetto is not chaotic or unorganized; its residents simply lack opportunities for power. Given such opportunities, they would construct there a world as healthy and productive as any other.[57]

In his study of representations of the ghetto in academic research and government policy, the French sociologist Loïc J. D. Wacquant, who lived on Chicago's South Side, makes this point forcefully. Quoting William Foote Whyte, Wacquant claims that, what appears to outsiders as social disorganization "often turns out to be simply a different form of social organization *if one takes the trouble to look closely*."[58]

> [F]ar from being disorganized, the ghetto is *organized according to different principles*, in response to a *unique set of structural and strategic constraints* that bear on the racialized enclaves of the city as on no other segment of American territory.[59]

These constraints include (1) "the unrelenting press of economic necessity and widespread material deprivation caused by the withering away of the wage-labor economy"; (2) "pervasive social and physical insecurity, fueled by the glaring failings of public sector institutions and the . . . debilitation of local organizations";

(3) "virulent racial antipathy conjoined with acute class prejudice resulting in a severe and systematic truncation of life chances"; (4) "symbolic taint and territorial stigmatization, contaminating every area of social endeavor"; which is reinforced by (5) "bureaucratic apathy and administrative ineptness made possible by the electoral expendability of the black poor."[60]

Eric Klinenberg has demonstrated how these normal human impulses toward social organization get repeatedly thwarted in the predominantly low-income African-American neighborhood of North Lawndale on Chicago's West Side. Despite poverty, unemployment, and discrimination, local residents there work hard to build community, improve security, and sponsor prosperity in their neighborhoods; and many become deeply engaged with public life. Klinenberg looks specifically at two of the most important sources of formal community participation in North Lawndale: the church and the block club.[61] In 1998, he reports, there were 120 of the former and 73 of the latter just in this one district. Unfortunately, these groups consistently lacked the financial and material resources needed to function adequately. Take, for example, the staffing of storefront churches in North Lawndale: unlike the Roman Catholic priests in mostly Latino South Lawndale, the preachers of these churches are typically not paid to be full-time religious leaders. Many take on "the Lord's work" in their spare time and find in the end that they simply do not have the resources to do what needs to be done in their communities, such as care for the elderly and poor. "North Lawndale residents," Klinenberg concluded, suffer "not from lack of knowledge about their neighbors or from disorganization, in the lay sense of the term, but from local pressures and challenges that [have] overwhelmed their capacity to respond."[62]

But probably the fullest study of the stressed social organization underlying a poor African-American neighborhood in Chicago is Sudhir Alladi Venkatesh's study of life in the Robert Taylor Homes, in which he shows how hard residents worked there, across multiple generations and against staggering odds, to try to create a safe, viable community on the South Side: "[c]oping with crime and socioeconomic hardship, battling local government agencies over inadequate service provision, and searching for external resources to meet local needs."[63] Certainly, admits Venkatesh, Taylor residents are in some respects at odds with the institutions of the "outside" world; living there, after all, is a singular experience, and hardships have unsurprisingly garnered most of the public's attention. But there are commonalities with the rest of the world as well: for example, "the ongoing challenge of . . . controlling the behavior of local youth" (9), which is, after all, a universal function of communities. As such, the project is not fundamentally different from the rest of society—if anything, its people have suffered from trying *too* hard to live up to social ideals without the resources to do so.

Venkatesh writes, for example, about how, immediately after the project opened in 1962, residents began to mobilize informally to monitor the neighborhood's many children and look out for the project's vulnerable common spaces (29–30). The most prevalent form that this early organizing took was "Mama's Mafias"—support networks of adult women based on simple propinquity. For a time, these groups helped deter gang recruitment efforts, provided babysitting and informal neighborhood watches, and took care of members during episodes of domestic violence (32). Next to develop at the project were more formal organizations, the most prominent of which were the building councils that the CHA itself put into place to help it manage the projects: bodies of elected and appointed tenants, mostly middle-aged and elderly females. Each floor of each Taylor high-rise elected a representative (or floor captain) who scheduled laundry use, assigned cleaning tasks, and sat on the building council, which was responsible for monitoring the elevators and supervising play around the building. Tenants also elected a building president who sat on a resident council for the whole project (34–35) and served in an advisory capacity for the CHA.

By the late 1960s, however, the more politicized residents at Robert Taylor were calling for greater tenant control of the project (43). This was also the time, as we saw in chapter 4, when the neighborhood was experiencing dramatic physical and social decline, with increasingly younger heads-of-household, fewer two-parent families, more apartments housing multiple families spanning two or more generations, and more and more joblessness (46ff). Tenants at Robert Taylor were trying to deal with this situation by demanding changes in housing policies and programs; and in 1969, the Chicago Housing Tenants Organization (CHTO) was formed, subsequently sponsoring marches and demonstrations and pressuring the CHA for greater resident control over the community (57). After nearly two years of protests, on April 8, 1971, CHA chairman Charles Swibel signed a landmark "Memorandum of Accord" giving Chicago's public housing tenants considerable powers to determine day-to-day operations and participate in policy decisions regarding their neighborhoods.[64] Out of this accord grew the LAC-CAC tenant management structure: in each building, tenants elected a building president who would represent them on the Local Advisory Council; each LAC president then sat on Chicago's Central Advisory Council, which had considerable power in public housing policies and programs in the city. The system was entirely funded by the CHA itself (60).

Unfortunately, in the 1970s, the problems faced by Chicago's public housing residents only increased: and the viability of life in Taylor came more and more to depend on two basic human activities: "locating material resources so that households could make ends meet and working with others to fulfill collective functions such as social control, policing, and law enforcement provision" (68).

Residents were increasingly involved in entrepreneurial activities (gambling, prostitution, drug trafficking, auto repair, jitney services, food provision, etc.) that mimicked business life outside the project but also put them in complex relations with authorities (70ff). Local resident leaders and Chicago police officers, for example, often helped one another: the police would ignore some activities if they received cooperation in controlling others. Gradually, writes Venkatesh, the LAC transformed itself from a democratic representative body to a powerful broker "for residents seeking access to resources in the outside world" (99–100).

In other words, project residents were not simply withdrawing from "official" society (though clearly they were increasingly excluded from its benefits). They were instead forging a new place *within* society: providing their own security when the police were absent (which was often) and becoming laborers in the new service economy by working "off the books" in a growing underground system (that is, "hustling") (106–8). Observers saw the ghetto moving away from the mainstream during this period and have focused therefore on the prevalence of such activities as "hanging out," public drinking, sexual promiscuity, and the formation of nonnuclear families. But, according to Venkatesh, they have ignored daily life there, which was all about securing resources and trying to build a habitable community—exactly what people *outside* the ghetto were doing. Life at Robert Taylor was not, in this sense, chaotic, pathological, or un-American: in fact, the problems of the project were arguably the result of its residents trying to be like everyone else, trying to secure for themselves American freedom and prosperity.

The early and mid-1980s saw only continued decline in the inner city, now accelerated by middle-class black flight, budget cuts in federal social programs, and a fatal mix of events that included the emergence of crack cocaine, the growth of a black male "incarceration culture," and, the rise of "corporate gangs" which produced high levels of black-on-black violence (133). The "hustling" of the 1970s was no longer capable of staving off complete disorder at Robert Taylor. To increase security, the CHA began organizing tenant patrols and tried to improve surveillance of the projects (124). But it failed to pursue less direct but ultimately more promising solutions: providing for adequate outdoor seating, supporting a vibrant local commercial sector, and forging stronger connections with the surrounding community.

In the early 1990s, gangs and the LACs were in open collaboration, largely to the former's benefit (186). The arrangement allowed a small measure of security to some residents but also eroded what trust there was between tenants and their leaders. Still, even in this context, many tenants fought on, attending meetings, organizing marches, signing petitions, starting community organizations, negotiating with gang leaders, forging connections within and outside the ghetto (234ff). The problems were too severe, however, and the resources, too few. By the mid-1990s, the project was essentially being emptied out, with dispersal and demolition the only foreseeable future. As confusion and uncertainty set in, social networks dissolved rapidly, and what civic organizations there were lost members (266).[65]

All human communities today require both internal organization and outside support to be viable; Venkatesh argues that public housing residents have probably been asked to provide too much of the former with too little of the latter (273). "Would residents of a suburb," he asks, "be expected to work largely on their own to curb gang activity, and, if they failed to do so, would most Americans then ask whether suburbs were no longer viable planned spaces of residence?" (274). From this point of view, the efforts of Robert Taylor families to cope with the obstacles thrown in their way have been nothing short of heroic. They devised there innovative techniques for surviving in a ghetto and fought to ensure their own welfare. "The result was the creation of fairly strong, cohesive networks, wherein individuals worked with one another to respond as best they could to their ever-present challenges" (275).

The experience of organizing a community against so many obstacles and with so little support has only made Chicago's public housing residents that much more insistent about their right to stay in these neighborhoods. Against the discourses we saw above, they have refused to see their tenancy in the projects as temporary and superficial, and they have constantly reminded others of their roots in these communities. As resident Barbara Moore says, "We poor people get uprooted a lot, but we are people with roots too. We want our grandchildren to grow up in our neighborhood. We don't want to be moved to a new place every year."[66] Similarly, resident leader Ferrell Freeman criticizes the ABLA redevelopment plan because "People with roots in the community will be moved to racially segregated and economically depressed areas of the city."[67] And in a 1997 interview with the *NewsHour with Jim Lehrer*, Cabrini Green LAC president Cora Moore defended her wish to stay put in the place she has called home for thirty years: "We still want to live here because our kids [have] grown up [here], three sets of families, you know, and you feel more comfortable."[68] Likewise, Cheryl Russon, another Cabrini Green resident, asked of the city's plans to demolish the project, "How can they take our roots from us without our input? They're planning to move the poor and destitute and build for rich folks."[69]

Attached to places that outsiders see as uninhabitable, residents claim a history in the projects: "We're proud of where we are from," says Verlee Gant, who has lived at Robert Taylor since 1970; and former resident Patricia Cathery refers to Taylor as "my roots."[70]

A People Empowered

Clearly, many current residents of Cabrini Green want to leave the project: some dream of moving to the suburbs; others, of living in a place like North Town Village. But, hard as it is for outsiders to believe, many of these families want to stay at Cabrini Green. They want the place to be improved, to be safer and cleaner, the local schools better, the crime rate lower, the commercial environment more vibrant, the job picture more promising—they want investment and renewal. But more than anything, they want to stay with their families and friends and have a voice in the governance of their community. Above all, they want to be treated with dignity and respect, as *subjects* of their own lives, rightful *citizens* of their city and neighborhood.

They want, that is, to revitalize the existing community of the neighborhood rather than sponsor its further break-up by either suburban relocation or mixed-income redevelopment, to work toward what John Calmore calls "spatial equality," which he defines as "a group-based remedy that focuses on opportunity and circumstances within black communities and demands that both be improved, enriched, and equalized."[71] For Calmore, such remedies are a viable alternative to "the tokenistic, gradualistic, and subordinating" impulse of "integration" projects.[72] The central idea behind them is *nonsegregation*: "both the right of people to remain where they are (even if in a ghetto) *and* the elimination of restrictions on moving into other areas."[73]

Calmore's skepticism about black integration into the American mainstream, and his advocacy of a kind of "separate but equal" policy on behalf of black communities, is part of an old debate among African Americans that goes back to at least the mid-nineteenth century,[74] when the nascent black bourgeoisie and laboring poor blacks in the North had similar aspirations for equality and full participation in American society but sometimes disagreed about whether this was best achieved by turning inward toward a self-sufficient community, based on a celebration of blackness and common African origins, or by integrating into the larger white society. The debate is evident in the late nineteenth century desire of Booker T. Washington and others to build a black society within America.[75] But it retains its hold even today: bell hooks has told the story, for example, of her childhood move "from beloved, all-black schools to white schools where black children were always seen as interlopers, as not really belonging."[76]

Keating associates this "separatist" position with the long-standing dream among some black Americans for a "gilded ghetto" in the central city, a healthy and prosperous urban community in which the minority are the majority but which isn't built on involuntary concentration or racial discrimination.[77] For nearly half a century now, a buzz word for this approach to urban revitalization has been "empowerment," defined as the acquisition of rights and resources of self-determination by a people or group previously denied such rights and resources.[78] The word first caught on in liberal and academic circles in Washington, DC, in the late 1950s and early 1960s, when the seeds were planted for the federal government's "community action" program. As Lemann tells the story, scholars and activists at the time began to think of poverty more as a political than an economic condition: if the poor could become politically self-governing, this theory ran, they would soon cease to be poor: "Empowerment would give [them] a new spirit of community; they would run their own lives, and their neighborhoods, with renewed purposiveness and vigor."[79] As it developed in the 1960s, empowerment rested on the belief that antipoverty programs should be located in poor neighborhoods, coordinate a wide variety of services in a single location, and be planned with the "maximum feasible participation" of the residents themselves.[80] Unfortunately, empowerment-type projects often faced steep obstacles; Matusow, for example, shows how big city mayors like Richard J. Daley resented the way federal funding for community action programs bypassed City Hall and went straight to neighborhood agencies and projects; by the end of the 1960s, the momentum for empowerment seemed to have died down.

But surprisingly, in the 1980s, the idea was revived on the right, most notably during the two Reagan administrations. And the notion that poor neighborhoods could be improved from the bottom up has persisted in the federal government into the present, though with much lower levels of material and ideological support than that provided demolition and mixed-income revitalization efforts, on the one hand, and voucherization and mobility programs, on the other. The U.S. Department of Housing and Urban Development, for example, has invested modestly in what it calls a "Community Building Project," which supports revitalization of public housing communities through programs based on (1) involving residents in planning, (2) building on their assets, (3) targeting manageable-size areas, (4) tailoring strategies for each neighborhood, (5) maintaining a holistic and integrative perspective, (6) building social and human capital, and (7) developing partnerships outside the relevant communities.[81]

Empowerment can also, of course, take on a more radical cast. In their book *Inside City Schools*, Sarah Warshauer Freedman and her colleagues tell the story of an African-American history class at a high school in Chicago that included students from the Cabrini Green project. Prompted by the Dantrell Davis killing, students in the class began reading and talking about the condition of public housing in their city. Many turned to black separatism as a solution to the problem of inner city poverty, arguing "that Blacks must band together to fight White plots to destroy the Black race, as evidenced in the creation of [the] projects." According to the authors, the students felt that blacks needed "to create their own all-Black society."[82]

But what would "empowerment" mean in terms of the Near North Redevelopment Initiative? Well, two things: first, as Calmore reminds us, any form of legal segregation or discrimination must be absolutely eliminated; that is, those black residents of Cabrini Green who want to resettle in white parts of the metropolis should be able to do so without undue difficulty. But second, there must also be a parallel project of self-enrichment that would allow residents to *stay* on the Near North Side if they wished and help transform it into a healthy community that they would run themselves.[83]

This strategy for revitalizing public housing in America has found its most visible expression in the idea of the "resident management corporation" (or RMC). In an RMC, control of a public housing building or project is turned over to the residents of that building or project themselves. As defined by Caprara and Alexander, "resident management is an empowerment process that places the responsibility for improving the quality of life in public housing properties into the hands of those who live there."[84] Structurally, an RMC is "a nonprofit corporation that contracts with a housing authority to manage a development. All tenants are members, with the right to participate, but the core of an RMC is its officers and board of directors. The board hires a director of the corporation, and many boards also take part in hiring and monitoring staff. Staff are usually hired from the tenant population."[85] Responsibilities that an RMC might take on include "resident screening, rent collection, budgetary authority, subsidy allocations and operating reserve investments, RMC management fees, hiring and firing of on-site management and maintenance staff, procurement of supplies and materials, design and supervision over modernization projects, access to business records, and other areas deemed necessary by the residents for successful administration of a development."[86]

At its most basic, then, an RMC is a means to improve living conditions in distressed public housing projects by giving tenants more power over their own environment. But the empowerment movement has been attached to more ambitious goals than this: according to longtime RMC advocate Bertha Gilkey, the best RMCs combine resident management with leadership training, social service provision, economic development, and homeownership options.[87] It is this expanded idea of resident empowerment in public housing projects, especially as it has played out in one building at Cabrini Green, that I want to examine next.

But, first, we need a little history. In 1969, residents of the Bromley-Heath public housing project in Boston, who had been organized since the mid-1960s, proposed taking over management of their project. The Boston Housing Authority agreed, and the conversion was accomplished in early 1971. It remains the oldest tenant-managed public housing development in the United States.[88] That same year, a famous "rent strike" begun by St. Louis public housing tenants was finally settled, resulting in the collapse and reorganization of the St.

Louis Housing Authority and the emergence of tenant management in that city's public housing. Two resident management corporations were formed there in 1973, two more in 1974, and a fifth soon after. The most famous is the Cochran Gardens RMC, founded and led by Bertha Gilkey since the mid-1970s.[89] The idea of resident empowerment spread quickly. As we saw above, in April, 1971, the Chicago Housing Authority agreed to recognize and financially support popularly elected Local Advisory Councils at its projects. Eventually, some of these bottom-up political organizations, which worked on behalf of tenant rights, morphed into full-fledged resident management corporations, the best known of which we will examine in some detail below.

Unfortunately, early enthusiasm for RMCs waned in the face of the steep challenges they faced. In the late 1970s, the Ford Foundation funded a National Tenant Management Demonstration Program whose lukewarm evaluation by the Manpower Demonstration Research Corporation (MDRC) persuaded many that resident empowerment did not warrant the enthusiasm with which it had first been met. According to that evaluation, RMCs (or TMCs—Tenant Management Corporations—as they were known at the time) were no better at rent collection, vacancy rates, and maintenance than local public housing authorities (PHAs),[90] although they were perceived by residents as stricter than their PHAs and produced additional benefits such as "(a) increased employment among residents, (b) a sense of personal development among participants in the tenant management organization, and (c) a greater overall satisfaction with the project management among residents."[91] The study also found, unfortunately, that RMCs were costly, due to their high demands for training and employment, that they suffered from high turnover among managers and officers, and that interest in project management among tenants was often low.[92] The MDRC report recommended continued support of the demonstration sites but not wider implementation.[93] Despite a few isolated success stories, in other words, RMCs seemed by the late 1970s to be an idea whose time had come and gone.

In the 1980s, however, thanks in part to the "conservative revolution" of the Reagan years, the idea of resident management was revived. Robert Woodson of the National Center for Neighborhood Enterprise, HUD Secretary Jack Kemp, and a public housing "star" named Kimi Gray from Washington, DC's Kenilworth-Parkside project all became visible proponents of the idea.[94] In 1987, resident management provisions were included in the Housing and Community Development Act, which provided up to $100,000 for RMCs; and in 1989, tenants at LeClair Courts in Chicago established the first RMC in Chicago.[95] Under the RMC, this 615-unit row-house project on Forty-third Street and Cicero Avenue came under the control of an elected, thirteen-member tenant board, which oversaw fifteen employees and a $1.5 million annual budget, used to support such initiatives as an on-site health care facility and various resident businesses.[96]

In 1990, Title IV of the National Affordable Housing Act of 1990 authorized funding to actually sell public housing buildings to RMCs, so that tenants would become homeowners in addition to project managers.[97] And in early 1991, residents of 1230 North Burling Street in Cabrini Green began a twelve-month training program to establish their own RMC. Also planning RMCs in Chicago at the time were residents of Dearborn Homes, Lathrop Homes, Ida B. Wells Homes, Wentworth Gardens, and Washington Park Homes.[98]

Against all odds, in other words, some public housing buildings and projects were finding a way to survive the deterioration and chaos of the 1980s inner city; these RMCs helped residents unite and work as a group against crime, physical blight, inadequate and inefficient government services, poor schools, and drug and alcohol abuse. They provided jobs and responsibility. They schooled residents in political participation and organization management. They also provided an extraordinary opportunity for leaders to emerge from the inner city, especially among African-American female residents. And, despite the uphill battle that every RMC faced, the secrets to success were becoming better known. According to Monti, the RMC must have adequate and continuing resources for operation, modernization, and technical assistance; it must arise from grass roots demand, not top-down fiat; an atmosphere of "creative tension" between residents and the public housing authority is needed; and residents must build and maintain strong and direct ties with non-governmental agencies in the community.[99]

1230 North Burling Street

Perhaps the best known resident management corporation in Chicago is the one at 1230 North Burling Street in the Cabrini Green complex (see figure 5). The building, which sits next door to North Town Village, is one of eight high-rises in the Green Homes (the so-called whites), a fifteen-story, 126-unit building dating from 1962; originally, it had 134 units but was rehabbed in 1995. Like many buildings at Cabrini Green, 1230 North Burling Street suffered astounding deterioration and lawlessness through the 1970s and early 1980s. When future tenant leader Arlene Williams moved to the building in the early 1980s, gang members were charging residents to ride the building's elevators, violence was a constant danger, there were no functioning lights in the building's public spaces, and as many as half the units were vacant.[100]

About that time, ten residents, mostly middle-aged women, all black, all single mothers and grandmothers,[101] all longtime residents of the projects, volunteered to begin a twenty-four-hour security watch at the building. They wanted, they would later say, to protect their children and their property. They asked the Chicago Housing Authority for lights and a phone in the lobby,[102] and they began an experiment that would last more than twenty years. Among those women was Cora Moore.

When I first met her in 2000, Cora Moore was a fifty-eight-year-old mother of six who had lived for thirty-one years at Cabrini Green. Born in Birmingham, Alabama, she had come to Chicago in 1949 at the age of seven. In 1969, she moved to one of the Cabrini Green "reds" and a decade later relocated to 1230 North Burling Street, where she was one of the founders of the RMC. She tells with pride the story of those early days, standing watch in the lobby with her friends: "ten of us took this building over; we were the first to do that in HUD. We fixed the doors and the lights. We became professional security officers." Moore was president of the building before becoming full-time manager of the RMC in 1992.[103]

Arlene Williams, forty-five years old when I met her, was born on the West Side of Chicago, but her mother had come to the city from Clarksdale, Mississippi, and her father, from Selma, Alabama. She had nine brothers and sisters. Arlene moved to Cabrini Green in 1978 and to 1230 North Burling Street in 1982. She raised four children there. Soon after she moved to the building, Arlene told me, she found a dead man in the lobby and began making plans to move once again. But after she attended a building council meeting to see if she could get free notebook paper for her eleven-year-old son, she began attending resident meetings twice monthly with other women to find out how they could make the building cleaner and safer. "We decided to come sit in the lobby to take care of our building. And we told the gang members to go away."[104] I heard similar stories from Dolores Wilson, who had been a Cabrini Green resident for forty-three years, and Bessie Rule, who had been there for thirty. Both had been active in the building's self-government, and both had held key posts in the RMC.[105]

The women's volunteer work in the 1980s on behalf of their building did not go unnoticed, though the CHA was always grudging in its respect for them. In 1989, an official tenant patrol was established at 1230 North Burling Street, the first of its kind at the CHA. The women were trained by HUD to be professional security guards and finally began to be paid for what they had been doing for so long as volunteers.[106]

But their appetite for self-government was not satisfied. Soon after instituting the tenant patrol, the women begin plotting to actually run the building themselves. In 1992, after a year of training from the CHA, HUD, and a group called Urban Women, Inc., led by Bertha Gilkey, they initiated a full-fledged Resident Management Corporation, signing a management contract with the CHA and taking control over not only building security and maintenance but also tenant screening, leasing, social service programs, and relations with the city.[107]

For more than a decade, these residents ran their own community within the project. As they put it in their RMC Mission Statement, "We, the residents of the 1230 North Burling Resident Management Corporation, will provide management programs and services, social, educational, cultural, and spiritual, to better the lives and living conditions of the 1230 North Burling residents."[108] The purpose of the organization, they wrote, is to "improve the living conditions of the residents of 1230 North Burling through resident management to ensure a decent, safe, and wholesome environment for the residents of these apartments."[109]

What is most extraordinary about the 1230 North Burling Street RMC, however, is not that these residents managed the day-to-day details of the building for so long, though that is not a minor accomplishment; it is that they developed at Cabrini Green, against staggering obstacles, a complete and functioning structure of self-government, with a seven-member elected board of directors, including a president, vice president, secretary, assistant secretary, treasurer, and sergeant of arms; seven full-time paid staff members, all residents of the building, including a manager, leasing clerk, accounting clerk, maintenance clerk/receptionist, maintenance mechanic, and two janitors; several security guards; twenty-four volunteer floor captains (two per floor); volunteer chairs of fifteen standing committees (including Grievance, Senior Citizen, Youth, Screening, Beautification, Security, Laundry Room, Newsletter, etc.); as well as chairs of special and advisory committees (see table 7.1).

With the help of a written constitution, regular elections, and monthly meetings of both the whole building and the board of directors, the residents of 1230 North Burling Street handled all building security, screening of new tenants, leasing, maintenance, and relations with other resident groups at Cabrini Green and across the city as well as with the CHA itself. On top of all that, they put on a variety of social service programs including summer youth programs and senior citizen groups. I have estimated that fully 50 percent of units in the building had an inhabitant actively involved in one way or another with the RMC, a much higher rate, I believe, than one would find in the typical Residential Community Association (RCA) described in chapter 3. Perhaps most important of all, the 1230 North Burling Street RMC became an extraordinary training ground for leaders in this neighborhood, especially for black women, who accounted for twelve of fourteen of the main officers of the building.

The upshot of all this? According to Cora Moore: "Before, we had fifty-four vacancies; now we have one. We did all of our own maintenance, got new blinds, a new elevator, a new laundry room. We've built a playground, planted flowers, kept the hallways free of graffiti. And we provide twenty-four hour a day security."[110] But the work of the RMC was not just managerial: "We stick together here, we have regular meetings, we stay on top of what the kids do."[112] In another place, she has described the community this way: "We're all

Table 7.1. Self-government at 1230 N. Burling Street: Resident Positions

Board of Directors	*Staff*
President	Manager
Vice President	Leasing Clerk
Secretary	Accounting Clerk
Asst. Secretary	Maintenance Clerk
Treasurer	Maintenance Mechanic
Sergeant at Arms	Janitor
Member	Janitor
Plus floor captains (2 per floor), committee chairs (about 15 total), and dozens of committee members	

Source: 1230 North Burling Street Resident Management Corporation, *By-Laws* (Chicago: December 1, 1999).

lit up at night. You won't see that at the other buildings. The elevators are running. And we got heat."[112]

Arlene Williams talked in similar terms about what the RMC had done for the most vulnerable members of the building: its children (through tutoring, a summer lunch program, a jump rope contest, awards, coat giveaways, a conflict resolution program, and trips to the zoo) and elderly (Thanksgiving dinner, winter wear, Christmas and Thanksgiving baskets, etc.).[113]

And there were dramatic personal stories about the effects of the RMC. Kelvin Cannon, thirty-eight years old, who was born and raised in Cabrini Green and has eight siblings and seven children here, was a gangbanger as a teenager and later served three years in prison for armed robbery. When he got out, he began working at the RMC as a janitor. "Cora Moore saved me, gave me a chance to start over. I want to protect this building at any cost. I'm dedicated to it."[114]

Again and again, when visiting the building and talking to its residents, I was told that 1230 North Burling Street was unique compared to the other buildings at Cabrini Green. As Cora Moore said, "this building is different, this is a family, this is our home." Kelvin Cannon told me, "This building is different."[115] And Linda Rule and Kenyetta Alexander said during one interview, "this building's always been different. It's the leaders. Other buildings have a project mentality; this is an ownership building; it's our building."[116] Richard Crayton put it in these words: "this place is the king of Cabrini Green."[117] And everyone offered the same explanation for the building's success: it is because of the RMC.

In the late 1990s, just as redevelopment was finally zeroing in on Cabrini Green itself, the 1230 North Burling Resident Management Corporation proposed to the Chicago Housing Authority that it be allowed to purchase its building for a nominal fee and convert it to a nonprofit resident-owned housing cooperative (or "co-op"). If accepted, the proposal would spare the building from demolition and let its residents stay in their own neighborhood, now as homeowners rather than tenants.[118]

According to the National Association of Housing Cooperatives, a housing co-op is what happens when people work with each other "on a democratic basis" to own or control the building(s) where they live.[119] If their building was converted to a co-op, according to the RMC homeownership plan, 1230 North Burling Street residents would be able to (1) continue to make decisions about how their building is run and learn skills by doing so; (2) participate in various self-sufficiency programs; (3) become homeowners; and (4) help keep affordable housing in the Near North area.[120] Above all, "conversion would allow the building's many residents to remain in their long-standing homes while achieving extraordinary affordability and eventual equity appreciation."[121]

Under the plan, residents would have a fifteen-year lease-to-purchase transition period, which would give them time to become more economically self-sufficient through a workforce development program. Meanwhile, the CHA would stop operating the building; and lease holders would be converted to the Section 8 voucher program. All co-op members would pay a small fee, and, during the interim period, the building would be owned by a limited equity partnership. After fifteen years, the partnership would sell the building to the cooperative.[122]

In addition, the building itself would undergo a $6–10 million rehabilitation. There would be new landscaping, lighting, a perimeter fence, a new vestibule, a curtain wall over open-air galleries, kitchen rehabs, new public spaces, new floors, and a reorganized ground floor, which would include a health clinic, child care facility, and community rooms. The building would go from 126 to 117 units after the conversion of the first and second floors to public use.[123]

The conversion proposal was approved by the CHA, reluctantly, and, in 2001, residents were waiting for funding to begin the physical rehabilitation. Ninety-one household heads, nearly the whole building, agreed to participate in the co-op.[124] And, on January 8, 2001, the RMC (with the help of the Holsten Real Estate Development Corporation) sent a $10 million proposal to the Illinois Housing Development Authority (IHDA) to rehabilitate the building and convert it to a Homeownership Cooperative. Letters of support came in from Bertha Gilkey, Jack Kemp, the principal of the local elementary school, the other RMCs at Cabrini Green, the Cabrini Green LAC, and local Chicago Alderman Walter Burnett.

Unfortunately, the proposal was turned down by both IHDA and the City of Chicago Department of Housing. Prospects appeared bleak: without conversion, 1230 North Burling Street would be subject to the viability test described in chapter 6 and torn down. The residents feared for their future. As Arlene Williams said to me, "we've been here the longest, we deserve to own our apartments. Then nobody could tell us we have to move. I'd like to stay here for the rest of my life. I've put too much of myself in 1230 North Burling. We run this building."[125] Likewise, Cora Moore told me: "People do not want to move out of here. We've lived here for so long; we deserve to own our apartments. I've put too much of myself in this building."[126] And Dolores Wilson said: "I like this building: it's companionable. I wouldn't trade it for the world. When people ask me where I'd like to live, I say 'Cabrini Green.' It's not a project for me, it's home. People do not want to move out of here."[127]

Assessment

In the mid- to late-1990s, resident-managed public housing projects and co-op conversions were not much on the radar screen in this country. Between 1988 and 1995, HUD provided $22 million to 328 RMCs, but only fifteen really took control of their developments.[128] A report claimed that half of all RMC efforts failed;[129] and even housing advocates were wary: were not RMCs and housing co-ops simply a way for the government to evade its responsibility and take more units out of the public housing inventory during an affordable housing crisis?[130] And there are ideological complaints as well. Nicholas Lemann, for example, has written that:

> Of all the simple ideas for helping the ghettos, probably the most common and persistent for the past quarter century has been the idea that they can be turned around, "developed" into thriving ethnic enclaves. . . . tax incentives will cause businesses to start up there, tenant management will save the housing projects, community-development corporations will shore up the housing stock, parents will fix the schools. . . .
>
> The clear lesson of experience, though, is that ghetto development hasn't worked. . . . The impressive record of black success in America's cities since the 1960s has been almost entirely bound up with leaving the ghettos rather than improving them.[131]

In chapter 5, we read similar reservations from James Traub, Owen Fiss, and William Julius Wilson.

Others have seen such efforts as only reinforcing racial segregation in the central city. Alexander Polikoff, the attorney for the *Gautreaux* plaintiffs, has been adamant in his opposition to any program that keeps poor black families in racially and economically homogeneous mid- and high-rise buildings in the ghetto.[132] Agreeing with him is the Habitat Corporation and other developers who stand to make money building new units on the site of the old high-rises.

There is also a certain irony about the empowerment strategy: the argument that has been most successful in helping public housing residents stay in their neighborhoods and fight for changes there—the argument that demolition, dispersal, and mixing are racially discriminatory—may give blacks a legal victory, rhetorical dignity, and greater resources; but it also leaves them back where they started: in racially homogeneous enclaves isolated from the rest of the city and the wider metropolitan region.

Of course, not all enclaves are the same.[133] The all-black, low- or moderate-income, democratically self-governed community envisioned at 1230 North Burling Street, a variant on the old "gilded ghetto" idea, reflects in important ways Christopher Alexander's vision of a "mosaic of subcultures" in the city.[134] It also conforms to Iris Marion Young's theory of "differentiated" subcommunities, internally homogeneous but intricately linked to other, diverse communities at the city or metropolitan level. For Young, forced segregation is clearly pernicious, but "integration" (when defined as either simple mixing or even dispersal) has problems, too. "Group-differentiated residential and associational clustering is not necessarily bad in itself, inasmuch as it may arise from legitimate desires to form and maintain affinity grouping," though she cautions that such spatial group differentiation should be "voluntary, fluid, without clear borders, and with many overlapping, unmarked, and hybrid places."[135]

Herbert Gans long ago proposed a similar kind of metropolitan layout: relatively homogeneous neighborhoods, like 1230 North Burling Street, *within* a highly heterogeneous city. In his 1967 study *The Levittowners*, he had written that "whereas a mixture of population types, and especially of rich and poor, is desirable in the community as a whole, heterogeneity on the block will not produce the intended tolerance, but will lead to conflict that is undesirable because it is essentially insoluble and thus becomes chronic. Selective homogeneity on the block will improve the tenor of neighbor relations, and will thus make it easier—although not easy—to realize heterogeneity at the community level."[136]

But the idea goes back even further than that and can be said to have originated, at least from a social scientific point of view, in Chicago urbanology itself. In an important 1915 paper, Robert Park had defined the city as "a mosaic of little worlds which touch but do not interpenetrate."[137] Later, Louis Wirth would echo the phrase in his introduction to the 1938 *Local Community Fact Book* for Chicago: "The modern metropolis is a city of cities. It is a mosaic of little worlds, an aggregate of local communities, each one differentiated from the others by its characteristic function in the total economy and cultural complex of city life."[138] And in his landmark article "Urbanism as a Way of Life," he wrote that "[t]he city consequently tends to resemble a mosaic of social worlds in which the transition from one to the other is abrupt. The juxtaposition of divergent personalities and modes of life tends to produce a relativistic perspective and a sense of toleration of differences which may be regarded as prerequisites for rationality and which lead toward the secularization of life."[139] There are differences, some subtle, some not-so-subtle, between the Park/Wirth/Gans image of self-contained "little worlds" and the Alexander/Young proposal of fluid but still differentiated subcultures, but what all these models share is the idea that there is a third way beyond the isolation and inequity of *segregation*, on the one hand, and the assimilation and homogenization of *integration*, on the other, that it is possible to build in our world a genuinely urban landscape in which *diversity*—with all of its liveliness, freedom, and provocation—is a daily fact of life but in which residents can still voluntarily group themselves into street- or even neighborhood-level subcommunities.

But even independent of this ideological defense of the public housing RMC, there are intriguing *rhetorical* benefits promised by the 1230 North Burling Street housing co-op and projects like it: opportunities for active participation by the dispossessed in communal self-determination; opportunities for leadership development, especially among African-American residents;[140] opportunities to represent local demands to outsiders in speech and writing and to develop the discursive abilities to do so; opportunities to lead lives devoted to communal, and not just personal, advancement; opportunities to increase the security, stability, and openness of literal and metaphoric "common grounds"; and opportunities to become positive role models for one's children. These are huge benefits not easily discounted by the obvious obstacles to, and expense of, empowerment strategies.

More to the point of this book, with its interest in how different metropolitan environments sponsor different scenes of social and political intercourse, the stories of 1230 North Burling Street are more than anything else stories of *civic* education. As Cora Moore put it, in learning to run their own building, "we learned HUD rules and regulations, CHA rules and regulations. We were trained in leadership, on running meetings."[141] Arlene Williams agrees: "I used to be a loner; this place made me get involved. I started traveling a lot. Bertha Gilkey taught me I could be anything. I had been good at writing before; but she taught me how to *say* that I could do it."[142] It would be a shame if the Near North Side no longer provided such remarkable schools of democracy.

In the summer of 1865, on the Sea Islands off the coast of South Carolina, Major Martin Delany, the highest-ranking black officer in the Union army, urged an audience of former lowcountry slaves to acquire land and "cultivate Rice and Cotton," beginning with one acre but expanding gradually their holdings and thus profits, all the while keeping their fields "in good order and well tilled and planted." It was the quintessential American dream articulated by a northern, urban, free man of color, fully committed to the integration of his people into mainstream society. His audience, rural blacks just freed from generations of slave labor, listened politely, no doubt delighted to see a black man wearing an officer's stripes.[143]

But when a Committee on Behalf of the People emerged on the islands several months later, the local blacks were not, apparently, as concerned as Major Delany was with "calculating the profitability of cotton and rice." Rather, what they requested of the government was "land enough to lay our Fathers bones upon." Ira Berlin's interpretation of the incident is eloquent:

> That striking figure spoke to the desire of plantation slaves to secure not just any land but *their* land, meaning specifically the land that they and their forebears had worked and in the process made part of themselves. It was not the hope of social mobility and a vision of opulence that animated the former slaves for whom the committee spoke. Rather, the committee articulated the freedpeople's desire to secure a competency and live on their own surrounded by their families.[144]

One hundred and forty years later, the people of Cabrini Green, descendants of those former slaves, want the same thing, nothing more nor less: "to secure a competency and live on their own surrounded by their families."

PART THREE

Lessons for Theory and Practice

EIGHT

Toward a New Sociospatial Dialectic

> For there is no creature whose inward being is so strong that it is not greatly determined by what lies outside it.
>
> —George Eliot, *Middlemarch*

The long tour of actual and proposed environments that we have just taken—full of Chicago politics, North American settlement patterns, federal housing policies, U.S. court decisions, twentieth-century economic developments, and large-scale architectural plans—probably read more like a local history lesson or a seminar in urban sociology than an analysis of situated discourse practices. Yet I wrote in chapter 1 that I was interested primarily in *rhetoric*, that is, in public discourse and civic education. What was all this about street grids and population densities, TIF funds, and housing vouchers? Certainly there were moments when these places were imagined specifically as sites of language use and political education—when we asked about the chances for healthy social interaction in neighborhoods where public space was literally life-threatening; or how thriving polities could form in places made up almost entirely of detached single-family homes surrounded by private lawns and accessible only by automobile. But that was probably not enough to justify the title of the book or the promises made in part 1. We need to consider more fully now the *rhetoric* of these proposals and their implications for the future of public discourse on the Near North Side and beyond.

In other words, we need to look at how the scenes just examined—a low-income African-American ghetto, an affluent white suburb, a mixed-income "urban village," a high-rise inner city housing co-op, as well as the overall metropolitan environment they (at least partially) constitute—*matter* for public discourse. We need to ask: What are the effects of these different kinds of social space on the ways we render and resolve conflict, on our attitudes toward public argument and our habits of political language? And we need to consider: Are there alternatives to these sociospatial arrangements that promise healthier interactions among us, better chances for our collective freedom, equality, and happiness? To answer those questions, I would like to consolidate what we have learned so far about social discourse and the built environment in the Chicago metropolitan area at the beginning of the twenty-first century.

The first two parts of this book described a human landscape beset by privatism and marked by highly decentralized, fragmented, and polarized social spaces. They told the story of a society in which, for the past century or more, the most privileged persons, families, and institutions have fled what is open, diverse, and complex—our cities—for what is, or at least appears to be, exclusive, homogeneous, and safe—our suburbs. The result of this centrifugal movement has been the deconcentration not just of our population but of our public life as well: the desertion of our shared centers; the division of once unitary, diverse polities into dispersed, fragmented, homogeneous ones; and the polarization of our communities so that the ones best situated become only more so, and the rest are consigned to seemingly eternal stagnation or decline.

In chapters 2 and 3, I examined what such an environment must mean for its residents, how they suffer from the loss of a middle ground between community and society, identity and difference, assimilation and separation, a place they can build together with different but equal others. And I argued that the teaching of politics in this country—the teaching, for example, of the habits and dispositions of public discourse—has contributed to this situation by privileging supposedly decontextualized skills of political expression and debate. We have failed, in other words, to help our young people appreciate and deal with the inevitable conflicts of living together in concrete space with people unlike themselves.

I proposed therefore that the *city*, with its metropolitan area and internal districts, could be an anchoring social scene capable of helping us invigorate our political lives and develop more centralized, integrated, and equitable public spheres: *commonplaces* that could balance our often-conflicting needs for unity and diversity, accessibility and power, belonging and anonymity. My goal was not to suggest that all human settlements be like cities, or that all rhetorical education be city-based, but to suggest that, in the menu of geopolitical options available to us, we have neglected such middle spaces, and that neglect has been detrimental for our physical landscape, our public life, and our common education.

I then looked in part 2 at an actual urban district on the Near North Side of Chicago, one at the crossroads of a troubled past, a conflicted present, and an uncertain future. What we discovered there was that, if Chicago is representative, Americans have not done a very good job of making space for diverse peoples to come together, openly and fairly, to determine together their shared destiny. If, as I argued in chapter 3, the dense, diverse, self-governing urban district of 50–100,000 residents offers the best chance for such public life, our contemporary landscape does not give us much hope. What is worse, even our most progressive ideas for improving that landscape seem to be driven by public philosophies motivated by either an impulse to separate or a naive dream of unity. Without a healthy attitude toward *conflict*, its inevitability and virtue, we will be unable to build either good cities in particular or good public spheres in general.

What we found on the site of the Cabrini Green public housing project and its immediate environs, at least up to 1995 or so, was a bona fide ghetto in which, over the course of several decades, low-income blacks were concentrated and isolated, by whites, through violence and intimidation, formal and informal discrimination, "urban renewal," and public housing site selection and tenant assignment policies. We saw further how, once they had been concentrated, isolated, and abandoned, blacks in places like Cabrini Green were hit especially hard by the deindustrialization (and suburbanization) of the U.S. economy in the late 1960s and early 1970s. By the end of the twentieth century, such neighborhoods had become communities of mostly poor, female-headed, African-American families living with high rates of joblessness, crime, substance abuse, school failure, and physical blight. Three specifically *rhetorical* problems with these places—isolation, fear, and silence—meant that residents were unable to sponsor the healthy public discourse, social interaction, and civic education they needed to flourish.

Unfortunately, our picture of suburbia—for many people the promised land in contemporary America and the opposite of the scene just described—was equally distressing. My purpose here was not to rehash old academic complaints but to look closely at one place during one historical period—Schaumburg, Illinois, over the past half century—and try to ascertain how open that place had been to the diversity of its own metropolitan region. What we found was a place that had self-consciously positioned itself *against* the city and the heterogeneity that it represented, that used zoning and other land use decisions to screen out the poor, that barred public housing from within its midst, that made no effort to attract or welcome blacks, and that, despite profiting enormously from the Chicago metropolitan economy, had been unwilling to share the burden of that economy's problems.

Of course, in many ways, suburbia is an attractive destination for the people of Cabrini Green, especially in terms of the safety, jobs, and schools it can offer them. But, in terms of the public sphere it enables, it too is a place mostly of isolation, fear, and silence. In this, it is surprisingly similar to Cabrini Green: racially and economically homogeneous, designed to depart from the comprehensible grid of urban settlement, a place lacking any kind of human scale in its structures, spaces, or activities. Both scenes, I believe, are built on prejudice, promote mistrust, and inspire social alienation both within and without.

Our next two options, fortunately, were more promising. They consciously work *against* the deconcentration, fragmentation, and polarization of the contemporary public sphere and *for* open social interaction and discursive exchange. Both celebrate the city, refuse to abandon it, refuse even to de-densify it; and both try to envision a distinctly American urban environment for the next century. Both also share a sense that the poorest and most vulnerable members of our society deserve a place in that environment and require support from the rest of us to keep it. Finally, both attend explicitly to the language of city life: to inter- and intragroup discourse, dialogue, and communication. My ultimate negative critique of both should not detract from their superiority to the first two options reviewed.

As an alternative to the classic twentieth century public housing project, North Town Village may be the most promising model for revitalizing the American public landscape in half a century. It is economically and racially diverse, scaled for individual human beings, and designed to encourage healthy social contact, both informal and formal, among its residents, including communal self-government of a sort. It is genuinely attractive and patently successful as a marketing proposition. One easily imagines it being replicated in other places and helping to foster a renewal of diverse central city residential communities across the country.

But I worry that North Town Village is just too expensive, too driven by the perceived need to cater to the mobile (and thus fickle) upper classes, too willfully blind to racial prejudice, too dependent on a public philosophy of social amalgamation, too beholden to the belief that intergroup conflict is something that can be and needs to be purified. It embraces the look of the city but not its heterogeneity or its politics, which it wishes away with a dream of unity and harmony. Rhetorically speaking, it is a community of narrative rather than argument, where difference is not so much rendered and resolved as (allegedly) transcended through the stories of its residents' common dreams and fears.

Of course, subcommunities within North Town Village or places like it, coalitions based on race, class, culture, family status, even musical preference, could emerge and engage one another. But the community is organized in a way that doesn't seem to allow for that: prior group characteristics are metaphorically "checked" at the gates of the development; and, inside, originally *different* individuals and families are interspersed evenly throughout, allegedly indistinguishable from one another, and united by shared dreams of living peacefully in the city.

As for 1230 North Burling Street, it succeeded for a time at least, more than any other place on the Near North Side, in constituting its residents not as private individuals pursuing their own desires but as genuine *citizens*, engaged in joint, nonprofit pursuits of personal *and* communal development. It may be the only model for the revitalization of the Near North Side that even comes close to seeing the city as truly public space and that acknowledges the deep and difficult conflicts over that space in our society. If there is a school for rhetoric on the Near North Side of Chicago, it is probably here, a community explicitly dedicated to training its residents in political problem-solving and inviting them to engage in that activity on a daily basis.

Unfortunately, the project seems to suggest that the only way to build a self-governing community in our society, a culture of argument that brings people together to work actively and discursively on common projects, is to make sure that they are all relatively similar in background and goals. Surely, we need something more inclusive for the twenty-first century city, something that more dramatically breaks with the troubled past of this particular neighborhood and is capable of greater involvement in the multicultural global economy. We need to find a way, in other words, to encourage participation by ordinary people in the self-determination of their own communities but within a context that forces them to work with others very different from themselves. In the end, 1230 North Burling Street is probably an enclave, and the liabilities of that kind of polis outweigh, I believe, its benefits.

Now, perhaps that wouldn't be a bad thing if enclaves like 1230 North Burling Street were positioned in close proximity to one another, if movement in and out of them were free and the distribution of problems and resources among them equal, and if there were a rich network of "official" publics *within*, *between*, and *beyond* such communities, including district-level polities where neighborhood-based decisions could, in a sense, be supervised. The resulting mosaic would thus be very different from the current configuration, in which our primary communities are completely alienated from one another, or a melting-pot model in which everyone is (supposedly) interspersed with everyone else. It would be a third way, with small groups of the like minded connected to and by larger, but still accessible, publics that are quite diverse.[1]

In the end, all the alternatives to the late twentieth-century ghetto we explored here—mobility, mixing, and empowerment—seemed to allow for innovation, selflessness, and even courage. We had glimpses, in all three, of a *better* metropolis: improved lives for some urban poor who relocate to the suburbs, a return to the central city by some middle- and upper-income whites, the empowerment of some public housing residents in communities of their own making. These are all good things. But can they really reverse the extreme fragmentation, decentralization, and polarization of our contemporary landscape and help us build thriving publics in this country, small enough to promote genuine access by ordinary citizens in the self-determination of their own communities but large enough to reveal their deepest conflicts and have a chance of actually resolving them? Schaumburg, for example, lacks the density, diversity, and publicity of a "real" city; it is a privatized version of social space with little public life. North Town Village, by contrast, is remarkably dense, diverse, and public for an American central city neighborhood, but there are not enough real political decisions for its residents to make and too much emphasis on their imagined union. In some ways, 1230 North Burling Street is the best of the bunch: lively, dense, public-spirited, gregarious. But in the end, it is probably too small, too homogeneous, and too disconnected from the wider world to really work.

What, then, have we learned from this tour of Chicago? Have we discovered anything that might inform, even improve, our theories, practices, and pedagogies of public life? We have certainly seen that the forces of decentralization, fragmentation, and polarization in this country are powerful, so powerful that it may be hard to come away from part 2 of this book with anything other than pessimism about the prospects of building a truly democratic civic sphere—grounded, unitary, and official—in the contemporary United States. But in fact, constantly reminding ourselves of that decentralization, fragmentation, and polarization, recognizing the negative effects of those phenomena on our social and political relations with one another, and acknowledging the impetus for them provided by both the unequal distribution of material resources in our society and our engrained ways of thinking and talking about community can still be useful, even liberating. That's because we benefit, I believe, from occasionally denaturalizing what otherwise appears innocent to us, making the world more open to our reflections, criticisms, and proposals for change. The case study provided here can remind us, that is, of both how *scenic* our political lives are, how inextricably embedded in the world around us, and how *thoughtful* they are, how reliant on the beliefs we harbor, often unexpressed, about our actual and ideal relations with one another. Teasing out these lessons will be the burden of this and the following chapter.

The case study at the heart of this book has presented strong evidence for a close relationship between physical location and individual and social welfare in our society and thus good reason to think that place and rhetorical well-being are linked as well. The scenes depicted in part 2 were materially so different from one another, and associated with such dramatic differences in socioeconomic status and opportunity that it seems noncontroversial to claim that different places in this country offer residents different chances for health, prosperity, and happiness. *Place matters*, and this is as true for rhetoric as for education and employment.[2]

And yet even this relatively tepid claim is routinely denied. We are constantly told, in a variety of ways, that poverty, unemployment, crime, and other social problems are the result of individual defects, inherited cultural patterns, even voluntary choice, and that success in our world is largely a function of personal virtue and hard work. Environment is at most a secondary factor; more likely, it is a complete irrelevance.[3] That is because, since the Enlightenment, we have tended to think of "man" as, in essence, a godlike creature: self-sufficient, self-governed, and self-motivating. And we have tended to mythologize that creature by putting *him* in narratives of autonomy and self-mastery, like that of Robinson Crusoe, in which the natural and built environment play an inauspicious role. For us moderns, our neighborhoods, cities, and metropolitan areas are merely backdrops for activities that could as well occur someplace else. We have therefore learned to treat our ties to the physical world as superficial: the real human "self" is immaterial, just as the most important human groups are ageographical, constituted less by shared space than by shared beliefs, knowledge, values, habits, and occupation.

This modern flight from place has only intensified of late. In the midst of a global economy that seems to have made political borders irrelevant and attachment to local community suspect; a technological revolution that appears to have dramatically reduced the role of space in human action and interaction; a philosophical modernism that has made universalism, cosmopolitanism, and proceduralism our supreme intellectual and ethical virtues; and a culture that celebrates, above all else, mobility and change; it is difficult to make the case that places still matter in human affairs. Yet they do. As we have seen again and again in this book, *where* people live, work, and play—the geographies they negotiate, the situations they find themselves in, the physical and human environments in which they think, act, and interact—these influence, directly and indirectly, subtly and forcefully, the experiences they have, the people they know, the skills and habits they develop, the values they acquire. The scenes in which we appear, that is, determine much about our opportunities, actions, and attitudes.[4]

True, those with more resources are often able to disattach themselves from scene, both because they can change scene more easily than other people and because they can insulate themselves to some degree from the deficiencies of any particular scene. And since the ideas of the most powerful are typically the most powerful ideas, the notion that human success is predicated on the ability to flourish *across* environments, to have one's way irrespective of place, has become the prevailing idea in our culture. Unfortunately, the mass of human beings cannot so easily move away, nor wall themselves off, from less than ideal environments. If local jobs are few and inferior, area schools substandard, neighborhood streets menacing, and neighbors desperate, the prospects for human flourishing will be bleak. This is especially true for the very young, the very old, the poor, the weak, and the afflicted, who are often less mobile than the rest of us and especially vulnerable in the face of an indifferent or hostile environment. But, in fact, environmental dependence is a condition that holds for everyone. Even at the peak of our mental and physical powers, even at the top of the socioeconomic ladder, we are all at the mercy of forces beyond our skin, and our greatest achievements are only successful responses to the world around us. "The apparent complexity of [human] behavior over time," Herbert Simon once wrote, "is largely a reflection of the complexity of the environment in which we find ourselves."[5]

We might add: apparent variations in the *quality* of human behavior *across space* are largely a reflection of differences in the environments in which that behavior occurs. Simply put, some environments provide their inhabitants with more and better resources for success than others. As Jared Diamond showed in *Guns, Germs, and Steel*, much of the variation in societal "progress" on earth can be explained by reference to environmental factors, such as the past availability of suitably domesticatable plant and animal species in different parts of the world and the superiority of an east-west land axis for the spatial diffusion of cultural innovations.[6] That there were, at the time when some human groups were beginning the march toward "civilization," no large mammals comparable to the horse or cow in sub-Saharan Africa, no cereal grains like wheat or rice in Australia, and a predominantly north-south land axis in South America—these facts go a long way in explaining the relative slowness with which cultures in those places developed. Advanced technologies like guns, Diamond argues, have only been invented and widely used in large, sedentary, highly stratified societies, which in turn have emerged only where there were reliable food surpluses, themselves a function of environmental conditions that varied widely on the planet 15,000 years ago:

> Europe's colonization of Africa had nothing to do with differences between European and African peoples themselves, as white racists assume. Rather, it was due to accidents of geography and biogeography—in particular, to the continents' different areas, axes, and suites of wild plant and animal species. That is, the different historical trajectories of Africa and Europe stem ultimately from differences in real estate.[7]

Considerations such as these should teach us humility when we compare the cultural and economic development of different groups on earth. "All human societies contain inventive people," says Diamond. "It's just that some environments provide more starting materials, and more favorable conditions for utilizing inventions, than do other environments."[8]

But our question here is this: Do the different human environments of the contemporary North American metropolis affect the *rhetorical* "inventiveness" of their inhabitants?[9] In answering that question, we would have to say, first, that there are some fairly obvious *indirect* effects of environment on the development of rhetorical habits and dispositions. For example, place can be said to affect the exercise and development of rhetorical and other political skills through its mediating influence on health. Lead-based paint, for example, and asthma-inducing air quality are not distributed in our society in a geographically neutral way, inner-city U.S. neighborhoods typically suffering high levels of both, relatively speaking.[10] It is not far-fetched to think that such factors could adversely affect the acquisition and use of rhetorical abilities in such places. Of course, there are attributes of suburban living that have an equally powerful effect on physical health and thus on civic capacities. Recent research suggests, for example, a link between suburban living and obesity.[11] And we should not limit ourselves here to the physical byproducts of environment: as we saw in chapter 5, researchers have found in the suburbs a "moral minimalism"—in which social confrontation is assiduously avoided—that may have negative costs for the mental well-being of residents there.[12]

Researchers have also documented strong links between housing and overall economic well-being, and this has obvious implications for rhetorical power as well. The so-called housing bundle[13]—whether one rents or owns, what proportion of the family budget is consumed by housing, as well as the characteristics of one's neighborhood and one's geographical access to local amenities like jobs and health care—is a key determinant, perhaps *the* key determinant, in one's overall opportunity for economic advancement in our society and thus for cultural and political voice.[14] Dreier, Mollenkopf, and Swanstrom demonstrate persuasively how residents of poor neighborhoods even pay more for consumer goods and services (everything from groceries to banking) than do residents of richer neighborhoods.[15] And there appears to be a relationship between one's tenure in a given location—the stability of one's geographical experience, which is tied to such things as homeownership—and one's involvement in local politics.[16] Such spatial inequalities only exacerbate the already-existing inequities in our society.

Proximity to jobs (as well as the capacity to search for jobs by changing location) is also an important factor in one's life chances, which in turn affect the development and exercise of civic skills like rhetoric. Obviously, many other things affect employment, but simply living close to a job, or being able to relocate so that one *is* close to it, is a key factor in being able to actually get and keep that job. Research shows, for example, that the fastest-growing locations for low-skill jobs in this country tend to be far away from the low-income adults who would most benefit from them.[17] A study of "spatial mismatch" in Boston found that, while 98 percent of welfare recipients lived within one-quarter mile of a public transit station, only 32 percent of entry-level *jobs* there were within one-quarter mile of a station. Meanwhile, none of the potential entry-level *employers* was within a thirty-minute public transit trip for residents of low-income Boston neighborhoods, and only 31 percent were within a ninety-minute trip.[18] Certainly, if economic independence is a function, in part, of environment (and if the function obtains more strongly for those least mobile), then we should expect a strong indirect effect of environment on political participation, since high rates of unemployment in a particular area cannot be good for the political vitality of either the neighborhood as a whole or the people who live there.

But the most obvious negative effect of place on individual and social flourishing, and thus on civic capacities, must surely be exposure to crime and violence. As we saw in chapter 6, living in a place where one is in constant danger of being hurt by other people is not good either for one's psychological health or for the public life of the community as a whole. And physical insecurity affects not only individual opportunities and resources; it shapes the kind of social community that people are able to build together, their capacities for trust and openness, and the kinds of discursive practices they learn and engage in.[19]

Another crucial environmental factor, especially for adolescents, turns out to be the socioeconomic characteristics of one's *neighbors*, as we saw in chapter 6. Recent research suggests, for example, that the proportion of one's neighbors who are affluent seems to be positively related to desired developmental outcomes for young people, such as high IQ and low rates of teenage pregnancy and school leaving;[20] similar claims have been made for the proportion of one's neighbors who are gainfully employed.[21] But, as we saw in previous chapters, our usual conclusions in this regard—for example, that hard-working, morally upstanding neighbors are good for the poor—may not always apply. The experience of racism has meant that for low-income blacks, and perhaps especially for low-income black male teenagers, having higher-income white neighbors may actually make things worse: some people you emulate, others you *resent*.[22]

The presence or absence of vibrant, accessible social organizations, institutions, and associations in one's midst can also affect whether and how one acquires particular rhetorical habits. Spurred on by the work of Robert Putnam and others, researchers and social activists have been interested lately in the role of local, voluntary, civic organizations (everything from parent-teacher associations to bowling leagues) in personal and communal well-being, the idea being that strong social networks prevent alienation, help individuals in times of trouble, and even facilitate local economic growth.[23] Eric Klinenberg has demonstrated vividly, for example, what happened to Chicago's North Lawndale neighborhood in the second half of the twentieth century when it lost, first, its white homeowners, then, its small businesses, then, its large employers, and finally, its middle-class black homeowners, who often took with them their churches and clubs.[24] During Chicago's deadly July 1995 heat wave, such socially depleted neighborhoods were affected especially acutely. Klinenberg compared heat wave mortality rates for North Lawndale and South

Lawndale, communities which have similar levels of poverty relative to the rest of Chicago, as well as similar numbers and proportions of seniors living in poverty and seniors living alone.[25] Despite these similarities, North Lawndale, which is 96 percent African-American, had a death rate of forty per 100,000 residents, while neighboring South Lawndale (or "Little Village"), which is 85 percent Latino, had a death rate of only four per 100,000. Can these differences in mortality be explained by the fact that Latinos are better able to deal with heat? or provide better familial support for their elders? Maybe; but, as Klinenberg points out, *all* people in South Lawndale, including white seniors living alone, did better than they did in North Lawndale. The explanation must be that one of the places was simply a worse place to live.

> In North Lawndale, the dangerous ecology of abandoned buildings, open spaces, commercial depletion, violent crime, degraded infrastructure, low population density, and family dispersion undermines the viability of public life and the strength of local support systems, rendering older residents particularly vulnerable to isolation. In Little Village, though, the busy streets, heavy commercial activity, residential concentration, and relatively low crime promote social contact, collective life, and public engagement in general and provide particular benefits for the elderly, who are more likely to leave home when they are drawn out by nearby amenities.[26]

Over and above race, ethnicity, income, education, religion, and culture, *place matters*. Dense, lively, gregarious neighborhoods—with places to go, things to look at, people to watch—are good for health, prosperity, and the development of genuinely civic skills and sensibilities. In fact, researchers have found that, controlling for individual characteristics like education and income, residents of distressed neighborhoods exhibit dampened political activity compared to residents of other places: they show decreased interest in political affairs, decreased levels of organizational membership, and decreased rates of electoral participation.[27] Physical marginalization is both cause and effect of social, economic, and political marginalization.

But no "indirect" effect of place is more important for the development and exercise of civic capacities than the quality and character of neighborhood *schools*. We have seen above how residence patterns in this country are stratified by both race and income. And because American public schooling is so closely tied to place, both in terms of student characteristics and fiscal resources, residential segregation directly affects educational segregation, which in turn affects the distribution of civic capacities and opportunities in our society, an especially pernicious effect since inferior schools seem to doom certain neighborhoods to a kind of perpetual distress.[28] The latest research from the Harvard Civil Rights Project documents how the nation's schools—after a period of some improvement, especially in the South—are now *re*segregating at an alarming rate, increasing metropolitan polarization between high-performing, suburban white schools and low-performing, inner-city minority ones.[29]

But what about *direct* effects of environment on rhetorical habits and dispositions? Does the physical organization of social space influence in any unmediated ways our discursive practices and civic dispositions? We know that *culture* matters in language development, that children typically acquire the rules, formulas, conventions, values, accents, and routines "natural" to their socioeconomic position in the world.[30] And clearly, certain kinds of built environment—for example, decentralized, fragmented, and polarized metropolitan areas—produce certain kinds of politics through their very economies (i.e., the high infrastructure needs of low-density settlement patterns means money not available for other purposes). But what about the effects of built environment on *individuals'* capacities and opportunities? Does a community's "ways with bricks" influence its members' "ways with words"?

Most teachers, I believe, would say yes; they know how important something as "trivial" as the arrangement of furniture in a classroom can be for generating student participation and increasing interaction. When teachers put desks or chairs in a circle in the belief that such a layout will make classroom discourse better, they are expressing belief in a direct connection between the physical organization of reality and human behavior. But does the way we organize larger *political* spaces matter for the civic discourse that takes place there?

I believe it does, and I have tried to specify here some of the broad scenic factors that may be most rhetorically powerful: for example, *accessibility*—how open a community is to the direct participation of ordinary, individual members in group affairs; *density*—the regularity with which community members are thrown into informal contact with one another; *diversity*—how different those members are from one another; *publicity*, the availability of shared space, information, and resources, open to all, for rendering and resolving difference; and *sovereignty*—the extent to which the community freely governs itself, solves its own problems, makes binding decisions about its own affairs, and determines its own past, present, and future.

What I suggested in chapter 3 was that a community high in both accessibility and diversity—a place small enough to welcome and even invite direct participation by all of its inhabitants in the sovereign decision-making of their community but large enough to actually reveal, elicit, and resolve the differences among them—would be an ideal location for developing and using *rhetoric*. And I suggested that the opposite would also be true: in a large community, individual citizens feel less welcome to participate and have diminished opportunities to raise their voices in public debate. Likewise, in an overly homogeneous community, members might have opportunities to participate in public life but no good reason to do so since there will be so few genuine conflicts to call participation forth. And we could say this about the other variables mentioned above: in a community without sovereignty, for example, vigorous public debate about local issues would be hard to sustain given that it would be so ineffectual.

A cursory review of the literature would lead one to believe that such sociospatial factors *do* have direct and independent influence on our civic relations and rhetorical opportunities. As we have seen, Dahl and Tufte reported strong effects for community size on both citizen effectiveness and system capacity more than thirty years ago.[31] And recently, Oliver found a relationship between community size and heterogeneity, on the one hand, and civic participation rates, on the other: smaller and more diverse communities seem to generate greater public life than do either large or homogeneous ones.[32] In addition, density has been shown to influence the amount and frequency of informal, unplanned contacts we have with others (and in a diverse community, the amount and frequency of contact we have with *different* others).[33]

The one thing that everyone seems to acknowledge about the landscape of contemporary North America is that it is segregated by race and class. And people are increasingly asking, not only whether such segregation is fair, but whether it might contribute to our overall political failure to deal with our differences. For Iris Marion Young, segregation not only limits choice and reproduces structures of advantage and disadvantage, it obscures the very privilege that it creates, encouraging the privileged to think that they do not have the problems that others have and do not need therefore to work with them to solve those problems.[34] Finally, and perhaps most obviously, segregation impedes communication. It limits the encounters we have with one another, exacerbating our mutual distrust and preventing opportunities to learn how we might better share the world we hold in common.

Perhaps the best proof I can offer here that places matter for civic life is that nearly everyone connected to the debate about Cabrini Green agrees that the physical organization of metropolitan Chicago is both cause and effect of intense social fragmentation and polarization, that no one has been hurt more from that arrangement than the region's low-income blacks, and that new ways of allocating social space are needed if we want a more equitable distribution of resources, increased opportunities for political participation and communal self-determination, more chances for diverse peoples to come into healthy contact with one another, more lively, gregarious *commonplaces* where all are welcome and can meet in freedom and equality.[35]

We would have to admit, however, that the effects of place on civic skills and virtues are complex and that any general conclusions about them should be approached with great caution. It is difficult to say, in any given situation, whether a trait like fear of conflict should be ascribed to life experiences, cultural background, the environment, or some combination of those; and even if we could agree that the built environment is an independent variable with causal power, we would still have many questions about it. I have found the approach of Susan Mayer and Christopher Jencks to be helpful here; they argue that the sociospatial environment does indeed affect human outcomes, independent of such variables as income and education, but that the effects are *contingent* (so that, for example, low-income blacks will respond differently to the same environment as low-income whites), *nonlinear* (so that extremely bad environments will be unusually influential on human outcomes, whereas moderately bad environments might not be), and *dynamic* (so that the effect of environment will change over the course of one's life, teenagers, for example, being more susceptible to neighborhood quality than either small children or middle-aged adults).[36] Let us take each of these qualifications in turn.

First, any influence that space has on rhetorical activity and the development of rhetorical habits and dispositions is obviously contingent on a variety of factors. As Kevin Lynch has put it, "One can be miserable in an island paradise and joyful in a slum."[37] So, for example, living on the upper floors of a central city high-rise building has been seen as harmful in the United States,[38] but in Europe such an environment is the preferred way of living for the middle and upper classes.[39] Likewise, the departure of town planning from the grid is something that *both* Cabrini Green and Schaumburg share, but the effects of that departure are very different: in one, it leads to decreased security and chaos; in the other, to increased security and privacy. And anyone who looks at North Town Village will say that design in such a place can only do so much to improve central city living in Chicago if the city does not also improve its public *schools* (though this, of course, depends in part on changes in residential patterns!).

Second, the effect of place on civic powers and habits is likely to be nonlinear: that is, the strongest effects will be at the top and bottom of the curve, where environments are extremely favorable or unfavorable. There might be a lower threshold, for example, beyond which "good" families are not able to compensate for bad neighborhoods. Above that threshold, the influence of a less-than-ideal environment might be offset by, say, parental income or education; but below it, environmental effects will be relatively independent of such variables. Another way to say this: if space matters, it matters most for those with the least.

Third, the effect of environment on human flourishing is likely to change over one's lifespan: researchers have found evidence that environmental influences are greatest during the teenage years, when children are, for the first time, spending large amounts of their time outside of the spaces that have previously shielded and supported them (family, school, church, etc.).[40] This is another reason why I think educators (and especially civic educators at the secondary and tertiary level) should be more involved in and concerned about the design of the built world: because it is so important in what and how our students learn and the kinds of adults they become. Rhetorical education in particular has been historically associated with the teenage years,[41] when children are already basically literate and culturally schooled but now need practice and instruction in taking on fuller roles in the public decision-making of their communities.

Given these caveats, perhaps we should give up on the idea that by *simply* manipulating the environment, we can achieve predetermined social ends: eradicate poverty, foster community, improve human character. Maybe Nathan Glazer was right: we should banish from our thinking "the assumption that the physical form of our community has social consequences."[42] Or maybe, we have just been asking the wrong question, which should be not whether environment changes human nature but whether it affects behavior and especially whether "bad" environments have negative effects on behavior.

> For us, that question is as obvious as asking whether locking a door keeps someone out of a room, or whether creating an environment in which nothing is nearby causes people to drive. One does not have to believe that front porches encourage sociability to accept that unwalkable streets discourage it. . . . Good design may not generate good behavior, but bad design can generate bad behavior.[43]

The virtue of this position, I believe, is that it avoids the environmental utopianism so tempting when looking at places like North Town Village but accepts nonetheless the *responsibility* that should always accompany invention and design in the public sphere.

So if there is no necessary link between environment and happiness—people can be miserable in an island paradise and joyful in a slum—there is, I believe, a clear link between environment and *opportunity*, especially at the negative end of the equation. Poverty researchers have consistently found, for example, that the main problems of the poor are not individual or cultural but *scenic*; put simply, the poor often lack *opportunities* to succeed, and those opportunities turn out to be unevenly distributed in space.

> [P]oor neighborhoods have an independent effect on social and economic outcomes of individuals even after taking account of their personal and family characteristics. . . . Of greatest concern are the

> effects that harsh neighborhood conditions have on children, whose choices in adolescence can have lifelong consequences.[44]

In other words, chronic poverty is caused primarily not by poor people themselves (as if they were born with a poverty gene) or the culture of their families and social groups (as if certain child-rearing practices consigned members to certain fates) but by the poor quality of the environments in which they live: their substandard neighborhood schools, the crime with which they daily battle, the lack of good jobs in their midst, the dearth of middle-class role models, the racial and economic segregation they experience.[45] Now, these things are not themselves *created* by place, as if a particular set of geographical coordinates produces inferior schools or job flight. But devalued places tend to perpetuate their devaluation—a process that Gunnar Myrdal used to refer to as "cumulative causation," the tendency of social differences to widen over time as the effects of a phenomenon like segregation become its cause.[46] The problems that students bring to school, for example, can make school a troubled place; but a troubled school, in turn, can contribute to the difficulties that its children and families experience in life, exacerbating problems already present and creating problems that did not exist before. In this sense, environment exerts an *independent* influence over its inhabitants. The biggest obstacle the poor face in turning their lives around, in other words, may well be the neighborhoods they live in.[47] And the biggest obstacle we all face in more equitably distributing *rhetorical* voice in our society may be the environments in which young people learn to speak, write, listen, read, tells stories, and argue.

So, if the effects of space are contingent, nonlinear, and dynamic, that should not mean that we simply give up on trying to make the world a better place for ourselves and others. By organizing the world in a certain way, we may not be able to guarantee that people will think or act as we would like them to. But we can certainly increase or decrease the opportunities they have to do so, and we can make the distribution of those opportunities, including opportunities to participate in genuinely "strong publics,"[48] more or less equitable in the society at large.

In the next chapter I suggest some ways that we might do that.

NINE

Cities of Rhetoric

> My goal has been to stimulate thinking about how we might replace the urban policy of fragmentation and division with one that can accommodate American diversity. Only if we do, can we, at long last, begin to rebuild what we have for so long sought to eradicate: the variety, temptation, stimulation, challenge, and vitality of city life.
>
> —Gerald Frug, *City Making*

The conclusions of the preceding chapter, if accepted, should leave us in an attitude of profound humility toward the built world. Designing environments that are conducive to human flourishing turns out to be an extremely difficult task. And yet, because our flourishing is so clearly dependent, at least in part, on our surroundings and because those surroundings are so clearly susceptible, at least in part, to our manipulation, we seem fated to keep trying.

This double lesson, combining the *modesty* appropriate to our limited powers with the *hopefulness* that always accompanies design, is one that the ancient Greeks taught as well. It shows up, for example, in one of their favorite myths, a creation story in which the human being starts out as a rather pitiful creature. When the gods distributed their gifts, according to this myth, it was *other* animals who got size, strength, and speed; who were blessed with sturdy hooves, sharp claws, and thick fur; who were granted the ability to soar through the air, glide beneath the waters, burrow underground, and swing from tree to tree.[1] Humans, by contrast, were left naked, unshod, clumsy, and weak. Eventually, of course, the gods realized their mistake and tried to compensate by giving fire to the poor creatures and distributing the practical arts, like carpentry and shoemaking, among them. But this only helped to a degree: bands of men, women, and children still wandered the earth, unsettled and uneasy, at the mercy of nature, chance, other animals, and one another.

Until, that is, someone—whether god or mortal, the accounts differ—had a revolutionary idea: he would gather people together into settlements, into *cities*, where, working side by side, they would build their own world: feeding, clothing, and sheltering themselves more efficiently, and defending themselves more effectively, than ever before. And once people had learned the arts and virtues of city life—once, that is, they had acquired justice and respect, politics and rhetoric—they began to prosper, both as individuals and collectives. In time, the city became humans' chief competitive advantage over nature, chance, and other animals, as well as the home of civilization itself: of music, poetry, art, commerce, athletics, drama, religion, science, and law. As we saw in chapter 1, Aristotle went so far as to make living in a free city and sharing in its rule the distinguishing feature of the entire species.[2]

Clearly, the city so seen was not simply (as we would have it) a *place*; it was also a *people*, bound together by shared ancestors, values, customs, institutions, and language: "You are . . . a city," said Nicias to the Athenians, "wherever you sit down."[3] But if the polis for the Greeks was something more than place, it was a place nonetheless. We are creatures, after all, with bodies, no matter how exalted the intellectual, social, and spiritual lives we lead; and the success of our communities depends as much on our physical situation in the world as on our relations with one another, time, and so on. The Greeks well knew, for example, that the wonders of the city were dependent, at least in part, on the raw materials produced in the hinterland. And, despite his disclaimers about place-based notions of citizenship,[4] Aristotle incorporated ideas about size and disposition of territory in his theory of the good regime.[5] He thought that democracies should be located on flat ground, for example, and described how best to lay out their streets and divide up their spaces.[6] And he made explicit recommendations about the size of his polis, arguing, as we saw in chapter 3, that it should not be so large that its citizens can't know one another's character[7] nor so small that it would be like a household, ruled by fiat rather than deliberation, which for Aristotle required a plurality of free and equal voices.[8]

Two and a half millennia later, we are still—as individuals, groups, and species—dependent on our cities. And those cities are still fundamentally *physical* entities: ways of organizing public and private space, systems for allocating and delivering material resources, scenes of mutual sustenance and even flourishing. The fact is that our individual and social needs have not changed substantially since the time of the Greeks. We still need, each of us, an immense array of basic goods that are nearly always in short supply, or at least difficult to provide affordably to all: clean air and water, nutritious food, and decent shelter, to say nothing of privacy, rest, security, exercise, laughter, friends, work, and love.

Meeting these basic human needs is especially pressing for the most vulnerable among us—the young, sick, poor, oppressed, old, different, and troubled. For them, just having clean shelter in a safe place can be the foundation on which everything else in their lives rests, from their mental and physical health on. Unfortunately, in the United States, despite the fifty-year-old promise of the federal government to ensure "a decent home and a suitable living environment for every American family,"[9] we have not done well at making sure that all of us have adequate, affordable housing in safe neighborhoods. Although we have a history, albeit mixed, of guaranteeing retirement benefits, unemployment assistance, food stamps, and basic education to all, we have never committed ourselves to ensuring even minimal housing for everyone in this country. Yet without a decent place to live, *no one* can secure the others things they need to survive, let alone flourish. Housing is, in this sense, prior to everything else. And the private economy can no more provide housing for all than it can meet the universal need for education, health care, and employment. The simple fact is that adequate, affordable housing, in safe neighborhoods, for all of us, should be a much higher public priority than it currently is.

Now, it is said by some that we cannot afford to subsidize any more housing for low- and moderate-income families in this country, especially on valuable central city land. But we are already heavily subsidizing, in innumerable ways, the building of middle- and upper-income suburban housing across the United States. In fact, over the course of the last century, federal, state, and local governments have literally sponsored (through zoning laws, tax policies, distribution of government services, highway construction, etc.) the suburbanization of the American landscape and the decline of our central cities.[10] We should, for starters, then, provide as much public support for cities and their residents as we currently do for suburbs and theirs.

But designing for people is not just about ensuring decent housing for the poor and disadvantaged; it is about designing for human beings in general. After all, we *all* have bodies; and none of those bodies, I would argue, is well served by the way we currently organize our sociospatial environment. We have seen in this book how dangerous, unhealthy, and unpromising so many of our low-income neighborhoods are; but, in fact, even our most prestigious residential spaces leave much to be desired from a human point of view. Many affluent suburbs, for example, are places where few people ever walk, where difference is rarely encountered, where children grow up thinking that the private automobile is the only legitimate means of transportation and the single-family detached home, the only truly human residence.[11]

To design for human beings is to design at a human scale; to help those humans be *near* one another, their jobs, schools, parks, shopping centers, and "third places,"[12] like libraries and cafes, where they can meet; to build communities that can be walked by creatures made for walking; to accommodate their need for privacy and intimacy but also acknowledge their desire to see and hear, to be seen and heard by, others. To design for human beings, in other words, is to design for the human body, that body's physical and mental needs, the social contact it craves, and the variety it desires. And it is to do this for *everybody*.[13]

But we also need to think about the kinds of *public* spheres that will support and sustain such creatures, places where people can interact not just with their family and friends but also with those "strange" others on whom they depend for the maintenance of their shared world. We need spaces, that is, where we can think and act not just as private individuals—as family members, friends, workers, shareholders, customers, and clients—but as *citizens* who are irreducibly different from one another but equally responsible for, and equally free to participate in, the governance of what we hold in common. As we saw with North Town Village, even when we design environments that promote greater social contact, something is often still missing from our communities: a genuinely *public* sphere where we can come together not just as fellow consumers or coreligionists or individuals with shared hobbies but as *equals* to talk about what belongs to all of us and render and resolve the differences that so easily divide us. We are rarely called on to participate in such a sphere, to talk with people not connected to us by bonds of blood, interest, or affinity, to participate with them in binding decision-making about public problems, and to remain together even when those decisions do not fully satisfy us. And we have too rarely considered that this kind of activity requires open, accessible, safe common spaces where we can gather to learn about and discuss our shared problems, where we always belong but where others always belong as well.

Designing such spaces means acknowledging, however, that each of us belongs to multiple publics at once; and that "publicity" can never be reduced to a single place, procedure, or criterion. People need access to a whole network of layered and interconnected publics to represent the many groups of which they are members, all (ideally) democratically governed to one degree or another. As Dahl and Tufte put it thirty years ago:

> Today and in the foreseeable future, people will live in a multiplicity of political units. Because democratic theorists, with notable exceptions, have focused on the problem of democratizing one sovereign unit—first the city, then the nation-state—they have overlooked the problem of democratizing a political system that consists of a collection of interacting units ranging from small primary associations in which direct democracy is at least theoretically possible to larger entities in which direct citizen rule is impossible. Rather than conceiving of democracy as located in a particular kind of inclusive, sovereign unit, we must learn to conceive of democracy spreading through a set of interrelated political systems, sometimes though

> not always arranged like Chinese boxes, the smaller nesting in the larger. The central theoretical problem is no longer to find suitable rules, like the majority principle, to apply within a sovereign unit, but to find suitable rules to apply among a variety of units, none of which is sovereign.[14]

Our political identities, theories, and practices should acknowledge, in other words, that we belong to multiple, overlapping public spheres. We need to recognize this multiplicity and help our young people understand and operate effectively within it.

That does not mean, however, that all publics are the same. They differ, as I argued in chapter 3, along several dimensions, and we need to think carefully about the implications of these differences and about the relative suitability of various publics for the different social projects we pursue. I claimed, for example, that our nearly all-consuming focus on the nation-state in U.S. civic education and our consequent neglect of city-based politics, including those at the metropolitan and district levels, have been harmful to us as a people.

In questioning the balance of power among the different publics in our political landscape, I am not alone. Others have argued recently, for example, that we need more powerful *regional* governments in the United States, sovereign entities that would encompass entire metropolitan areas, including central cities and all their suburbs, and be better equipped to work across the local boundaries that often divide us.[15] The logic of regionalism has merit; this book, in fact, has been very much about seeing the United States, and its educational system, through a specifically metropolitan lens, about devolving to regions some of the power we currently reserve for states but also about not allowing affluent suburbanites in those regions to wall themselves off from their neighbors, especially their central city neighbors, and perpetuate their privilege by excluding everything that threatens their property values, tax revenues, or homogeneous schools. Anything we can do to limit the decentralization, fragmentation, and polarization of our sociospatial landscape is good; and if creating and empowering metropolitan governments will achieve that, I am all for it.

But if regionalism makes sense for some projects, like equalizing school funding, it makes less sense for others. For the development and exercise of healthy *rhetorical* skills, for example, the metropolis is just too big. We need smaller publics where individual citizens can feel that they belong, publics they know and understand, where they are themselves known and understood, and where they have a reasonable chance of participating, regularly and directly, in the governance of a world that is dear to them. By this logic, of course, we should be privileging, in both our political procedures and curricula, *very* small publics, neighborhood-size polities where our voice can always be heard and we are surrounded by people who know, recognize, and value us—people literally *familiar* with us. David Brooks has argued that, whether we like it or not, Americans prefer such places to other kinds of social settings.[16] And even Iris Marion Young has defended certain kinds of intimate, homogeneous communities on the grounds that they satisfy our basic human need for "safe havens," places where we are shielded from the tensions and animosities that often characterize society in general.[17]

Unfortunately, small publics often lack the conflict that prompts healthy political and rhetorical interaction to begin with, and they typically lack the resources to actually solve the problems that most trouble their members. For some observers, in fact, they are simply anachronistic; Robert Halpern, for example, has claimed that our desire for local empowerment is nostalgic and irrational; the forces controlling us, he writes, are almost all national and global in scale, and it is quixotic to think that local governments, of whatever size, can resist them.[18] As we have seen here, the federalism of the U.S. national constitution, in which all power resides in the central and state governments, actually *proscribes* sovereignty for cities and regions.[19]

Even the nation-state is probably too small these days. After all, humans now inhabit a single global public in which all are interconnected and every action has unpredictably wide repercussions.[20] But there are many things to keep in mind when gauging the political implications of globalization: for example, that ordinary individuals should be able, as a matter of principle, to freely, actively, regularly, and *directly* participate in the political decision-making that most concerns them; that public problems, however extensive in cause or effect, are probably best approached from *multiple* directions, with due consideration for local customs and resources; that large publics, however powerful and inclusive, can be slow, ineffective, and impersonal; and that smaller, more agile publics are sometimes needed to complement them. The great paradox of contemporary globalization, in fact, is that it has opened up so many new *local* spaces for the agency of individuals and groups. Advanced societies are said to depress opportunities for participating in political decision-making; but, according to Mark Warren:

> [A]s societies become more complex, individuals find themselves inhabiting multiple and pluralistic roles for which traditional identities are unsuited. Under these circumstances, new identities must be generated by individuals themselves. Moreover, the performance of complex institutions increasingly requires that identities be discursively negotiated, which in turn requires appropriate institutional spaces. In political language, this means that democratic empowerment [. . .] is increasingly necessary for modern societies to function.[21]

There is nothing inconsistent, in other words, with encouraging among us a political identity that is simultaneously cosmopolitan *and* civic, responsible to our "world brothers and sisters"[22] *and* to people and places nearby.

We should probably, then, abandon all zero-sum theories of political authority, in which power gravitates to one or a few places and leaves all the rest enfeebled. Sovereignty turns out to be a generous entity, like the sun; attaining its benefits need not mean less for others. We should design our political system, therefore, to have *multiple* centers, each one relatively empowered *and* relatively constrained to deal with the problems that affect it most.[23]

And yet, given our historical tendency to privilege the very small and very large, the face-to-face primary group, on the one hand, and the maximally diverse cosmos, on the other, middle-size publics like the city may need special attention and care from us. These are publics that are unusually conducive, I believe, to the development of civic virtue in ourselves and others because, at their best, they mediate the conflicting values of accessibility and diversity, allowing individuals opportunities for both voice and edification, chances to participate directly in communal self-government but to encounter meaningful differences along the way. That is why I have had so much to say here about the *urban district*, a public with (prototypically speaking) a medium-sized population (50,000–100,000), settled in a medium-size space (e.g., 1,000 acres), with, ideally, both a coherent identity (its own history and traditions, natural and artificial features, schools, etc.) and substantial internal diversity (of people, structures, uses, etc.). It is a political sphere located between the neighborhood, on the one hand, and the state, on the other—between, that is, the community of the like-minded and the society of laws. If provided meaningful decision-making authority, such places can allow ordinary people, perhaps for the first time in their lives, to have a real voice in a free and open public where genuine disagreements are rendered and resolved.

Now, such publics probably need their own kind of political practice, one distinct from both the spectatorial procedures of representative democracies and the private government of residential community associations, systems we examined in chapter 3 under the headings "nation-state" and "neighborhood." They would need, I believe, something like what Archon Fung and Erik Olin Wright call "empowered participatory governance," a political practice motivated by three principles—a focus on specific, tangible problems; the direct involvement of ordinary people and officials close to those problems; and the use of deliberative problem-solving techniques[24]—and supported by three design features—the devolution of decision authority to local groups, decentralized coordination across those groups, and new state institutions to support and oversee them.[25]

Democratic reforms structured along these lines can produce demonstrable gains not only in terms of political participation but also in terms of equity and effectiveness. But perhaps the key benefit of such publics, from the point of view of this book, is the kind of human relationship they both entail and sponsor, the close contact of individuals who are neither intimates nor strangers; people who have a concrete social connection with one another but are not necessarily "friends." Such people are fellow *citizens* in a very real sense, and their political relationship—exemplified, for me at least, by the intense but limited interactions of the jury—is a neglected kind of social relationship that, I believe, has enormous and far-reaching developmental consequences. To work closely with people who are manifestly different from you but who nonetheless share your world and the responsibility for governing it is to see both how interconnected we all are and how irreducibly distinct. It is to realize that we need not *be* the same to *have* things in common and that we need not always *agree* on those things in order to *keep* them in common. And it is to have a full public life to complement the private ones we already have—to be able to think and argue with others about issues that affect everyone in the community and, through discourse, to reach binding decisions together about those issues.

The great tragedy of our contemporary political system is that most of us grow up without ever being members of such publics and without ever developing the kinds of skills and virtues rewarded there. Accompanying any new plans for the physical reorganization of the human landscape, in other words, must be new opportunities for the inhabitants of that landscape to work together, directly and regularly, in formal, official, "strong publics" of decision-making. This is what I meant in the Preface when I described the revitalization of civic life in this country as a necessarily *unified* project. We need to not only design and build new concrete public spheres capable of literally grounding our political interconnectedness; we also need new public institutions and practices that can enable the free and equal citizens who meet in those spheres to effectively and responsibly enact their political will together.

But we need something else as well: a new way of thinking and talking about politics that can help us live nonviolently with diverse others and see that cohabitation as natural, even desirable. We need, that is, new "public philosophies"[26] that pay equal attention to our plurality *and* our unity, our undeniable bonds *and* our inevitable conflicts—theories of everyday political life that can help us appreciate our commonalities even as we confront our differences.

This is clearly a tall order. We are a culture of extraordinary diversity that is becoming more and more diverse everyday; and yet, even in our most enlightened moments, we still envision our differences as either a reason to separate or an accident to be transcended by some overarching (but usually superficial) unity. As we have seen in this book, we have not yet succeeded in imagining, let alone building, a world where our conflicts are actually and literally *faced*, seen as part of who we are: a diverse people who live together, despite and even through our differences.

I do not go so far here as John Dewey, who wrote three-quarters of a century ago that "the problem of a democratically organized public is primarily and essentially an intellectual problem,"[27] but I do believe that how we think and talk about these issues turns out to be as crucial as how we plan and build our physical surroundings. The fact is that we don't really know how to live with our differences; we do not even know how to talk responsibly about them; and if the solution to that ignorance is partly environmental—new designs and policies that bring us together without assimilating us to one another—it is also partly educational—new pedagogies that can develop in us the habits and dispositions of nonviolent coexistence.

In other words, questions about setbacks and TIF districts, urban grids and income mixes, are irrelevant if we also lack a theory of public life that can motivate truly democratic relations among us, an image of the good community that can bring us, literally and figuratively, together. As it is, the very language of civic community used in this country makes it difficult for us to plan and build a public world here. In my research on Cabrini Green, I detected at least three linguistic obstacles to our building the kind of civic culture envisioned in this book.

First, in debates and discussions about community, Americans consistently privilege mobility over stability. By that, I do not mean simply that we see ourselves as a nation of movers, a people constantly shuttling in and out of social (and other) situations; I mean that we assume this mobility even when we are trying to develop *places* of all things. The best example of that here was North Town Village, whose plan was based on the perceived need to attract residents who could live elsewhere. The result is a community that often seems to be built on sand, a place designed to ignore those most likely to stay and appeal to those most likely to leave.[28] The proposal for 1230 North Burling Street was just the opposite, being all about physical and temporal continuity, about supporting those residents who had lived on the Near North Side the longest, who had suffered there the most and whose roots were the deepest, and allowing them to *stay*. Unfortunately, that language of depth turns out to be surprisingly uncommon in discourses about city-building. In general, our political philosophies and pedagogies—to say nothing of our economic policies—privilege the mobile subject: he or she whose skills and habits foster a radical disattachment from particular local worlds. This may be a useful strategy for making oneself employable in the global economy; but for the design and maintenance of the good city, we need residents who are more fully situated in place, willing to develop social ties, grow roots, and establish reliable allegiances to place and people. On this score, Chicago's public housing families are way ahead of the rest of us. For them, mobility is almost always a fraught condition, a sign of rootlessness and insecurity—which is why the so-called renewal of central Chicago raises so many suspicions among that city's poorest residents: because, for them, "revitalization" has too often meant displacement, relocation, and homelessness.

A second way that our language creates obstacles for building genuine "publicity" in the metropolitan areas, cities, and urban districts of this country is that we routinely associate political position with self-interest. When we imagine civic involvement, in other words, we too often imagine the autonomous individual fighting for his or her rights.[29] It is easy to see how such a discourse would leave us with insufficiently thick ties to one another and the communities we share. To sustain a more broad-based public sphere, we need to learn to speak a language in which political positions are by definition relational, and the general interest is as compelling a value in our debates and deliberations as self-interest. A healthy public sphere in this view would involve a large number of diverse members unified by what they share even when their points of view on that shared thing are different, a sphere that is never so large that its members are not always personally committed to it or so diverse that they cannot literally see their interconnections.[30] The public interest I am describing here is well captured by something former Missoula, Montana mayor Daniel Kemmis once wrote about Athens: democracy took root and flourished there because its citizens taught themselves to act and speak "as if they cared more about Athens than they cared about winning."[31]

Finally, we lack a language that recognizes and celebrates *conflict* and imagines ways of dealing with that conflict that do not involve assimilation or separation. This third linguistic consideration is crucial because the second is often interpreted as favoring communities that absorb, even tyrannize, the individual; the Kemmis quote above, in fact, comes close to expressing what is most discomfiting about communitarianism for many theorists. We need to temper our appeals to the public interest, then, with an acknowledgment and even celebration of conflict. And this is where *rhetoric* can be helpful because it provides a theory and pedagogy of political life in which disagreement, debate, and conflict—as well as uncertainty, doubt, confusion, ignorance, and contingency—are the central facts of our social existence, *not* an excuse for us to break up into "communities" or throw our hands up in the face of the problems attendant on living together in the real world. Conflict, from this point of view, is the very basis of our union; and the rendering and resolving of conflict is the means by which, paradoxically, we stay together. Conflict is also, of course, a source of tension and discomfort, which may be why contemporary North America culture seems so often to be conflict-averse.[32] But unless we learn to see conflict as inevitable and even valuable, it will be hard for us to build a thriving public sphere on the Near North Side of Chicago—or anywhere else for that matter.[33]

So, we need to learn a language of civic life that privileges depth over mobility, publicity over self-interest, and conflict over harmony. If developing such a language will be difficult given the "habits of our heart"[34]—and the fragmented and polarized condition of our built world—the benefits of having such a discourse available to us will make the effort, I believe, worthwhile.

I would like to end this chapter by thinking about how public schools might participate in the project just described, how a revitalized civic education might be part of a broader place-based reform of our society. Now, we saw in chapter 3 how political and rhetorical education in this country have been organized for more than a century now from the point of view of the nation-state and how that scene has tended to promote a spectatorial conception of public life among its residents, who are invited to consume and express their opinions about the affairs of the nation but not to actively participate in its actual, day-to-day decision-making. The question is, what would an education look like that was designed to support a truly direct, deliberative democracy?

In simplest terms, it would be, I believe, a fundamentally *civic* (that is, literally city-based) education, adapted to the practical and ethical demands of living with others in an open, free, diverse, relatively sovereign, but always accessible community—large, dense, and heterogeneous, but also known, lived in, and loved. It would be an education well-suited for a public small enough to encourage and reward the active participation of ordinary people in its governance but large enough to possess the diversity—and power—to make that governance matter. It would be an education oriented to the "strong publics" of decision-making rather than the "weak publics" of opinion formation.[35]

But what would that mean in everyday pedagogical terms? It would mean, I believe, that our schools need to do a better job of practicing our young people in using language to effectively, responsibly, and publicly render their experiences, values, and opinions. But, it would also mean—what is less well done in contemporary political education—practicing them in the arts of listening to and understanding the experiences, values, and opinions of others. And, finally, it would mean—what may be the most neglected civic art of all—giving them practice in responsibly *resolving* the conflicts that arise from the interaction of these different experiences, values, and opinions. It would mean helping young people learn to share a common world with equally free but irreducibly different others and not to use those differences as an excuse for alienation, assimilation, or worse.

We need in our schools, that is, a rhetoric oriented neither to personal expression nor victory in debate but to reasoning with others about shared problems, an art that is as much about listening and learning as talking and persuasion, and which is useful not just for rendering but also for resolving our differences, however provisionally, contingently, and imperfectly. This would be a departure for rhetorical education, which has often, I believe, overemphasized opinion expression—as if the point of developing public discourse skills were to see who could speak and write the clearest, loudest, and most passionately. Fortunately, rhetorical theories of the last several decades have begun to pursue more dialogic imperatives in public discourse, promoting arguments that not only find adherents because they are persuasive, but that tolerate, even generate, alternative arguments precisely because they are couched in language that makes them accessible, reasonable, even refutable, to others.[36] Such theories have been less helpful, however, in teaching us to work *beyond* dialogue and conflict, to reason with our interlocutors toward the decisions that *end* dialogue and conflict (however provisionally), that allow actual communities to actually resolve (however contingently) the problems they face without literally coming apart. This third level of argumentation, the management of conflict beyond claim-making, on the one hand, and dialogue, on the other, is difficult to stage; but it may be the practice most needed in the democratic polities envisioned here.

The full development of these skills and dispositions can only take place, of course, in the actual neighborhood, district, municipal, and metropolitan assemblies, councils, juries, boards, and committees that would govern the political landscape described in this book. But there is still a place, I believe, for *school* in helping future citizens acquire these practices. For one thing, schools are nearly inescapable in transmitting to children and young adults the *substantive* political knowledge they need about their world, its people, history, and customs, as well as knowledge about the other political communities they are members of and those which it would be helpful for them to know something about. By "substantive" knowledge, I mean here the formal content that schools are especially adept at providing—facts, laws, procedures, and so forth—as well as the informal knowledge about a community's beliefs, habits, and problems that is perhaps best learned through stories, case studies, and projects. There is obviously overlap here with what Vico called a civil education: "simply growing up as part of a city's life, coming to know its streets and its buildings, learning its language and its lore, its history and its ways, and in time being trained in its schools, especially in the company of one's peers. There is nothing . . . that can instruct one better in that *sensus communis*, which is the norm of all prudence and eloquence."[37]

Students also need of course to develop the *skills* of deliberative democratic politics: how to listen well to others; ask good questions; locate resources; summarize facts; evaluate evidence; consider alternative interpretations of that evidence; make coherent claims; support those claims with reasons; acknowledge counterarguments and rebut, concede, or integrate them with one's own arguments; effectively introduce and conclude one's remarks; adapt discourse to audience, occasion, and purpose; and so on. This is the *procedural* knowledge citizens need in order to participate effectively and responsibly in their publics. Such knowledge comes through normal social and cognitive development, as well as trial and error; but it can also be acquired in formal situations: by working with experienced partners and teachers who prompt, encourage, coach, model, and evaluate as well as provide occasional direct instruction.[38]

Finally, besides substantive and procedural knowledge, young people preparing to take on full civic roles in their local publics need to acquire the *dispositions* of direct, deliberative democracy itself. Here, I am thinking about the kinds of values that encourage us to talk and listen to one another in the first place and to see that activity as normal, productive, even pleasurable. Without such values, people will believe that political conflicts are best resolved by appealing to expertise, authority, or tradition; or by simply aggregating individual preferences; or by calling on the state's police power to uphold one set of interests and quash all others. So, we need to pay attention not just to *what* people know about politics and *how* they use language and reason to understand and manage their disagreements, but also to whether or not they even *value* the practices I have been describing here. Reflection on these values is an undeniable responsibility of our public schools.[39]

Let me briefly suggest four projects in "civic" education that I believe can help students acquire the political knowledge, skills, and dispositions described above.

1. *Memory*: Civic discourse is about more than just arguing positions and making decisions; it also involves learning about one's community and its members. And this includes learning not just about its present makeup and problems but also about its past: memorializing its former residents and long-ago events, uncovering its lost histories and forgotten conflicts, and asking questions about how it has come to be the way it is. Listening to and telling stories about one's own world, stories often hidden from us and at risk of never being told, is not only a rich and powerful way to learn about one's community, it is also a way to make history itself come alive for young people. Take, for example, the stories Doria Dee Johnson has told about her great-great-grandfather, Anthony Crawford, a 1916 southern lynching victim,[40] stories that are also very much about a particular place—Abbeville, South Carolina—that had not publicly *remembered* Johnson's ancestors very well before she began conducting her research. I wonder why we do not more often ask our students today to elicit such stories from themselves and others and reconstruct similar moments in their community's past. It is sad how little we know about our own histories, about the histories of our own families and fellows, about the histories of our own cities; and it is remarkable how powerful such knowledge can be in helping us better understand the present and build together a more just future.

2. *Mapping*: One of the biggest problems students have in producing their own "public" discourse is that they do not know enough about what they

are writing and speaking about. The projects in collective memory described above would go some distance in correcting that situation, giving students a deeper and more concrete historical sense regarding their own communities; but students also need practice in researching the *present*, in observing, recording, interrogating, theorizing, and understanding the world around them. Just as jurors need to learn everything they can about the cases they decide, future citizens need to learn to inquire closely, accurately, and responsibly into the way things are, amassing information about the public issues they are called on to adjudicate. The century-old research conducted by Jane Addams and her colleagues in Chicago's tenement neighborhoods, collected in *Hull House Maps and Papers*, remains inspirational in this regard.[41] Evident there is the immense argumentative power that comes from closely and fearlessly *surveying* one's world. Just to take one small but potentially rich contemporary example: researchers in Madison, Wisconsin, have mapped the location of grocery stores in that town and have been able to show, visually and verbally, the dramatic inequality of access to nutritious food there,[42] a fact of lived local life that is surprisingly invisible to so many of us so much of the time but which could be profitably revealed to young people by simply inviting them to pay attention to their own cities, look around, ask questions, and take notes. Unfortunately, "research" in our schools, especially outside of the sciences, remains today an inert, derivative, and abstract affair, usually conducted by students working alone in libraries and on the internet. We need to turn our students loose in their communities, encouraging them to uncover what usually goes unseen, develop hypotheses, and account for what they see and hear.

3. *Judgment*: The democratic politics I have focused on in this book are about more than just opinion consumption and formation; they are also about deliberating and decision making among free equals in sovereign but accessible communities. The best example we have of such politics remains, I believe, jury deliberations. In fact, the jury room may be the only place in the contemporary public sphere where ordinary people, working in groups of their peers, make binding decisions about important and complex problems in the world around them. And yet, the jury is largely (and inexplicably) absent from our educational system, where preparing young people to serve in decision-making groups is so far from a prominent developmental objective that we might as well say the schools are hostile to it. In my own teaching, mock jury deliberations play an important role in helping young people acquire the knowledge, skills, and dispositions of civic discourse. In such classrooms, students work together on "real" cases (reading documents, writing summaries, weighing arguments, developing opinions, debating among themselves), render collaborative judgments on those cases, and reflect on their practices in doing so.[43]

4. *Design*: In addition to learning about the history of their communities, deepening their knowledge of the present, and practicing decision making in

groups of peers, students need to develop skills in inventing, planning, and building solutions to the problems they face. They need exercises, that is, in collaborative *design*, working with their fellow citizens to reflectively define the problems they share, invent creative, feasible solutions to those problems, and honestly and critically evaluate progress in implementing those solutions. If the pedagogies of public discourse in this country have been too often too abstract—mere words about decontextualized ideas uttered from the remove of the classroom—the educational projects envisioned here must be practical through and through. The political problems explored by students should be very much the problems of their own *city*, and the solution to those problems should be articulated through design of some kind, through plans that contemplate the actual betterment of their world.

Our schools, in other words, can accomplish a great deal in democratic community-building, even independent of the reforms laid out in the previous chapter; and I hope the brief remarks above suggest how we might reimagine public education in this country to serve the democratic goals described in this book. But just as we need to make our schools more *civic*, more oriented toward and devoted to the cities in which they are situated, we need to make our *cities* more educational, more edifying to the people who live and interact in them. That is because, as important as formal schooling is in the acquisition of genuinely civic knowledge, skills, and dispositions, it pales next to society itself, next to the "real world" where our children and young adults develop as citizens.

Our cities already educate us, of course, by their layout and design: they teach us today, for example, that social conflicts are best managed by physical separation and that the way to deal with our differences is for us to live and work in different parts of the landscape. But cities can teach other lessons as well. They can teach us that we hold the world in common, that our different points of view on that common world are inevitable and even useful, and that if we devote some of our shared time and space to regularly meeting as free equals to deliberate openly and fairly about our differences, we might learn to make good decisions about our commonalities.

Take ancient Athens. Moses Finley has argued that although the classical polis did very little to *formally* teach its young—there was nothing like what we would call public schooling there—its ordinary citizens were nonetheless very well educated.[44] Some of that *paideia* came from listening to the stories of the poets, attending the theater, participating in shared rituals, and so forth. But young Athenians also learned about their city by participating in its everyday politics, in the open structures of decision-making that the city had developed to promote its security and prosperity and protect its citizens' freedom and equality. In such a society

> [I]t was perfectly valid to call the basic institutions of the community—the family, the dining-club, the gymnasium, the Assembly—agencies for education. A young man was educated by attending the Assembly; he learned not necessarily the size of the island of Sicily . . . but the political issues facing Athens, the choices, the arguments, and he learned to assess the men who put themselves forward as policy-makers, as leaders. There was thus continuing contact from childhood with public life: hence, given the extension of political rights to peasants, craftsmen and shopkeepers, there was a larger element of political education in the process of growing up than in most other societies before or since. It was inherent in the system.[45]

And this political education involved more than just attendance at the assembly. In any decade in the fifth and fourth centuries, BCE, according to Finley, between a fourth and a third of the total Athenian citizenry over thirty would have been members of the executive council (or *boulé*), serving daily through the year as councilors and for a tenth of the year as "presidents."[46] Given the range and importance of council business, says Finley, we are right in calling such a body a veritable "school of democracy."[47] Add to this the thousands who had court experience and the hundreds of magistrates, also selected by lot, and "the idea of a multitude deciding from ignorance melts away."[48]

In the nineteenth century, John Stuart Mill concluded that this kind of public duty "raised the intellectual standard of the average citizen beyond anything known since. He was called upon to weigh interests not his own, to be guided, in case of conflicting claims, by another rule than his private partialities."[49] This is perhaps the ultimate compliment we could pay to a city: that it is not only a stage for our freedom, equality, security, prosperity, and happiness, but that it also makes us better people. "*Polis andra didaskei*," said Simonides: "The city teaches us."[50]

What lessons do we learn from our cities today? Can they be refashioned to impart *better* lessons to our children and our children's children? I hope the answers offered in this book can be of use as the twenty-first century unfolds.

TEN

Afterword

> The Congress declares that the general welfare and security of the Nation and the health and living standards of its people require . . . the realization as soon as feasible of the goal of a decent home and a suitable living environment for every American family.
>
> —U.S. Housing Act of 1949 (as amended)

Even before September 11, 2001, housing had begun to disappear as an issue in the public life of the United States. Despite soaring costs and other problems, it was becoming invisible in national political debates. One observer, for example, called 1996, the "year that housing died," after an especially precipitous drop in federal funding.[1] Regardless of why this happened—because public housing was by then considered a failed experiment by most Americans, because of the rise of a postentitlement mentality among the population in general, because of the increasing dominance of discourses of mobility in our society, or because of the continuing "secession of the affluent" into their own communities—we seem increasingly unable to treat our embodied lives together, our literal cohabitation of space, as a legitimate and important topic of public talk. That is a shame because recent years have seen only growing diversity in our metropolitan areas, rising economic and social inequality in society at large, and increasingly obvious problems associated with our increasingly centrifugal settlement patterns.

And since September 11, 2001, problems like urban poverty, suburban sprawl, residential racial segregation, and geographically based income inequality have been pushed almost completely off the national radar screen. The enormity of that event, combined with the subsequent wars in Afghanistan and Iraq and the leadership of a president who was probably not much interested in domestic policy to begin with, have meant that our most pressing social and physical problems have gone largely unattended and undiscussed. Hurricane Katrina in 2005 exposed the environmental plight of America's urban poor, especially its minority urban poor; and the immediate aftermath of that tragedy brought issues of housing, urban design, and community development to the fore, at least for a few weeks. But the attention was too little, too late, and, by mid-2006, already seemed to have waned.

The neglect of domestic public life under this administration has been doubly unfortunate because, first, urban poverty and homelessness in this country have actually worsened while our attention was focused elsewhere; and, second, the exorbitant cost of our new international adventures has made fixing those problems even more difficult than before since more and more of an increasingly tight budget must now be devoted to military spending, foreign aid, and the national defense.

My point in this book has *not* been that we should not think globally, that we should not be always intensely aware of the rest of the world and our place in it, both as individuals and as communities. As I have tried to suggest here, considering more carefully our metropolitan lives together and thinking more creatively about our civic responsibilities to one another is not about simply shifting our political allegiance from one public to another, from the globe or nation-state to the city or urban district; it is rather about developing and protecting the full, multilayered set of publics in which we are always already embedded, as well as being able to distinguish among those different publics in terms of which projects they are best equipped to sponsor. That said, I believe that we suffer in general from an impoverished "middle-range" of public activity in our society, *between* community and society, neighborhood and nation. And that is why I have had so much to say here about our cities, their metropolitan surroundings, and internal districts.

When we turn our gaze to such places, what we find is that, first, too many of their residents cannot afford to live in "a decent home and suitable living environment," to use the words of the 1949 Housing Act; and, second, there is continuing, even accelerating, movement toward socioeconomic fragmentation and polarization in our society. In the 1990s, there was some improvement in urban poverty in this country: less concentration, rising employment, and so on. But those years saw an especially good economy and, comparatively speaking, a liberal federal government; and even under those favorable conditions, the gains in civic welfare in the United States were in most cases quite small, typically only bringing the country back to 1970s levels. What is worse, the last few years have seen a reversal in whatever gains there were in the 1990s, with rising unemployment, increasing numbers of individuals and families without health insurance, scarcer affordable housing, higher rates of poverty, a "meaner" national government.

Unfortunately, most of our solutions to the problems of social inequality remain individualistic and private. No publics will help us, we are told: we just need more private enterprise, individual initiative, and mobility of both capital and labor, strategies which, I am afraid, will only exacerbate the segregation and alienation of both our lives and our landscape. The most prominent alternative to such privatism has been a vague call to "community," a hope that we might somehow sublimate our differences by appealing to the shared human experiences that transcend them. We continue, that is, to be afraid of our diversity and to imagine that the most progressive response to social alienation is its opposite—a melding of disparate experiences into unity. We lack attractive models of public life *between* fragmentation and harmony, separation and togetherness; and we lack the concrete *places* where such middle grounds can be nurtured, as well as the language that would help us recognize them for what they are.

What has happened with the three options for metropolitan Chicago that we examined in part 2 of this book? Well, the Gautreaux program is now officially over: in fact, it ended before the recent demolition frenzy in Chicago forced thousands of public housing families out of their longtime homes and into uncertain futures. By the end of 2006, it is estimated, all the high rises at both Robert Taylor and Cabrini Green will be gone; and what is being built in their place does not even come close to housing the numbers that once lived in those buildings. Where have those families gone? The answers are not reassuring.

The latest statistics on Schaumburg, meanwhile, show that it is still racially and economically segregated. Metropolitan inequality in Chicago, and elsewhere in the United States, persists and even grows. The suburbs are *not* the key to our future together.

At North Town Village, the much vaunted "Storytelling Project" was dropped before the development even opened its doors, and most of the attempts at social integration there are now confined to leisure activities: fieldtrips to the skating rink, Halloween parades, wine and cheese parties. Financially, the community is a huge success, and now the model for the much larger Parkside of Old Town rising nearby. But the real winners here, I believe, are the white childless couples who have scored cheaper housing than they would have found in Lincoln Park and are even closer to the Loop.

As for 1230 North Burling Street, on June 9, 2003, the Chicago Housing Authority fired the entire RMC and transferred management of the high-rise to an outside contractor. That building will now be demolished with the rest of the Cabrini Green "reds" and "whites." The journey of those remarkable women and their volunteer security patrol has now come to an end. The CHA cited a failed inspection at the building, apparently involving exposed electrical wires, uncovered garbage chutes, and unlighted common areas. Resident leaders and local activists, on the other hand, were convinced that the housing authority simply wanted to remove a potentially troublesome obstacle to more gentrification in this part of the city.

All that is a shame. Central city neighborhoods like the Near North Side of Chicago remain our most promising spaces for what Michael Sorkin calls "authentic urbanity," spheres of human sociality based on physical proximity, free movement, and a desire for collectivity.[2] What we are left with—the social and physical separation of groups and the increasing polarization among them—is bad for the poor and powerless, bad for the rich and powerful, bad for all of us and the earth we live on. To bring us closer together, physically and discursively, we will need to devote ourselves much more vigorously to building healthy, strong, diverse publics. And *that* will require, I believe, a new appreciation for our cities and a new interest in developing the practical policies and public philosophies that can help them flourish.

Looking back on these stories, I realize that the prospects do not, on their surface, look good. The forces that keep us apart and repress our public interactions seem overwhelming and overdetermined. But I remain hopeful for at least three reasons. First, design is, by its very nature, a countervailing force against large-scale economics and politics. It is almost by definition an affair of the local, the embodied, the here-and-now. That is not to say that the design of buildings, neighborhoods, and other concrete human spaces is not always impacted by distant forces—sometimes to the good, as we have seen with public housing residents' successful appeals to the U.S. Constitution—but it does suggest ever-present possibilities for experimentation and initiative. With apologies to the late Tip O'Neill, *all design is local*, which should give us some hope for at least scattered and piecemeal progress in trying to improve the world around us.

Second, if readers are not convinced by the sociological, political, and rhetorical reasons given here in support of resisting sociospatial decentralization, fragmentation, and polarization in our world, they may well come to such a view because of the need to save our *natural* environments. Ironically, dense, centered cities—as "un-natural" as they often seem to us—may be our best hope in fighting global warming and, ultimately, saving Earth as a habitable planet.[3]

Third, as a teacher—rather than a designer, activist, or politician—it is hard for me not be hopeful about the future. To have those young faces in front of you everyday—their lives partly composed by past experiences and current situations but partly also malleable—is to be always mindful of the power of invention, creation, and change in human life, the opportunities always before us for a better tomorrow. Perhaps if young people experience, even just within the walls of a high school or college classroom, what it can be like to be members of a strong public, they will grow up and demand such publics in the "real world."

Acknowledgments

This book was written mainly in Madison, Wisconsin, from 1998 to 2006. But the journey that produced it began much earlier and included stops in many other places. Along the way, I have been helped by numerous friends, family members, students, teachers, colleagues, and acquaintances.

First among them is David Hackett, whom I met in Washington, DC, more than twenty years ago and whose ideas and example continue to influence and inspire me. In 1985, I was two years out of college and looking for a job as a political writer when I found a position at an out-of-the-way, nonprofit, nonpartisan, "think tank" called the Youth Policy Institute, which tracked governmental and nongovernmental affairs related to children, youth, and families, especially in terms of health, education, employment, juvenile justice, housing, and welfare. Soon, I was attending congressional hearings, reading research reports from nongovernmental organizations, searching the *Federal Register* for available funds, and helping to write and publish newsletters and journals for policy analysts, program officers, child advocates, and others trying to solve some of the nation's most intractable social problems.

It was low-paying, time-consuming, and difficult work. The mid-1980s was an era of increasing socioeconomic polarization in this country. Some people in some places were doing well—the "yuppies," for example, were helping revive city neighborhoods that had been in decline for decades. But other Americans in other places were suffering, not only from crime, unemployment, school failure, and family breakdown, which had worsened in low-income, minority, urban neighborhoods since the mid-1960s, but from a whole new set of problems, including AIDS and crack cocaine, which had appeared on the scene just as the Reagan administration was beginning its historic assault on U.S. social programs. At YPI, we felt like we were in the thick of all this, even if we were not exactly major players. In fact, we were just a handful of underpaid twenty-somethings, working on a shoestring budget out of a cluttered office in a half-abandoned building on the campus of the Catholic University of America. We were convinced, however, that we were opening windows onto the problems of the nation's children and youth. The best part of it all for me, though, was my boss: a thin, rumpled, sixty-year-old man with a booming voice, stained shirts, an incoherent but captivating eloquence, and a dedication to his work the likes of which I had never seen before.

David Hackett had been Robert F. Kennedy's best friend in the early 1940s when both were students at Milton Academy outside Boston; he was a legendary prep school athlete, the model for Phineas in John Knowles's *A Separate Peace*, and, later, a star on the 1948 and 1952 U.S. Olympic hockey teams. He was in Montreal, publishing a small *New Yorker*–style magazine, when, in 1959, his old friend Robert Kennedy called him up to help with his brother's presidential campaign. Later assigned to direct the president's Committee on Juvenile Delinquency and Youth Crime in Robert Kennedy's Justice Department, Hackett essentially, and improbably, invented the U.S. government's 1960s antipoverty effort. His main idea, developed after extensive discussion with experts and visits to programs across the country, was that the poor suffered from lack of opportunity and that what they needed was neither a lecture on good behavior nor another massive governmental program but the resources to improve their own lives and revitalize their own neighborhoods. This was best achieved, Hackett thought, through "community action": antipoverty projects that were located *in* poor neighborhoods themselves and built there from the ground up; that integrated and coordinated the services and programs that the poor relied on (housing, health care, education, employment, etc.); and that were planned and managed with the "maximum feasible participation" of the residents themselves.

The Committee on Juvenile Delinquency (whose enthusiastic young staffers were known as "Hackett's guerrillas") had, by late 1963, decided on a handful of demonstration projects to fund; and Hackett was all set to unveil the plan to the president at the end of that year—when history intervened. A few months later, when it looked like the new president was taking community action (now called "the War on Poverty") in directions he had not intended, Hackett left government altogether. He stayed close to Robert Kennedy, however, working with him on his presidential campaign and accompanying him to Los Angeles in June, 1968. After that, Hackett wandered in the wilderness for awhile until becoming executive director of the Robert F. Kennedy Memorial, a position he left in the late 1970s to found the Youth Policy Institute. That is where I came to know him and where he continues to work, dogged as ever, today.[1]

In 1987, I left YPI—no one stayed there long, and I probably stayed longer than most. Besides, I had always dreamed of going back to school to become a teacher or professor. So I returned to North Carolina to pursue a master's degree in English, immersing myself in the study of literature. I missed the world of politics, though, and felt unsettled in the program until a professor named Erika Lindemann introduced me to a part of English Studies I had never heard of, called "rhetoric and composition," which was less about literary texts and theory and more about "practical" discourse, social action, and civic education. It was life-changing for me.

But by then I was married, a parent, and in need of steady income. So, after finishing the master's degree, I began looking for a teaching job, eventually finding one at a community college in South Texas, on the U.S.-Mexico border. There, in the years just before NAFTA, my family and I saw the beginnings of a new global economy, with its incessant movement of people, trucks, and commodities and its seeming apathy toward the health of local communities. We spent our summers, however, in a village in Spain, my wife's hometown, a place with fewer than 10,000 inhabitants but a more lively civic life, more gregarious public sphere, and more vibrant political culture than cities ten times its size in the United States. I was beginning to see how different human environments taught radically different lessons about social and political life.

In 1991, we left Texas, and I enrolled in the Rhetoric PhD program at Carnegie Mellon University, where I finally found the intellectual home I had been looking for. I also found Pittsburgh, the first city I truly fell in love with. To this day, I retain my membership card for the Fourteenth Ward Democratic Club; I still root for the Steelers; and in my mind's eye, I still stroll the long blocks of shops along Forbes and Murray Avenues in Squirrel Hill. Our children were small then, and we walked the neighborhood every night: to the library, the park, the grocery store. Meanwhile, at school, I was studying how ordinary people, using everyday language, reason their way through shared problems. And my dissertation on the argument practices of graphic designers, written under the direction of David Kaufer, was revealing to me a rich world of visual communication and reviving a love of art and architecture I had nourished in college. But I still was not making explicit connections between rhetoric and the city. I knew that the former had its origins in the polis, that people need contact with difference to develop rhetorically, and that such contact is facilitated by literally setting aside time and place for *public* discourse. But the idea for this book was still years away.

In 1996, when I accepted a faculty position at New Mexico State University in Las Cruces, we moved yet again, this time to a place warmed by the sun and surrounded by mountains and desert. The city itself, though, was something of a shock after Pittsburgh: it was extraordinarily dispersed, almost centerless. So when I heard of a project to revitalize the downtown there, I was interested both because I thought it could help make my new home more livable and because I thought it would be a chance to extend what I had learned in my dissertation about the rhetoric of design. I began attending meetings and talking to the participants, and I came to see that Las Cruces' desire to revitalize its center was really a dream of free and open social discourse. It was then that I began to imagine what a *rhetoric of the city*—and, by extension, a *city of rhetoric*—might look like. I was fortunate during these years to have Reed Way Dasenbrock as my department chair and role model; his early encouragement was crucial in many ways.

Unfortunately, I had to abandon the downtown revitalization project in 1998, when I took a position at the University of Wisconsin–Madison and moved north again. The idea of a rhetoric/city connection, though, stayed with me, and, in early 1999, while thumbing through a UW alumni magazine, I came across an article about Peter Holsten and his work building affordable housing in impoverished Chicago neighborhoods. I wondered if the research I had wanted to do in Las Cruces might be done instead in Chicago. So, I drove down to meet Peter and learned about his Halsted North project. I also walked across the street and saw Cabrini Green for the first time. Soon, I was driving to Chicago as often as I could, reading its newspapers, visiting its libraries, and walking its streets. It is a city I came to admire greatly.

Over the next eight years, numerous Chicagoans helped me with this book; I owe thanks to the following for their time and expertise: at the Chicago Housing Authority: John Tuhey, Francisco Arcaute, Lorri Newson, and, especially, Olusegun Obasanjo; at the National Center on Poverty Law, Bill Wilen; at Holsten Real Estate Development Corporation, Peter Holsten, Candice Howell, and David Greenbeck; at Horner Homes: Sarah Ruffin; at the Cabrini row houses: Carole Steele; and at 1230 North Burling Street: Cora Moore, Arlene Williams, Bessie Rule, Linda Rule, Kenyatta Alexander, Dolores Wilson, and Kelvin Cannon. I also thank Dave Coogan and Annie Knepler for their own work on rhetoric and public housing in Chicago.

At the University of Wisconsin–Madison, there are many people to thank. Three English Department chairs supported my work on this project: Thomas Schaub, Susan Stanford Friedman, and Michael Bernard-Donals. Terry Kelley, Lynn Keller, Russ Castronovo, and Ceci Ford, among others, read parts or all of this manuscript and gave helpful advice. As for my colleagues in Composition and Rhetoric, Martin Nystrand, Deborah Brandt, and Michael Bernard-Donals read more drafts of this book than I had the right to expect of anyone, and they always came through with the perfect mix of challenge and encouragement. Martin Nystrand included an early essay from this project in a book he co-edited with John Duffy, and for that I am grateful. Michael Bernard-Donals was a steadfast colleague; I hope he knows how appreciative I am of his wide-ranging support, professional and personal. Brad Hughes provided valued friendship and inspiration. Other Wisconsin colleagues who helped include Rob Asen, John Drake, and Aarthi Vaade. I thank also my many undergraduate and graduate students there. And I want to express my gratitude as well to the UW–Madison Graduate School, and especially Dean Judith Kornblatt, for financial assistance at various points during this project.

Many people wrote letters supporting me; in addition to those named above, they include Carolyn Miller, Michael Halloran, Carl Herndl, and

Maureen Daly Goggin. Audiences at the Conference on College Composition and Communication, the Rhetoric Society of America, the Ontario Society for the Study of Argumentation, and the American Society for the History of Rhetoric listened helpfully to presentations of this work. Joseph Petraglia and Deepika Bahri were gracious hosts at Emory University, where I delivered a talk. At the University of Massachusetts Amherst, meanwhile, I have received important support to finally finish this project. I want especially to thank my new colleagues in composition and rhetoric: Anne Herrington, Donna LeCourt, Haivan Hoang, and Janine Solberg.

Through it all, my family in North Carolina never wavered in their support. My father showed constant interest in this book; and my brother Lee helped me through a rough patch, spending a memorable holiday with me in Chicago years ago. My mother and siblings Mark and Susie deserve my gratitude as well. Moira Amado Miller, Wendy Hecht, and Rachael Bower were good friends while I struggled through this project. And Wendy Hopfenberg, who long ago showed me New York City and then accompanied me on my first trip to Europe, remains a treasured friend. Juana Gamero de Coca never stopped believing that I could finish this book.

Last, but not least, I want to thank my daughters Carmen (who also helped with the index) and Isabel. They have been more patient, good-natured, and loving than a distracted father deserved. They have lived in and visited many different cities with me; I hope they will continue to explore the world and feel at home wherever they find themselves—to enjoy the cities of their own souls, as Plato put it. But I also hope they will find and help settle real *places*—good, human places—that will deserve and reward their gifts. And I hope they will be better *citizens* than I have been, in a world where such citizenship will matter even more than it does now.

Appendix

Table A.1. The Chicago Housing Authority: Public Housing Projects, 1938–1999

Project	*Year*	*Place*	*Units*	*Orig. Race*	*Building Type*	*Plan for Transformation*
PWA[a] Projects						
Jane Addams Homes (ABLA)[b]	1938	W	1,027	94% white	3–4 story AB[d] & 2-story RH[e]	To be redeveloped as MIC[g]
Julia Lathrop Homes	1938	N	925	white	3–4 story AB & 2-story RH	To be determined
Trumbull Park Homes	1938	S	426	white	4-story AB & 2-story RH	To be rehabilitated
Ida B. Wells Homes (MPWD)[c]	1941	S	1,662	black	3–4 story AB & 2-story RH	To be redeveloped as MIC
CHA: The War Years (1937 Housing Act)						
Frances Cabrini Homes	1942	N	586	80% white	2–3 story RH	To be rehabilitated
Lawndale Gardens	1942	W	128	white	2-story RH	To be determined
Bridgeport Homes	1943	S	141	white	2-story RH	To be rehabilitated
Brooks Homes (ABLA)	1943	W	834	80% black	2-story RH	To be redeveloped as MIC
Altgeld Gardens	1945	S	1,500	black	2-story RH	To be rehabilitated
Wentworth Gardens	1946	S	422	black	3-story AB & 2-story RH	To be rehabilitated
Dearborn Homes	1950	S	800	black	6–9 story AB	To be determined
City-State Slum Clearance/Relocation						
LeClair Courts	1950	S	316	white	2-story RH	To be determined
Harrison Courts	1952	W	140	black	7-story AB	NA
Maplewood Courts	1952	W	140	black	7-story AB	NA

Ogden Courts	1952	W	140	black	7-story GS	NA
Archer Courts	1952	S	126	black	7-story GS	NA
Loomis Courts (ABLA)	1950	W	126	black	7-story GS	To be redeveloped as MIC
Prairie Avenue Courts	1952	S	343	black	7, 14-story GS, 2-story RH	NA
1949 Housing Act						
Victor Olander Homes (Lake Parc)	1953	S	300	black	15-story AB	To be redeveloped as MIC
Altgeld Ext. (Philip Murray Homes)	1954	S	500	black	2-story RH	To be rehabilitated
LeClaire Extension	1954	S	300		2-story RH	To be redeveloped
Frank Lowden Homes		S	128		2-story RH	To be rehabilitated
Harold Ickes Homes	1955	S	797	black	7- & 9-story AB	To be determined
Ida B. Wells Extension (MPWD)	1955	S	641	black	7-story AB	To be redeveloped as MIC
Grace Abbott Homes (ABLA)	1955	W	1,200	black	15-story AB & 2-story RH	To be demolished and redeveloped as MIC
Henry Horner Homes & Annex	1957	W	1,029	black	7- & 15-story AB	To be redeveloped as MIC
Stateway Gardens	1958	S	1,684	black	10- & 17-story GS	To be demolished and redeveloped as MIC
Cabrini Extension	1958	N	1,925	black	7-, 10-, & 19-story AB	To be demolished and redeveloped as MIC
Rockwell Gardens	1961	W	1,126	black	10- & 13-story GS	To be demolished and redeveloped as MIC

(continued on next page)

Table A.1. The Chicago Housing Authority: Public Housing Projects, 1938–1999 *(continued)*

Project	*Year*	*Place*	*Units*	*Orig. Race*	*Building Type*	*Plan for Transformation*
1954 Housing Act						
Prairie Ave. Courts Extension	1958	S	203	black	13-story GS	NA
Clarence Darrow Homes (MPWD)	1961	S	479	black	14-story GS	To be demolished and redeveloped as MIC
Brooks Extension (ABLA)	1961	W	449	black	16-story GS	To be demolished and redeveloped as MIC
Horner Extension	1961	W	736	black	8- & 14-story AB	To be demolished and redeveloped as MIC
Green Homes	1962	N	1,096	black	15- & 16-story GS	To be demolished and redeveloped as MIC
Robert Taylor Homes	1962	S	4,415	black	16-story GS	To be demolished and redeveloped as MIC
Washington Park Homes	1962	S	1,443	black	16-story GS & 2-story RH	To be redeveloped as MIC
Lake Michigan Homes	1963	S	457	black	16-story GS	To be demolished and redeveloped as MIC
Raymond Hilliard Homes	1966	S	346	black	22-story GS	To be rehabilitated
Madden Park Homes (MPWD)	1970	S	450	black	3- & 9-story AB	To be demolished and redeveloped as MIC
TOTALS			**29,526**			

[a]PWA = Public Works Administration; [b]ABLA= Addams, Brooks, Loomis, & Abbott Homes; [c]MPWD = Madden Park, Wells, & Darrow Homes; [d]AB = apartment buildings; [e]RH = row houses; [f]GS = gallery-style buildings; [g]MIC = mixed-income community.

In 1999, the Chicago Housing Authority was the third largest public housing authority in the country with approximately 41,000 units, including 28,000 family units, 10,000 elderly units, and 3,000 "scattered-site" units. In addition, it administered 28,000 Section 8 certificates for a total of 67,000 households served (about 130,000 residents). That year, it unveiled a $1.5 billion *Plan for Transformation* that foresaw the following changtes over the subsequent decade:

Unit Type	*Existing Units*	*(Number Occupied)*	*– To Be Demolished*	*= Units Retained*	*(Families Relocated)*	*+ New Units*	*= Final Units*	*(Total Units Lost)*
Family	26,374	14,046	18,296	8,078	5,968	4,529	12,607	13,767
Elderly	9,480	8,044	0	9,480	0	0	9,480	0
Scattered	2,922	2,400	236	2,686	0	0	2,686	236
Total	38,776	24,490	18,532	20,244	5,968	4,529	24,773	14,003

Sources: Devereaux Bowly, Jr., *The Poorhouse: Subsidized Housing in Chicago, 1895–1976* (Carbondale: Southern Illinois University Press, 1978); Chciago Housing Authority, *Plan for Transformation* (Chicago: January 6, 2000); Chicago Housing Authority, "Family Developments," http://www.thecha.org/housingdev/family)_sites.html.

Notes

Preface

1. For an expansion of this argument, see Fleming, "Streets of Thurii."

2. For the history of modern North American city planning, see Jon Peterson, *Birth of City Planning*; for the Progressive Era reform of municipal government, see Adrian, "Forms of Local Government"; for the late nineteenth century rise of postsecondary composition instruction, see Connors, *Composition-Rhetoric*.

3. Bledstein, *Culture of Professionalism*; Schön, *Reflective Practitioner*; and Sies, "City Transformed," which relates these trends to the rise of the "Professional-Managerial Class," a formulation she borrows from Barbara and John Ehrenreich.

4. Boyer, *Dreaming the Rational City*, 7.

5. Donovan, "City and the Garden."

6. Bender, "Erosion of Public Culture." The disconnection has continued up to the present. According to Benson and Harkavy, the recent history of the university in the United States has been the story of an "increasingly obvious, increasingly embarrassing, increasingly immoral contradiction between the increasing status, wealth, and power of American higher education (particularly its elite research university component) and the increasingly pathological state of American cities" ("Higher Education's Third Revolution," 48). See also Bender, *University and the City*, and the various reports of the Kellogg Commission on the Future of State and Land-Grant Universities at http://www.nasulgc.org/Kellogg/kellogg.htm.

1. Introduction

1. Whether the great Chicago architect and urban planner actually said these words is the subject of debate, though they are widely attributed to him. See Kenneth Kolson, *Big Plans: The Allure and Folly of Urban Design* (Baltimore: Johns Hopkins University Press, 2001), 189.

2. Chicago is "naturally" divided into three parts. With Lake Michigan to the east and the Illinois prairie to the west, the Chicago River and its North and South Branches partition the city into South, North, and West Sides, with the "Loop" at their intersection (see Donald Miller, *City of the Century*, 266). These divisions can themselves be broken down further: in the 1930s, sociologist Louis Wirth and his colleagues

at the University of Chicago drew a map of the city with 77 "community areas," one of which, the section between the Chicago River and North Avenue—between, that is, the Loop and Lincoln Park—they called the "Near North Side" (Wirth and Furez, *Local Community Fact Book*). In 2000, 73,000 people lived here, in one of the most diverse areas of the city (see the Chicago Fact Finder at http://www.nd.edu/~chifacts/). The poorest part of the Near North Side remains its northwest corner, sometimes called "North Town" or "the Lower North." Defined to be coextensive with Mayor Daley's Near North Redevelopment Initiative area, bounded by Wells Street, Chicago Avenue, the North Branch of the Chicago River, and North Avenue, it is about 330 acres in size. A good source on Chicago social geography in general is Grossman, Keating, and Reiff, *Encyclopedia of Chicago*.

3. For the history of the Near North Side, see the CHA, "Cabrini-Green Homes"; Hunter, *Tenement Conditions*; Marciniak, *Reclaiming the Inner City*; Donald Miller, *City of the Century*; Seligman, "Near North Side"; and Zorbaugh, *Gold Coast and Slum*.

4. During the 1870s and '80s, the neighborhood had the largest Swedish 'town' outside of Sweden and Finland (CHA, "Cabrini-Green Homes").

5. Zorbaugh, *Gold Coast and Slum*, 40 (hereafter cited parenthetically in the text).

6. According to the CHA, the church was established in 1904 at the peak of Italian immigration and overseen for years by Rev. Luigi Giambastiani ("Cabrini-Green Homes").

7. Ten years after Zorbaugh's book was published, the *WPA Guide to Illinois* included the corner in its tour of the Near North Side, describing it as "the scene of more slayings during the prohibition era than any other point in the city" (Federal Writers' Project, *WPA Guide*, 246); see also Seligman, "Near North Side." The CHA locates "Death Corner" at Oak and *Milton* Streets, just east of St. Philip Benizi ("Cabrini-Green Homes"); Wikipedia, meanwhile, puts it at Locust and Sedgwick (http://en.wikipedia.org/wiki/Cabrini-Green, accessed January 14, 2007).

8. See also Edith Abbott, *Tenements of Chicago*, 106–10.

9. Bowly, *Poorhouse*, 41; CHA, "Cabrini-Green Homes"; and NTRAC, *North Town, I*, 37.

10. See Hirsch, *Making the Second Ghetto*, 36, 45, for evidence of sporadic interracial fighting on the Near North Side. Thomas Guglielmo's *White on Arrival: Italians, Race, Color, and Power in Chicago, 1890–1945* (New York: Oxford University Press, 2003) details racial tensions on the Near North Side during these years and paints an unflattering portrait of Rev. Giambastiani's relations with the neighborhood's blacks.

11. On this last possibility, see Drake and Cayton, *Black Metropolis*, 42–3.

12. De Wit, "Rise of Public Housing," 234. In the 1920s, by contrast, 227,786 new apartments were built in the city, a number never approached since (Bowly, *Poorhouse*, 8).

13. Federal Writers' Project, *WPA Guide*, 236.

14. Bowly, *Poorhouse*, 35.

15. Since 683 old units were demolished to make room for the 586 new ones, the project actually resulted in a net *loss* of low-income housing in the neighborhood (Bowly, *Poorhouse*, 35).

16. CHA, "Cabrini-Green Homes."

17. For the history of Cabrini Green (and the CHA in general), see Bowly, *Poorhouse*, passim.

18. NTRAC, *North Town*, *I*, 29.

19. On the 80:20 ratio at the Cabrini row houses, see note 9 above; on the "Neighborhood Composition Rule," see Bowly, *Poorhouse*, 27; Cohen and Taylor, *American Pharaoh*, 71–3; and Meyerson and Banfield, *Politics, Planning, and the Public Interest*, 121–2.

20. Lillian Davis Swope as quoted in Whitaker, *Cabrini Green*, 13.

21. Hauser and Kitagawa, *Local Community Fact Book*, 38.

22. Changes at the Cabrini Homes lagged; in 1949, proportions there were still only 40 percent black and 60 percent white (CHA, "Cabrini-Green Homes"; Cohen and Taylor, *American Pharaoh*, 73).

23. Arzula Ivy in Whitaker, *Cabrini Green*, 14.

24. Margaret Wilson in Whitaker, *Cabrini Green*, 14.

25. See interviews with Mother Vassar, Ramsey Lewis, Zora Washington, and Margaret Wilson in Whitaker, *Cabrini Green*, 13, 20. One young resident of the row houses, Richard Sennett, would grow up to become a noted sociologist of city life; on Sennett's days in Cabrini, see Sudhir Venkatesh, "Making Connections: 50 Years Removed from his Cabrini-Green Childhood," *Chicago Tribune*, February 16, 2003; and Elizabeth Taylor, "Music, Life, and Playing Together: Richard Sennett Believes Society Must Shift Focus," *Chicago Tribune*, March 23, 2003.

26. According to one study from the time, in the neighborhood adjacent to the Cabrini row houses, there were 1,300 more families than housing units (NTRAC, *North Town*, *I*, 32).

27. Bowly, *Poorhouse*, 116–8.

28. "It's heaven here," said one early resident (quoted in NTRAC, *North Town*, *I*, 34). There were still whites in the neighborhood, and 25 percent of the Extension was reserved for them. One building in particular, 500 W. Oak, was known as the "international building" because of its multicultural population (CHA, "Cabrini-Green Homes").

29. Bowly, *Poorhouse*, 118–9.

30. For these and other projects, there was massive demolition and clearance throughout the 1940s, '50s, and '60s. Edward Marciniak claims that 90 percent of the housing stock present in the neighborhood in 1930 had been razed by 1970 (*Reclaiming the Inner City*, 31). Some of that land was obviously built up again, especially by the CHA; but in 1997, one report claimed that 47 percent of Lower North lots were vacant (City of Chicago, *Near North Tax Increment*). Meanwhile, the neighborhood had become disattached from the Chicago grid (NTRAC, *North Town*, *II*).

31. Whitaker, *Cabrini Green*, 5.

32. CHA, "Cabrini-Green Homes."

33. Hunt, "What Went Wrong?" 108–9.

34. In his study of the deterioration of Chicago's ghetto neighborhoods during this time, Hunt ignores the King riots, probably because they impacted the South Side, where he focuses his research, less than they did the Near West and Near North Sides.

35. Inez Gamble in Whitaker, *Cabrini Green*, 25–6.

36. Zora Washington in Whitaker, *Cabrini Green*, 26.

37. Arzula Ivy in Whitaker, *Cabrini Green*, 27.

38. Of course, good things happened here as well: individuals from Cabrini Green—Curtis Mayfield, Jerry Butler, and Ramsey Lewis, for example—became noted performers; the film *Cooley High* was set and shot nearby; and the television show *Good Times* was about a Cabrini family (see, e.g., Whitaker, *Cabrini Green*, 4).

39. See, for example, Cohen and Taylor, *American Pharaoh.*

40. See, for example, Jargowsky, *Poverty and Place*; and Wilson, *Truly Disadvantaged.*

41. Wilson, *Truly Disadvantaged*, 26; cf. Salama, "Redevelopment," 107 n. 13.

42. NTRAC, *North Town, I*, 37.

43. Marciniak, *Reclaiming the Inner City*, 115. See also NTRAC, *North Town, II*, 18; Myron Orfield, *Chicago Metropolitics*; and Wilson, *Truly Disadvantaged.*

44. NCSDPH, *Final Report*; see also "Severely Distressed Public Housing" in the "Glossary of HOPE VI Terms" at http://www.hud.gov/offices/pih/programs/ph/hope6/pubs/glossary.pdf.

45. The period saw several "popular" accounts of Chicago ghetto life, most notably Jones and Newman, *Our America*; Kotlowitz, *There Are No Children Here*; and Lemann, *Promised Land.*

46. On this last trend, see, for example, Asen, *Visions of Poverty*; and Gans, *War Against the Poor.*

47. Salama, "Redevelopment," 135.

48. See Coulibaly, Green, and James, *Segregation in Subsidized Housing*; Hirsch, *Making the Second Ghetto*; Robert Starks, "Blacks and the Chicago Land Grab," *Chicago Tribune*, Nov. 9, 1992; and David Peterson, "A Great Chicago Land Grab," *Z Magazine*, April, 1997.

49. Schill, "Distressed Public Housing," 498, n. 9; see also the U.S. Housing Act of 1949.

50. The fight over Cabrini Green was waged primarily through words and images, one of the reasons I became so interested in it; for more, see Fleming, "Subjects of the Inner City."

51. On ancient rhetoric and its contemporary relevance, see Barthes, "Old Rhetoric"; Billig, *Arguing and Thinking*; Conley, *Rhetoric*; and Sloane, *On the Contrary.*

52. The phrase is "*politikon zoon*" (Aristotle, *Politics*, 1253a3). On "politikos" as "city-living," see "πολιτικοσ," note 4, in the Liddell-Scott *Greek-English Lexicon* (Oxford, 1996).

53. The Greeks privileged cities in their stories of human progress and saw language as central to city life. In Plato's *Protagoras*, for example, the title character argues that cities are humans' main competitive advantage over nature, chance, and other animals; but their inhabitants need to acquire the "political" virtues of justice and respect, which are enacted largely through discourse (320d). For more on cities and rhetoric in Greek thought, see Carolyn Miller, "*Polis.*"

54. Bookchin, *From Urbanization to Cities*, 60.

55. Joseph Petraglia has labeled the dominant mode of contemporary composition pedagogy "General Writing Skills Instruction," criticized its formality and abstraction ("Introduction"), and disparaged school writing as "pseudo-transactional" ("Spinning Like a Kite"). Kaufer and Young have similarly referred to the subject of composition

as "writing with no content in particular" ("Writing in the Content Areas"). True, compositionists today often begin their work from the premise that humans exist in concrete space and time, grow up in specific social, economic, and cultural circumstances, and use language to pursue particular purposes; in the classroom, this has meant a new appreciation for the diverse sites and functions of discourse. But the field remains blind, I believe, to the everyday scenes of our embodied lives, especially the neighborhoods, cities, and metropolitan areas where we actually live and work.

56. Sam Bass Warner, *Private City*, 3–4. Warner is sometimes credited with first using this word in the late 1960s, but the *Oxford English Dictionary* gives examples from the 1950s: it seems to be an American coinage, applied disparagingly to the excessive individualism of our culture.

57. "What is characteristic of our city-building is to wall off the differences between people, assuming that these differences are more likely to be mutually threatening than mutually stimulating" (Sennett, *Conscience of the Eye*, xii).

58. See, for example, Frug, *City Making*; Geoghegan, *Secret Lives of Citizens*; Lazare, *America's Undeclared War*; and White and White, *Intellectual Versus the City*.

2. The Placelessness of Political Theory

1. Center for Civic Education, *National Standards*, "9–12 Content Standards," §IIC. The *Standards* were a joint project of the U.S. Department of Education, the Center for Civic Education, and the Pew Charitable Trusts and are still used as a model for state standards and curricula in civic education. They were also the basis for the 1998 and 2006 "Report Cards" of the National Assessment of Educational Progress (NAEP) in Civics and Government. For more information on the Standards, see http://www.civiced.org/stds.html; for more on NAEP's Civics Report Cards, see http://nces.ed.gov/nationsreportcard/civics/.

2. Smith, *Civic Ideals*, 15.

3. Conrad, "Citizenship," 103.

4. Not being born in the United States is no bar if one's parent is a citizen, and it need not be a permanent obstacle to naturalization.

5. See the "Naturalization" home page of the U.S. Citizenship and Immigration Services: http://uscis.gov/graphics/services/natz/index.htm.

6. Ibid.

7. See, for example, the American Political Science Association, Task Force on Inequality and American Democracy, *American Democracy in an Age of Rising Inequality* (Washington, DC, 2004).

8. Rawls, *Theory of Justice*; Habermas, "Remarks on Discourse Ethics."

9. See, for example, Dietz, "Context Is All"; Fraser, "Rethinking the Public Sphere"; and Young, *Justice*.

10. In other words, proceduralism has often taken bias out of the conversation even as it continues to act behind the scenes. For this reason, some philosophers have begun to promote theories of *differentiated* citizenship, in which particularity, specificity, and difference play as big a part in civic identity as "universal" human nature (see, e.g., Young, *Justice*, 96–121).

11. Smith, *Civic Ideals*, 12.

12. Mouffe, *Democratic Paradox*, 36–59. She derives her argument partly from the work of Carl Schmitt, for whom democracy required "tracing a line of demarcation between those who belong to the demos—and therefore have equal rights—and those who, in the political domain, cannot have the same rights because they are not part of the demos" (40). For Mouffe, this moment of demarcation need not, however, be the simple acknowledgement of preexisting empirical differences—it can and should be the result of politics itself. The moment of rule, in other words, is inseparable from defining "the people," a struggle which should be kept open even if the process of articulating who belongs and who does not is unavoidable for democratic equality to be meaningful (53–57). The problem is "how to envision a form of commonality strong enough to institute a 'demos' but nevertheless compatible with certain forms of pluralism: religious, moral and cultural pluralism, as well as a pluralism of political parties" (55).

13. Carl Schmitt, as quoted by Mouffe, *Democratic Paradox*, 41.

14. Smith argues that the failure of liberals to acknowledge particularist political visions, their belief that appeals to the special characteristics of particular groups are always hostile to universal, cosmopolitan rights, has been a liability for them (*Civic Ideals*, 9).

15. "Politics is a process by which a group of people, whose opinions or interests might be divergent, reach collective decisions that are generally regarded as binding on the group and enforced as common policy . . . Politics necessarily arises whenever groups of people live together" (Center for Civic Education, *National Standards*, "9–12 Content Standards," §IA).

16. Mouffe, *Democratic Paradox*, 37 (quoting Richard Falk).

17. Nussbaum, *For Love of Country*. See also Held, *Models of Democracy*, 353–360.

18. On our "natural" bilateral symmetry, see Turner, *Reading Minds*; on humans' universal needs and resources, see Diamond, *Guns, Germs, and Steel*, which argues that the basic grains that form the mainstay of human diets the world over have not changed substantially in millennia.

19. A fortuitous association is "a group of people in which individuals simply find themselves, one that demands an ability to get along with the other members of the group no matter how different they are" (Frug, *City Making*, 174).

20. Cf. Emmanuel Levinas' argument that "proximity" is the origin of our ethical responsibility for one another (as quoted in Crosswhite, *Rhetoric of Reason*, 67).

21. Solomon, *Global City Blues*, 2–3.

22. "To live together in the world means that a world of things is between those who have it in common, as a table is located between those who sit around it" (Arendt, *Human Condition*, 52).

23. Robert McC. Adams, as quoted in Kotkin, *City*, 149.

24. Just to take one example: from the early 1990s, when the North American Free Trade Agreement took effect and the World Trade Organization was formed, until 2002, more than 140,000 jobs left the state of North Carolina alone. During these years, Fieldcrest Cannon moved production of its kitchen and bath towels from Kannapolis to India and Pakistan (laying off 950 workers); Hamilton Beach/Proctor Silex moved manufacture of its toasters from Washington to Mexico (laying off 1,800 workers); and

Gerber relocated production of its baby pajamas from Lumberton to Guatemala (laying off 294 workers) (Karin Rives, "No End in Sight to N.C. Job Losses," *The News and Observer* [Raleigh, NC], August 18, 2002).

25. Sennett, *Corrosion of Character*. Robert Reich has written less critically about the rise of the postmodern "symbolic-analytical" worker, whom he describes as able to define problems, assimilate data, make deductive and inductive leaps, ask questions, work collaboratively to find solutions, and convince others to adopt them (*Work of Nations*). But see Hull, "Hearing Other Voices," on the intellectual reality of the new low-wage, service-sector work.

26. For versions of this binary scheme, see Benhabib, "Toward a Deliberative Model"; Habermas, "Three Normative Models"; Hauser, "Politics"; and Held, *Models of Democracy*. Republicanism and liberalism do not exhaust modern democratic theory, of course. Nor do all theorists even recognize an opposition between the two—see Dagger's "republican liberalism" (*Civic Virtues*) and Sunstein's "liberal republicanism" ("Beyond"). And many thinkers reject *both*. Smith shows, for example, that the *practice* of forming publics, as opposed to theorizing them, has often employed ascriptive notions of citizenship that have more to do with race, class, ethnicity, religion, and gender than political philosophies admit (*Civic Ideals*, 5–8).

27. Pocock, *Machiavellian Moment*, 550.

28. Ibid., 59–60. So seen, the bête-noir of republicanism is *tyranny*, defined as anything that impedes freedom, whether that be a foreign power, a ruthless dictator, an oligarchy of wealth, the masses, or a despotism of administrators and bureaucrats. Freedom, meanwhile, is defined in both external and internal terms, that is, the freedom of the group as a whole from other groups and the freedom of individual citizens to participate in their own government (on this distinction, see Arendt, *Human Condition*; Finer, *Ancient Monarchies*; Hansen, *Athenian Democracy*; Alan Ryan, "City as a Site"; and Sandel, "Procedural Republic"). The best way to protect both freedoms, according to republicans, is for each individual to take an active interest in politics, to delegate nothing when it comes to civic rights and duties, and to defend his or her freedom by enacting it in public life.

29. Pocock, "Civic Humanism," 85.

30. See, for example, Isaiah Berlin, "Two Concepts of Liberty."

31. Habermas, "Three Normative Models," 23.

32. But see Berkowitz, *Virtue*, for a more generous view of liberalism's ethical basis.

33. Habermas, *Structural Transformation*.

34. Although Habermas's civil society is a place of association and debate, liberals have usually glorified something else: the individual, a decontextualized rational agent who preexists society, bears inalienable natural rights, and seeks only to realize his or her individual capabilities and goals (see, e.g., Dietz, "Context Is All").

35. Rahe, *Republics Ancient and Modern*, 7.

36. Arendt, *Human Condition*; Pocock, "Civic Humanism," 85–6.

37. See, for example, Sandel, "Procedural Republic"; and Rawls, *Theory of Justice*.

38. Foucault, "Space, Knowledge, and Power."

39. I borrow the phrase from Soja, *Postmodern Geographies*, 76ff.

40. Foucault, "Of Other Spaces," 22.

41. Soja, *Postmodern Geographies*; Gross, "Space, Time, and Modern Culture" 65; Jameson, *Postmodernism*, 16; and Friedman, *Mappings*.

42. See, for example, Bhaba, *Location of Culture*.

43. On 1963, see DeLillo, *Libra*; on 1972, see Jencks, *Language of Post-modern Architecture*; 1972 is also seen as a watershed year by Harvey, though for him it marks the economic shift from Fordism to "flexible accumulation" (*Condition of Postmodernity*).

44. Cf. Castells' notion of an economy and culture based on "flows" (*Informational City*).

45. Asen and Brouwer, *Counterpublics*; Fraser, "Rethinking the Public Sphere"; and Hauser, *Vernacular Voices*.

46. Sandel, "Procedural Republic."

47. Foucault, "Of Other Spaces," 24; Jameson, *Postmodernism*; and Davis, "Fortress Los Angeles." See also Blakely and Snyder, *Fortress America*; Caldeira, *City of Walls*; and Marcuse, "Enclave."

48. Eberly, "Writers, Audiences, and Communities"; Miller, "Polis," 239; and Wells, "Rogue Cops," 326–7.

49. Pensky, "Universalism and the Situated Critic," 71.

50. Sennett, *Conscience of the Eye*, xi.

51. Oliver, *Democracy in Suburbia*, 189.

52. Sassen, *Global City*; Castells, *Informational City*.

53. On "creative centers," see Florida, *Rise of the Creative Class*; on "ideopolises," see Judis and Teixeira, *Emerging Democratic Majority*; on "latte towns," see Brooks, *Bobos in Paradise*.

54. Myron Orfield, *American Metropolitics*, 31–46.

55. "Every American metropolitan area is now divided into districts that are so different from each other they seem to be different worlds. Residential neighborhoods are African American, Asian, Latino, or white, and upper-middle-class, middle-class, or poor. . . . Traveling through this mosaic of neighborhoods, metropolitan residents move from feeling at home to feeling like a tourist to feeling so out of place that they are afraid for their own security. . . . Everyone knows which parts of the metropolitan area are nice and which are dangerous. We all know where we don't belong" (Frug, *City Making*, 3).

56. See, for example, Ray Boshara, "The $6,000 Solution" *The Atlantic Monthly*, January/February 2003; Paul Krugman, "For Richer," *New York Times*, October 20, 2202; and Phillips, *Politics of Rich and Poor*.

57. See, for example, Popenoe, *Private Pleasure, Public Plight*.

58. The average size of a single family house in the United States grew from 800 square feet in 1950 to 1,500 square feet in 1970 to 2,250 square feet in 1999, nearly a three-fold increase in just fifty years (see Hayden, "Model Houses," 1; and Deborah Kades, "The Thing About a Lot of New Houses Is They're Big," *Wisconsin State Journal*, June 24, 2001).

59. See, for example, Daskal, *In Search of Shelter*; and the Millennial Housing Commission, *Meeting Our Nation's Housing Challenges*.

60. Suro, "Movement at Warp Speed."

61. The romanticization of mobility by academics may derive as much from *their* relatively ageographical existence as from anything else (in *Country of Exiles*, Leach refers to American academics as the "nomads" of the twentieth century).

62. Sennett, *Corrosion of Character*.

63. Arendt, *Human Condition*, 52; elsewhere, Arendt wrote, "Freedom, wherever it existed as a tangible reality, has always been spatially limited" (*On Revolution*, 275). See also Fleming, "Streets of Thurii," on "bounded democracy."

64. Frug, *City Making*, 174; Williamson, Imbroscio, and Alperovitz, *Making a Place*, 2; and Young, *Inclusion and Democracy*, 222.

3. A New Civic Map for Our Time

1. Aristotle, *Nicomachean Ethics*, 1170b29–1a7. This is my own loose translation.

2. Mancur Olson, *Logic of Collective Action*, 20.

3. Center for Civic Education, *National Standards*, §§II–III.

4. Almond and Verba, *Civic Culture*; and Verba, Schlozman, and Brady, *Voice and Equality*, where "political participation" is defined as an "activity that has the intent or effect of influencing government action," a formulation that neatly separates citizen from ruler.

5. See, for example, Anderson, *Imagined Communities*; Shumway, *Creating American Civilization*; and Michael Warner, *Letters of the Republic*.

6. Clifford Adelman, *The New College Course Map and Transcript Files: Changes in Course-Taking and Achievement 1972–1993* (Washington, DC: U.S. Department of Education, Office of Educational Research and Improvement, 1995), 232.

7. Through such projects as land grants to universities, the G.I. Bill, and funding for research and student loans.

8. Connors, *Composition-Rhetoric*, 69–111.

9. The textbooks examined in the paragraphs that follow are from Bedford/St. Martin's, the leading publisher of college composition textbooks in the United States.

10. Diana Hacker, *A Writer's Reference*, 4th ed. (Boston: Bedford/St. Martin's, 1999).

11. See, for example, James Berlin, "Rhetoric and Ideology"; Bloom, "Freshman Composition"; Brodkey, *Writing Permitted*; Douglas, "Rhetoric for the Meritocracy"; Fusfield, "Refusing to Believe It"; and Ohmann, *English in America*.

12. On the history of "unidirectional English monolingualism" in U.S. college composition, see Horner and Trimber, "English Only."

13. Annette T. Rottenberg, *Elements of Argument*, 6th ed. (Boston: Bedford/St. Martin's, 2000).

14. Notwithstanding its use of British philosopher Stephen Toulmin's theory of argument.

15. The anthologies are revealing in this regard because they present public discourse as a fundamentally *literary* phenomenon, a matter of reading and writing *essays*, an appropriate genre (monologic, spectatorial) for a nationalistic enterprise like

college composition. In Lynn Bloom's "Essay Canon," nineteen of the top twenty-five anthologized essays are by Americans, and twenty-four of the twenty-five were originally written in English. On the essay as dominant school genre, see Farr, "Essayist Literacy"; and David Olson, "From Utterance to Text."

16. Emig, *Composing Processes*, 97.

17. Fraser, "Rethinking the Public Sphere," 134. Similarly, Young complains that "welfare capitalist society" has made public policy formation the province of experts and confined political conflict to "bargaining among interest groups," a paradigm that depoliticizes public life "by failing to bring issues of decision-making power . . . into explicit public discourse" (*Justice*, 10). An alternative conception of politics can be found among the Greeks, for whom "ruling" was decision-making (see, e.g., Aristotle, *Politics*, 1278b8), and politics, "a practical art . . . concerned with enabling practical judgment" (Hauser, "Politics," 613). It is perhaps only since Machiavelli and Hobbes that politics has become so thoroughly impersonal, intimidating, and remote, a matter of parties, politicians, bureaucracies, and mass movements. If there is a role for ordinary people in such an activity, it is indirect: consuming opinions and voting for representatives. The difference between these two approaches is summed up nicely in the *Oxford Classical Dictionary*, which contrasts the ancient notion of politics as "ritualized decision-making" with its modern sense as "the struggle for power" (Murray, "Politics," 1207).

18. Aristotle, *Politics*, 1275a22. According to Schudson (*Good Citizen*), the best we can hope from our fellow citizens these days is that they be "informed," though even that weak conception is being supplanted by one that defines citizens in exclusively rights-bearing terms and thus removes them even further from active, collaborative, public decision-making.

19. Ervin, "Encouraging Civic Participation." Patricia Roberts-Miller's recent *Deliberate Conflict* also fails to acknowledge, I believe, the extent to which our political philosophies, and the pedagogies derived from them, are inextricably *scenic*.

20. Of course, I could have gone here in the other direction, finding the solution to the problems of the nation-state in *larger* publics (see, e.g., Paehlke, *Democracy's Dilemma*). After all, many people today think of themselves as "cosmopolites" (Nussbaum, *For Love of Country*) whose primary public is the earth itself, and its inhabitants, their "world brothers and sisters." Cosmopolitanism certainly solves some of the problems of nation-based publics, but it does little to moderate the spectatorial identity expected of citizens. In this sense, the nation-state and the "globe" are equally inaccessible to the individual and thus equally "weak" in Fraser's sense.

21. Arendt, *On Revolution*, 215–81.

22. "Freedom, wherever it existed as a tangible reality, has always been spatially limited" (ibid., 275).

23. Cf. Mouffe, *Democratic Paradox*, 36–59.

24. Citizenship in a free polis, Aristotle wrote, cannot be delegated (see Garver, *Aristotle's Rhetoric*, 18–51).

25. Arendt, *On Revolution*, 246.

26. Ibid., 232–9.

27. Ibid., 248–9.

28. Ibid., 235. On the anti-urbanism of the American political tradition, see chapter 1 above, note 58.

29. Kelbaugh, *Common Place*, 5.

30. For these units, see Linklater, *Measuring America*; on the neighborhood, see Hall, "Global City," 43; Lynch, *Good City Form*, 239–50; Mumford, "Neighborhood," passim, and *City in History*, 499ff; Rykwert, *Seduction of Place*, 171ff; and Vale, *From the Puritans*, 142ff.

31. Jacobs in *Death and Life*, Alexander et al. in *A Pattern Language*, and Lynch in *Good City Form* all use "neighborhood" to refer to very small geopolitical entities, just a street or two with a few hundred inhabitants. Taking the point of view of the planner, I see the neighborhood as larger and more self-sufficient, with institutions like schools, churches, stores, and parks.

32. See, for example, Fleming, "Streets of Thurii"; and Mumford, *City in History*.

33. Although the "Garden City" movement in nineteenth century England is a precursor.

34. See, for example, Mumford, "Neighborhood," 259ff.

35. My summary of Perry's ideas comes mainly from Banerjee and Baer, *Beyond the Neighborhood Unit*.

36. "The neighborhood is based, essentially, on the needs of families; particularly on the needs of mothers and children from the latters' infancy up to adolescence" (Mumford, "Neighborhood," 264).

37. Duany and Plater-Zyberk, "Neighborhood, District, and Corridor." On the New Urbanism, see Fleming, "Space of Argumentation."

38. Plato, *Laws*, 746d.

39. Hansen, *Athenian Democracy*, 94.

40. Fleming, "Streets of Thurii."

41. Aristotle, *Politics*, 1326b.

42. Hansen, *Athenian Democracy*, 60.

43. Ibid.

44. Alexander et al., *Pattern Language*, 70–74. Using a rule of thumb developed by Paul Goodman that no citizen be more than two friends away from the highest member of his or her local unit, they compute this to roughly 5,000 people, assuming twelve good friends per person, each friend representing a household of 3, thus: $12^3 \times 3 = 5{,}184$ (72).

45. Dahl and Tufte, *Size and Democracy*, 63.

46. Oliver, *Democracy in Suburbia*, 52.

47. See http://www.census.gov/geo/www/cen_tract.html.

48. Jacobs, *Death and Life*; and Webber, "Order in Diversity."

49. Oliver, *Democracy in Suburbia*, 84, 95, 202.

50. On "community" as ideally harmonious, see, Harris, "Idea of Community"; Pratt, "Linguistic Utopias"; Sandercock, *Towards Cosmopolis*, 190ff; and Young, *Justice*, 226–56.

51. See McKenzie, *Privatopia*.

52. See the Web site of the Community Association Institute: http://www.caionline.org/.

53. Michael Heller, quoted in Franzese, "Does It Take a Village?"

54. See, for example, Bell, "Civil Society"; Blakely and Snyder, *Fortress America*; Dilger, *Neighborhood Politics*; McKenzie, *Privatopia*; and Tamir, "Revisiting the Public Sphere."

55. McKenzie, *Privatopia*, 25.

56. Ibid, 139.

57. Ibid, 25.

58. Ibid.

59. Bell, "Civil Society"; Schragger, "Limits of Localism."

60. Quoted in McKenzie, *Privatopia*, 139.

61. Young, *Inclusion*, 230.

62. Oliver, *Democracy in Suburbia*, 208.

63. Roberts-Miller, *Deliberate Conflict*, 190–1.

64. Dahl and Tufte, *Size*, 138 (emphases in original). Dahl revisits the dilemma in *On Democracy* (105ff).

65. Dahl and Tufte, *Size*, 140.

66. Aristotle, *Nicomachean Ethics*, 1170b29–1a7.

67. Aristotle, *Politics*, 1252b15.

68. Ibid., 1326b.

69. Ibid., 1261a15, and 1277a5.

70. Ibid., 1261a15.

71. According to Aristotle, human beings, unlike other social creatures (e.g., ants and bees), have an innate capacity for reasoned speech, which leads them, *naturally*, to argue with one another (Yack, "Community and Conflict," 100). Thus, Black's criticism of Aristotle that "It is easy to develop a rhetorical system out of commonplace topics if one lives in a walled city, many days journey from the nearest settlement, with well-established and clearly understood traditions and a culture almost tribal in its cohesiveness" (*Rhetorical Criticism*, 125) is off the mark: the Greeks in general, and the Athenians in particular, were a highly litigious, incessantly argumentative people, for whom conflict, faction, and dispute were a way of life. Nothing in the Greek polis, writes Nussbaum, happened without an argument ("Kant and Cosmpopolitanism," 52, n. 6).

72. The distinction is due to Tönnies, *Community and Society*.

73. Mouffe, *Democratic Paradox*, 55; Young, *Inclusion*, x. On the place of strangers in city life, see Frug, *City Making*: "the primary function of cities is to teach people how to interact with unfamiliar strangers" (140); Jacobs, *Death and Life*: "cities are by definition full of strangers" (30); Sennett, *Fall of Public Man*: "a city is a human settlement in which strangers are likely to meet" (39); Young, *Justice*: city life is "the being together of strangers" (237); and Lofland, *World of Strangers*: "To live in a city is, among many other things, to live surrounded by large numbers of persons whom one does not know. To experience the city is, among many other things, to experience anonymity. To cope with the city is, among many other things, to cope with strangers" (ix–x). What I have tried to suggest here, though, is that our social geography is not exhausted by the world of intimates, on the one hand, and strangers, on the other. There is also *politics*—in which equals meet to discuss and manage their common affairs. These equals are neither really friends nor strangers—I am tempted to say they are "civic friends" (Rahe, *Republics Ancient and Modern*, 57) or "political friends" (Allen, *Talking to Strangers*, 119–39), but I find those phrases too warm. The best word we have is probably the old standby "citizen," he or she who *combines* a commitment to *procedure* with an ethical concern for his or her fellows. The kind of social relationship that develops among citizens in a good city is thus more virtuous than the bonds of a contract but

more conflictual than the ties of camaraderie (Yack, "Community and Conflict"). It is this kind of relationship, I believe, that lies behind Aristotle's theory of rhetorical "ethos," which has always given rhetoricians trouble precisely because they lack a middle term between friend and stranger. In his *Rhetoric*, but nowhere else, *ethos* for Aristotle is discursive: "There is persuasion through character (ethos) whenever the speech is spoken in such a way as to make the speaker worthy of credence. . . . And this should result from the speech, not from a previous opinion that the speaker is a certain kind of person" (*On Rhetoric*, 1.2.3–4), a notion that contemporary theorists have used to suggest that virtue is discursively constructed. But that is not quite right. Everywhere else that Aristotle talks about ethos, it refers to an attribute of a *person* and not the result of a discursive presentation. In the *Rhetoric*, Aristotle clearly wants ethos to be artistically available, but if we look at his political and ethical writings, the community where rhetoric functioned was a place where citizens *knew* one another's character extra-discursively. "A city's acts," Aristotle wrote, "are those of its people, judgment and rule, and to do these things well, and not offhandedly, citizens must know what each other is like" (*Politics*, 1326b). To govern well in a polis, in other words, we need more than rhetorical artifice; we need the practical wisdom that is attuned to time and place, to our fellow-citizens and their behavior, and to what is good, right, and true in the situations in which we find ourselves. This kind of social knowledge is not confined to small-scale, tightly knit, homogeneous, face-to-face communities. The population of fourth century, BCE, Athens was above 100,000, and audiences for political speeches probably contained 10,000 people or more (Hansen, *Athenian Democracy*). You cannot "know" speakers in such a context the way you know family and friends. But you *can* know them well enough to judge their discourse in practically wise ways.

74. Carolyn Miller, "*Polis*," 239.

75. Mouffe, *Democratic Paradox*, 55

76. Young, *Justice*, 227.

77. Mary Ryan, *Civic Wars*, 4.

78. Wirth, "Urbanism as a Way of Life," 8. Like Tönnies, Wirth saw the modern city as a place that induced isolation and anomie; but his definition, I believe, can just as easily direct us to the virtues of the city, at least once we reject his disparagement of heterogeneity.

79. See, for example, De Romilly, *Great Sophists*; Fleming, "Space of Argumentation" and "Streets of Thurii"; Garver, *Aristotle's "Rhetoric"*; Hansen, *Athenian Democracy*; Kerferd, *Sophistic Movement*; Carolyn Miller, "*Polis*"; Poulakos, *Speaking for the Polis*; and Schiappa, *Protagoras and Logos*.

80. See, for example, John Parker, "A Survey of Cities," *The Economist*, July 29, 1995, 1–18; and the United Nations Population Fund at http://www.unfpa.org/pds/urbanization.htm.

81. See, for example, Porter, "Competitive Advantage of the Inner City."

82. Lately, for example, there has been a surge of interest in "community literacy," which often focuses on the language practices of specifically *urban* writers and speakers (see, e.g., Adler-Kassner, Crooks, and Waters, *Writing the Community*; Cintron, *Angels' Town*; Cushman, *Struggle and the Tools*; Peck, Flower, and Higgens, "Community Literacy").

83. Dagger, *Civic Virtues*, 155.

84. See also Bookchin, *From Urbanization to Cities*; Frug, *City Making*; Geoghegan, *Secret Lives of Citizens*; Lazare, *America's Undeclared War*; Ryan, "City as a Site"; Sennett, *Fall of Public Man* and *Conscience of the Eye*; and Young, *Inclusion*.

85. See "Metropolitan statistical area (MSA)" in the "Glossary" of the *Geographic Areas Reference Manual*, available at http://www.census.gov/geo/www/garm.html. For more information, see http://www.census.gov/population/www/estimates/metroarea.html.

86. See also Downs, *Opening Up the Suburbs* and *New Visions*; Bruce Katz, "Reviving Cities"; Myron Orfield, *American Metropolitics*; and Rusk, *Cities Without Suburbs*.

87. See, for example, Young, *Justice*, 252, and *Inclusion*, 232; Popenoe, *Private Pleasure*, 93–108; and Alexander et al., *Pattern Language*, which proposes that the world be organized politically into a thousand metropolitan areas, or "regions," of two to ten million people each (10–14).

88. Frug, *City Making*, 3.

89. See also Banerjee and Baer, *Beyond the Neighborhood Unit*; and Jacobs, *Death and Life*.

90. I am defining "public" here as all those who are affected, directly or indirectly, by the consequences of an act (Dewey, *Public*, 15–16).

91. Young, *Inclusion*, 229. Of course this argument could be used to support *global* politics since things like air pollution are planetary in their scope. What I am trying to locate here, though, is a public that can comprehend such effects but still hear the individual voices of ordinary citizens.

92. Hansen, *Athenian Democracy*, 60. Of course, the polity I am imagining here would be governed also by juries, committees, boards, and various officials. Still, the direct assembly remains the *sine qua non* of democracy, which is why I have based my calculations largely on it.

93. See Dahl, "Procedural Democracy," x.

94. Hansen thought attendance of one-fifth of the citizens at assembly meetings in fourth century, BCE, Athens was pretty good (cf. Finley, "Politics," 29). Interestingly, a study by Frank Bryan of 1,215 town meetings held between 1970 and 1994 in 210 Vermont towns found that, on average, 19 percent (that is, roughly one-fifth) of a town's eligible voters were present at any given meeting and that 37 percent of them (or 7 percent of eligible voters) spoke out at least once (Dahl, *On Democracy*, 110–11). Outside of small town Vermont, though, most of us would see even one-tenth attendance at a civic meeting as impressive, which is why I have used that proportion here.

95. Jacobs, *Death and Life*, 117–32.

96. Dahl, "City," 960. See also Spanish planner Jordi Borja's "*barrio grande*" and Richard Dagger's "districts" of 50,000, subdivided into ten wards of recognizably neighborhood size. Danielle Allen imagines a polis of 99,999 within South Chicago (*Talking to Strangers*, 172ff).

97. See, for example, http://www.ci.nyc.ny.us/html/dcp/html/lucds/cdstart.shtml.

98. Now, a political unit this large can still be suburban: Anthem, Arizona will eventually have 12,500 homes on 3,000 acres; Levittown, NJ, originally had ten neighborhoods of 1,200 units each; and Levittown, NY, had 17,400 homes on 4,000 acres with 82,000 residents.

99. Oliver, *Democracy in Suburbia*, 361.

100. On district-level governance in New York City, see Sanjek, *Future of Us All*, 11, 46ff. On Chicago's Local School Councils, see Fung and Wright, *Deepening Democracy*.

101. His "local transport area" seems to be the size of what I'm calling an urban district.

102. See, for example, Laslett, "Face to Face Society."

4. Ghetto

1. DuBois, *The Souls of Black Folk*, 359.

2. Kerner Commission, *Report*, 6, n. 1. By comparison, Jargowsky and Bane define "ghetto" as "an area in which the overall poverty rate . . . is greater than 40 percent," an approach that Wacquant says is arbitrary, asociological, deracialized, and bureaucratic ("Three Pernicious Premises," 342). Wacquant's own definition is similar to the Kerner Commission's: ghettoization is "involuntary, permanent, and total residential separation premised on caste as basis for the development of a *parallel (and inferior) social structure*" (343, emphasis in original). From this point of view, a ghetto is neither a topographic entity nor a simple aggregation of poor individuals; it is rather "an *institutional form*, a historically determinate, spatially based concatenation of mechanisms of *ethnoracial closure and control* . . . a bounded, racially and/or culturally uniform sociospatial formation based on (1) the forcible relegation of (2) a 'negatively typed' population . . . to (3) a reserved, 'frontier territory' . . . in which this population (4) develops under duress a set of parallel institutions that serve both as a functional substitute for, and a protective buffer against, the dominant institutions of the encompassing society . . . but (5) duplicate the latter only at an incomplete and inferior level while (6) maintaining those who rely on them in a state of structural dependency" (343, emphases in original). Marcuse defines ghetto, meanwhile, as "a spatially concentrated area used to separate and to limit a particular involuntarily defined population group (usually by race) held to be, and treated as, inferior by the dominant society" ("Enclave"). He makes important distinctions between the "classic" ghetto and Chicago's black belt today, an "outcast ghetto." And he compares these two to "enclaves" and "citadels" (see chap. 7).

3. Wright, "Introduction," xvii.

4. Klinenberg, *Heat Wave*, 22. See also Abbott and Wurr, "Chicago Studied."

5. For the story of Du Sable, see http://www.chipublib.org/004chicago/timeline/dusable.html; Drake and Cayton, *Black Metropolis*, 31–2; Donald Miller, *City of the Century*, 55–6; Spear, *Black Chicago*, 5; and Spinney, *City of Big Shoulders*.

6. Starks's brief history of "land grabs" in Chicago suggests that Du Sable was defrauded of his homestead when he left the area (see chap. 1 above, note 48); similar stories have been told about the 1795 Treaty of Greenville, by which the six square miles around the mouth of the Chicago River were "ceded" by the Potawatomi Indians to the United States, a deal that some historians have found ethically suspect (see, e.g., Cronon, *Nature's Metropolis*).

7. See, for example, Jacqueline Peterson, "Wild Chicago," 50ff.

8. Donald Miller, *City of the Century*, 56–7. This early heterogeneity is something we will see repeatedly in the history examined here: in the beginning is class and race mixing; it is only later that separation and homogeneity are *imposed* on the landscape. Jacqueline Peterson and Donald Miller both attest to this for early Chicago; but it is evident later on as well. Spear writes about how, from 1890 to 1920, "a relatively fluid pattern of race relations gave way to a rigid pattern of discrimination and segregation" in Chicago (*Black Chicago*, ix). We've already seen (in chap. 1) how the Lower North became homogeneously black only *after* World War II, thanks in large part to the Chicago Housing Authority; and Fidel shows how the Lincoln Park neighborhood lost much of its original economic and racial diversity during the government-sponsored gentrification of the 1970s and '80s ("End of Diversity"). All of this is persuasive evidence against any theory of a "natural" separation of races or classes. For other stories of how an "original" condition of racial, ethnic, economic, cultural, religious, and linguistic diversity is quashed, see Ira Berlin's *Generations of Captivity* about racial integration in seventeenth-century New York City, which he describes as a "farrago of nationalities, tongues, allegiances" (32); Mike Davis's "Fortress Los Angeles" about a 1940s downtown where "crowds of Anglo, black, and Mexican shoppers of all ages and classes mingled" (159); Mark Mazower's *Salonica, City of Ghosts*, about the religious, cultural, and linguistic mixing in that city from the fifteenth to twentieth centuries; Maria Rosa Menocal's *The Ornament of the World* about religious, ethnic, and linguistic diversity in medieval Spain; and Sam Bass Warner's *The Private City* about class integration in early Philadelphia.

9. Drake and Cayton, *Black Metropolis*, 32 (hereafter cited parenthetically in the text).

10. There was also an active abolitionist movement in Chicago, so much so that the town was known as "nigger-loving" in southern Illinois (Drake and Cayton, *Black Metropolis*, 33).

11. See also Spear, *Black Chicago*, 5–7.

12. Spear, *Black Chicago*, 20 (hereafter cited parenthetically in the text).

13. Cronon, *Nature's Metropolis*.

14. Miller, *City of the Century*, passim.

15. In 1890, almost 80 percent of the city's population was foreign-born or of foreign parentage (Spear, *Black Chicago*, 4).

16. According to Spear, 65 percent of black men and 80 percent of black women in Chicago at the turn of the nineteenth century were in domestic service, working as porters, servants, waiters, janitors, maids, and laundresses (*Black Chicago*, 29).

17. Chicago recorded an increase of almost 40,000 blacks between 1880–1910, the population nearly doubling every decade.

18. This was also the year of the Springfield race riots, which prompted some violence in Chicago.

19. Spear, *Black Chicago*, 151. Most of those working in the factories were classified as unskilled, and unionization efforts among them generally failed.

20. Ibid., 142. According to Stanley Lieberson, the black isolation index, which measures the percentage of blacks in the ward of the average black person, rose from 15.1 to 38.1 percent between 1910 and 1920; it would double again, to 70.4 percent, between 1920 and 1930 (quoted in Massey and Denton, *American Apartheid*).

21. Hirsch, *Making the Second Ghetto*, 3.

22. By 1958, 91% of Chicago elementary schools would have a racially homogeneous population (Spinney, *City of Big Shoulders*, 228).

23. On whether a young Richard J. Daley, future president of the Hamburg Athletic Club in Bridgeport, was involved in this violence, see Cohen and Taylor, *American Pharaoh*, 35ff.

24. See also Hirsch, *Making of the Second Ghetto*, 1. According to Hirsch, the racial breakdown was as follows: 23 blacks dead, 342 injured; 15 whites dead, 195 injured (276, n. 3).

25. See also Drake and Cayton, *Black Metropolis*, 73.

26. Massey and Denton, *American Apartheid*, 36. See also McKenzie, *Privatopia*; and Plotkin, " 'Hemmed In,' " 41.

27. Massey and Denton, *American Apartheid*, 36.

28. CHA vice-chairman Robert Taylor put the figure at 80 percent in 1939, but Plotkin suggests that this number is too high ("Hemmed In," 44–5; cf. McKenzie, *Privatopia*). For many of the Irish and Polish neighbors to the west of the black belt, covenants were a sign of *weakness*: the better way to prevent black residential incursions was violence (see Plotkin, "Hemmed In" and Hirsch, *Making the Second Ghetto*). When the U.S. Supreme Court finally dealt with covenants in *Shelly v. Kraemer* (1948), it only ruled that their *enforcement* by the courts was unconstitutional.

29. In 1934, there were 6.8 persons per black household in Chicago, 4.7 in white ones (Hirsch, *Making the Second Ghetto*, 18).

30. On the Near North Side, meanwhile, one of a handful of "satellite" neighborhoods created by the overflow of the South Side ghetto, an Urban League survey of 500 black families in 1925 found that most lived in rundown dwellings with no heat, falling plaster, and outside toilets. More than 60 percent lived in rear flats or basements with an average rent of less than $4 per room. Most moved frequently: 63 percent of the families had been at their present address less than a year. Nearly 90 percent of these blacks were native to the rural South, 55 percent had come to Chicago since 1918, and 63 percent had only been on the North Side since 1922. The majority of adults were young wage-earners; most had irregular employment as unskilled laborers, and 85 percent earned less than $32 per week. Poverty and mortality rates were both high (Zorbaugh, *Gold Coast*, 148).

31. Spear calls them the "halcyon days" (*Black Chicago*, 221); Drake and Cayton, the "fat years" (*Black Metropolis*, 78).

32. Drake and Cayton, *Black Metropolis*, 80–1. The 1939 *WPA Guide to Illinois* paints a vivid portrait of Bronzeville's side streets: "small shops selling mystic charms and potions; curbstone stands with smoke rising from wood fires over which chicken and spareribs are being barbecued; lunchrooms serving hot fish, sweet potato pie, gumbo, and other Southern dishes, markets bulging with turnip tops, mustard greens, and chitterlings; taverns and nightclubs that resound with blues-singing and hot-foot music" (Federal Writers' Project, 296).

33. Lemann, *Promised Land*, 64.

34. Wilson, *Truly Disadvantaged*, 3.

35. Ibid., 49, 143.

36. De Wit, "Rise of Public Housing," 234.

37. Bowly, *Poorhouse*, 30.

38. Ibid., 18.

39. For more on the history and structure of the U.S. public housing program, see Fleming, "Subjects of the Inner City."

40. Wood was a graduate of Fred Newton Scott's rhetoric program at the University of Michigan (Cohen and Taylor, *American Pharaoh*, 69).

41. See chap. 1 above, note 19.

42. Bowly, *Poorhouse*, 30. Drake and Cayton, *Black Metropolis*, 207.

43. Lemann, *Promised Land*, 3–7, 70.

44. Ibid., 70.

45. In its *Annual Report* of 1945, the CHA anticipated that there would be 32,500 homeless veteran families in the city within a year (De Wit, "Rise of Public Housing," 238).

46. See Jackson, *Crabgrass Frontier*.

47. Condit, *Chicago 1930–1970*, 286–7; Hirsch, *Making the Second Ghetto*, 27–8.

48. Hirsch, *Making the Second Ghetto*, 31.

49. Ibid., 1–16 (hereafter cited parenthetically in the text).

50. Bowly, *Poorhouse*, 49.

51. Condit, *Chicago 1930–1970*, 206.

52. Ibid.

53. Research shows that these residents were part of the movement into Hyde Park Kenwood that would later prompt drastic "protection" efforts there (Hirsch, *Making the Second Ghetto*, 122).

54. Hirsch, *Making the Second Ghetto*, 120. In a comment eerily applicable to today, Condit says, "Chicago has never developed a relocation program" (*Chicago 1930–1970*, 206).

55. Other projects from the time include the 1,677-unit Prairie Shores complex, built from 1959–62 on South Parkway from Twenty-eighth to Thirty-first Streets, and the IIT-led South Commons housing project, located between Michigan and Prairie Avenues from Twenty-sixth to Thirty-first Streets, which was somewhat more economically and racially integrated than the others. The 1958 Kenwood Hyde Park Urban Renewal Plan was another large-scale project of this type. There were also similar projects, most notably Carl Sandburg Village, on the Near North Side. What all of these projects shared was not only government-supported profits for private developers and a net loss of housing for poor and working-class blacks; they were all notoriously slow-moving (Condit, *Chicago 1930–1970*).

56. Condit, *Chicago 1930–1970*, 220.

57. Massey and Denton, *American Apartheid*, 56.

58. Ibid.

59. Matusow, *Unraveling of America*, 103. All this, of course, will sound familiar to anyone following the "revitalization" of Cabrini Green today. In the year 2000, we would also hear about plans to reattract "solvent" populations downtown and reclaim the central city, and there would also be skeptics wondering if these were not code phrases for the displacement of the poor, a net loss of housing units in the city, and racial turnover in other places. In an eerie foreshadowing of events half a century in

the future, Drake and Cayton asked in 1945, about a revitalization plan of that time, "What [does the city] plan to do with the Negroes who now live in the blighted areas?" (*Black Metropolis*, 207).

60. Condit, *Chicago 1930–1970*, 150ff; he is speaking of Racine Courts, LeClair Courts, and Ogden Courts (all since sold). Hunt and Venkatesh both see Chicago public housing as viable up to the early or mid-1960s and becoming only unredeemable much later, in the 1970s and '80s.

61. Schill and Wachter, "Spatial Bias," 1291–1300.

62. Fleming, "Subjects of the Inner City."

63. Of the 1948 sites, five of nine were in white areas, but they were smaller than the black projects, in out-of-the-way locations, and had a 10 percent ceiling on black tenancy (Hirsch, *Making the Second Ghetto*, 224).

64. See also Hirsch, *Making the Second Ghetto*, 213ff; and Bowly, *Poorhouse*, 77–80.

65. Schill, "Distressed Public Housing," 498, n. 9; the phrase is still part of federal law (see 42 U.S.C. §1441).

66. CHA, *Plan for Transformation*, 14.

67. See chap. 5 for the story of *Gautreaux v.* CHA. Cf. Solomon, *Global City Blues*, for a critique of Corbusian superblocks, but see Venkatesh (*American Project*) and Hunt ("What Went Wrong?") for a more nuanced story of the high rises.

68. Bowly, *Poorhouse*, 112.

69. Ibid., 124–129.

70. Condit, *Chicago 1930–1970*, 163. The language used to talk about Robert Taylor and the other State Street projects is often hyperbolically derogatory: Mayer and Wade, for example, write that "[t]he cancer stretched for miles" (*Chicago: Growth of a Metropolis*, 378).

71. "A de facto purpose of public housing in Chicago, at least after Elizabeth Wood left the Chicago Housing Authority in 1954, was to isolate the poor and especially the black population away from the white middle-class areas of the city" (Bowly, *Poorhouse*, 225).

72. Massey and Denton, *American Apartheid*.

73. Hunt, "What Went Wrong?" 108 (hereafter cited parenthetically in the text).

74. ADC was the forerunner of Aid to Families with Dependent Children (AFDC), today's Temporary Assistance for Needy Families (TANF).

75. Originally, the CHA did not accept families on relief at all. From 1947–1967, it tried to keep the percentage of welfare families at 25 percent of each project (Hunt, "What Went Wrong?" 121, n. 55).

76. Venkatesh, *American Project*. When Ruby Haynes saw the Robert Taylor Homes for the first time in the early 1960s, she thought they were magnificent: "tall, sturdily constructed buildings with elevators and balconies, fresh paint and central heating." As Ruby's son Larry, twelve years old at the time, later put it: "I thought that was the beautifullest place in the world" (Lemann, *Promised Land*, 106–7). So too LaJoe Rivers's memories of the Henry Horner Homes, which, when it opened in the late 1950s, was a dazzling place to her. Kotlowitz imagines her vision this way: "The building's brand-new bricks were a deep and luscious red, and they were smooth and solid to the touch. The

clean windows reflected the day's movements with a shimmering clarity that gave the building an almost magical quality" (*There Are No Children Here*, 19–20). And in an interview with the *Chicago Reporter*, Patricia Reed remembered: "I'll never forget the day my father called all of us together and asked if we wanted to live in the projects, and we were so excited, we just started saying, 'yes, yes' " (Brian Rogal, "Survey Casts Doubt on CHA Plans," *The Chicago Reporter*, June, 1999).

77. Clarence Wood also dates the collapse to this time: "[T]he black ghetto . . . was still a functioning community as late as 1966. Blacks still provided most of the community services, they still owned the small shops and businesses, and black professionals still provided help to black citizens. There was a vertical integration" (quoted in Marcuse, "Enclave").

78. Venkatesh, *American Project*, 46ff.

79. Kasarda claims that his "extreme poverty" tracts are almost 60 percent black ("Inner-City Concentrated Poverty," 264).

80. Jargowsky, *Poverty and Place*, 29ff.

81. Ibid., 257ff.

82. Lemann, *Promised Land*, 282. Nationally, black unemployment increased from 5.9 percent to 14.4 percent between 1948 and 1984 (Wilson, *Truly Disadvantaged*, 31 [table 2.4]).

83. Wilson, *When Work Disappears*, 19–20.

84. Lemann, *Promised Land*, 283; Wilson, *Truly Disadvantaged*, 27. Looking at all black families, the percentage headed by a female increased from 34.5 percent in 1970 to 48 percent in 1980 to 55 percent in 1990 (Kasarda, "Inner-City Concentrated Poverty," 270). But the change in family structure in Chicago's public housing projects during these years was more dramatic: according to CHA annual reports, Robert Taylor Homes in 1963 housed 2,734 two-parent families and 1,441 one-parent families; in 1982, the respective numbers were 322 and 3,523 (Natalie Y. Moore, "The Good Ol' Days," *The Chicago Reporter*, July/August, 2006).

85. Lemann, *Promised Land*, 283. Wilson reports similar numbers: in 1959, 15 percent of black births were out of wedlock; in 1982, it was 57 percent (*Truly Disadvantaged*, 28).

86. Wilson, *Truly Disadvantaged*, 29.

87. Lemann, *Promised Land*, 282.

88. Ibid., 283.

89. Jargowsky, *Poverty and Place*; Kasarda, "Inner-City Concentrated Poverty," 272.

90. Lemann, *Promised Land*, 283.

91. Wilson, *Truly Disadvantaged*, 22–25. When Ricketts and Sawhill looked at U.S. census tracts whose populations were above the national mean on the first four characteristics above—male joblessness, female-headed families, receipt of federal aid, and school leaving—they found an increase of 230 percent in the nation's "underclass" population from 1970 to 1980, much of it in the urban northeast and north central regions.

92. Wilson, *When Work Disappears*, 17–24; according to Drake and Cayton, in 1934, more than 50 percent of the families in the black belt were on relief (*Black Metropolis*, 203).

93. Lemann, *Promised Land,* 283.

94. Jargowsky, *Poverty and Place,* 30, 139.

95. There was also a string of court decisions, beginning in 1967, that made eviction or rejection from public housing difficult (Hunt, "What Went Wrong," 110).

96. See also Wilson, *Truly Disadvantaged,* 36–9.

97. Massey and Denton, *American Apartheid,* viii.

98. Darden, "Segregation," 524.

99. Massey and Denton, *American Apartheid,* 33, 49?

100. Ibid., 2.

101. Wilson, *Truly Disadvantaged,* 29–62; Wilson, *When Work Disappears,* 3–50; Jargowsky, *Poverty and Place,* passim.

102. Wilson, *When Work Disappears,* 25–34.

103. Ibid., 29, 37.

104. Klinenberg, *Heat Wave,* 93.

105. Wilson, *When Work Disappears,* 35.

106. Ibid., 34–35.

107. Klinenberg, *Heat Wave,* 95.

108. Wilson, *When Work Disappears,* 35. See Klinenberg's *Heat Wave* for the "natural" disaster that befell this community in 1995, aggravated by the neighborhood's social and physical decay.

109. Wilson, *When Work Disappears,* 25.

110. Ibid., 30.

111. The term is from Wilson, *Truly Disadvantaged,* 46–62.

112. Jargowsky calls this "neighborhood filtering" (*Poverty and Place*).

113. Wilson, *Truly Disadvantaged,* 49–55.

114. Ibid., 50.

115. Wilson, *When Work Disappears,* 6.

116. Wilson, *Truly Disadvantaged,* 56.

117. Ibid., 55–62. The Wilson of the 1980s and '90s probably romanticizes the Bronzeville of the 1940s and '50s, in the same way that Bronzeville residents of the 1920s and '30s romanticized the neighborhood of the 1890s and 1900s (Drake and Cayton, *Black Metropolis,* 73, which is, overall, a worrisome report of the neighborhood circa 1945, a community cut off from the mainstream economy, housing market, etc.—see, e.g., 202ff).

118. Jargowsky, *Poverty and Place,* 118–32.

119. Ibid., 157.

120. Ibid., 161.

121. Venkatesh, *American Project,* 110ff. The CHA budget fell 87 percent during this period (116).

122. Ibid., 131.

123. Edward Marciniak, "Why Perpetuate Chicago's High-Rise Hell?" *Chicago Tribune,* Nov. 26, 1993; and Jorge Casuso, "CHA Flat Vacancies Soaring," *Chicago Tribune,* July 26, 1988.

124. *Henry Horner Mothers Guild v.* CHA, No. 91 C 3316 (N.D. Ill. 1995); see also Hunt, "What Went Wrong?"; Kotlowitz, *There Are No Children Here*; and Lemann, *Promised Land.*

125. Lemann, *Promised Land*, 296.

126. Massey and Denton, *American Apartheid*, 77.

127. Ibid., 161; cf. Wilson, *Truly Disadvantaged*, 60–62.

128. Lemann, *Promised Land*, 266–7; emphasis in original.

129. Massey and Denton, *American Apartheid*, 161.

130. Darden, "Segregation," 523. Isolation is also a feature of affluent, white neighborhoods; Dreier, Mollenkopf, and Swanstrom, for example, cite studies showing that affluent families in this country are "considerably more isolated from other groups than the poor" (*Place Matters*, 54); and Young argues that isolation among the wealthy makes their own privilege invisible to them, allowing them to think that the problems of others are not their problems (*Inclusion and Democracy*, 204ff). The isolation of the wealthy is clearly different from the isolation of the poor, however, given that the former generally have access to resources that make them less dependent on environment (see e.g., Dreier et al., *Place Matters*, 4; and Marcuse, "Enclave").

131. Oliver, *Democracy in Suburbia*.

132. This is just as true for the white suburbs of Chicago, as we'll see in chapter 5.

133. Rubinowitz and Rosenbaum, *Crossing the Class and Color Lines*, 90ff; see also 219, n. 24.

134. Metropolitan Planning Council, *Untapped*, 35; cf. Venkatesh, *American Project*.

135. Newman, *Defensible Space*; Jacobs, *Death and Life*.

136. Klinenberg, *Heat Wave*, 79–128.

137. Fleming, "Streets of Thurii."

138. NTRAC, *North Town, II*.

139. City of Chicago, *Draft Near North Redevelopment Initiative*.

140. Kotlowitz, *There Are No Children Here*, 55 (also 13, 18, 34, 55). Cf. Wilson, *Truly Disadvantaged* and *When Work Disappears*; Klinenberg, *Heat Wave*; and Popkin, et al., *Hidden Wars*.

5. Suburbia

1. William Levitt, as quoted in McKenzie, *Privatopia*, 71.

2. On the Gautreaux case and its aftermath, see Rubinowitz and Rosenbaum, *Crossing the Class and Color Lines*, 17–48 (hereafter cited parenthetically in the text); also, Bowly, *Poorhouse*, 189–94; Business and Professional People, "Gautreaux Information" and "Gautreaux"; Peroff, Davis, and Jones, *Gautreaux Housing Demonstration*, passim; Polikoff, *Housing the Poor*, 147–59; and Cohen and Taylor, *American Pharaoh*, 486–89, 549–50.

3. Austin also ruled that future CHA projects had to be limited to 120 persons, could comprise no more than 15 percent of the total residential units in a single census tract, and could not house families with children above the third floor (Rubinowitz and Rosenbaum, *Crossing*, 26) (see also Sandra Newman, "Introduction and Overview"; and *Gautreaux v. CHA*, 304 F. Supp. 736 [N.D. Ill. July 1, 1969] at http://www.bpichicago.org/pht/pubs/1969_judgment_order.pdf).

4. According to Hirsch, between 1969 and 1980, the CHA built only 114 new apartments (*Making the Second Ghetto*, 265); see also Bennett, "Do We Really?"

5. See also Brian J. Rogal, "The Habitat Co.: Private Firm Keeps Tight Grip on Public Housing," *The Chicago Reporter*, November, 1999. The Gautreaux court has since waived restrictions on building new public housing units in segregated neighborhoods where new development is likely to increase economic and racial integration and where the reconcentration of low-income blacks is avoided, as long as the proportion of public housing units is not more than 30 percent of the total, and as long as some of those units are reserved for higher-income public housing families (with incomes 30–80 percent of a.m.i.). See Business and Professional People, "Gautreaux"; and the 1998 HOPE VI ruling in *Gautreaux v.* CHA, No. 66 C 1459 (N.D. Ill. February 25, 1998) at http://www.bpichicago.org/pht/pubs/hopeIV_ruling.pdf.

6. The court supported its decision in part by pointing to the deconcentration goals laid out in the 1974 Housing and Community Development Act, which set up the Section 8 program. Only two years earlier, however, the court had denied metropolitan relief in a school desegregation case, *Milliken v. Bradley* (Rubinowitz and Rosenbaum, *Crossing*, 37; for more on *Milliken*, see Irons, *Jim Crow's Children*, 234–88; for more on legal challenges to suburban residential segregation, see Kirp, Dwyer, and Rosenthal, *Our Town*, passim).

7. This was a one-year, metropolitan-wide, experimental housing initiative. It was renewed annually several times thereafter and finally institutionalized in 1981 by a consent decree in federal district court (*Gautreaux v. Landrieu*, affirmed in 1982 at the appeals court level in *Gautreaux v. Pierce*) (Rubinowitz and Rosenbaum, *Crossing*, 38–9).

8. See Cohen and Taylor, *American Pharaoh*, 357–429, for the story of the open housing movement in Chicago in the 1960s; and the LCMOC website at http://www.lcmoc.org/.

9. Lemann, *Promised Land*, 347.

10. James Traub, "What No School Can Do," *New York Times Magazine*, January 16, 2000.

11. Fiss, "What Should Be Done?" See also Downs, *New Visions*; and Marciniak, *Reclaiming the Inner City*.

12. Its authorization was Section 8 of the 1974 Housing and Community Development Act.

13. HUD, "Housing Choice Vouchers Fact Sheet"; see also CBPP, "Introduction."

14. See CBPP, "Introduction." Though any family whose income is below 50 percent (sometimes 80 percent) of a.m.i. is eligible, current law reserves 75 percent of vouchers for the extremely poor, that is, those below 30 percent a.m.i. Preference is also given to the homeless, those paying more than 50 percent of income for rent, and the involuntarily displaced. The median income for the Chicago metropolitan area in 2002 was $75,400 for a family of four (http://www.huduser.org/datasets/il.html).

15. HUD's 2002 fair market rents for the six-county Chicago metropolitan area, calculated for the fiftieth percentile, were as follows: $747 for one bedroom, $891 for two bedrooms, $1,114 for three bedrooms, and $1,247 for four bedrooms (see http://www.huduser.org/datasets/fmr.html). The PHA has some flexibility to adjust payment standards and make exceptions. If the rent for the unit is greater than the payment standard, the

family must pay the additional amount itself (but may not pay more than 40 percent of its income for housing). If the rent is less than the local payment standard, the family can keep some or all of the difference.

16. Schill, "Distressed Public Housing"

17. See, for example, Hendrickson, "Racial Desegregation"; Sard and Fischer, "Housing Voucher Block Grant Bills"; Schill, "Distressed Public Housing"; Schill and Wachter, "Principles"; and Weicher, *Privatizing Subsidized Housing.*

18. CBPP, "Introduction." Between 1996 and 2003, Congress added more than 650,000 new vouchers, almost half to families losing other types of federal housing subsidies; recently, however, the number of new vouchers added has dropped dramatically, from 130,000 in 2001 to only 30,000 a year for 2003–2005—this despite the fact that demand for vouchers far exceeds supply. The CBPP claims that only one-fourth of eligible families receive federal housing assistance (see "Growth in Housing Voucher Costs" at http://www.cbpp.org/pubs/housing.htm).

19. Lawyers Committee for Better Housing, "Locked Out," 4. Unlike, say, Social Security or Medicare, decent housing is not an entitlement in this country despite the express goal of the 1949 U.S. Housing Act to ensure "a decent home and a suitable living environment for every American family." According to a 2000 report, more than 5 million low-income households with severe housing needs, paying more than 50 *percent* of their income on rent and utilities, receive no housing assistance whatsoever and would benefit from vouchers. Unfortunately, there is a long waiting list to enroll in Section 8—the national average is over two years; in New York City, eight years; and in Los Angeles, ten (HUD, "Section 8").

20. See also Daskal, *In Search*; NLIHC, *Out of Reach 2005*; and HUD, *Widening Gap*. The problem is worsened by the recent conversion of so many urban apartments to condominiums.

21. Tests by the Lawyers' Committee for Better Housing revealed that Section 8 voucher holders in Chicago routinely experienced discrimination based on source of income, illegal in that city, and that black and Latino voucher holders suffered additional discrimination based on race and ethnicity, illegal everywhere in the United States ("Locked Out").

22. Brian J. Rogal, "CHA Residents Moving to Segregated Areas," *The Chicago Reporter*, July–August, 1998. Similarly, Paul Fischer from Lake Forest College found strikingly similar results in 1999: of 1,000 Section 8 relocatees in the city, 80 percent had moved to census tracts that were over 90 percent black, and over 90 percent had relocated to census tracts whose median income was under $15,000 per year ("Section 8"; see also his 2003 update, "Where Are the Families Going?"). The top four destinations for Section 8 holders in the city were all in low-income minority neighborhoods: South Shore, Austin, Auburn-Gresham, and Woodlawn (Kate N. Grossman, "Neighborhoods Fear Influx of Poor Renters," *Chicago Sun-Times*, March 27, 2001). For those relocating outside the city limits, three of the top four Section 8 destinations were predominantly black southern suburbs (Harvey, Calumet City, and Chicago Heights) (the other top destination was Evanston).

23. CHAC, Inc., the private company that administers the Housing Choice Voucher Program for the CHA, reported that 93 percent of recent relocatees from Chicago public housing have settled in communities that are majority African-American, and 75 percent in high-poverty neighborhoods (cited in Alex Kotlowitz, "Where

Is Everyone Going?" *Chicago Tribune Magazine*, March 10, 2002). See also Melita Marie Garza, "Study Plots Effect of CHA Housing Rehab Plan," *Chicago Tribune*, November 23, 1999; Jamie Kalven, "Where Will All the People Go?" *View from the Ground*, June 6, 2001; National Housing Law Project, *False HOPE*; and Christopher Swope, "Rehab Refugees," *Governing Magazine*, May 2001. In a 2000 report, HUD denied that there was a *national* trend toward the reconcentration of poor blacks due to Section 8 relocations (HUD, "Section 8"); and a 2001 Urban Institute study of Section 8 relocatees reported a lessening of racial and economic concentration as a result of relocation: nationwide, there was a drop in the neighborhood poverty rate of Section 8 holders from 61 percent to 27 percent, although 16 percent of relocates were still in high-poverty census tracts (Kingsley, Johnson, and Petit, "HOPE VI"). The minority figures are not as encouraging: families moved from neighborhoods with an average 88 percent minority population to neighborhoods with an average 68 percent minority population.

24. See, for example, Fiss, "What Should Be Done?"; and Bradford McKee, "Public Housing's Last Hope," *Architecture*, August 1, 1997.

25. Polikoff, "Chicago's Not About to Give Up On a Bad Idea," 215.

26. Linnet Myers, "From a World of Despair to Life of Promise," *Chicago Tribune*, December 30, 1998.

27. See, for example, Martinson, *American Dreamscape*, though there appears to be a trend of late to see the suburbs in a more favorable light (e.g., Baxandall and Ewen, *Picture Windows*; Gordon and Richardson, "Are Compact Cities Desirable?"; Iver Peterson, "Some Perched in Ivory Tower Gain Rosier View of Suburbs," *New York Times*, December 5, 1999; Rybczynski, *City Life*; and D. J. Waldie, "Do the Voters Really Hate Sprawl?" *New York Times*, March 3, 2000). Sharpe and Wallock refer to this as the new "suburbanophilia" ("Bold New City," 13–7).

28. For "suburb," see Appendix A to the 1999 American Housing Survey at http://www.census.gov/hhes/www/housing/ahs/ahs99/appendixa.pdf; for "metropolitan area," see http://www.census.gov/population/www/estimates/aboutmetro.html and chapter 3 above, note 85; for "urbanized area," see http://www.census.gov/population/censusdata/urdef.txt.

29. Oliver, *Democracy*, 35.

30. Sies, "City Transformed," 83–4, 89–90.

31. Jackson, *Crabgrass Frontier*.

32. See, for example, Duany, Plater-Zyberk, and Speck, *Suburban Nation*.

33. See, for example, Downs, *Opening Up*; but cf. Bruegmann, "Schaumburg": suburbia was the driving force in the rise of the automobile rather than the other way around (166).

34. Warner, *Private City*, 3–4.

35. Downs, *New Visions*.

36. Martinson, *American Dreamscape*; William Schneider, "The Suburban Century Begins," *The Atlantic Monthly*, July, 1992: 33–44.

37. Lazare, *America's Undeclared War*. Sharpe and Wallock argue that functional approaches to suburbia, emphasizing, for example, the rise of office space there, mask the continuing social impulse (race and class segregation) behind this landscape ("Bold New City," 6–13).

38. Hayden, *Building Suburbia*, 8; she calls it Americans' "triple dream." As an example of the early twenty-first century North American suburb, consider Anthem, Arizona, a private development of 12,500 homes being built on 6,000 acres north of

Phoenix, which conforms to all three of our definitions above. It is outside Phoenix but still within commuting distance of it, is comprised almost entirely of single-family detached residences, built at low density, with curving streets and a golf course, and is homogeneous in appearance, use, and population. Most of the land not given over to housing is dedicated to recreation; the development will include a 43,000-square-foot community center with a climbing wall, fitness center, water park, and community park with a kid's train, fishing lake, playground, and sports fields. Surely, *this* is *par excellence* the physical manifestation of American privatism. Other than a school and some "community rooms" where residents can learn origami, nothing here will engage people in differentiation and resolution, debate and discussion; such things are unneeded given the homogeneity of the population. For more, see http://www.delwebb.com/anthemarizona/.

39. See, for example, Bruegmann, "Schaumburg"; Fishman, *Bourgeois Utopias*; Garreau, *Edge City*; Hayden, *Building Suburbia*; Christopher B. Leinberger and Charles Lockwood, "How Business is Reshaping America," *Atlantic Monthly*, October, 1986: 43–52; and Von Hoffman and Felkner, "Historical Origins."

40. Myron Orfield, *American Metropolitics*, 28.

41. Ibid., 31–46.

42. For a different typology, see Lang and Sanchez, "New Metro Politics," which classifies metropolitan counties according to their density, growth, and proportion of non-Hispanic whites. Five regional types are derived: cores, inner suburbs, mature suburbs, emerging suburbs, and exurbs; residents vote Democratic in proportion to their county's "urban intensity."

43. For example, Schaumburg is "a bustling suburban community" (Village Web site, "Introduction").

44. See, for example, Alison Mitchell, "Two Parties Prepare for Biggest Battle Yet in Fight for Suburbs," *New York Times*, May 4, 1999.

45. Downs, *Opening Up*.

46. Squires, "Urban Sprawl."

47. See also Von Hoffman and Felkner, "Historical Origins."

48. See, for example, Dreier, Mollenkopf, and Swanstrom, *Place Matters*; Gyourko and Sinai, "Spatial Distribution"; Hanchett, "U.S. Tax Policy"; Jackson, *Crabgrass Frontier*; Kemper, "Home Inequity"; and Von Hoffman and Felkner, "Historical Origins."

49. Bruce Katz, "Reviving Cities"; Oliver, *Democracy in Suburbia*; Myron Orfield, *American Metropolitics*; Philips, *Wealth and Democracy*; and Rusk, *Cities Without Suburbs*.

50. Von Hoffman and Felkner, "Historical Origins."

51. See Frug, *City Making*; and Teaford, *City and Suburb*.

52. See Heikkila, "Are Municipalities Tieboutian Clubs?"; Booza, Cutsinger, and Galster, "Where Did They Go?"

53. Heikkila, "Are Municipalities Tieboutian Clubs?"

54. Neil Harris, "The City That Shops," 179; the single biggest drop occurred in the 1950s.

55. Bruegmann also traces the movement of Chicago businesses away from the center toward the periphery during this time ("Schaumburg"; cf. Wilson, *When Work Disappears*).

56. Leachman et al., *Black, White and Shades of Brown*, 31.

57. Johnson, *Chicago Metropolis 2020*, 46; Oliver, *Democracy in Suburbia*; Myron Orfield, *Chicago Metropolitics*; Teaford, *City and Suburb*.

58. Pamela A. Lewis and Leah Samuel, "Exclusionary Codes: In Northwest Suburbs, Zoning Shuts Door on Affordable Housing," *Chicago Reporter*, June, 2002.

59. Johnson, *Chicago Metropolis 2020*, 41.

60. Myron Orfield, *American Metropolitics*, Map 2–3.

61. Ibid., 37–8. Meanwhile, business taxes on a 100,000-square-foot office building in mostly white DuPage County were $212,639, compared with $468,000 in mostly black south suburban Cook County. As for sales taxes: in 1997, Oak Brook had sales tax revenues of $1,167 per resident; Schaumburg, $341; Chicago, $59; and Brookfield, $30 (Johnson, *Chicago Metropolis 2020*, 55).

62. Myron Orfield, *Chicago Metropolitics*, 31–2.

63. Ibid., 16–7, 23.

64. In 1993, Robbins, a black suburb, had a tax base per household of $23,616; in Oak Brook, a white suburb, it was $885,186. Cicero's schools had annual operating expenditures of $4,031 per student; Winnetka's, $8,829. Homeowners in Harvey paid $5,437 in taxes on a $100,000 house; in Barrington Hills, they paid $1,738 (ibid., 30–32).

65. See also the 2004 comparison of Naperville, Illinois, and Gary, Indiana in the U.S. Census Bureau's "Children and the Households They Live In," which reveals that, in 2000, only 9 percent of Naperville's children did not live with two married parents; while in Gary, the proportion was 70 percent (16–18). Naperville also figures in Dreier, Mollenkopf, and Swanstrom's three-way comparison of a poor central city congressional district in New York City's South Bronx, an older inner-ring suburban district outside of Los Angeles, and a wealthy outer-ring suburban district (Naperville) (*Place Matters*, 4–18). Finally, see the comparison between Chicago's census tract #3805, which includes the Robert Taylor Homes, and the suburbs Kenilworth, Ford Heights, and Naperville in Ebner, "Suburbs and Cities."

66. Scott Baldauf, "When Zoning Becomes Segregation Tool, " *Christian Science Monitor*, August 11, 2000; Jackson, *Crabgrass Frontier*; and Kirp, Dwyer, and Rosenthal, *Our Town*.

67. Leachman et al., *Black, White and Shades of Brown* (hereafter cited parenthetically in the text).

68. See also Nyden et al., "Neighborhood Diversity"; and Stuart, *Integration or Resegregation*, 17ff.

69. In suburban Cook County, for example, there was an increase of 131,000 blacks between 1990 and 1998 (Leachman et al., *Black, White and Shades of Brown*, 14) (cf. Frey, "Melting Pot Suburbs," at the national level).

70. Two-thirds of all blacks in the Chicago metropolitan area live in just 20 of the city's 77 community areas and 18 of its 269 suburbs (Johnson, *Chicago Metropolis 2020*, 41).

71. See also Logan, "Separate and Unequal."

72. In Lake County, for example, the high average price of a single family dwelling discourages the building of housing affordable to anyone making less than 80 percent a.m.i. (Leachman et al., *Black, White and Shades of Brown*, 24).

73. Most suburbs explicitly discourage housing construction targeted to young families with children, minority households, single-parent households, low-wage workers, and retirees on fixed income because they require more expenditures for education and other services (ibid., 24–5).

74. Ibid., 33. Meanwhile, 38 percent of the affordable homes and 44 percent of the rental units are in the twenty-two suburban municipalities which experienced job loss between 1980 and 1990. Considering the entire region (that is, throwing economically stagnant Chicago in the mix, with its "wealth" of affordable units), only 20 percent of total affordable homes and 6 percent of affordable rental units were located in municipalities with high job growth (ibid., 33–4).

75. Ibid., 36. In addition, Blacks are overrepresented in municipalities with the lowest tax bases and under-represented in those with the highest tax base, that is, those better able to provide good schools and services and to have moderate tax rates (ibid., 36–8). In 1990, there were twenty-eight municipalities in the region where blacks constituted 10 percent or more of the population; twenty-four of these fell into the two lowest tax base per household categories (37). All this is evidence for the spatial mismatch thesis (31): lower-wage and lower-skilled jobs are developing far from the neighborhoods where the most potential job seekers live. Transportation costs to the suburbs and lack of affordable housing there clearly limit employment opportunities for low-income inner-city residents. What is happening, then, is that minorities who are leaving central Chicago for the northern and western suburbs are concentrating in older cities (e.g., Elgin), which have become bedroom communities for workers in the wealthier suburbs (e.g., Hoffman Estates).

76. Leachman et al.'s research was based mostly on 1980 and 1990 U.S. Census numbers. What do we know about suburban diversity in the Chicago metropolitan area from more recent data? According to Frey, the 2000 U.S. Census showed a rise in the minority proportion of the nation's suburban population from 19.3 percent in 1990 to 27.3 percent in 2000 ("Melting Pot," 2), but much of that change was caused by Asian and Hispanic immigrant growth in just thirty-five metropolitan areas (6–12), of which Chicago's suburbs recorded the second lowest minority share (14), trailing only Fort Worth, Texas. Stuart's research confirms this: he found that, in 2000, 27 percent of the Chicago metropolitan area's African-Americans lived in the suburbs, up from 19 percent in 1990, a 58 percent increase (for Latinos, 39 percent lived in the suburbs, up from 29 percent in 1990, a 128 percent increase; for whites, 75 percent lived in the suburbs, up from 67 percent in 1990). But 50 percent of suburban African Americans lived in just 13 of the area's 264 suburbs (50 percent of the Latinos lived in just 17 suburbs) (*Integration or Resegregation*, 1). McArdle's work, also using 2000 data, focused more on the skyrocketing Latino population in the Chicago metropolitan area: although the area remains one of the most segregated in the country for blacks, the largest increase in overall segregation in the area from 1990–2000 was actually for suburban Latinos (*Race, Place, and Opportunity*, i).

77. It is also, admittedly, on the I-90 corridor that I traveled from south central Wisconsin to downtown Chicago while writing this book.

78. Village of Schaumburg Web site, "Introduction." Information in the rest of this paragraph also comes from this page.

79. Similarly, Naperville, Illinois, grew from 7,000 residents in 1950 to 128,358 in 2000 (Dreier, Mollenkopf, and Swanstrom, *Place Matters*, 16).

80. Village of Schaumburg Web site, "History." Information in this and the following paragraph comes from this page.

81. Bruegmann, "Schaumburg," 169.

82. Village of Schaumburg Web site, "Introduction." Information in this and the next four sentences comes from this page.

83. Village of Schaumburg Web site, "Government." Information in this and the rest of the sentences in this paragraph come from this page.

84. Village of Schaumburg Web site, "Introduction." Information in the rest of this paragraph comes from this page.

85. Garreau, *Edge City*, 6–7. This is similar to what Fishman has called a "technoburb" (*Bourgeois Utopias*, 184); Hayden, a "taxopolis" ("Model Houses," 9); and Gottdiener and Kephart, one nucleus in a "multinucleated" metropolitan region (quoted in Sharpe and Wallock, "Bold New City," 4); see also Bruegmann, "Schaumburg"; Myron Orfield, *American Metropolitics*; and Jackson, *Crabgrass Frontier*.

86. Thall, *New American Village*, 6 (hereafter cited parenthetically in text).

87. Charles Lockwood, "Putting the Urb in the Suburbs," *Planning* 63, no. 6 (1997): 18–21.

88. Village of Schaumburg, Web site, "Publications": press release from February 1, 2001: "Edge City Expert and Author Joel Garreau to Headline Schaumburg Conference June 3–5" (http://www.ci.schaumburg.il.us/vos.nsf/schaumburg/EMUR-58KU42).

89. Lockwood, "Putting the Urb in the Suburbs" (see n. 87 above).

90. Most such projects are modeled on Reston, Virginia, which in the late 1980s built its own Town Center: a one-acre plaza with 530,000 square feet of office space, 200,000 square feet of stores and restaurants, an eleven-screen movie theater, and a 514-room Hyatt Hotel (ibid.).

91. See also Dirk Johnson, "Town Sired by Malls Creates Downtown," *New York Times*, August 7, 1996: A8.

92. Leinberger and Lockwood, 49 (full reference available in note 39 above).

93. Village of Schaumburg Web site, "Population." Information in the rest of this paragraph and the next come from this page.

94. Village of Schaumburg, 2000 Census Tables.

95. Village of Schaumburg, 2000 Census Tables, which indicates a total of 31,799 households in the village; blacks were 3.4 percent of the total population.

96. Village of Schaumburg Web site, "Housing." Of 32,851 units, 84.5 percent were built since 1970.

97. Ibid. Currently, single family dwellings make up 36 percent of the village housing stock, with multifamily housing (apartments, townhouses, etc., most of them owner-occupied) comprising 64 percent.

98. Ibid. As for housing costs, the average price for a detached, single family dwelling in the village in 1999 was $215,000. The average rent for a two bedroom apartment, meanwhile, was $996 per month (compare HUD's 2000 Fair Market Rent for a similar sized unit in Cook County: $762 per month—see http://www.huduser.org/datasets/fmr.html).

99. Leachman et al., *Black, White and Shades of Brown*, Appendix B, Table 11.

100. The Urban Institute, *Assessment*. (According to critics, the program was designed to keep federal funds in the hands of governors and mayors and away from community development corporations and other grassroots organizations founded during the 1960s.)

101. Ibid.; and HUD, "CDBG Entitlement Communities Overview." These communities received approximately $3 billion in FY2000 out of a total $4.75 billion CDBG appropriation nationwide ("CDBG Entitlement Communities Program").

102. HUD, "CDBG Entitlement Communities Program." The block funding itself (i.e., the disbursement of money to states and cities) is automatic and not contingent on federal approval of the actual proposed projects: "[r]ather, the choice of the type of development to fund, the agencies to carry out funded activities, and the neighborhoods that would benefit [is] left almost entirely to local jurisdictions" (see The Urban Institute, *Assessment*).

103. That is, states and "local entitlement communities," which can be central cities of a metropolitan area, other cities in a metropolitan area with populations of at least 50,000 (like Schaumburg), and qualified urban counties (HUD, "CDBG Entitlement Communities Program").

104. HUD, "CDBG Entitlement Communities Overview."

105. Ibid. In annual reports to HUD, the grantee must certify that at least 70 percent of funds received over a one-, two-, or three-year period were used for activities that benefited low- and/or moderate-income persons (that is, individuals or families making below 80 percent of the area median income) and that it "affirmatively furthers" fair housing. The grantee must also "develop and follow a plan which provides for and encourages citizen participation and which emphasizes participation by persons of low- or moderate-income, particularly residents of predominantly low- and moderate-income neighborhoods, slums, or blighted areas" (ibid.).

106. Village of Schaumburg, *Consolidated Plan, 2000–2005*, 19–20.

107. Ibid., 24.

108. In 1999, a two-bedroom apartment there rented for $1,100, a little over the village average of $980 (ibid., 21) and well above the metropolitan area fair market rent of $737 (see http://www.huduser.org/datasets/fmr.html).

109. Village of Schaumburg, *Consolidated Plan, 2000–2005*, 25.

110. Village of Schaumburg Web site, "Housing."

111. Village of Schaumburg, *Consolidated Plan, 2000–2005*, 25.

112. On its Web site ("Housing"), the Village claims that three apartment complexes have set aside 20 percent of their apartments for moderate income families (this would include #1 in the list provided and two of the complexes in #4). But the next two sentences suggest to me a distaste for this arrangement on the part of the Village: "These apartment complexes received federal loans for construction and are required to do so [that is, set aside apartments for the poor]. When these obligations are complete, the question of affordable housing will once again become more crucial."

113. In Schaumburg's Annual Plan for its FY 2001 grant of almost $400,000 in CDBG funds, the village lists the activities to be undertaken. They include housing assistance for the elderly and homeless and child care (e.g., the village plans to use $350,000 from its FY2002–03 CDBG funds to build a YMCA day-care center) (Village of Schaumburg, *Annual Action Plan, FY 2001*).

114. See 42 U.S.C. §5305(c). "Low or moderate income" residents are individuals or families making below 80 percent of the area median income (in 1999, $47,800 per year for a four-person family in the Chicago metropolitan area—see Village of Schaumburg, *Consolidated Plan*, 10). For HUD's income categories, see http://www.huduser.org/datasets/il/IL06/index.html.

115. Ibid. See Village of Schaumburg, *Action Plan*, 9. The village claims that it has fourteen neighborhoods with from 21–56 percent low or *moderate* income residents, and apparently Hartung Road goes through one of them.

116. See also Patrick Kerkstra, "Funding for Federal Grants in Suburbs," *Philadelphia Inquirer*, August 5, 2001, for a similar story of a well-to-do municipality using CDBG funds against the clear *intent* of the legislation that created the program.

117. Jackson, "Gentleman's Agreement," 210.

118. See "Derivation of the Village of Schaumburg Logo" at http://www.ci.schaumburg.il.us/vos.nsf/schaumburg/JSCP-593PP5.

119. Rubinowitz and Rosenbaum, *Crossing the Class and Color Lines* (hereafter cited parenthetically in the text).

120. See also MTO research: "getting away from drugs and gangs" was the main reason for seeking relocation assistance, more than either jobs or better schools.

121. See, for example, Polikoff, " 'Chicago's Not About' "; Downs, *Opening Up*.

122. MTO's mandate was thus to facilitate *economic* integration, whereas Gautreaux's was racial: the two kinds of integration are, of course, difficult to separate for this particular population. For more on the MTO program, see Brennan, "Background"; Kling, *Moving to Opportunity*; HUD, *Moving to Opportunity: Current Status* and *Moving to Opportunity: Interim Impacts*; Shroder, "Moving to Opportunity"; and Del Conte and Kling, "Synthesis."

123. Pettit and McLanahan, "Social Dimensions," 7–9.

124. Del Conte and Kling, "Synthesis," 4.

125. Leventhal and Brooks-Gunn, "Moving to Better Neighborhoods," 12.

126. Del Conte and Kling, "Synthesis," 4.

127. Emily Rosenbaum, "Social Context," 17–18; the Boston study also showed striking effects for health and safety (Del Conte and Kling, "Synthesis," 4).

128. Del Conte and Kling, "Synthesis," 5.

129. Ludwig, Duncan, and Ladd, "Effect of MTO," 13–4.

130. Del Conte and Kling, "Synthesis," 3–4.

131. Ludwig, Duncan, and Ladd, "Effect of MTO," 13–5.

132. Emily Rosenbaum, "Social Context," 19.

133. Pettit and McLanahan, "Social Dimensions," 9.

134. Ibid., 8, table 1. Though most of my references to MTO data are from around 2001, the more recent 2003 HUD "midterm" evaluation of the program continued to find nonexistent, mixed, and even disturbing effects for suburban moving among former public housing families. True, the experimental group families moved to neighborhoods with higher percentages of adults employed, two-parent families, and high school graduates, and nearly twice the rate of homeownership (viii–ix); they reported higher levels of satisfaction with their neighborhoods, greater perception of safety, and lower rates of crime victimization (ix); and both adults and female children experienced improvements in mental and physical health (x). But there were increased behavior problems among boys in the experimental group families (xi); small or no effects on educational outcomes (at least at the short- and mid-term); and no effects on employment, earnings, or receipt of public assistance (xii–xiii). A final evaluation study will be done ten years after the end of implementation (around 2008) (HUD, *Moving to Opportunity: Interim Impacts*).

135. According to Rubinowitz and Rosenbaum, crime and fear in the suburbs is often automobile-related: taunting and things thrown from car windows, and so on.

Another problem with cars in the suburbs is that many of the movers did not own one: Kasarda's research shows that 59 percent of black households in extreme poverty tracts, like those including and surrounding Cabrini Green, did not own a car in 1990 ("Inner-City," 279); Wilson's figure is even lower: only 18 percent of black households in extreme poverty tracts own a car (*When Work Disappears*, 39).

136. See also "Housing Policy: From Ghetto to Suburb," *The Economist*, October 7, 1995: "Newcomers to the suburbs complain of isolation, lack of child care and the reluctance of suburban hospitals to accept Medicaid. . . . Racism also crops up" (33).

137. See also Popkin et al., "Gautreaux Legacy," 929–30.

138. For example, Cicero and Berwyn (James Rosenbaum, "Changing," 257).

139. See also Flynn McRoberts, "A New World—Down the Block," *Chicago Tribune*, October 8, 1998.

140. Bill Rumbler, "Integration Project Leads to a Sense of Community," *Chicago Sun-Times*, March 15, 1998; Danielle Gordon and James Ylisela Jr., "Court Ruling Puts More Teeth in Public Housing Plan," *The Chicago Reporter*, March, 1998; and Jerry Adler and Maggie Malone, "Toppling Towers," *Newsweek*, November 4, 1996, 70–2.

141. Fiss, "What Should Be Done?"

142. And see Linnet Myers, "From a World of Despair to Life of Promise," *Chicago Tribune*, December 30, 1998.

143. Andrew Martin, and Flynn McRoberts, "Scattered CHA sites? Hardly," *Chicago Tribune*, December 8, 1998; James L. Tyson, "Self-Help: The New Tenet at Chicago Housing Project," *Christian Science Monitor*, June 28, 1996.

144. Jewish Council on Urban Affairs, "Public Housing: Voices Rising Above the Bulldozers," *Community Views: Voices from Chicago's Neighborhoods* (Chicago: October, 1999).

145. Ibid.

146. Bezalel, *Voices of Cabrini.*

147. See also Brian Rogal, "Survey Casts Doubt on CHA Plans," *The Chicago Reporter*, June, 1999: in a survey, 68 percent of Robert Taylor families did not rank Section 8 among top three housing options; Cory Oldweiler, "Cabrini Changes Come All Too Slowly," *Chicago Reporter*, March 1998; and Ranney and Wright, "Race, Class, and State Power," 14–7.

148. Sharpe and Wallock, "Bold New City," 23.

149. For example, Baumgartner, *Moral Order*; Leachman et al., *Black, White and Shades of Brown*; and Oliver, *Democracy in Suburbia.*

150. See Reich's discussion the "secession of the successful," in *Work of Nations*, 243–315.

151. Duany, Plater-Zyberk, and Speck, *Suburban Nation*; Thall, *New American Village*.

152. Lynch, *Good City Form.*

153. Garreau, *Edge City*.

154. Fishman, *Bourgeois Utopias*.

155. See, for example, Duany, Plater-Zyberk, and Speck, *Suburban Nation*; Jackson, *Crabgrass Frontier*; Sies, "City Transformed," 93; and Southworth and Owens, "Evolving Metropolis."

156. Ewing, "Is Los Angeles-Style Sprawl Desirable?"; Southworth and Parthasarathy, "Suburban Public Realm I" and "Suburban Public Realm II."

157. Mumford, *Culture of Cities*, 215.

6. The New Urbanism

1. Mary Schmich, "Mixed-Income Developer Screens for Right Attitude," *Chicago Tribune*, July 2, 2000; John Handley, "Moving to Cabrini: A Mixed-Income Model for Redevelopment Rises in the Shadows of Dilapidated CHA Buildings," *Chicago Tribune*, August 12, 2000; and Don Debat, "A Nostalgic Tour of North and Halsted," *Chicago Sun-Times*, August 10, 2000.

2. City of Chicago Department of Housing, *Near North Development Initiative*, 5.

3. Flynn McRoberts, "A New World—Down the Block," *Chicago Tribune*, October 8, 1998; and CBS News, "Tearing Down Cabrini-Green," *60 Minutes II*, December 11, 2002. See also Robert Sharoff, "Chicago Tries to Upgrade a Neighborhood," *New York Times*, September 10, 2000.

4. City of Chicago Department of Housing, *Request for Proposals*.

5. See http://www.thecha.org/housingdev/family_sites.html and http://www.thecha.org/transformplan/plan_summary.html.

6. See chapter 4 above, notes 7–8.

7. Europe, incidentally, has much more economically integrated urban residence patterns than the United States; public housing there, for example, contains a much broader socioeconomic mix of residents than do the rigidly means-tested projects of the United States (Nivola, *Laws*, 22).

8. Hunt, "What Went Wrong?" 102.

9. See, for example, Jacobs, *Death and Life*, 72, 143–51.

10. For example, the Kerner Commission's 1968 call for *racially* integrated housing in the suburbs (*Report*) and the 1969 Gautreaux ruling expressly forbidding *racial* concentration in Chicago's public housing (Business and Professional People, "Gautreaux"). In the 1970s, interest in mixed-*income* housing was modest at best (though see the 1974 law cited in Spence, "Rethinking the Social Role," and Schill, "Chicago's Mixed-Income Communities," and the 1974 Boston program cited in Brophy and Smith, "Mixed-Income Housing."

11. Although we should be careful here about oversubscribing to a uniformly negative portrayal of public housing in the United States. As advocates frequently note, most public housing in this country is well-maintained and serves a vital function.

12. For more on this, see chapter 4.

13. Wilson, *Truly Disadvantaged*.

14. See, for example, his "Waiting for Gautreaux," 7–8.

15. See, for example, Jamie Kalven, "Where Will All the People Go?" *View From the Ground*, June 6, 2001.

16. See, for example, *Cabrini-Green LAC v.* CHA; *Concerned Residents of ABLA v.* CHA; *Henry Horner Mothers Guild v.* CHA; and *Wallace v.* CHA. For more on these

and other legal actions, go to the website of the National Center on Poverty Law at http://www.povertylaw.org/advocacy/housing.

17. Salama, "Redevelopment," 96; Ranney and Wright, "Race, Class, and State Power" 13.

18. Though, according to residents, because of its neglect of the projects during the 1970s and '80s and the increasing vacancy rates that resulted, the CHA was engaged in "de facto demolition" of its developments long before the rule change, which made it easier for the agency to pursue mixed-income model since the number of poor people living on its sites had by then been so drastically reduced—see, for example, Jorge Casuso, "CHA Flat Vacancies Soaring," *Chicago Tribune*, July 26, 1988; and *Henry Horner Mothers Guild v. CHA*.

19. Ranney and Wright, "Race, Class, and State Power," 12–13. See also Fleming, "Subjects of the Inner City" and "Changes to Admission and Occupancy Requirements in the Public Housing and Section 8 Housing Assistance Programs (Proposed Rule)," 64 Fed. Reg. 23460ff (1999, April 30) (to be codified at 24 C.F.R. § 5.603) and "Cuomo Issues Policy Directive" (HUD Press release, March 23, 2000).

20. On the NCSDPH, see Spence, "Rethinking the Social Role." On the "conversion rule," see http://www.hud.gov/offices/pih/centers/sac/section_202/.

21. See CHA's *Plan for Transformation*; also Flynn McRoberts, "CHA May Be Forced to Raze 18,000 Units: Federal Mandates Could Send 34,000 Into New Housing," *Chicago Tribune*, July 24, 1997.

22. "HOPE" stands for "Homeownership Opportunities for People Everywhere." For more on HOPE VI, see http://www.hud.gov/offices/pih/programs/ph/hope6/. From 1993–2005, more than $6 billion in grants were awarded (http://www.hud.gov/offices/pih/programs/ph/hope6/about/). See also Solomon, *Global City Blues*, Part 7; and http://www.housingresearch.org/. For critiques, see the National Housing Law Project, *False HOPE*, and the Center for Community Change, *A HOPE Unseen*.

23. See chapter 5 above, note 5.

24. For more on this and other issues in financing new-style developments, see Salama, "Redevelopment"; and the U.S. General Accounting Office, "HOPE VI Leveraging."

25. Patrick Reardon, "CHA Chief Criticizes Demolition Proposal," *Chicago Tribune*, July 16, 1988; Ed Marciniak, "Empty the CHA's Poverty Towers," *Chicago Tribune*, July 3, 1990.

26. Ed Marciniak, "Why Perpetuate Chicago's High-Rise Hell?" *Chicago Tribune*, Nov. 26, 1993.

27. CHA, *Plan for Transformation*; see also Melita Marie Garza and Flynn McRoberts, "Leaner, Cleaner CHA Envisioned in Overhaul," *Chicago Tribune*, October 1, 1999, and the response from both tenant leaders and HUD in Melita Marie Garza, "CHA Tenant Leaders Decry Major Makeover," *Chicago Tribune*, October 5, 1999, and Melita Marie Garza, "CHA Rehab Re-Ignites Oversight from U.S.," *Chicago Tribune*, October 8, 1999. The plan was finally ratified by HUD in early February, 2000: William Claiborne, "HUD, Chicago Ink Deal to Reconstruct Public Housing," *Washington Post*, February 6, 2000; see also David Heinzmann, "$1.5 Billion CHA Rebuilding Plan Draws Mix of Fans and Foes," *Chicago Tribune*, February 7, 2000; and Cory Oldweiler and Brian J. Rogal, "Public Housing: Reading Between the Lines," *Chicago Reporter*, March 2000. In chapter

1, I discuss some of the large-scale societal changes that may have been behind the move to demolition and mixed-income redevelopment at urban public housing projects. For a "macroeconomic" view of public housing under the late twentieth century "new world order," see Ranney and Wright, "Race, Class, and State Power."

28. On Harbor Point, see Breitbart and Pader, "Establishing Ground"; Schubert and Thresher, "Lessons from the Field"; and Vale, *From the Puritans to the Projects*. For Techwood Homes, see Salama, "Redevelopment"; and Schubert and Thresher, "Lessons from the Field." For Lake Parc Place, see Rosenbaum, Stroh, and Flynn, "Lake Parc Place"; and Schill, "Chicago's Mixed-Income Communities."

29. HUD, *Public Housing that Works*.

30. Oscar Newman, *Defensible Space*.

31. See, for example, Congress for the New Urbanism, *Principles for Inner City Design*, and HUD, *New American Neighborhoods*; also: Solomon, *Global City Blues*, Part 7; Talen, "Social Goals"; Peter Katz, *The New Urbanism*; and Fleming, "Space of Argumentation."

32. See, for example, Porter, "Competitive Advantage."

33. See Thall, *Perfect City*.

34. But see Dreier, Mollenkopf, and Swanstrom, *Place Matters*, for skepticism about an urban "comeback."

35. Pam Belluck, "Chicago Reverses 50 Years of Declining Population," *New York Times*, March 15, 2001.

36. According to Coulibaly, Green, and James, public housing in this country has never been about social welfare; it has always been about removing the poor from central business districts "as part of the transition from the industrial to the corporate city" (*Segregation*, 35).

37. Formal recommendations to do something about the Near North Side slum were made as early as the 1909 *Plan of Chicago* by Burnham and Bennett, which expressed concern about congestion and poverty around the Halsted Street/Chicago Avenue intersection. And some early philanthropy was provided to this district from the wealthy families on the Gold Coast, the Catholic Church, and, after 1934, the Lower North Center for social services (Zorbaugh, *Gold Coast*; and Marciniak, *Reclaiming the Inner City*). But otherwise, the area was left to its own devices. The first large-scale efforts to revitalize the Near North Side slum came in the 1930s with three massive private building projects: the Merchandise Mart on the north bank of the Chicago River, once the largest commercial building in the world; the Chicago Avenue headquarters of Montgomery Ward, for years the largest employer on the Near North Side; and the privately funded Marshall Field Garden Apartments on Sedgwick Avenue, at the time the largest moderate-income housing development in the country (see Marciniak, *Reclaiming the Inner City*, 21–4, and Bowly, *Poorhouse*). But the effort was piecemeal and plodding because of diminished construction activity during the Depression and World War II and because only one of the projects was specifically designed to do something about housing in the area.

38. In the 1980s, George Hicks, one of the key informants in Lemann's *Promised Land*, spoke of the valuable real estate under the project and its attraction for the white people living nearby: "They want Cabrini *bad* . . . They think about it in their sleep. If black folks don't hold on, they'll lose what they have" (280; emphasis in original).

39. See, for example, Connie Lauerman, "The Clybourn Experiment: The Fit May Not Be Perfect, But the Goal Is to Gentrify an Urban Wasteland Without Losing its Industrial Muscle," *Chicago Tribune*, February 18, 1990; John McCarron, "Rich, Poor Rub Elbows in Cabrini-Green's Shadow," *Chicago Tribune*, December 12, 1990; Patrick Reardon, "U.S. to Sell Huge Low-Income Site in Lincoln Park," *Chicago Tribune*, April 1, 1991.

40. Marciniak, *Reclaiming the Inner City*.

41. See, for example, Patrick Reardon, "Cabrini Is Prime Real Estate, But Not For Sale," *Chicago Tribune*, October 16, 1992; and comments by resident Mark Pratt in Ronit Bezalel's 1999 film *Voices of Cabrini*. My own calculation, using the 1998 sale price of the Halsted North parcel, suggests a gross value at that time, just for the land under the seventy-acre housing project, of $134 million—3 million square feet at $44 per square foot.

42. See NTRAC, *North Town, I* and *II*. On the NTRAC plans, see also Bennett, "Do We Really"; Wright et al., "Plan to Voucher Out."

43. Klinenberg, *Heat Wave*, 62.

44. See chapter 4 above, notes 123–4.

45. Matthew Nickerson, "Sniper Kills Cabrini Kid Steps from School," *Chicago Tribune*, October 14, 1992; Jennifer Lenhart and John O'Brien, " 'We're Crying for Help': Cabrini, the Day After," *Chicago Tribune*, October 15, 1992; and George Papajohn and Mary Hill, "A Heartbreaking Death—and Life—in Cabrini," *Chicago Tribune*, October 25, 1992.

46. David Silverman, "Sniper Ends Girls' Dream to Flee Cabrini," *Chicago Tribune*, July 25, 1992; Curtis Lawrence, "Cabrini Residents Call for an End to Snipers," *Chicago Tribune*, August 12, 1992.

47. See, for example, the *Chicago Tribune*'s editorial of November 15, 1992: "Tear Down the CHA High-Rises." See also chapter 7.

48. "A New Tribune Competition," *Chicago Tribune*, February 21, 1993. The winner, a design team from North Dakota State University, was announced four months later: Blair Kamin, "Rebuilding the Community: New Ideas in Public Housing Are a Return to the Basics," *Chicago Tribune*, June 20, 1993: the top entries, according to Kamin, shared with the CHA a desire to end the project's physical isolation, reintroduce the old street grid, attract middle-class residents, and so forth. The competition was only symbolic, but it forced attention both in Chicago and beyond on rethinking the neighborhood.

49. Frank James, "CHA Plans a Facelift for Cabrini," *Chicago Tribune*, December 25, 1992; Patrick Reardon and Paul Sloan, "CHA Aim: Make Cabrini 'a Normal Neighborhood,' " *Chicago Tribune*, February 6, 1993.

50. Lane's rehabilitation of the former Victor Olander Homes on the South Side involved a mix of "working" families with incomes between 50–80 percent of area median income (a.m.i.) and families earning less than 50 percent a.m.i. in 282 units in two fifteen-story buildings, renamed Lake Parc Place. See John McCormick, "Chicago Housecleaning: How the City Is Winning Back Crime-Ridden Projects," *Newsweek*, August 19, 1991: 58–9; idem, "A Housing Program that Actually Works: Chicago's Lake Parc Place, One Year Later," *Newsweek*, June 22, 1992: 61–3; Rosenbaum, Stroh, and Flynn, "Lake Parc Place"; and Schill, "Chicago's Mixed-Income Communities."

51. My recounting of this somewhat convoluted story relies on articles in the *Chicago Tribune* and *Sun-Times* (cited below); Bennett, "Do We Really"; Ranney and Wright, "Race, Class, and State Power"; Salama, "Redevelopment"; and Wright et al., "Plan to Voucher Out."

52. For details, see Patrick Reardon, "Some in Cabrini to Get New Homes," *Chicago Tribune*, October 27, 1993, Patrick Reardon, "Daley and CHA Taking City in a New Direction," *Chicago Tribune*, December 7, 1993; and Joel Kaplan, "Lane's 'Vision' for Cabrini Made HUD Blink," *Chicago Tribune*, June 9, 1995.

53. As critics pointed out, however, this was not exactly one-for-one replacement, since virtually *all* Cabrini Green families were "very low income" (see Wright et al., "Plan to Voucher Out").

54. Patrick Reardon, "Daley and CHA Taking City in a New Direction," *Chicago Tribune*, December 7, 1993.

55. On residents' concerns, see, for example, Jerry Thornton, "Cabrini Vow: A Fight to Stay," *Chicago Tribune*, February 26, 1993. In an editorial published the same day, the *Tribune* called resident fears of redevelopment "paranoia" ("Toward a New Legacy of Renewal," *Chicago Tribune*, February 26, 1993). On the reservations of the local U.S. congressman, see Patrick Reardon, "Some in Cabrini to Get New Homes," *Chicago Tribune*, October 27, 1993.

56. Lou Carlozo, "HUD Hints CHA Should Look to '94," *Chicago Tribune*, August 27, 1993.

57. Patrick Reardon, "Daley and CHA Taking City in a New Direction," *Chicago Tribune*, December 7, 1993.

58. Flynn McRoberts and Blair Kamin, "Cabrini's New Beginning Marked at CHA Ceremony," *Chicago Tribune*, July 19, 1994. The homes sold for around $300,000 each, $50,000 less than other townhouses in the neighborhood, and $200,000 less than in Lincoln Park, mostly because title to the land remained with the city and was then rented to buyers at low cost (Bill Rumbler, "Integration Project Leads to a Sense of Community," *Chicago Sun-Times*, March 15, 1998).

59. Only 3 percent of the $137 million spent for all of the Near North Side during those years, although the neighborhood contains 25 percent of the district's land.

60. City of Chicago, *Near North Tax Increment*, 14.

61. J. Linn Allen and William Gaines, "A Buildup of High Pressure: As Upscale Development Marches Relentlessly to Cabrini-Green's Border, Values Are Starting to Clash," *Chicago Tribune*, August 6, 1995. Neil Steinberg and Fran Spielman reported in 1998 that vacant lots in the area that sold for $32,000 in 1986 were now going for $350,000 ("Grass Is Greener in Hot Cabrini Area," *Chicago Sun-Times*, September 23, 1998).

62. Units at Mohawk North were selling for $300,000–$450,000 per unit (Wright et al., "Plan to Voucher Out").

63. The earlier plan was shelved, apparently, because Shuldiner thought it involved too much resident displacement; there were also apparently lingering questions about Vince Lane's financing scheme and alleged corruption in his management of the CHA (Joel Kaplan, "Lane's 'Vision' for Cabrini Made HUD Blink," *Chicago Tribune*, June 9, 1995).

64. Flynn McRoberts and Blair Kamin, "Developers Peek at Cabrini Future," *Chicago Tribune*, December 21, 1995; see also Cornelia Grumman, "CHA Watch: The McLean-Davis Plan: A Detailed Look," *Chicago Tribune*, March 30, 1996.

65. John Kass and Flynn McRoberts, "Daley Unveils Cabrini-Green Facelift Plan," *Chicago Tribune*, June 27, 1996; Blair Kamin and John Kass, "Daley's Cabrini Dream: Financing, Support from Residents Seem to Be Lacking," *Chicago Tribune*, June 28, 1996. The plan's estimated cost was later lowered from $1 billion to $700 million (James Hill, "CHA Chief Lowers Cost Estimate," *Chicago Tribune*, June 29, 1996).

66. Wright et al., "Plan to Voucher Out," 38. See also Jim McNeill and J. S. Fuerst, "Creative Destruction? Plan by Politicians and Private Developers to Demolish CHA High-Rises Is Flawed," *Chicago Tribune*, July 10, 1996. For related concerns, see chapter 5 nn. 22–3.

67. Blair Kamin and John Kass, "Daley's Cabrini Dream: Financing, Support from Residents Seem to Be Lacking," *Chicago Tribune*, June 28, 1996.

68. Ranney and Wright, "Race, Class, and State Power," 19–20; Wright et al., "Plan to Voucher Out."

69. *Cabrini-Green LAC v. CHA.*

70. Nancy Ryan, "Cabrini Alternative is Proposed: Residents Seeking Limit on Demolitions," *Chicago Tribune*, March 28, 1997.

71. Flynn McRoberts and J. Linn Allen, "When Two Worlds Collide at Cabrini," *Chicago Tribune*, July 30, 1998.

72. "On Cabrini, A Deal Best Not Made," *Chicago Tribune*, August 3, 1998. For more on this editorial, see chapter 7.

73. Leon Pitt, "Judge Stalls Cabrini Renewal Deal: CHA 'Mini-War' with Developer Cited," *Chicago Sun-Times*, July 31, 1998; see also Brian Rogal, "The Habitat Co.: Private Firm Keeps Tight Grip on Public Housing," *Chicago Reporter*, November, 1999.

74. See consent decree in *Cabrini-Green LAC v. CHA* at http://www.povertylaw.org/poverty-law-library/case/52100/52181/52181z-2.rtf. See also Curtis Lawrence, "OK Today for Cabrini Plan," *Chicago Sun-Times*, August 15, 2000; and Mickey Ciokajlo, "New Cabrini Agreement May End Residents' Suit," *Chicago Tribune*, August 16, 2000.

75. The decree made it clear, however, that no Cabrini family would be excluded from a new unit because it did not have a working member.

76. Each "lease-compliant" Cabrini Green resident or displaced resident, then, would have the following relocation options: (1) a rehabilitated unit within the HOPE VI revitalization area, (2) a new public housing or affordable unit in the area, (3) a Section 8 voucher with mobility assistance for use anywhere in the private housing market, or (4) a scattered-site unit somewhere in the city. First priority would be given to families displaced by the demolition of Cabrini Extension North; second priority would go to nondisplaced families from other Cabrini Green properties; third priority would go to other CHA families; and fourth priority, to families on the CHA waiting list (see consent decree in *Cabrini-Green LAC v. CHA*).

77. City of Chicago Department of Housing, *Request for Proposals.*

78. Kate N. Grossman, "Money Flows for New Cabrini Homes: 18 Acres Will Become Mixed-Income Area for 650 Families," *Chicago Sun-Times*, October 30, 2002;

for more information, see http://www.parksideofoldtown.com; and http://www.thecha.org/housingdev/cabrini_green_homes.html.

79. City of Chicago Department of Housing, *Near North Development Initiative* (hereafter cited parenthetically in the text).

80. The RFP noted that the CHA had two kinds of funds available for these units: development funds of about $100,000 per unit for construction, and operating subsidies of about $450 per unit per month for rent and utilities, including the tenant's contribution (capped at 30 percent of income) (ibid., 6).

81. Using $63,800, the HUD-determined median annual income for a family of four in Chicago in 1999 (see http://www.huduser.org/datasets/il.html), renters eligible for "affordable" units would have to have an income below $51,040, with their total housing costs no higher than $1,276 per month. For these units, developers were urged to pursue federal LIHTC and tax exempt bond financing (see note 90 below) to help pay for construction and upkeep (City of Chicago Department of Housing, *Near North Development Initiative*, 7).

82. The idea, clearly based on New Urbanist principles, was to create a "street pattern and hierarchy that helps define a compact and identifiable character for the neighborhood while meeting the need to connect the Near North Side to the rest of the city" (ibid., 9) and to connect each block to both the sidewalk network and to other paths, greenways, parks, and public spaces.

83. For the latter, the RFP noted that most ground-floor units should have three or more bedrooms with a private yard enclosed by fence and that the majority of CHA units should contain two or more bedrooms each, with half of the units ideally containing three or more bedrooms (ibid., 10).

84. This represents an implicit critique of "tower in the park" public housing with its lack of private entrances.

85. Developers were also encouraged to vary masonry color, break rows of houses every 120–160 feet to allow for views into courtyards, and avoid too much "massing"; provide individually landscaped front yards for each building marked by a wrought iron fence; and provide porches and balconies for units lacking private yards (ibid., 11).

86. Holsten Real Estate Development Corporation (abbreviated in these notes as "HREDC"), *Proposal for Redevelopment of Halsted North Community*, cover letter, 1. This proposal will hereafter be cited parenthetically in the text, with page numbers preceded by one of the following section titles: cover letter, Development Team Approach, Development Team Qualification, Proposed Use and Concept, Overall Unit Counts, Detailed Unit Mix, Homeowner Deed Restrictions, Management Plan, Screening Criteria, Long-Term Affordability Strategy, Pre-Approval Community Seminar, Halsted North Community Amenities, Job Opportunities, Economic Impact, Drawings and Plans, Budget and Financing Plan, and Total Development Cost.

87. For this, Holsten had elicited the participation of the Kenard Corporation, which was more experienced in market-rate development (ibid., Development Team Qualification, 3).

88. As discussed further on, race is *never* mentioned in either the city's RFP or Holsten's proposal; see Fleming, "Subjects of the Inner City," for a discussion of this absence in discourses surrounding urban revitalization.

89. Originally, all market-rate customers at Halsted North would have been owners, but this was changed to achieve a better income mixture in the development: in the end, 91 percent of the market-rate units were for sale; 9 percent were rentals (HREDC, *Reply*).

90. The Low Income Housing Tax Credit (LIHTC) allows developers, over a ten-year period, to recover 30 percent of their costs in building low-income housing. See the NLIHC's *2006 Advocates' Guide to Housing and Community Development* at http://www.nlihc.org/advocates/lihtc.htm and the following HUD Web sites: http://www.huduser.org/datasets/lihtc.html; and http://www.hud.gov/offices/cpd/affordablehousing/training/web/lihtc/basics/.

91. A point made by Brophy and Smith in "Mixed-Income Housing," an article that had a strong influence on Peter Holsten, as evidenced by the heavily-annotated copy he showed me during our January 9, 2003, interview.

92. In this, Holsten reverses Jane Jacobs who, in *Death and Life*, had argued that the health of formal public organizations depended on the prior establishment of trust during informal sidewalk life. Holsten seems to believe that the formal interactions organized at North Town Village will lay the foundation for closer *informal* relations later on.

93. HREDC, *Reply* (hereafter cited parenthetically in the text).

94. Tom Cruze and Scott Stewart, "A Glimpse of Cabrini's Future," *Chicago Sun-Times*, July 20, 1998.

95. Abdon M. Pallasch, "Developer Building a Dream at Cabrini," *Chicago Tribune*, September 20, 1998.

96. Rick Hepp, "CHA Shows Off Complex Near Cabrini," *Chicago Tribune*, June 5, 2001.

97. See http://www.holstenchicago.com/buildings/Management/ntownvillage.htm.

98. See note 3 above.

99. Flynn McRoberts, "A New World—Down the Block," *Chicago Tribune*, October 8, 1998.

100. This is especially evident in Holsten's design for North Town Park, the nineteen-acre Cabrini North site (see http://www.parksideofoldtown.com; and http://www.thecha.org/housingdev/cabrini_green_homes.html).

101. See also HREDC, *Proposal*, Job Opportunities, 1–2.

102. See also ibid.; and HREDC, *Reply*, 11–12, where the Cabrini Green LAC's priority is clearly on jobs and the role of social services in mixed-income developments.

103. Peter Holsten, interview by author, January 9, 2003.

104. The poor, it is apparently assumed, need all the bedrooms they can get just for their children.

105. David Roeder, "Developer Puts New Spin on Affordable," *Chicago Sun-Times*, July 26, 1999. Cf. Brophy and Smith's study of seven mixed-income housing developments, including Harbor Point in Boston: the successful ones used excellent design, location, and management to attract "renters with choices" ("Mixed-Income Housing").

106. See, for example, U.S. General Accounting Office, "HOPE VI Leveraging": HOPE VI projects have been good at leveraging funds, but most of the funds leveraged turn out to be public (4, 10–12).

107. Flynn McRoberts, "A New World—Down the Block," *Chicago Tribune*, October 8, 1998.

108. Note that in Holsten's *Proposal*, "Good Value in Sales Price" is the top "amenity" listed for prospective homebuyers (Halsted North Community Amenities, 1).

109. See also Fleming, "Subjects of the Inner City."

110. Schill, "Chicago's Mixed-Income Communities," 149.

111. Sarkissian, "Idea." Cf. David Brooks on "cultural" integration in New Orleans: "The only chance we have to break the cycle of poverty is to integrate people who lack middle-class skills into neighborhoods with people who possess these skills and who insist on certain standards of behavior" ("Katrina's Silver Lining," *New York Times*, September 8, 2005). Note that Brooks's evidence for this view comes in part from the Gautreaux experiment in Chicago (see chap. 5).

112. Wilson, *Truly Disadvantaged*, 56.

113. Sarkissian, "Idea of Social Mix," 243.

114. See chapter 7; and Cory Oldweiler, "Residents Lack Role in Revamped Public Housing," *Chicago Reporter*, April 2002.

115. On the lack of participation by residents in planning or managing mixed-income developments, see Bennett, "Do We Really"; National Housing Law Project, *False HOPE*; Salama, "Redevelopment"; Cory Oldweiler, "Residents Lack Role in Revamped Public Housing," *Chicago Reporter*, April 2002; and Schubert and Thresher, "Lessons from the Field."

116. Salama, "Redevelopment," 97.

117. See also Spence, "Rethinking the Social Role," on the NCSDPH; and Putnam (*Bowling Alone*) and Wilson (*Truly Disadvantaged*) on the importance of social capital.

118. See the National Housing Law Project, *False HOPE*; the Center for Community Change, *HOPE Unseen*; and the U.S. General Accounting Office, "HOPE VI Leveraging."

119. Brophy and Smith, "Mixed-Income Housing"; Schwartz and Tajbakhsh, "Mixed-Income Housing"; Popkin et al., "Gautreaux Legacy"; Von Hoffmann, "High Ambitions," 439; and Sandra Newman, "Introduction."

120. Schill, "Chicago's Mixed-Income Communities."

121. James E. Rosenbaum, Linda K. Stroh, and Cathy A. Flynn, "Lake Parc Place."

122. Mayer and Jencks, "Growing Up"; Brooks-Gunn et al., "Do Neighborhoods Influence"; Luttmer, "Neighbors as Negatives"; and Ellen and Turner, "Does Neighborhood Matter?"

123. In fact, the absence of affluent neighbors turned out to be more influential than the presence of low-income ones (Brooks-Gunn et al., "Do Neighborhoods Influence").

124. Luttmer, "Neighbors as Negatives." Cf. John Cassidy, "Relatively Deprived," *The New Yorker*, April 3, 2006, 42–7; and Rubinowitz and Rosenbaum, *Crossing the Lines*, 104.

125. See, for example, Mulroy's study: in the 20 percent poor/80 percent market-rate developments she examined, low-income residents were more likely to be female, single, nonwhite, have children, and not hold a professional job ("Mixed-Income Housing," 4).

126. Brophy and Smith, "Mixed-Income Housing."

127. See note 3 above.

128. Bennett, "Do We Really?"

129. Flynn McRoberts, "A New World—Down the Block," *Chicago Tribune*, October 8, 1998.

130. Bill Rumbler, "Integration Project Leads to a Sense of Community," *Chicago Sun-Times*, March 15, 1998.

131. Alexander, Ishikawa, and Silverstein, *Pattern Language*, 42–50; Gans, "Balanced Community."

132. Alexander, Ishikawa, and Silverstein, *Pattern Language*, 43–4.

133. Young, *Justice*, 231.

134. Gans, *Levitttowners* and "Urbanism and Suburbanism"; Marcuse, "Enclave."

135. HREDC, *Proposal*, Community Building Storytelling Project, 1 (hereafter cited parenthetically in the text).

136. If there is harmony at North Town Village, it will come about *not* because of physical interspersal or storytelling but through screening and control of the CHA families, including observation, surveillance, and strict rule-enforcement. Management must meet the standards of the market-rate customers, Holsten writes; "[W]e therefore take an extremely aggressive position with respect to eviction and relocation of residents who have a pattern of disruption of the quiet enjoyment of the entire population" (Development Team Qualifications, 1). Screening and control show up in several places in the proposal: in the community covenant; in tenant selection, income verification, and credit checks; in drug tests; and in the lengthy rules governing life in the development. Prospective residents can be denied access, meanwhile, because of an unsatisfactory rent payment history, inadequate income (this does not apply to CHA families), failed home inspection, bad credit history, or a criminal record. In addition, prospective tenants must attend a preapproval seminar, agree to attend three monthly tenant meetings during a one-year lease; and, if in affordable or CHA units, agree to provide information on employment and income. As Vincent Scully has written about Seaside, Florida, "Architecture is fundamentally a matter not of individual buildings but of the shaping of community, and that is done by the law" ("Architecture," 229). Similarly, on the Near North Side, it's all about setting rules for behavior (Flynn McRoberts, "A New World—Down the Block," *Chicago Tribune*, October 8, 1998). According to Pallasch, Holsten's buildings work because of strict management (see note 95 above; cf. Brophy and Smith, "Mixed-Income Housing").

137. Historically, as we have seen, urban renewal has never really increased the supply of housing in this country or helped the poor enter the mainstream; in fact, it is hard not to see it as a way for elites to reclaim the inner city for themselves.

7. Home

1. It is probably more accurate to say that they are dispersed across valued communities but still concentrated in devalued ones.

2. Data for this analysis come from more than 200 written documents concerning Halsted North and similar developments, including business plans, government reports and regulations, position papers, legal documents, articles from the mass media,

and scholarly and historical materials. An earlier and fuller version of this analysis is available in Fleming, "Subjects of the Inner City."

3. See U.S. Housing Act of 1937 (as amended), 42 U.S.C. § 1437a(a)(1) and (b)(2). As I detail in "Subjects of the Inner City," however, the average income of public housing residents is well below 30 percent of a.m.i. For income statistics, see http://www.huduser.org/datasets/il.html.

4. See, for example, Bowly, *Poorhouse*; Hays, *Federal Government*; Meyerson and Banfield, *Politics, Planning, and the Public Interest*; Mitchell, "Historical Overview"; Schill, "Distressed Public Housing"; and Schill and Wachter, "Spatial Bias." The legislative means for effecting this restriction was to impose income ceilings on tenancy. According to the 1937 Act, "[N]o family shall be accepted as a tenant in any such project whose aggregate income exceeds five times the rental [including utilities] of the quarters to be furnished such family" (as quoted in Fisher, "Origins," 241).

5. See U.S. Housing Act of 1937 (as amended), 42 U.S.C. § 1437a(b)(1).

6. According to the CHA, 99 percent of Cabrini Green residents in 1998 were black; for ABLA, Henry Horner, and Robert Taylor, the figures were 97 percent, 100 percent, and 99.9 percent respectively ("Cabrini-Green Demographics," http://www.thecha.org/Cabrini_Demo.htm, November 20, 1998).

7. Note that most urban areas of extreme poverty are not just places where there are many poor people, they are the direct heirs of yesteryear's black belts. "To say that they are ghettos because they are poor is to reverse social and historical causation: it is *because they were and are ghettos* that joblessness and misery are unusually acute and persistent in them—not the other way around" (Wacquant, "Three Pernicious Premises," 343: emphasis in original).

8. Schorr, *Common Decency*, 7, 28–9.

9. Ibid., 28–9, 32.

10. Meyerson and Banfield, *Politics, Planning, and the Public Interest*, 25.

11. Schorr, *Common Decency*, 7. In Europe, most programs already operate this way. For example, two to three times the U.S. percentage live in public housing there, in developments which contain a much broader socioeconomic mix of residents than do the means-tested projects of the United States (Nivola, *Laws of the Landscape*, 22).

12. Since such an income corresponds roughly to the government's "poverty" threshold, defined as three times the cost of an "economy food plan." In 1998, that was $16,530 for a family of four with two children, or $13,133 for a family of three (U.S. Census Bureau, "Poverty").

13. A single mother with two children living at the poverty line in Chicago (that is, at about 30 percent of a.m.i.) would pay almost 50 percent of her income for "fair market" housing (in 1999, $737 per month for a two-bedroom apartment [http://www.huduser.org/datasets/il/fmr99rev/index.html]), a "severe" rent burden (HUD, *Rental Housing Assistance*, "Appendix B"; see also Daskal, *In Search of Shelter*; and the NLIHC's annual *Out of Reach* reports). Even someone at 50 percent of U.S. median family income in 1999 ($23,900) would still pay approximately 30 percent of his or her income for housing at the fair market rate, the "affordable" threshold for HUD (although by European standards this is still a high rent level [Meehan, "Evolution," 296]).

14. In 1999, someone could have been employed full time at the minimum wage and still make below 30 percent of area median income in fifty-four of the nation's

fifty-five largest metropolitan areas (Lubell and Sard, "Proposed Housing Legislation"; see also Daskal, *In Search of Shelter*).

15. Peter Holsten, as quoted in David Roeder, "Developer Puts New Spin on Affordable," *Chicago Sun-Times*, July 26, 1999, para. 3.

16. "On Cabrini, A Deal Best Not Made," *Chicago Tribune*, August 3, 1998; Kamin, "Who Controls the Future of Cabrini-Green?" *Architectural Record* 185 (September, 1997), 62.

17. Flynn McRoberts and Abdon M. Pallasch, "Neighbors Wary of New Arrivals," *Chicago Tribune*, December 28, 1998.

18. My own Google search of the exact phrase "notorious Cabrini Green" in 2006 yielded 310 separate hits; Mary Schmich has written that the phrase comes so naturally to reporters it is as if the project's name begins with the word "notorious" ("Future Closes in on Cabrini," *Chicago Tribune*, July 4, 2004).

19. Bradford McKee, "Public Housing's Last Hope," *Architecture*, August 1, 1997.

20. Blair Kamin, "Can Public Housing Be Reinvented?" *Architectural Record* 185 (February, 1997): 87.

21. Witold Rybczynski, "Bauhaus Blunders: Architecture and Public Housing," *Public Interest* 11, no. 3 (Fall 1993): 82–90.

22. Quoted in Kotlowitz, *There Are No Children Here*, 259. I am sure that I have inadvertently participated in such pathologizing of the projects in this book.

23. Sam Walker, "US Eyes Public Housing—And Begins to Remodel," *Christian Science Monitor*, September 9, 1997.

24. Edward Marciniak, "More Than a Roof: Promising Moves in Public Housing," *Commonweal* 123, no. 11 (June 1, 1996): 11–13.

25. Kotlowitz, *There Are No Children Here*, 45.

26. Lemann, *The Promised Land*, 296–7.

27. U.S. Housing Act of 1937 (as amended), 42 U.S.C. § 1437v(h) (compare description of projects as "blighted" for TIF designation). See also chapter 1 of this book.

28. Wacquant, "Three Pernicious Premises," 345.

29. See, for example, McCormick, "Chicago Housecleaning" in chapter 6 above, note 50.

30. Ibid.

31. Marciniak, "More Than a Roof," 11 (above, note 24).

32. Chicago Housing Authority, "History," at http://www.thecha.org/History.htm (accessed October 26, 1999). Similarly, for Alexander Polikoff, public housing began "as a temporary way station for working families down on their luck because of the Depression. . . . In the post-war years, however, the public clientele began to change . . . becoming the landlord for hard-core poverty families" ("Chicago's Not About to Give Up On a Bad Idea").

33. Jewish Council on Urban Affairs, "Public Housing: Voices Rising Above the Bulldozers," *Community Views: Voices from Chicago's Neighborhoods* (Chicago: October, 1999). Unfortunately for people like Steele, although Americans tend to consider stability a good thing, when it comes to housing, we believe in what Howard Husock calls the "housing ladder" ("Public Housing as a 'Poorhouse,' " *The Public Interest*, Fall

1997; see also Downs, *Opening Up*): as a family rises up the socioeconomic scale, it changes residence as it goes, from tenement to walk-up rental to duplex to single-family detached house, and so on. By this logic, public housing residents aren't even in the same story as the rest of us.

34. "CHA Vote Belies Housing Dilemma," *Chicago Sun-Times*, December 25, 1995.

35. "On Cabrini, A Deal Best Not Made," *Chicago Tribune*, August 3, 1998.

36. Meyerson and Banfield, *Politics, Planning, and the Public Interest*, 34.

37. Ann Scott Tyson, "Rehab of Chicago High Rises Aims to Lure Working Class," *Christian Science Monitor*, July 7, 1995: 1.

38. Jerry Adler and Maggie Malone, "Toppling Towers," *Newsweek*, November 4, 1996: 70–72.

39. Blair Kamin, "Can Public Housing Be Reinvented?" *Architectural Record* 185 (February, 1997): 84–89.

40. Elizabeth Brackett, "Rethinking Public Housing," *The NewsHour with Jim Lehrer*, Public Broadcasting Service, July 3, 1997.

41. "High-rise brought low at last," *The Economist*, July 11, 1998.

42. Melissa Herron, "Brave New World," *Builder Online*, July 1998.

43. Andrew Martin, and Flynn McRoberts, "Scattered CHA Sites? Hardly," *Chicago Tribune*, December 8, 1998.

44. Abdon M. Pallasch, "Fall of High-Rises Lifts Hopes of Area," *Chicago Tribune*, December 11, 1998.

45. Polikoff, " 'Chicago's Not About,' " 211.

46. Ibid., 214.

47. HUD, *Public Housing that Works*.

48. Kamin, "Can Public Housing Be Reinvented?" 89 (see note 39 above).

49. Sudhir Alladi Venkatesh, "An Invisible Community: Inside Chicago's Public Housing," *The American Prospect* 34 (September/October, 1997): 35–40.

50. See chapter 5 above, note 147.

51. Jewish Council on Urban Affairs, "Public Housing," 2 (see note 33 above).

52. Cabrini-Green Local Advisory Council, "Vision 2000."

53. Flynn McRoberts and Abdon M. Pallasch, "Neighbors Wary of New Arrivals," *Chicago Tribune*, December 28, 1998.

54. Jewish Council on Urban Affairs, "Public Housing" (see note 33 above).

55. Cabrini-Green Local Advisory Council, "Vision 2000." Perhaps nowhere has the rhetorical agency of public housing residents been more powerfully exercised than in the federal courts, where they have consistently presented themselves not as poor, black, or socially disordered, but as *plaintiffs*, that is, individuals who put forth *claims* and seek relief (see Fleming, "Subjects of the Inner City"; cf. Allen, *Talking to Strangers*, 192, n. 12). There, they are seen as having control over their world, something that, as we saw above, is typically denied them in other contexts. And this control is often literal: as we saw in chapter 6, according to the terms of the 1998 Cabrini Green consent decree, later voided, the Cabrini Green LAC would have been cogeneral partner in the redevelopment of the Lower North neighborhood with a 51 percent interest, participating fully in profits, personnel decisions, planning, and so forth. In that document, public housing families also had (as they did not in the RFP for the

Halsted North parcel) *options*: they had the right to choose whether they would stay in a rehabilitated building, move to a new unit in the neighborhood, move to a "scattered-site" unit somewhere else in Chicago, or take a Section 8 rent oucher for use anywhere on the private market. And they had the right to job training, employment opportunities, and full participation in all decision-making concerning the project. As Ferrell Freeman, forty-year resident of ABLA Homes and president of the Concerned Residents of ABLA, put it after that group filed a class action discrimination lawsuit in 1999 against the CHA, "We can't allow our homes to be torn down without having a say in the decision and without the opportunity to live in any new units that are built" (National Center on Poverty Law, "Chicago Housing Authority and U.S. Department of Housing and Urban Development sued for racial discrimination," press release, July 29, 1999). Henry Horner plaintiffs also sued the city, CHA, and HUD in 1991, alleging de facto demolition of their project without being provided replacement housing. In 1995, they won a comprehensive revitalization of the entire Horner development (*Henry Horner Mothers Guild v. CHA*) and were given the right to determine whether the annex would be demolished or rehabilitated. Other residents in the Horner complex were given their choice of a scattered site unit, a Section 8 certificate, an apartment in a rehabilitated high- or mid-rise, or a new replacement unit on site. Further, the consent decree requires that the CHA consult and attempt to agree with the plaintiffs on all aspects of the revitalization program, including location and design of new units, the hiring of developers and managers, and the determination of management and security policies: "No site for new construction or acquisition shall be selected, no design approved, and no development or management entity selected, and no management plan . . . or security plan adopted unless the CHA defendants first agree with the HRC [Horner Residents Committee]" (31–2).

56. NTRAC, *North Town, I.*

57. See, for example, Bennett, "Do We Really"; Bezalel, *Voices of Cabrini*; Breitbart and Pader, "Establishing Ground"; Calmore, "Spatial Equality"; DeFillipis, "Myth of Social Capital"; Porter, "Competitive Advantage"; Dante Ramos, "Hud-dled Masses," *New Republic*, March 14, 1994, 12–14); Ranney and Wright, "Race, Class, and State Power"; Venkatesh, *American Project*; Wacquant, "Three Pernicious Premises"; Whitaker, *Cabrini Green*; and Wilen and Stasell, "Gautreaux and Chicago's Public Housing Crisis."

58. Wacquant, "Three Pernicious Premises," 346 (emphasis in original).

59. Ibid. (emphasis in original).

60. Ibid., 346–7.

61. Klinenberg, *Heat Wave*, 105.

62. Ibid., 104.

63. Venkatesh, *American Project*, 4 (hereafter cited parenthetically in the text).

64. Ibid., 59–60; HUD had pressured CHA by threatening to freeze $8.2 million in modernization funds unless the board agreed to management changes.

65. See Susan Chandler, "Gangs Built on Corporate Mentality," *Chicago Tribune*, June 13, 2004.

66. Jewish Council on Urban Affairs, "Public Housing," 2 (see note 33 above).

67. National Center on Poverty Law, "Chicago Housing Authority" (see note 55 above).

68. Quoted in Elizabeth Brackett, "Rethinking Public Housing," *The Newshour with Jim Lehrer*, Public Broadcasting Service, July 3, 1997.

69. Cory Oldweiler, "Cabrini Changes Come All Too Slowly," *Chicago Reporter*, March 1998.

70. Brian Rogal, "Survey Casts Doubt on CHA Plans," *The Chicago Reporter*, June 1999.

71. Calmore, "Spatial Equality," 1495.

72. Ibid., 1492.

73. Ibid., 1498, quoting Robert F. Forman. On this idea of nonsegregation, especially as it relates to Chicago, see also Wilen and Stasell, "Gautreaux and Chicago's Public Housing Crisis."

74. Ira Berlin, *Generations of Captivity*, 239.

75. Cf. Drake and Cayton, *Black Metropolis*, on the "world within a world" theory of Bronzeville.

76. bell hooks, *Teaching to Transgress*, "Introduction," 4.

77. Keating, *Suburban Racial Dilemma.*

78. For more on both the word and concept of "empowerment," and how they have played out in debates about public housing reform, see Peterman, "Meanings of Resident Empowerment."

79. Lemann, *The Promised Land*, 122.

80. Ibid., 133. See also Cohen and Taylor, *American Pharaoh*; Lemann, *Promised Land*; Matusow, *Unraveling*; and Bradford McKee, "Public Housing's Last Hope," *Architecture*, August 1, 1997. See also my Acknowledgments in this book.

81. HUD, *Community Building in Public Housing.*

82. Freedman et al., *Inside City Schools*, 99.

83. For other arguments against demolition, dispersal, and mixed-income revitalization, see Jim McNeill and J. S. Fuerst, "Creative Destruction? Plan by Politicians and Private Developers to Demolish CHA High-Rises Is Flawed," *Chicago Tribune*, July 10, 1996.

84. Caprara and Alexander, *Empowering Residents of Public Housing*, 1.

85. Peterman, "Resident Management," 164.

86. Caprara and Alexander, *Empowering*, 4.

87. Ibid., 2.

88. Peterman, "Resident Management," 162; Caprara and Alexander, *Empowering*, 10–4, 49–51.

89. On Cochran Gardens, see Peterman, "Resident Management," 162; Caprara and Alexander, *Empowering*, 10–14, 47–49; and MDRC, *Tenant Management*. On Carr Square, see Monti, "People in Control." On Bertha Gilkey, see Sandercock, *Towards Cosmopolis*, 152–4.

90. MDRC, *Tenant Management*, 5–6

91. Ibid., 6.

92. Ibid., 6–8.

93. Ibid., 8–9.

94. For more on Kenilworth-Parkside, see Caprara and Alexander, *Empowering*, 10–4, 54–7.

95. Gary Marx, "CHA Lets Tenants Take Charge of Their Homes," *Chicago Tribune*, May 7, 1989; Michael Gillis, "Tenant-Run CHA Housing is Pushed," *Chicago Sun-Times*, May 9, 1989, 28. For more on LeClair Courts, see Caprara and Alexander, *Empowering*, 44–6; and Monti, "People in Control."

96. One year after it began operation, the LeClair RMC seemed to be a success; see Michael Gillis, "Pilgrims' Progress: How Management by Tenants Is Working at LeClair Courts," *Chicago Sun-Times*, June 3, 1990, 56. But within six years, the entire RMC would be fired and the CHA reinstalled as manager of the complex (see Leon Pitt, "CHA Fires Manager of LeClaire," *Chicago Sun-Times*, July 16, 1996).

97. For the statutory and regulatory background to resident management and ownership of public housing, see 42 U.S.C. § 1437 et seq., section 20, available at http://www4.law.cornell.edu/uscode/42/ch8.html; also 24 CFR part 964 as amended by sec. 532 of Public Housing Reform Act of 1998 (QHWRA), available at http://www4.law.cornell.edu/cfr/24p5.htm#start. See also HUD's Resident Opportunities and Self Sufficiency (ROSS) Program at http://www.hud.gov/offices/pih/programs/ph/ross/.

98. Terry Wilson, "Tenant Management Transforming Some CHA Developments," *Chicago Tribune*, March 18, 1991.

99. Monti, "Organizational Strengths and Weaknesses."

100. Arlene Williams, interview by author, February 22, 2002.

101. For the ways in which women's roles in public housing revitalization have been consistently erased, see Breitbart and Pader, "Establishing Ground."

102. Arlene Williams, interview by author, February 22, 2002.

103. Cora Moore, interview by author, June 21, 2000, and July 28, 2000.

104. Arelene Williams, interview by author, June 21, 2000, and February 22, 2002.

105. Dolores Wilson, interview by author, February 22, 2002; Bessie Rule, interview by author, June 30, 2000.

106. Cora Moore, interview by author, June 21, 2000.

107. James L. Tyson, "Self-Help: The New Tenet at Chicago Housing Project," *Christian Science Monitor*, June 28, 1996: 1; Cora Moore, interview by author, June 21, 2000; Arlene Williams, interview by author, June 21, 2000, and February 22, 2002.

108. 1230 N. Burling RMC, *By-Laws*, Article II: Mission Statement.

109. 1230 N. Burling RMC, *By-Laws*, Article III: Purpose.

110. Cora Moore, interview by author, June 21, 2000.

111. Cora Moore, interview by author, July 28, 2000.

112. Martha Irvine, "Can't Beat 'Em? Buy 'Em," *Chicago Sun-Times*, March 15, 1999: 20.

113. Arlene Williams, interview by author, February 22, 2002.

114. Kelvin Cannon, interview by author, March 8, 2002.

115. Ibid.

116. Linda Rule and Kenyatta Alexander, interview by author, June 30, 2000.

117. Richard Crayton, interview by author, July 28, 2000.

118. 1230 N. Burling RMC, *Homeownership Plan*, Summary.

119. On "cooperative housing," see the National Association of Housing Cooperatives at http://www.coophousing.org/; on "cohousing," see the Cohousing Association of the United States at http://www.cohousing.org/; on "mutual housing," see the Chicago

Mutual Housing Network at http://www.chicagomutual.org/; and on "community land trusts," see the Institute for Community Economics at http://iceclt.org/.

120. 1230 N. Burling RMC, *Homeownership Plan*, Summary; and *Homeownership Cooperative*.

121. Ibid.

122. 1230 N. Burling RMC, *Homeownership Plan*, Summary; and *Homeownership Cooperative*.

123. 1230 N. Burling RMC, *Homeownership Plan*, Summary; and *Homeownership Cooperative*.

124. 1230 N. Burling RMC, *Homeownership Cooperative*.

125. Arlene Williams, interview by author, February 22, 2002.

126. Cora Moore, interview by author, July 28, 2000.

127. Dolores Wilson, interview by author, February 22, 2002.

128. James L. Tyson, "Self-Help: The New Tenet at Chicago Housing Project," *Christian Science Monitor*, June 28, 1996: 1. According to the same HUD audit, "Although there have been notable accomplishments by some tenant organizations, the overall success of the Resident Mangagement Program has been minimal" (ibid.).

129. Gary Marx, "CHA Lets Tenants Take Charge of Their Homes," *Chicago Tribune*, May 7, 1989.

130. Martha Irvine, "Can't Beat 'Em? Buy 'Em," *Chicago Sun-Times*, March 15, 1999: 20.

131. Lemann, *The Promised Land*, 347.

132. See chapter 6.

133. We may in fact want to adopt Marcuse's four-part distinction between a *classic ghetto* ("a spatially concentrated area used to separate and to limit a particular involuntarily defined population group [usually by race] held to be, and treated as, inferior by the dominant society"); an *outcast ghetto* ("a ghetto in which ethnicity is combined with class in a spatially concentrated area with residents who are excluded from the mainstream of the economic life of the surrounding society, which does not profit significantly from its existence"); an *enclave* ("a spatially concentrated area in which members of a particular population group, self-defined by ethnicity or religion or otherwise, congregate as a means of enhancing their economic, social, political and/or cultural development"); and a *citadel* ("a spatially concentrated area in which members of a particular population group, defined by its position of superiority, in power, wealth, or status, in relation to its neighbors, congregate as a means of protecting that position").

134. Alexander, Ishikawa, and Silverstein, *Pattern Language*, 42ff.

135. Young, *Inclusion and Democracy*, 197.

136. Quoted in McKenzie, *Privatopia*, 189; see also Gans, "Balanced Community," 141–2. Further support for the black enclave idea comes from the "integration fatigue" experienced by some members of minority groups, who yearn therefore for "racial comfort zones" (see, e.g., Briggs, *Geography of Opportunity*). For a "white" view on the attractions of living among the like-minded, see David Brooks, "People Like Us," *Atlantic Monthly*, September, 2003: 29–32. And yet, as I will argue in chapter 9, the tension and conflict that arise when people very different from one another live in close proximity—in the context of equality and in a system in which resources for nonviolent conflict resolution are readily available—have positive benefits. And enclaves

have serious drawbacks, including rhetorical ones: in them, we never learn, for example, to listen well to difference, to test our views, to genuinely try to persuade others (Jane Mansbridge as quoted in Roberts-Miller, *Deliberate Conflict*, 41–3, 186ff).

137. Park, "City," 608.

138. Wirth and Furez, *Local Community Fact Book.*

139. Wirth, "Urbanism as a Way of Life."

140. Oldweiler, Cory. "Residents Lack Role in Revamped Public Housing." *Chicago Reporter*, April 2002.

141. Cora Moore, interview by author, July 28, 2000.

142. Arlene Williams, interview by author, February 22, 2002.

143. Ira Berlin, *Generations of Captivity*, 269.

144. Ibid., 270.

8. Toward a New Sociospatial Dialectic

1. See ch. 7 above, notes 133–39.

2. For a good summary of this issue, see Dreier, Mollenkopf, and Swanstrom, *Place Matters.*

3. One of the most persuasive studies of this ideology remains Bellah et al., *Habits of the Heart.*

4. My use of the word "scene" here derives from Burke, *Grammar of Motives*, passim.

5. Simon, *Sciences of the Artificial*, 53.

6. Diamond, *Guns, Germs, and Steel.*

7. Ibid., 400.

8. Ibid., 408.

9. I take the word "inventive" here from Diamond, but it has a long tradition in rhetoric as well: see, for example, Cicero's *De Inventione.*

10. See, for example, Obasanjo, *Impact of the Physical Environment.*

11. See, for example, Bradford McKee, "As Suburbs Grow, So Do Waistlines," *New York Times*, September 4, 2003; Martha T. Moore, "The Way Cities and Suburbs Are Developed Could Be Bad for Your Health," *USA Today*, April 22, 2003; Lauran Neergaard, "Suburban Sprawl Is Tied to Human Sprawl," *Wisconsin State Journal*, August 29, 2003; and David F. Williamson, "Editorial: The Prevention of Obesity," *The New England Journal of Medicine* 341, no. 15 (October 7, 1999). For other resources on the health effects of place, see Dreier, Mollenkopf, and Swanstrom, *Place Matters*, chapter 3; and the HUD, "Is Where We Live."

12. Baumgartner, *Moral Order of a Suburb.*

13. Shlay, "Family Self-Sufficiency."

14. See, for example, Millennial Housing Commission, *Meeting Our Nation's Housing Challenges*; and National Low Income Housing Coalition, *Out of Reach 2005.*

15. Dreier, Mollenkopf, and Swanstrom, *Place Matters.*

16. Oliver, *Democracy in Suburbia.*

17. See, for example, Jargowsky, *Poverty and Place*, 123–5.

18. Bernstein, Brocht, and Spade-Aguilar, "How Much Is Enough?" 29.

19. Ironically, the original impetus for city life was probably security.

20. Brooks-Gunn et al., "Do Neighborhoods Influence?"

21. Cf. Wilson's argument about poor children learning "planfulness" from being surrounded by working adults (*Truly Disadvantaged* and *When Work Disappears*).

22. For a summary of this issue, see Sandra Newman, "Introduction," 3.

23. Putnam, *Bowling Alone*. We saw in chapter 3, however, the social liabilities associated with some civic organizations.

24. Klinenberg, *Heat Wave*, 79–128.

25. North Lawndale had higher poverty and crime rates; but South Lawndale had risks as well, namely linguistic and cultural isolation and high numbers of seniors living alone (ibid., 86–90).

26. Ibid., 91.

27. Alex-Assensoh, "Race, Concentrated Poverty, Social Isolation."

28. Education is an important means to correct inequality, but gross inequalities make some schools less capable of serving this function; see Downey, Broh, and von Hippel, "Are Schools the Great Equalizer?"

29. Gary Orfield and Nora Gordon, *Schools More Separate*; see also Kozol, *Shame of the Nation*; and, for a local angle on this, Brian J. Rogal and Dan Weissmann, "Commuter Students: CHA Parents Seek Stability as Housing Falls," *The Chicago Reporter*, April, 2001.

30. On the cultural, economic, and geographical specificity of our "ways with words," see Anyon, "Social Class and the Hidden Curriculum"; Corsaro and Rizzo, "Disputes"; Hart and Risley, *Meaningful Differences*; and Heath, *Ways with Words*.

31. Dahl and Tufte, *Size and Democracy*.

32. Oliver, *Democracy in Suburbia*.

33. So, for example, Putnam has claimed that the longer commute times characteristic of suburban living are associated with lower levels of civic associationism (*Bowling Alone*).

34. Young, *Inclusion and Democracy*, 204ff.

35. For one side of this debate, see Von Hoffman, "High Ambitions," who argues that liberal housing policy in this country suffers from "environmental determinism," the "belief that an ideal or improved residential environment will better the behavior as well as the condition of its inhabitants" (423–4), and writes that such a view has consistently overstated the potential of housing policies and designs to solve the problems of the poor. He suggests that housing advocates "not promote large-scale politically controversial programs (such as Moving to Opportunity) as panaceas for deep-rooted social problems" (442). For the other side, see Dreier, Mollenkopf, and Swanstrom, *Place Matters*, who acknowledge that the research on how places affect people's lives is "full of thorny methodological and conceptual disputes" but argue nonetheless that "[t]he evidence on the contextual effects of place is overwhelming" (65). They amass a wealth of data to support claims for the impact of place on individuals' jobs and income, mental and physical health, access to private goods and services, and crime (64–102), as well as public goods and services like education (152–215). And because government policies have so clearly supported place-based differences in citizens' life

chances (103–51), they hold out more hope than Von Hoffman does for the power of *alternative* public policies and environmental designs to improve the lives of the poor or at least to level the playing field (216–309).

36. Mayer and Jencks, "Growing Up in Poor Neighborhoods."

37. Lynch, *Good City Form*, 99—though I have often thought there was an asymmetry in the statement: I am more willing to accept the first part than the second.

38. Oscar Newman, *Defensible Space*; and Alexander, Ishikawa, and Silverstein, *Pattern Language*.

39. Jim McNeill and J. S. Fuerst deconstruct the old "high-rises are bad" argument by pointing to both the historic low performance of Los Angeles' mostly low-rise public housing projects and the high performance of New York City's mostly high-rise ones ("Creative Destruction? Plan by Politicians and Private Developers to Demolish CHA High-Rises Is Flawed," *Chicago Tribune*, July 10, 1996). Of course, this doesn't make such effects random; it may mean we just need to qualify them more carefully.

40. Brooks-Gunn et al., "Do Neighborhoods Influence?"; and Ellen and Turner, "Does Neighborhood Matter?"

41. Fleming, "Rhetoric as a Course of Study."

42. Duany, Plater-Zyberk, and Speck, *Suburban Nation*, 239.

43. Ibid., 238–9.

44. Jargowsky, *Poverty and Place*, 4.

45. Ibid., 144.

46. Dreier, Mollenkopf, and Swanstrom, *Place Matters*, 30.

47. Jargowsky, *Poverty and Place*, 193. See also Dreier, Mollenkopf, and Swanstrom, who argue that we should focus not on behaviors but "opportunity structures" (*Place Matters*, 66). This need not mean, however, that we favor mobility programs like Gautreaux. I do not dispute here Rubinowitz and Rosenbaum's claim (in *Crossing the Class and Color Lines*) that environment causes most of the distress in the inner city; what I have disputed is their conclusion that the solution to that problem is flight.

48. Fraser, "Rethinking the Public Sphere."

9. Cities of Rhetoric

1. For the sources of the story that follows, see Plato, *Protagoras*, 320d; Isocrates, *Nicocles*, 5; Cicero, *De Inventione*, 1.2; Kerferd, *Sophistic Movement*, 139–62; and Carolyn Miller, "*Polis*."

2. See chapter 1 above, note 52.

3. Thucydides, *History of the Peloponnesian War*, 7.77

4. Aristotle, *Politics*, 1275a5. Citizenship in Aristotle's polis was determined not by residence, as if everyone who merely lived in a place constituted its *demos*, but by a particular kind of social union: a fellowship of beings of a certain type (in his case, free-born adult males), related to one another in a particular way (i.e., as equals), engaged in a specific kind of activity (i.e., practical judgment), and devoted to a shared ethical project (i.e., "living well").

5. Ibid., 1325b33.

6. Ibid., 1330b15ff.

7. Ibid., 1326b7.

8. "A city is made up not only of many human beings but also of human beings who differ in kind" (*Politics*, 1261a22; see also 1255b16, 1261a15). See also chapter 3 above, notes 66–70.

9. Schill, "Distressed Public Housing," 498, note 9; see also U.S. Housing Act of 1949.

10. See, for example, Scott Baldauf, "When Zoning Becomes Segregation Tool," *Christian Science Monitor*, August 11, 2000; Gyourko and Sinai, "Spatial Distribution"; Hanchett, "U.S. Tax Policy"; Jackson, *Crabgrass Frontier*; Kemper, "Home Inequity"; Kirp, Dwyer, and Rosenthal, *Our Town*; Schill and Wachter, "Spatial Bias"; and Von Hoffman, "High Ambitions."

11. It is relevant to note here that, during the spate of school shootings that occurred in this country at the end of the twentieth century, most of the shooters were not inner-city gangbangers but middle-class white teenage boys from segregated, automobile-dependent suburbs, places where adolescents often have nowhere to go and nothing to do, where middle- and upper-class, mostly white, nuclear families live in communities comprised entirely of other middle- and upper-class, mostly white, nuclear families, and where the socioeconomic segregation of the world "outside" is echoed in the segregation of students into social cliques inside (see Timothy Egan, "Shooting Shakes the Myth of Safety in Suburbs," *New York Times*, March 9, 2001; and William L. Hamilton, "How Suburban Design Is Failing Teen-Agers," *New York Times*, May 6, 1999; but cf. Alan Wolfe, "Littleton Takes the Blame," *New York Times*, May 2, 1999).

12. Oldenburg, *Great Good Place*.

13. Such design need not mean that we go bankrupt; in *Making a Place*, Williamson, Imbroscio, and Alperovitz argue persuasively for locally and publicly owned businesses, interstate compacts against job-poaching, small business development, co-operative economic structures, community development corporations, community land trusts, and so on.

14. Dahl and Tufte, *Size and Democracy*, 135.

15. Dreier, Mollenkopf, and Swanstrom, *Place Matters*; Bruce Katz, "Reviving Cities"; Myron Orfield, *American Metropolitics*; Rusk, *Cities Without Suburbs*; Young, *Justice*, 252, and *Inclusion*, 232.

16. David Brooks, "People Like Us," *The Atlantic Monthly*, September 2003: 29–32; cf. McPherson, Smith-Lovin, and Cook, "Birds of a Feather."

17. See chapter 7.

18. Halpern, *Rebuilding the Inner City*.

19. The anti-urbanism of the powerful U.S. Senate—the way it gives as many votes to Wyoming as it does to New York—probably makes much of what I've been arguing for here seem simply naïve (see, e.g., Dahl, *How Democratic?* and Rosenfeld, "What Democracy?").

20. See, e.g., Paehlke, *Democracy's Dilemma*.

21. Warren, "Self in Discursive Democracy," 168.

22. Nussbaum, "Kant and Cosmopolitanism."

23. Frug, *City Making*. Cf. Dewey, *Public and its Problems*; and Oliver, *Democracy in Suburbia*. Iris Marion Young prefers talking about empowerment rather than autonomy, since the latter implies for her privacy and atomism, while the former suggests broad and

full participation in decision-making (*Justice*, 248–55); she also applauds Frug's theory of "decentered decentralization," with its focus on "relational autonomy" rather than a decentralization that often results in increased inequity. But Young is clear in both books that the lowest level of sovereign power in her proposed system is the region or metropolitan area, while the districts I am arguing here for here are lower down on the scale, between the neighborhood and the metropolis.

24. Fung and Wright, *Deepening Democracy*, 15.

25. Ibid., 22.

26. Sandel, *Democracy's Discontent*.

27. Dewey, *Public and Its Problems*, 126.

28. See, for example, Sennett, *Corrosion of Character*; and Fullilove, *Root Shock*.

29. See, for example, Glendon, *Rights Talk*; and Schudson, *Good Citizen*.

30. On the ways in which our discourses privilege independence and neglect the inevitability and value of our interdependencies with others, see Fineman, *Autonomy Myth*; and Readings, *University in Ruins*.

31. Kemmis, *Good City and Good Life*, 198.

32. See, for example, Corsaro and Rizzo, "Disputes." But cf. Tannen, who sees our culture as hyperargumentative (*Argument Culture*). Most writing and speech teachers probably find our culture not argumentative *enough* (see, e.g., Graff, *Clueless in Academe*).

33. See, for example, Arendt, *Human Condition*; Billig, *Arguing and Thinking*; Burke, *Rhetoric of Motives*; Coser, *Functions of Social Conflict*; Crick, *In Defense of Politics*; Crosswhite, *Rhetoric of Reason*, chapter 4; Graff, *Clueless in Academe*; Kuhn, *Skills of Argument*; Light, *Making the Most of College*, chapters 7–8; Mill, *On Liberty*, chapter II; Mouffe, *Democratic Paradox*; Popper, "Science"; and Roberts-Miller, *Deliberate Conflict*.

34. Bellah et al., *Habits of the Heart*.

35. Fraser, "Rethinking the Public Sphere," 134.

36. See, for example, Neel's definition of "strong discourse" in *Plato, Derrida, and Writing*, 208; see also note 33 above.

37. Mooney, *Vico*, 84; see also Fleming, "Becoming Rhetorical"; and Lakoff, *Don't Think of an Elephant*. On the substantive knowledge that schools should be imparting to citizens, see Galston, "Political Knowledge."

38. Fleming, "Very Idea of a Progymnasmata"; and Graff, *Clueless in Academe*.

39. In her study of "real-world" argument skills and dispositions, Kuhn found that subjects fell into three epistemological camps: "absolutists," "multiplists," and "evaluativists," the last being the one that Kuhn considers most conducive to a flourishing public life. Unlike absolutists, evaluativists deny the possibility of certain knowledge on issues that come up for debate in public life; but unlike multiplists, they also believe that viewpoints can be compared and judged. This is not the place to pursue this question, but I do believe that *some* kind of commendatory attitude toward argumentation itself, the very act of reasoning with others on contentious issues, is needed if young people are to learn to meet the demands of direct, deliberative democracy.

40. See the interview with Johnson at "Senate Lynching Apology," *The News-Hour with Jim Lehrer*, broadcast June 13, 2005 (http://www.pbs.org/newshour/bb/race_relations/jan-june05/anti-lynching_6-13.html). For "The Lynching of Anthony Crawford"

by Doria Dee Johnson, see http://www.ccharity.com/acarter.php; and for the "Anthony Crawford Remembered" Web site, see http://home.comcast.net/~doriajohnson/.

41. Hull House was the social settlement founded by Jane Addams in Chicago; see Residents of Hull House, *Hull-House Maps and Papers* (New York: T. Y. Crowell & Co., 1895).

42. Heather Stouder, "Grocery Stores in City Neighborhoods: Supporting Access to Food Choices, Livable Neighborhoods, and Entrepreneurial Opportunities in Madison, Wisconsin" (Madison: Office of the Mayor, 2004) at http://www.cityofmadison.com/planning/Grocery Store.pdf and http://ncgrocery.org/newsReports/MadCityGrocReport.pdf.

43. See syllabus for English 236 at http://people.umass.edu/dfleming.

44. Finley, *Politics in the Ancient World*, 28.

45. Finley, *Democracy Ancient and Modern*, 31.

46. Finley, *Politics in the Ancient World*, 74.

47. Ibid.

48. Ibid., 75. Cf. Ober, *Mass and Elite*, 159–65.

49. As quoted in Finley, *Democracy Ancient and Modern*, 31–2. The quotation comes from Mill's *Considerations on Representative Government*.

50. Simonides was an ancient Greek lyric poet from the island of Ceos, whose years are usually given as 556–469 BCE. For this quotation, see Hansen, *Athenian Democracy*, 320, n. 271.

10. Afterword

1. Briggs, *The Geography of Opportunity*, 5.

2. Sorkin, "Introduction," xv.

3. Cieslewicz, "City Ethic"; see also David Owen, "Green Manhattan," *The New Yorker*, October 18, 2004: 111–23.

Acknowledgments

1. For more about Hackett, see Lemann, *Promised Land*, 123–8; Matusow, *Unraveling of America*, 107–26; and Schlesinger, *Robert Kennedy and His Times*, 48–9, 440–48.

Bibliography

Abbott, Andrew, and Jolyon Wurr. "Chicago Studied: Social Scientists and Their City." In Grossman, Keating, and Reiff, *Encyclopedia of Chicago*, 148–51.

Abbott, Edith. *The Tenements of Chicago, 1908–1935*. Chicago: University of Chicago Press, 1936.

Adler-Kassner, Linda, Robert Crooks and Ann Waters, eds. *Writing the Community: Concepts and Models for Service-Learning in Composition*. Washington, DC: American Association for Higher Education, 1997.

Adrian, Charles R. "Forms of Local Government in American History." In *Forms of Local Government: A Handbook on City, County and Regional Options*, edited by Roger L. Kemp, 47–62. Jefferson, NC: McFarland & Co., 1999.

Alex-Assensoh, Yvette. "Race, Concentrated Poverty, Social Isolation, and Political Behavior." *Urban Affairs Review* 33, no. 2 (1997): 209–27.

Alexander, Christopher, Sara Ishikawa, and Murray Silverstein (with Max Jacobson, Ingrid Fiksdahl-King, and Shlomo Angel). *A Pattern Language: Towns, Buildings, Construction*. New York: Oxford University Press, 1977.

Allen, Danielle S. *Talking to Strangers: Anxieties of Citizenship since* Brown v. Board of Education. Chicago: University of Chicago Press, 2004.

Almond, Gabriel A., and Sidney Verba. *The Civic Culture: Political Attitudes and Democracy in Five Nations*. Princeton: Princeton University Press, 1963.

Anderson, Benedict. *Imagined Communities: Reflections on the Origin and Spread of Nationalism*, rev. ed. London: Verso, 1991.

Anyon, Jean. "Social Class and the Hidden Curriculum of Work." *Journal of Education* 162 (1980): 67–92.

Arendt, Hannah. *The Human Condition*. Chicago: University of Chicago Press, 1958.

———. *On Revolution*. New York: Penguin, 1963.

Aristotle. *Nicomachean Ethics*. Translated by Terence Irwin. Indianapolis: Hackett, 1985.

———. *The Politics*. Translated by Peter L. Phillips Simpson. Chapel Hill: University of North Carolina Press, 1997.

———. *On Rhetoric: A Theory of Civic Discourse*. Translated by George A. Kennedy. Oxford: Oxford University Press, 1991.

Asen, Robert. *Visions of Poverty: Welfare Policy and Political Imagination*. East Lansing: Michigan State University Press, 2002.

Asen, Robert, and Daniel C. Brouwer, eds. *Counterpublics and the State*. Albany: State University of New York Press, 2001.

Banerjee, Tridib, and William C. Baer. *Beyond the Neighborhood Unit: Residential Environments and Public Policy*. New York: Plenum Press, 1984.

Barthes, Roland. "The Old Rhetoric: An Aide-Mémoire." In *The Semiotic Challenge*. Translated by Richard Howard. New York: Hill & Wang, 1988. First published 1970.

Baumgartner, M. P. *The Moral Order of a Suburb*. New York: Oxford University Press, 1988.

Baxandall, Rosalyn, and Elizabeth Ewen. *Picture Windows: How the Suburbs Happened*. New York: Basic Books, 2000.

Bell, Daniel. "Civil Society versus Civic Virtue." In *Freedom of Association*, edited by Amy Gutmann, 239–272. Princeton, NJ: Princeton University Press, 1998.

Bellah, Robert N., Richard Madsen, William M. Sullivan, Ann Swidler, and Steven M. Tipton. *Habits of the Heart: Individualism and Commitment in American Life*. New York: Harper & Row, 1985.

Bender, Thomas. "The Erosion of Public Culture: Cities, Discourses, and Professional Disciplines." In *The Authority of Experts: Studies in History and Theory*, edited by T. L. Haskell, 84–106. Bloomington: Indiana University Press, 1984.

———, ed. *The University and the City: From Medieval Origins to the Present*. New York: Oxford University Press, 1988.

Benhabib, Seyla. "Toward a Deliberative Model of Democratic Legitimacy." In *Democracy and Difference: Contesting the Boundaries of the Political*, edited by Seyla Benhabib, 67–94. Princeton, NJ: Princeton University Press, 1996.

Bennett, Larry. "Do We Really Wish to Live in a Communitarian City? Communitarian Thinking and the Redevelopment of Chicago's Cabrini-Green Public Housing Complex." *Journal of Urban Affairs* 20, no. 2 (1998): 99–116.

Benson, Lee, and Ira Harkavy. "Higher Education's Third Revolution: The Emergence of the Democratic Cosmopolitan Civic University." *Cityscape: A Journal of Policy Development and Research* 5, no. 1 (2000): 47–57.

Berkowitz, Peter. *Virtue and the Making of Modern Liberalism*. Princeton, NJ: Princeton University Press, 2000.

Berlin, Ira. *Generations of Captivity: A History of African-American Slaves*. Cambridge, MA: Harvard University Press, 2003.

Berlin, Isaiah. "Two Concepts of Liberty." In *The Proper Study of Mankind: An Anthology of Essays*, edited by Henry Hardy and Roger Hausheer, 191–242. New York: Farrar, Straus and Giroux, 1998. First published 1969.

Berlin, James. "Rhetoric and Ideology in the Writing Class." *College English* 50 (1988): 477–94.

Bernstein, Jared, Chauna Brocht, and Maggie Spade-Aguilar. "How Much Is Enough? Basic Family Budgets for Working Families." Washington, DC: Economic Policy Institute, 2000.

Bezalel, Ronit. *Voices of Cabrini*. Documentary film. 1999.

Bhaba, Homi. *The Location of Culture*. London: Routledge, 1994.

Billig, Michael. *Arguing and Thinking: A Rhetorical Approach to Social Psychology*, 2nd ed. Cambridge: Cambridge University Press, 1996.

Black, Edwin. *Rhetorical Criticism: A Study in Method*. Madison: University of Wisconsin Press, 1978. First published 1965.

Blakely, Edward J., and Mary Gail Snyder. *Fortress America: Gated Communities in the United States*. Washington, DC: Brookings Institute Press and Cambridge, MA: Lincoln Institute of Land Policy, 1997.

Bledstein, Burton J. *The Culture of Professionalism: The Middle Class and the Development of Higher Education in America*. New York: Norton, 1976.

Bloom, Lynn Z. "The Essay Canon." *College English* 61 (1999): 401–30.

———. "Freshman Composition as a Middle Class Enterprise." *College English* 58 (1996): 654–75.

Bookchin, Murray. *From Urbanization to Cities: Toward a New Politics of Citizenship*. London: Cassell, 1995.

Borja, Jordi. "Cities: New Roles and Forms of Governing." In *Preparing for the Urban Future: Global Pressures and Local Forces*, edited by Michael A. Cohen, Blair A. Ruble, Joseph S. Tulchin, and Allison M. Garland, 242–263. Washington, DC: Woodrow Wilson Center Press, 1996.

Bowly, Devereaux, Jr. *The Poorhouse: Subsidized Housing in Chicago, 1895–1976*. Carbondale: Southern Illinois University Press, 1978.

Boyer, M. Christine. *Dreaming the Rational City: The Myth of American City Planning*. Cambridge, MA: MIT Press, 1983.

Breitbart, Myrna Margulies, and Ellen J. Pader. "Establishing Ground: Representing Gender and Race in a Mixed Housing Development." *Gender, Place, & Culture: A Journal of Feminist Geography* 2, no. 1 (1995): 5–24.

Brennan, Brian. "Background on MTO." Available at http://www.nber.org/~kling/mto/background.htm#Gautreaux.

Briggs, Xavier De Souza, ed. *The Geography of Opportunity: Race and Housing Choice in Metropolitan America*. Washington, DC: Brookings Institution Press, 2005.

Brodkey, Linda. *Writing Permitted in Designated Areas Only*. Minneapolis: University of Minnesota Press, 1996.

Brooks, David. *Bobos in Paradise: The New Upper Class and How They Got There*. New York: Simon & Schuster, 2000.

Brooks-Gunn, Jeanne, Greg J. Duncan, Pamela Kato Klebanov, and Naomi Sealand. "Do Neighborhoods Influence Child and Adolescent Development?" *American Journal of Sociology* 99, no. 2 (1993): 353–95.

Brophy, Paul C., and Rhonda N. Smith. "Mixed-Income Housing: Factors for Success." *Cityscape: A Journal of Policy Development and Research* 3, no. 2 (1997).

Bruegmann, Robert. "Schaumburg, Oak Brook, Rosemont, and the Recentering of the Chicago Metropolitan Area." In Zukowsky, *Chicago Architecture and Design*, 159–77.

Burke, Kenneth. *A Grammar of Motives*. Berkeley: University of California Press, 1969. First published 1945.

———. *A Rhetoric of Motives*. Berkeley: University of California Press, 1969. First published 1950.

Burnham, Daniel H., and Edward H. Bennett. *Plan of Chicago*. Edited by Charles Moore. Introducation by Wilbert R. Hasbrouck. New York, Da Capo Press, 1970. First published 1909.

Business and Professional People for the Public Interest. "Gautreaux Information." (January 6, 2000). Appendix 15 to the City of Chicago Department of Housing's *Request for Proposals for Cabrini Extension North Property* (see reference below).

———. "Gautreaux." Available at http://www.bpichicago.org/pht/gautreaux.html.

Cabrini-Green Local Advisory Council. "Vision 2000: The Future Is Now." Agenda for August 5, 1999, public meeting. July 16, 1999.

Cabrini-Green Local Advisory Council v. Chicago Housing Authority and City of Chicago, No. 96 C 6949 (N.D. Ill. Oct. 23, 1996).

Caldeira, Teresa P. R. *City of Walls: Crime, Segregation, and Citizenship in Sao Paolo.* Berkeley: University of California Press, 2000.

Calmore, John O. "Spatial Equality and the Kerner Commission Report: A Back-to-the-Future Essay." *North Carolina Law Review* 71 (1993): 1487–98.

Caprara, David, and Bill Alexander. *Empowering Residents of Public Housing: A Resource Guide for Resident Management.* Washington, DC: National Center for Neighborhood Enterprise, 1989.

Castells, Manuel. *The Informational City: Information Technology, Economic Restructuring, and the Urban-Regional Process.* Oxford: Blackwell, 1989.

CBPP—see Center on Budget and Policy Priorities.

Center on Budget and Policy Priorities. "Growth in Housing Voucher Costs Has Slowed Sharply." Washington, DC, 2005.

———. "Introduction to the Housing Voucher Program." Washington, DC, 2003.

Center for Civic Education. *National Standards for Civics and Government.* Calabasas, CA, 1994.

Center for Community Change. *A HOPE Unseen: Voices from the Other Side of HOPE VI.* Washington, DC: Everywhere and Now Public Housing Residents Organizing Nationally Together (ENPHRONT), 2003.

CHA—See Chicago Housing Authority.

Chicago Fact Book Consortium. *Local Community Fact Book: Chicago Metropolitan Area: Based on the 1970 and 1980 Censuses.* Chicago: Chicago Review Press, 1984.

———. *Local Community Fact Book: Chicago Metropolitan Area, 1990.* Chicago: University of Illinois at Chicago Press, 1995.

Chicago Housing Authority. "Cabrini-Green Homes." Available at http://www.thecha.org/housingdev/cabrini_green_homes.html. Chicago, 2001.

———. *Cabrini-Green HOPE VI Revitalization Plan.* Chicago, June 20, 1997.

———. *Plan for Transformation.* Chicago, January 6, 2000.

Cicero. *De Inventione.* Translated by H. M. Hubbell. Cambridge, MA: Harvard University Press [Loeb Classical Library], 1968.

Cieslewicz, Dave. "City Ethic: Urban Conservation and the New Environmentalism." Madison, WI: 1000 Friends of Wisconsin, April, 2000. Available at http://www.1kfriends.org/Publications/Online_Documents/City_Ethic.htm.

Cintron, Ralph. *Angels' Town: Chero Ways, Gang Life, and Rhetorics of the Everyday.* Boston: Beacon, 1997.

City of Chicago. *Draft Near North Redevelopment Initiative.* Prepared by JJR/Inc.; Goody, Clancy & Associates, and others. June 1996; February 1997, December 10, 1997.

———. *Near North Tax Increment Redevelopment Plan and Project.* Prepared by Camiros, Ltd., et al., June 1997.

———. *Near North Redevelopment Initiative Update*. January 1998.

City of Chicago Department of Housing. *Near North Development Initiative. Request for Proposals for Purchase and Redevelopment of the Halsted North Property*. January 30, 1998.

———. *Request for Proposals for Mixed-Income Redevelopment of Cabrini Extension North Property*. October 19, 2001.

Cohen, Adam, and Elizabeth Taylor. *American Pharaoh: Mayor Richard Daley and His Battle for Chicago and the Nation*. Boston: Little Brown, 2000.

Concerned Residents of ABLA v. Chicago Housing Authority and United States Department of Housing and Urban Development, No. 99 C 4959 (N.D. Ill. July 29, 1999).

Condit, Carl W. *Chicago 1930–1970: Building, Planning, and Urban Technology*. Chicago: University of Chicago Press, 1974.

Congress for the New Urbanism. *Principles for Inner City Neighborhood Design: HOPE VI and the New Urbanism*. Washington, DC, June, 2000.

Conley, Thomas M. *Rhetoric in the European Tradition*. New York: Longman, 1990.

Connors, Robert J. *Composition-Rhetoric: Backgrounds, Theory, and Pedagogy*. Pittsburgh, PA: University of Pittsburgh Press, 1997.

Conrad, Stephen A. "Citizenship." In *The Oxford Companion to American Law*, edited by Kermit L. Hall, 101–104. New York: Oxford University Press, 2002.

Corsaro, William A., and Thomas A. Rizzo. "Disputes in the Peer Culture of American and Italian Nursery-School Children." In *Conflict Talk: Sociolinguistic Investigations of Arguments in Conversations*, edited by Allen D. Grimshaw, 21–66. Cambridge: Cambridge University Press, 1990.

Coser, Lewis A. *The Functions of Social Conflict*. New York: The Free Press, 1956.

Coulibaly, Modibo, Rodney D. Green, and David M. James. *Segregation in Federally Subsidized Low-Income Housing in the United States*. Westport, CT: Praeger Publishers, 1998.

Crick, Bernard. *In Defense of Politics*, 4th ed. Chicago: University of Chicago Press, 1992.

Cronon, William. *Nature's Metropolis*. New York: Norton, 1991.

Crosswhite, James. *The Rhetoric of Reason: Writing and the Attractions of Argument*. Madison: University of Wisconsin Press, 1996.

Cushman, Ellen. *The Struggle and the Tools: Oral and Literate Strategies in an Inner City Community*. Albany: State University of New York Press, 1998.

Dagger, Richard. *Civic Virtues: Rights, Citizenship, and Republican Liberalism*. New York: Oxford University Press, 1997.

Dahl, Robert A. "The City in the Future of Democracy." *American Political Science Review* 61, no. 4 (1967): 953–70.

———. *How Democratic Is the American Constitution?* New Haven, CT: Yale University Press, 2001

———. *On Democracy*. New Haven, CT: Yale University Press, 1998.

———. "Procedural Democracy." In *Philosophy, Politics, and Society, Fifth Series*, edited by Peter Laslett and James Fishkin, 97–133. New Haven, CT: Yale University Press, 1979.

Dahl, Robert A., and Edward R. Tufte. *Size and Democracy*. Palo Alto, CA: Stanford University Press, 1973.

Darden, Joe T. "Segregation." In *The Encyclopedia of Housing*, edited by Willem van Vliet, 523–25. Thousand Oaks, CA: Sage, 1998.

Daskal, Jennifer. *In Search of Shelter: The Growing Shortage of Affordable Rental Housing*. Washington, DC: Center on Budget and Policy Priorities, 1998.

Davis, Mike. "Fortress Los Angeles: The Militarization of Urban Space." In Sorkin, *Variations on a Theme Park*, 154–80.

DeFilippis, James. "The Myth of Social Capital in Community Development." *Housing Policy Debate* 12, no. 4 (2001): 781–806.

Del Conte, Alessandra, and Jeffrey Kling. "A Synthesis of MTO Research on Self-Sufficiency, Safety and Health, and Behavior and Delinquincy." *Poverty Research News*, 5, no. 1 (2001): 3–6.

DeLillo, Don. *Libra*. New York: Viking, 1988.

Denton, Nancy. "Are African Americans Still Hypersegregated?" In *Residential Apartheid: The American Legacy*, edited by Robert D. Bullard, J. Eugene Grigsby III, and Charles Lee, 49–81. Los Angeles: Center for Afro-American Studies at the University of California at Los Angeles, 1994.

De Romilly, Jacquelline. *The Great Sophists in Periclean Athens*. Translated by Janet Lloyd. Oxford: Clarendon Press, 1992.

Dewey, John. *The Public and Its Problems*. Denver, CO: Alan Swallow, 1927.

de Wit, Wim. "The Rise of Public Housing in Chicago, 1930–1960." In Zukowsky, *Chicago Architecture and Design*, 233–45.

Diamond, Jared. *Guns, Germs, and Steel: The Fates of Human Societies*. New York: W. W. Norton, 1999.

Dietz, Mary G. "Context Is All: Feminism and Theories of Citizenship." *Daedalus* 116, no. 4 (1987): 1–24.

Dilger, Robert Jay. *Neighborhood Politics: Residential Community Associations in Neighborhood Governance*. New York: New York University Press, 1992.

Donovan, Brian R. "The City and the Garden: Plato's Retreat from the Teaching of Virtue." *Educational Theory* 45, no. 4 (Fall 1995): 453–64.

Douglas, Wallace. "Rhetoric for the Meritocracy." In Ohmann, *English in America*, 97–132.

Downey, Douglas B., Beckett A. Broh, and Paul T. von Hippel. "Are Schools the Great Equalizer? Cognitive Inequality During the Summer Months and the School Year," *American Sociological Review* 69 (2004): 613–35.

Downs, Anthony. *New Visions for Metropolitan America*. Washington, DC: The Brookings Institution and Cambridge, MA: Lincoln Institute of Land Policy, 1994.

———. *Opening Up the Suburbs: An Urban Strategy for America*. New Haven, CT: Yale University Press, 1973.

Drake, St. Clair, and Horace R. Cayton. *Black Metropolis: A Study of Negro Life in a Northern City*, rev. ed. 2 vols. New York: Harper & Row, 1962. First published 1945.

Dreier, Peter, John Mollenkopf, and Todd Swanstrom. *Place Matters: Metropolitics for the Twenty-first Century*, 2nd ed. Lawrence: University Press of Kansas, 2004.

Duany, Andres, and Elizabeth Plater-Zyberk. "The Neighborhood, the District, and the Corridor." In Katz, *The New Urbanism*, xvii–xx.

Duany, Andres, Elizabeth Plater-Zyberk, and Jeff Speck. *Suburban Nation: The Rise of Sprawl and the Decline of the American Dream.* New York: North Point Press, 2000.

Du Bois, W. E. B. *The Souls of Black Folk.* In *Writings.* Edited by Nathan Huggins. New York: Library of America, 1986. First published 1903.

Eberly, Rosa A. "From *Writers*, *Audiences*, and *Communities* to *Publics*: Writing Classrooms as Protopublic Spaces." *Rhetoric Review* 18, no. 1 (1999): 165–78.

Ebner, Michael. "Suburbs and Cities as Dual Metropolis" In Grossman, Keating, and Reiff, *Encyclopedia of Chicago*, 798–802.

Ehrenreich, Barbara and John Ehrenreich. "The Professional-Managerial Class." *Radical America* 11, no. 2 (1977): 7–31.

Ellen, Ingrid Gould, and Margery Austin Turner. "Does Neighborhood Matter? Assessing Recent Evidence." *Housing Policy Debate* 8, no. 4 (1997): 833–66.

Emig, Janet. *The Composing Processes of Twelfth Graders.* Urbana, IL: NCTE, 1971.

Ervin, Elizabeth. "Encouraging Civic Participation among First-Year Writing Students." *Rhetoric Review* 15 (1997): 382–99.

Ewing, Reid. "Is Los Angeles-Style Sprawl Desirable?" *Journal of the American Planning Association* 63, no. 1 (1997): 107–26.

Farr, Marcia. "Essayist Literacy and Other Verbal Peformances." *Written Communication* 10, no. 1 (1993): 4–38.

Federal Writers' Project of the Works Progress Administration. *The WPA Guide to Illinois.* New York: Pantheon Books, 1983. First published 1939.

Fidel, Kenneth. "End of Diversity: The Long-Term Effects of Gentrification in Lincoln Park." In *Gentrification and Urban Change*, edited by Ray Hutchison, 145–64. *Research in Urban Sociology: A Research Annual*, vol. 2. Greenwich, CT: JAI Press, 1992.

Fineman, Martha A. *The Autonomy Myth: A Theory of Dependency.* New York: The New Press, 2004.

Finer, S. E. *Ancient Monarchies and Empires. The History of Government from the Earliest Times*, vol. 1. Oxford: Oxford University Press, 1997.

Finley, Moses I. *Democracy Ancient and Modern*, rev. ed. New Brunswick, NJ: Rutgers University Press, 1985. First published 1973.

———. "Politics." In *The Legacy of Greece: A New Appraisal*, edited by M. I. Finley, 22–36. Oxford: Clarendon Press, 1981.

———. *Politics in the Ancient World.* Cambridge: Cambridge University Press, 1983.

Fischer, Paul B. "Section 8 and the Public Housing Revolution: Where Will the Families Go?" Chicago: Metropolitan Planning Council, July 1999.

———. "Where Are the Public Housing Families Going? An Update." Chicago: National Center on Poverty Law, 2003.

Fisher, Robert B. "Origins of Federally Aided Public Housing." In Mitchell, *Federal Housing Policy and Programs*, 231–244. First published 1959.

Fishman, Robert. *Bourgeois Utopias: The Rise and Fall of Suburbia.* New York, Basic Books, 1987.

Fiss, Owen. "What Should Be Done for Those Who Have Been Left Behind?" *Boston Review*, Summer, 2000.

Fleming, David. "Becoming Rhetorical: An Education in the Topics." In *The Realms of Rhetoric: Inquiries into the Prospects for Rhetoric Education*, edited by Deepika Bahri and Joseph Petraglia, 93–116. Albany: State University of New York Press, 2003.

———. "Rhetoric as a Course of Study." *College English* 61, no. 2 (1998): 169–91.

———. "The Space of Argumentation: Urban Design, Civic Discourse, and the Dream of the Good City." *Argumentation* 12, no. 2 (1998): 147–66.

———. "The Streets of Thurii: Discourse, Democracy, and Design in the Classical *Polis*." *Rhetoric Society Quarterly* 32, no. 3 (2002): 5–32.

———. "Subjects of the Inner City: Writing the People of Cabrini-Green." In *Towards a Rhetoric of Everyday Life: New Directions in Research on Writing, Text, and Discourse*, edited by Martin Nystrand and John Duffy, 207–44. Madison: University of Wisconsin Press, 2003.

———. "The Very Idea of a *Progymnasmata*." *Rhetoric Review* 22, no. 2 (2003): 105–20.

Florida, Richard L. *The Rise of the Creative Class and How It's Transforming Work, Leisure, Community and Everyday Life*. New York: Basic Books, 2002.

Foucault, Michel. "Of Other Spaces." Translated by Jay Miskowiec. *Dialectics* 16, no. 1 (1986): 22–27. First published 1984 from 1967 lecture.

———. "Space, Knowledge, and Power." In *The Foucault Reader*, edited by Paul Rabinow, 237–56. New York: Pantheon, 1984.

Franzese, Paula. "Does It Take a Village? Privatization, Patterns of Restrictiveness, and the Demise of Community." *Villanova Law Review* 47 (2002): 553ff.

Fraser, Nancy. "Rethinking the Public Sphere: A Contribution to the Critique of Actually Existing Democracy." In *Habermas and the Public Sphere*, edited by Craig Calhoun, 109–142. Cambridge, MA: MIT Press, 1992.

Freedman, Sarah Warshauer, Elizabeth Radin Simons, Julie Shalhope Kalnin, Alex Casareno, and the M-Class Teams. *Inside City Schools: Investigating Literacy in Multicultural Classrooms*. New York: Teachers College Press, 1999.

Frey, William. H. "Melting Pot Suburbs: A Census 2000 Study of Suburban Diversity." Washington, DC: The Brookings Institute, 2001.

Friedman, Susan Stanford. *Mappings: Feminism and the Cultural Geographies of Encounter*. Princeton, NJ: Princeton University Press, 1998.

Frug, Gerald E. *City Making: Building Communities Without Building Walls*. Princeton, NJ: Princeton University Press, 1999.

Fullilove, Mindy Thompson. *Root Shock: How Tearing Up City Neighborhoods Hurts America, and What We Can Do About It*. New York: Ballantine, 2004.

Fung, Archon, and Erik Olin Wright. *Deepening Democracy: Institutional Innovations in Empowered Participatory Governance*. London: Verso, 2003.

Fusfield, William D. "Refusing to Believe It: Considerations on Public Speaking Instruction in a Post-Machiavellian Moment." *Social Epistemology* 11, no. 3–4 (1997): 253–314.

Galston, William A. "Political Knowledge, Political Engagement, and Civic Education." *Annual Review of Political Science* 4 (2001): 217–34.

Gans, Herbert J. "The Balanced Community: Homogeneity or Heterogeneity in Residential Areas?" In *Housing Urban America*, edited by Jon Pynoos, Robert Schafer

[and] Chester W. Hartman, 135–46. Chicago: Aldine Publishing, 1973. First published 1961.

———. *The Levitttowners: Ways of Life and Politics in a New Suburban Community*. New York: Pantheon, 1967.

———. "Urbanism and Suburbanism as Ways of Life: A Re-evaluation of Definitions." In *Human Behavior and Social Processes: An Interactionist Approach*, edited by Arnold M. Rose, 625–648. Boston: Houghton Mifflin, 1962.

———. *The War Against the Poor: The Underclass and Antipoverty Policy*. New York: Basic Books, 1995.

Garreau, Joel. *Edge City: Life on the New Frontier*. New York: Doubleday, 1991.

Garver, Eugene. *Aristotle's "Rhetoric": An Art of Character*. Chicago: University of Chicago Press, 1994.

Geoghegan, Thomas. *The Secret Lives of Citizens: Pursuing the Promise of American Life*. New York: Pantheon Books, 1998.

Glendon, Mary Ann. *Rights Talk: The Impoverishment of Political Discourse*. New York: The Free Press, 1991.

Gordon, Peter, and Harry W. Richardson. "Are Compact Cities a Desirable Planning Goal?" *Journal of the American Planning Association* 63, no. 1 (1997): 95–106.

Graff, Gerald. *Clueless in Academe: How Schooling Obscures the Life of the Mind*. New Haven, CT: Yale University Press, 2003.

Gross, David. "Space, Time, and Modern Culture." *Telos* 50 (Winter 1981–82): 59–78.

Grossman, James R., Ann Durkin Keating, and Janice L. Reiff, eds. *The Encyclopedia of Chicago*. Chicago: University of Chicago Press, 2004. Available online at http://www.encyclopedia.chicagohistory.org/.

Gyourko, Joseph, and Todd Sinai. "The Spatial Distribution of Housing-Related Tax Benefits in the U.S." Washington, DC: Brookings Institution, 2001.

Habermas, Jürgen. "Remarks on Discourse Ethics." *Justification and Application: Remarks on Discourse Ethics*, 19–111. Translated by Ciaran Cronin. Cambridge, MA: MIT Press, 1993.

———. *The Structural Transformation of the Public Sphere: An Inquiry into a Category of Bourgeois Society*. Translated by Thomas Burger with Frederick Lawrence. Cambridge, MA: MIT Press, 1989.

———. "Three Normative Models of Democracy." In *Democracy and Difference: Contesting the Boundaries of the Political*, edited by Seyla Benhabib. Princeton, NJ: Princeton University Press, 1996.

Hall, Peter. "The Global City." *International Social Science Journal* 48, no. 1 (1996): 15–23.

Halpern, Robert. *Rebuilding the Inner City: A History of Neighborhood Initiatives to Address Poverty in the United States*. New York: Columbia University Press, 1995.

Hanchett, Thomas W. "U.S. Tax Policy and the Shopping-Center Boom of the 1950s and 1960s." *American Historical Review* 101, no. 4 (1996): 1082–110.

Hansen, Mogens Herman. *The Athenian Democracy in the Age of Demosthenes*. Translated by J. A. Crook. Oxford: Blackwell, 1991. First published 1977–81.

Harris, Joseph. "The Idea of Community in the Study of Writing." *College Composition and Communication* 40, no. 1 (1989): 11–22.

Harris, Neil. "The City That Shops: Chicago's Retailing Landscape." In Zukowsky, *Chicago Architecture and Design*, 179–200.

Hart, Betty, and Todd R. Risley. *Meaningful Differences in the Everyday Experiences of Young American Children*. Baltimore: P. H. Brookes, 1995.

Harvey, David. *The Condition of Postmodernity: An Enquiry into the Origin of Cultural Change*. Cambridge, MA: Blackwell, 1990.

Hauser, Gerard A. "Politics: An Overview." In *Encyclopedia of Rhetoric*, edited by Thomas O. Sloane, 612–616. Oxford: Oxford University Press, 2001.

———. *Vernacular Voices: The Rhetoric of Publics and Public Spheres*. Columbia: University of South Carolina Press, 1999.

Hauser, Philip M., and Evelyn M. Kitagawa, eds. *Local Community Fact Book for Chicago, 1950*. Chicago: University of Chicago Press (for the Chicago Community Inventory), 1953.

Hayden, Dolores. *Building Suburbia: Green Fields and Urban Growth, 1820–2000*. New York: Pantheon, 2003.

———. "Model Houses for the Millions: The Making of the American Suburban Landscape, 1820–2000." Cambridge, MA: Lincoln Institute of Land Policy, 2000.

Hays, R. Allen. *The Federal Government and Urban Housing: Ideology and Change in Public Policy*, 2nd ed. Albany: State University of New York Press, 1995.

Heath, Shirley Brice. *Ways with Words: Language, Life, and Work in Communities and Classrooms*. Cambridge: Cambridge University Press, 1983.

Heikkila, Eric J. "Are Municipalities Tieboutian Clubs?" *Regional Science and Urban Economics* 26 (1996): 203–26.

Held, David. *Models of Democracy*, 2nd ed. Palo Alto, CA: Stanford University Press, 1996.

Hendrickson, Cara. "Racial Desegregation and Income Deconcentration in Public Housing." *Georgetown Journal on Poverty Law and Policy* 9, no. 1 (Winter 2002): 35ff.

Henry Horner Mothers Guild v. Chicago Housing Authority, No. 91 C 3316 (N.D. Ill. August 31, 2001).

Hirsch, Arnold R. *Making the Second Ghetto: Race and Housing in Chicago, 1940–1960*. Cambridge: Cambridge University Press, 1983.

Holsten Real Estate Development Corporation. *Proposal for Redevelopment of Halsted North Community*. Chicago: March 30, 1998.

———. *Reply to City's Questions*. Chicago: June 10, 1998.

hooks, bell. *Teaching to Transgress: Education as the Practice of Freedom*. New York: Routledge, 1994.

Horner, Bruce, and John Trimbur. "English Only and U.S. College Composition." CCC 53, no. 4 (2002): 594–630.

HREDC—see Holsten Real Estate Development Corporation.

HUD—see U.S. Department of Housing and Urban Development.

Hull, Glynda. "Hearing Other Voices: A Critical Assessment of Popular Views on Literacy and Work." *Harvard Educational Review* 63, no. 1 (1993): 20–49.

Hunt, D. Bradford. "What Went Wrong with Public Housing in Chicago? A History of the Robert Taylor Homes." *Journal of the Illinois State Historical Society* 94, no. 1 (2001): 96–123.

Hunter, Robert. *Tenement Conditions in Chicago*. Chicago: City Homes Association, 1901.

Irons, Peter. *Jim Crow's Children: The Broken Promise of the* Brown *Decision*. New York: Viking, 2002.

Isocrates. *Nicocles*. In *Isocrates I*, translated by David C. Mirhady and Yun Lee Too. Austin: University of Texas Press, 2000.

Jackson, Kenneth T. *Crabgrass Frontier: The Suburbanization of the United States*. New York: Oxford University Press, 1985.

———. "Gentleman's Agreement: Discrimination in Metropolitan America." In *Reflections on Regionalism*, edited by Bruce Katz, 185–217. Washington, DC: Brookings Institution Press, 2000.

Jacobs, Jane. *The Death and Life of Great American Cities*. New York: Vintage, 1961.

Jameson, Frederic. *Postmodernism, or, The Cultural Logic of Late Capitalism*. Durham, NC: Duke University Press, 1991. Chapter 1 first published 1984.

Jargowsky, Paul A. *Poverty and Place: Ghettos, Barrios, and the American City*. New York: Russell Sage Foundation, 1997.

Jencks, Charles A. *The Language of Post-modern Architecture*. New York: Rizzoli, 1977.

Johnson, Elmer W. *Chicago Metropolis 2020: Preparing Metropolitan Chicago for the Twenty-first Century*. The Commerical Club of Chicago in association with the American Academy of Arts and Sciences, 1999. Chicago: University of Chicago Press, 2001.

Jones, LeAlan, and Lloyd Newman (with David Isay; photographs by John Anthony Brooks). *Our America: Life and Death on the South Side of Chicago*. New York: Scribner, 1997.

Judis, John B., and Ruy Teixeira. *The Emerging Democratic Majority*. New York: Scribner, 2002.

Kasarda, John D. "Inner-City Concentrated Poverty and Neighborhood Distress: 1970 to 1990." *Housing Policy Debate* 4, no. 3 (1993): 253–302.

Katz, Bruce. "Reviving Cities: Think Metropolitan." Washington, DC: The Brookings Institution, 1998.

Katz, Lawrence F., Jeffery R. Kling, and Jeffrey B. Liebman. "Moving to Opportunity in Boston: Early Results of a Randomized Mobility Experiment." *Quarterly Journal of Economics* 116, no. 2 (2001): 607–54.

Katz, Peter, ed. *The New Urbanism: Toward an Architecture of Community*. New York: McGraw-Hill, 1994.

Kaufer, David, and Richard E. Young. "Writing in the Content Areas: Some Theoretical Complexities." In *Theory and Practice in the Teaching of Writing: Rethinking the Discipline*, edited by Lee Odell, 71–104. Carbondale: Southern Illinois University Press, 1993.

Keating, W. Dennis. *The Suburban Racial Dilemma: Housing and Neighborhoods*. Philadelphia: Temple University Press, 1994.

Kelbaugh, Douglas. *Common Place: Toward Neighborhood and Regional Design*. Seattle: University of Washington Press, 1997.

Kemmis, Daniel. *The Good City and the Good Life*. Boston: Houghton Mifflin, 1995.

Kemper, Vicki. "Home Inequity." *Common Cause Magazine* 29 (1994).

Kerferd, G. B. *The Sophistic Movement*. London: Cambridge University Press, 1981.

Kerner Commission. *Report of the National Advisory Commission on Civil Disorders*. Washington, DC: Government Printing Office, March 1, 1968.

Kingsley, Thomas, Jennifer Johnson, and Kathryn L. S. Petit. "HOPE VI and Section 8: Spatial Patterns in Relocation." Washington, DC: The Urban Institute, 2001.

Kirp, David L., John P. Dwyer, and Larry A. Rosenthal. *Our Town: Race, Housing, and the Soul of Suburbia*. New Brunswick, NJ: Rutgers University Press, 1995.

Kitagawa, Evelyn M., and Karl E. Taeuber. *Local Community Fact Book: Chicago Metropolitan Area, 1960*. Chicago: University of Chicago Press (for the Chicago Community Inventory), 1963.

Klinenberg, Eric. *Heat Wave: A Social Anatomy of Disaster in Chicago*. Chicago: University of Chicago Press, 2002.

Kling, Jeffrey. *Moving to Opportunity Research*. A Web site of resources. Available at http://www.nber.org/~kling/mto/.

Kotkin, Joel. *The City: A Global History*. New York: Modern Library, 2005.

Kotlowitz, Alex. *There Are No Children Here: The Story of Two Boys Growing Up in the Other America*. New York: Anchor/Doubleday, 1991.

Kozol, Jonathan. *Shame of the Nation: The Restoration of Apartheid Schooling in America*. New York: Crown, 2005.

Kuhn, Deanna. *The Skills of Argument*. Cambridge: Cambridge University Press, 1991.

Lakoff, George. *Don't Think of an Elephant! Know Your Values and Frame the Debate*. White River Junction, VT: Chelsea Green Publishing, 2004.

Lang, Robert E., and Thomas W. Sanchez. "The New Metro Politics: Interpreting Presidential Elections Using a County-Based Regional Typology." Alexandria: Virginia Tech University's Metropolitan Institute, 2006.

Laslett, Peter. "The Face to Face Society." In *Philosophy, Politics, and Society*, edited by Peter Laslett, 157–184. Oxford: Basil Blackwell, 1956.

Lawyers Committee for Better Housing. "Locked Out: Barriers to Choice for Housing Voucher Holders." Chicago, 2002. Available at http://www.lcbh.org/ (click on "Reports").

Lazare, Daniel. *America's Undeclared War: What's Killing Our Cities and How We Can Stop It*. New York: Harcourt, 2001.

Leach, William. *Country of Exiles: The Destruction of Place in American Life*. New York: Pantheon Books, 1999.

Leachman, Mike, Phil Nyden, Bill Peterman, and Darnell Coleman. *Black, White and Shades of Brown: Fair Housing and Economic Opportunity in the Chicago Region*. Chicago: Leadership Council for Metropolitan Open Communities, 1998.

Lemann, Nicholas. *The Promised Land: The Great Black Migration and How It Changed America*. New York: Vintage, 1992.

Leventhal, Tama, and Jeanne Brooks-Gunn. "Moving to Better Neighborhoods Improves Health and Family Life among New York Families." *Poverty Research News* 5, no. 1 (2001): 11–12.

Light, Richard J. *Making the Most of College: Students Speak Their Minds*. Cambridge, MA: Harvard University Press, 2001.

Linklater, Andro. *Measuring America*. New York: Walker, 2002.

Lofland, Lyn H. *A World of Strangers: Order and Action in Urban Public Space*. New York: Basic Books, 1973.

Logan, John R. "Separate and Unequal: The Neighborhood Gap for Blacks and Hispanics in Metropolitan America." Albany, NY: Lewis Mumford Center for Comparative Urban and Regional Research, SUNY-Albany, Oct. 13, 2002.

Lubell, Jeff, and Barbara Sard. "Proposed Housing Legislation Would Divert Subsidies from the Working Poor and Weaken Welfare Reform Efforts." Washington, DC: Center on Budget and Policy Priorities, August 3, 1998.

Ludwig, Jens, Greg Duncan, and Helen Ladd. "The Effect of MTO on Baltimore Children's Educational Outcomes." *Poverty Research News* 5, no. 1 (2001): 13–15.

Luttmer, Erzo F. P. "Neighbors as Negatives: Relative Earnings and Well-Being." *Quarterly Journal of Economics* 120, no. 3 (2005): 963–1002.

Lynch, Kevin. *Good City Form*. Cambridge, MA: MIT Press, 1981.

Manpower Demonstration Research Corporation. *Tenant Management: Findings from a Three-Year Experiment in Public Housing*. Cambridge, MA: Ballinger, 1981.

Marciniak, Edward. *Reclaiming the Inner City: Chicago's Near North Revitalization Confronts Cabrini-Green*. Washington, DC: National Center for Urban Ethnic Affairs, 1986.

Marcuse, Peter. "The Enclave, the Citadel, and the Ghetto: What Has Changed in the Post-Fordist U.S. City." *Urban Affairs Review* 33, no. 2 (1997): 228–64.

Martinson, Tom. *American Dreamscape: The Pursuit of Happiness in Postwar Suburbia*. New York: Carroll & Graf, 2000.

Massey, Douglas S., and Nancy A. Denton. *American Apartheid: Segregation and the Making of the Underclass*. Cambridge, MA: Harvard University Press, 1993.

Matusow, Allen J. *The Unraveling of America: A History of Liberalism in the 1960s*. New York: Harper & Row, 1984.

Mayer, Harold M., and Richard C. Wade. *Chicago: Growth of a Metropolis*. Chicago: University of Chicago Press, 1969.

Mayer, Susan E., and Chrisopher Jencks. "Growing Up in Poor Neighborhoods: How Much Does It Matter?" *Science* 243 (1989): 1441–45.

Mazower, Mark. *Salonica, City of Ghosts: Christians, Muslims and Jews 1430–1950*. New York: Alfred A. Knopf, 2005.

McArdle, Nancy. *Race, Place, and Opportunity: Racial Change and Segregation in the Chicago Metropolitan Area, 1990–2000*. Cambridge, MA: the Civil Rights Project of Harvard University, 2002.

McKenzie, Evan. *Privatopia: Homeowner Associations and the Rise of Residential Private Government*. New Haven, CT: Yale University Press, 1994.

McPherson, Miller, Lynn Smith-Lovin, and James M. Cook. "Birds of a Feather: Homophily in Social Networks." *Annual Review of Sociology* 27, no. 1 (2001): 415–44.

MDRC—see Manpower Demonstration Research Corporation.

Meehan, Eugene J. "The Evolution of Public Housing Policy." In Mitchell, *Federal Housing Policy and Programs*, 287–318.

Menocal, Maria Rosa. *The Ornament of the World: How Muslims, Jews, and Christians Created a Culture of Tolerance in Medieval Spain*. New York: Little, Brown, 2002.

Metropolitan Planning Council. Task Force on CHA Rehabilitation and Reinvestment. *Untapped Potentials: The Capacities, Needs, and Views of Chicago's Highrise Public Housing Residents*. Chicago, 1986.

———. Housing Subcommittee on Cabrini Redevelopment. *Cabrini of the Future*. Chicago, 1996.

———. Housing Subcommittee on Cabrini Redevelopment. *The Road to Redevelopment: Cabrini of the Future II*. Chicago, 1996.

Meyerson, Martin and Edward Banfield. *Politics, Planning, and the Public Interest: The Case of Public Housing in Chicago*. Glencoe, IL: The Free Press, 1955.

Mill, John Stuart. *On Liberty*. Edited by David Bromwich and George Kateb. New Haven, CT: Yale University Press, 2003. First published 1859.

Millennial Housing Commission. *Meeting Our Nation's Housing Challenges*. Washington, DC, 2002. Available at http://govinfo.library.unt.edu/mhc/.

Miller, Carolyn R. "The *Polis* as Rhetorical Community." *Rhetorica* 11 (1993): 211–40.

Miller, Donald L. *City of the Century: The Epic of Chicago and the Making of America*. New York: Simon & Schuster, 1996.

Mitchell, J. Paul. "Historical Overview of Direct Federal Housing Assistance." In Mitchell, *Federal Housing Policy and Programs*, 187–206.

———, ed. *Federal Housing Policy and Programs: Past and Present*. New Brunswick, NJ: Center for Urban Policy Research at Rutgers University, 1985.

Monti, Daniel J. "The Organizational Strengths and Weaknesses of Resident-Managed Public Housing Sites in the United States." *Journal of Urban Affairs* 11 (1989): 39–52.

———. "People in Control: A Comparison of Residents in Two U.S. Housing Developments." In *Ownership, Control, and the Future of Housing Policy*, edited by R. Allen Hays, 177–94. Westport, CT: Greenwood P, 1993.

Mooney, Michael. *Vico in the Tradition of Rhetoric*. Princeton, NJ: Princeton University Press, 1985.

Mouffe, Chantal. *The Democratic Paradox*. London: Verso, 2000.

Mulroy, Elizabeth A. "Mixed-Income Housing in Action." *Urban Land* 50, no. 5 (May 1991): 2–7.

Mumford, Lewis. *The City in History: Its Origins, Its Transformations, and Its Prospects*. San Diego: Harcourt, 1989. First published 1961.

———. *The Culture of Cities*. New York: Harcourt, Brace and Company, 1938.

———. "The Neighborhood and the Neighborhood Unit." *The Town Planning Review* 24 (1953–1954): 256–70.

Murray, Oswyn. "Politics." In *The Oxford Classical Dictionary*, edited by Simon Hornblower and Anthony Spawforth, 1207–08, 3rd ed. Oxford: Oxford University Press, 1996.

National Center on Poverty Law. "Chicago Housing Authority and U.S. Department of Housing and Urban Development Sued for Racial Discrimination." Press release. Chicago: July 29, 1999.

National Commission on Severely Distressed Public Housing. *Final Report to the Congress and the Secretary of Housing and Urban Development*. Washington, DC, 1992.

National Housing Law Project. *False HOPE: A Critical Assessment of the HOPE VI Public Housing Redevelopment Program*. Oakland, CA, June, 2002.

National Low Income Housing Coalition. *Out of Reach 2005*. Washington, DC, 2005. Available at http://www.nlihc.org/oor2005/.

NCSDPH—see National Commission on Severely Distressed Public Housing.

Neel, Jasper. *Plato, Derrida, and Writing*. Carbondale: Southern Illinois University Press, 1988.

Newman, Oscar. *Defensible Space: Crime Prevention Through Urban Design*. New York: Macmillan, 1972.

Newman, Sandra J. "Introduction and Overview." In *The Home Front: Implications of Welfare Reform for Housing Policy*, edited by Sandra J. Newman, 1–28. Washington, DC: The Urban Institute Press, 1999.

Nivola, Pietro. *Laws of the Landscape: How Policies Shape Cities in Europe and America*. Washington, DC: Brookings Institution Press, 1999.

North Town Redevelopment Advisory Council. *North Town Community Redevelopment Plan, Phase I: Policy Issues, Goals, and Recommendations*. Chicago: Near North Development Corporation, 1990.

———. *North Town Community Plan, Phase II: Policy Issues, Goals, and Recommendations*. Chicago: Near North Development Corporation, 1991.

NTRAC—see North Town Redevelopment Advisory Council.

Nussbaum, Martha C. (with respondents). *For Love of Country: Debating the Limits of Patriotism*, edited by Joshua Cohen. Boston: Beacon Press, 1996.

———. "Kant and Cosmopolitanism." In *Perpetual Peace: Essays on Kant's Cosmopolitan Ideal*, edited by James Bohman and Matthias Lutz-Bachman, 25–58. Cambridge, MA: MIT Press, 1997.

Nyden, Philip, John Lukehart, Michael T. Maly, and William Peterman. "Neighborhood Racial and Ethnic Diversity in U.S. Cities." *Cityscape: A Journal of Policy Development and Research* 4, no. 2 (1998): 1–17.

Obasanjo, Olusegun Olutosin. *The Impact of the Physical Environment on Adolescents in the Inner City*. Dissertation. Ann Arbor: School of Architecture of the University of Michigan, 1998.

Ober, Josiah. *Mass and Elite in Democratic Athens: Rhetoric, Ideology and the Power of the People*. Princeton, NJ: Princeton University Press, 1989.

Ohmann, Richard. *English in America: A Radical View of the Profession*. New York: Oxford University Press, 1976.

Oldenburg, Ray. *The Great Good Place*. New York: Paragon, 1989.

Oliver, J. Eric. *Democracy in Suburbia*. Princeton, NJ: Princeton University Press, 2001.

Olson, David R. "From Utterance to Text: The Bias of Language in Speech and Writing." *Harvard Educational Review* 47 (1977): 257–81.

Olson, Mancur. *The Logic of Collective Action: Public Goods and the Theory of Groups*. Cambridge, MA: Harvard University Press, 1965.

Orfield, Gary. "Housing Segregation: Causes, Effects, Possible Cures." Presentation given at the National Press Club, April 3, 2001.

Orfield, Gary, and Nora Gordon. *Schools More Separate: Consequences of a Decade of Resegregation*. Cambridge, MA: The Civil Rights Project, Harvard University Graduate School of Education, 2001.

Orfield, Myron. *American Metropolitics: The New Suburban Reality*. Washington, DC: Brookings Institution Press, 2002 See the Metropolitan Area Research Corporation Web site at http://www.metroresearch.org/.

———. *Chicago Metropolitics: A Regional Agenda for Members of the U.S. Congress.* Washington, DC: Brookings Institution, 1998.

Paehlke, Robert C. *Democracy's Dilemma: Environment, Social Equity, and the Global Economy*. Cambridge, MA: MIT Press, 2003.

Park, Robert E. "The City: Suggestions for the Investigation of Human Behavior in the City Environment." *American Journal of Sociology* 20, no. 5 (1915): 577–612.

Peck, Wayne C., Linda Flower, and Lorraine Higgins. "Community Literacy." *College Composition and Communication* 46, no. 2 (1995): 199–222.

Pensky, Max. "Universalism and the Situated Critic." In *The Cambridge Companion to Habermas*, edited by Stephen K. White, 67–94. Cambridge: Cambridge University Press, 1995.

Peroff, Kathleen, Cloteal L. Davis, and Ronald Jones (in collaboration with others). *Gautreaux Housing Demonstration: An Evaluation of Its Impact on Participating Households*. Washington, DC: U.S. Department of Housing and Urban Development, Office of Policy Development & Research, 1979.

Peterman, William. "The Meanings of Resident Empowerment: Why Just About Everybody Thinks It's a Good Idea and What It Has to Do with Resident Management." *Housing Policy Debate* 7, no. 3 (1996): 473–90.

———. "Resident Management and Other Approaches to Tenant Control of Public Housing." In *Ownership, Control, and the Future of Housing Policy*, edited by R. Allen Hays, 161–75. Westport, CT: Greenwood P, 1993.

Peterson, Jacqueline. " 'Wild' Chicago: The Formation and Destruction of a Multiracial Community on the Midwestern Frontier, 1816–1837." In *The Ethnic Frontier: Essays in the History of Group Survival in Chicago and the Midwest*, edited by Melvin G. Holli and Peter d'A. Jones, 25–71. Grand Rapids, MI: William B. Eerdmans Publishing Co., 1977.

Peterson, Jon A. *The Birth of City Planning in the United States, 1840–1917*. Baltimore: Johns Hopkins University Press, 2003.

Petraglia, Joseph. "Introduction: General Writing Skills Instruction and its Discontents." In *Reconceiving Writing, Rethinking Writing Instruction*, edited by Joseph Petraglia, xi–xvii. Mahwah, NJ: Lawrence Erlbaum, 1995.

———. "Spinning Like a Kite: A Closer Look at the Pseudotransactional Function of Writing." *Journal of Advanced Composition* 15, no. 1 (1995): 19–33.

Pettit, Becky, and Sara McLanahan. "Social Dimensions of Moving to Opportunity." *Poverty Research News* 5, no. 1 (2001): 7–10.

Phillips, Kevin. *The Politics of Rich and Poor: Wealth and the American Electorate in the Reagan Aftermath*. New York: Random House, 1990.

———. *Wealth and Democracy: A Political History of the American Rich*. New York: Broadway Books, 2002.

Plato. *Laws*. Translated by R. G. Bury. Cambridge, MA: Harvard University Press, 1968.

———. *Protagoras*. Rev. ed. Translated by C. C. W. Taylor. Oxford: Clarendon Press, 1991.

Plotkin, Wendy. " 'Hemmed In': The Struggle Against Racial Restrictive Covenants and Deed Restrictions in Post-WWII Chicago." *Journal of the Illinois State Historical Society* 94, no. 1 (Spring 2001): 39–69.

Pocock, J. G. A. "Civic Humanism and Its Role in Anglo-American Thought." In *Politics, Language, and Time: Essays on Political Thought and History*, 80–103. New York: Atheneum, 1973.

———. *The Machiavellian Moment: Florentine Political Thought and the Atlantic Republican Tradition.* Princeton, NJ: Princeton University Press, 1975.

Polikoff, Alexander. " 'Chicago's Not About to Give Up On a Bad Idea': The Future of Public Housing High-Rises." In *Affordable Housing and Public Policy: Strategies for Metropolitan Chicago*, edited by Lawrence B. Joseph, 195–218. Chicago: The University of Chicago Center for Urban Research and Policy Studies, 1993.

———. *Housing the Poor: The Case for Heroism*. Cambridge, MA: Ballinger, 1978.

———. "Waiting for Gautreaux: Reflections and Conundrums about Chicago's Long-Running Public Housing Desegregation Case." Presentation at the Northwestern University Institute for Policy Research Colloquium, November, 2002. Available at http://www.bpichicago.org/pht/phtcr_pubs.html.

Popenoe, David. *Private Pleasure, Public Plight: American Metropolitan Community Life in Comparative Perspective*. New Brunswick, NJ: Transaction Books, 1985.

Popkin, Susan J., Larry F. Buron, Diane K. Levy, and Mary K. Cunningham. "The Gautreaux Legacy: What Might Mixed-Income and Dispersal Strategies Mean for the Poorest Public Housing Tenants?" *Housing Policy Debate* 11, no. 4 (2000): 911–42.

Popkin, Susan J., Victoria E. Gwiasda, Lynn M. Olson, Dennis P. Rosenbaum, and Larry Buron. *Hidden Wars: Crime and the Tragedy of Public Housing in Chicago*. New Brunswick NJ: Rutgers University Press, 2000.

Popper, Karl R. "Science: Conjectures and Refutations." In *Conjectures and Refutations: The Growth of Scientific Knowledge*, 33–65. New York: Harper & Row, 1968.

Porter, Michael E. "The Competitive Advantage of the Inner City." *Harvard Business Review* 75 (1995): 55–71.

Poulakos, Takis. *Speaking for the Polis: Isocrates' Rhetorical Education*. Columbia: University of South Carolina Press, 1997.

Pratt, Mary Louise. "Linguistic Utopias." In *The Linguistics of Writing: Arguments Between Language and Literature*, edited by Nigel Fabb, Derek Attridge, Alan Durant, and Colin MacCabe, 48–66. New York: Methuen, 1987.

Putnam, Robert D. *Bowling Alone: The Collapse and Revival of American Community*. New York: Simon & Schuster, 2000.

Rahe, Paul A. *Republics Ancient and Modern: Classical Republicanism and the American Revolution*. 3 vols. Chapel Hill: University of North Carolina Press, 1992.

Ranney, David C., and Patricia A. Wright. "Race, Class, and the Abuse of State Power: The Case of Public Housing in Chicago." *SAGE Race Relations Abstracts* 25 (2000): 3–32.

Rawls, John. *A Theory of Justice*. Cambridge, MA: Harvard University Press, 1971.

Readings, Bill. *The University in Ruins*. Cambridge, MA: Harvard University Press, 1996.

Reich, Robert B. *The Work of Nations: Preparing Ourselves for Twenty-first Century Capitalism*. New York: Alfred A. Knopf, 1991.

Roberts-Miller, Patricia. *Deliberate Conflict: Argument, Political Theory, and Composition Classes*. Carbondale: Southern Illinois University Press, 2004.

Rosenbaum, Emily. "The Social Context of New Neighborhoods Among MTO Chicago Families." *Poverty Research News* 5, no. 1 (2001): 16–9.

Rosenbaum, James E. "Changing the Geography of Opportunity." *Housing Policy Debate* 6, no. 1 (1995).

Rosenbaum, James E., Linda K. Stroh, and Cathy A. Flynn. "Lake Parc Place: A Study of Mixed-Income Housing." *Housing Policy Debate* 9, no. 4 (1998): 703–40.

Rosenfeld, Richard N. "What Democracy? The Case for Abolishing the United States Senate." *Harper's Magazine* 308, no. 1848 (May, 2004): 35–44.

Rubinowitz, Leonard S., and James E. Rosenbaum. *Crossing the Class and Color Lines: From Public Housing to White Suburbia.* Chicago: University of Chicago Press, 2000.

Rusk, David. *Cities Without Suburbs: A Census 2000 Update*, 3rd ed. Washington, DC: Woodrow Wilson Center Press, 2003.

Ryan, Alan. "The City as a Site for Free Association." In *Freedom of Association*, edited by Amy Gutmann, 314–29. Princeton, NJ: Princeton University Press, 1998.

Ryan, Mary P. *Civic Wars: Democracy and Public Life in the American City During the Nineteenth Century*. Berkeley: University of California Press, 1997.

Rybczynski, Witold. *City Life: Urban Expectations in a New World.* New York: Scribner, 1995.

Rykwerk, Joseph. *The Seduction of Place: The City in the Twenty-first Century*. New York: Pantheon, 2000.

Salama, Jerry J. "The Redevelopment of Distressed Public Housing: Early Results from HOPE VI Projects in Atlanta, Chicago, and San Antonio." *Housing Policy Debate* 10, no. 1 (1999): 95–142.

Sandel, Michael J. *Democracy's Discontent: America in Search of a Public Philosophy*. Cambridge, MA: Belknap Press of Harvard University Press, 1996.

———. "The Procedural Republic and the Unencumbered Self." *Political Theory* 12, no. 1 (1984): 81–96.

Sandercock, Leonie. *Towards Cosmopolis: Planning for Multicultural Cities*. Chichester, England: John Wiley & Sons, 1998.

Sanjek, Roger. *The Future of Us All: Race and Neighborhood Politics in New York City*. Ithaca, NY: Cornell University Press, 1998.

Sard, Barbara, and Will Fischer. "Housing Voucher Block Grant Bills Would Jeopardize An Effective Program and Likely Lead to Cuts in Assistance for Low-income Families." Washington, DC: Center on Budget and Policy Priorities, 2003.

Sarkissian, Wendy. "The Idea of Social Mix in Town Planning: An Historical Review." *Urban Studies* 13 (1976): 231–46.

Sassen, Saskia. *Global City: New York, London, Tokyo*, 2nd ed. Princeton, NJ: Princeton University Press, 2001.

Schaumburg, IL—see Village of Schaumburg, IL.

Schiappa, Edward. *Protagoras and Logos: A Study in Greek Philosophy and Rhetoric*. Columbia: University of South Carolina Press, 1991.

Schill, Michael H. "Chicago's Mixed-Income New Communities Strategy: The Future Face of Public Housing?" In *Affordable Housing and Urban Redevelopment in the United States*, edited by Willem Van Vliet, 135–157. Thousand Oaks, CA: Sage, 1997.

———. "Distressed Public Housing: Where Do We Go from Here?" *University of Chicago Law Review* 60, no. 2 (1993): 497–554.

Schill, Michael H., and Susan M. Wachter. "Principles to Guide Housing Policy at the Beginning of the Millennium." *Cityscape: A Journal of Policy Development and Research* 5, no. 2 (2001): 5–19.

———. "The Spatial Bias of Federal Housing Law and Policy: Concentrated Poverty in Urban America." *University of Pennsylvania Law Review* 143, no. 5 (1995): 1285–342.

Schlesinger, Arthur M., Jr. *Robert Kennedy and His Times*. New York: Ballantine, 1979.

Schön, Donald A. *The Reflective Practitioner: How Professionals Think in Action*. New York: Basic Books, 1983.

Schorr, Alvin L. *Common Decency: Domestic Policies After Reagan*. New Haven, CT: Yale University Press, 1986.

Schragger, Richard. "The Limits of Localism." *University of Michigan Law Review* 100 (2001): 371ff.

Schubert, Michael F., and Alison Thresher. "Lessons from the Field: Three Case Studies of Mixed-Income Housing Development." Chicago: Great Cities Institute, College of Urban Planning and Public Affairs of the University of Illinois at Chicago, 1996.

Schudson, Michael. *The Good Citizen: A History of American Civic Life*. New York: The Free Press, 1998.

Schwartz, Alex, and Kian Tajbakhsh. "Mixed-Income Housing: Unanswered Questions." *Cityscape: A Journal of Policy Development and Research* 3, no. 2 (1997): 71–92.

Scully, Vincent. "The Architecture of Community." In Katz, *The New Urbanism*, 221–30.

Seligman, Amanda. "Near North Side." In Grossman, Keating, and Reiff, *Encyclopedia of Chicago*, 561–62.

Sennett, Richard. *The Conscience of the Eye: The Design and Social Life of Cities*. New York: Alfred A. Knopf, 1990.

———. *The Corrosion of Character: The Personal Consequences of Work in the New Capitalism*. New York: W. W. Norton: 1998.

———. *The Fall of Public Man*. New York: Alfred A. Knopf, 1977.

Sies, Mary Corbin. "The City Transformed: Nature, Technology, and the Suburban Ideal, 1877–1917." *Journal of Urban History* 14, no. 1 (1987): 81–111.

Sharpe, William, and Leonard Wallock. "Bold New City or Built-up 'Burb? Redefining Contemporary Suburbia." *American Quarterly* 46, no. 1 (1994): 1–30.

Shlay, Anne B. "Family Self-Sufficiency and Housing." *Housing Policy Debate* 4, no. 3 (1993): 457–95.

Shroder, Mark. "Moving to Opportunity: An Experiment in Social and Geographic Mobililty." *Cityscape: A Journal of Policy Develpment and Research* 5, no. 2 (2001): 57–67.

Shumway, David R. *Creating American Civilization: A Genealogy of American Literature as an Academic Discipline*. Minneapolis: University of Minnesota Press, 1994.

Simon, Herbert A. *The Sciences of the Artificial*, 3rd ed. Cambridge, MA: MIT Press, 1996.

Sloane, Thomas O. *On the Contrary: The Protocol of Traditional Rhetoric*. Washington, DC: The Catholic University of America Press, 1997.

Smith, Rogers. *Civic Ideals: Conflicting Visions of Citizenship in U.S. History*. New Haven CT: Yale University Press, 1997.

Soja, Edward. *Postmodern Geographies: The Reassertion of Space in Critical Social Theory*. London: Verso, 1989.

Solomon, Daniel. *Global City Blues*. Washington, DC: Island Press, 2003.

Sorkin, Michael. "Introduction: Variations on a Theme Park." In Sorkin, *Variations*, xi–xv.

———, ed. *Variations on a Theme Park: The New American City and the End of Public Space*. New York: Hill & Wang, 1992.

Southworth, Michael, and Peter M. Owens. "The Evolving Metropolis: Studies of Community, Neighborhood, and Street Form at the Urban Edge." *Journal of the American Planning Association* 59, no. 3 (1993): 271–88.

Southworth, Michael, and Balaji Parthasarathy. "The Suburban Public Realm I: Its Emergence, Growth and Transformation in the American Metropolis." *Journal of Urban Design* 1, no. 3 (1996): 245–64.

———. "The Suburban Public Realm II: Eurourbanism, New Urbanism and the Implications for Urban Design in the American Metropolis." *Journal of Urban Design* 2, no. 1 (1997): 9–35.

Spear, Allan H. *Black Chicago: The Making of a Negro Ghetto, 1890–1920*. Chicago: University of Chicago Press, 1967.

Spence, Lewis H. "Rethinking the Social Role of Public Housing." *Housing Policy Debate* 4, no. 3 (1993): 355–68.

Spinney, Robert G. *City of Big Shoulders: A History of Chicago*. DeKalb: Northern Illinois University Press, 2000.

Squires, Gregory D. "Urban Sprawl and the Uneven Development of Metropolitan America." In *Urban Sprawl: Causes, Consequences, and Policy Responses*, edited by Gregory D. Squires. Washington, DC: The Urban Institute Press, 2002.

Stuart, Guy. *Integration or Resegregation: Metropolitan Chicago at the Turn of the New Century*. Cambridge, MA: the Civil Rights Project at Harvard University, 2002.

Sunstein, Cass R. "Beyond the Republican Revival." *Yale Law Journal* 97 (1988): 1539–90.

Suro, Roberto. "Movement at Warp Speed: Technology and Global Markets Are About to Reshape America's Metropolitan Landscapes." *American Demographics* 22, no. 8 (August 2000).

Talen, Emily. "The Social Goals of New Urbanism." *Housing Policy Debate* 13, no. 1 (2002): 165–88.

Tamir, Yael. "Revisiting the Civic Sphere." In *Freedom of Association*, edited by Amy Gutmann, 214–38. Princeton, NJ: Princeton University Press, 1998.

Tannen, Deborah. *The Argument Culture: Moving from Debate to Dialogue*. New York: Random House, 1998.

Teaford, Jon C. *City and Suburb: The Political Fragmentation of Metropolitan America, 1850–1970*. Baltimore: Johns Hopkins University Press, 1979.

Thall, Bob. *The New American Village*. Baltimore: Johns Hopkins University Press, 1999.

———. *The Perfect City*. Baltimore: Johns Hopkins University Press, 1994.

Thucydides. *History of the Peloponnesian War*. Edited by W. Robert Connor. Translated by Richard Crawley. London: J. M. Dent, 1993.

Tönnies, Ferdinand. *Community and Society*. Translated by Charles P. Loomis. Lansing: Michigan State University Press, 1957.

Turner, Mark. *Reading Minds: The Study of English in the Age of Cognitive Science*. Princeton, NJ: Princeton University Press, 1991.

1230 North Burling Street Resident Management Corporation. *By-Laws*. Chicago: December 1, 1999.

———. *Homeownership Cooperative*. Trust fund application to the Illinois Housing Development Authority. Chicago: January 8, 2001.

———. *Homeownership Plan*. Chicago: March 23, 2000.

———. *Management Plan*. Chicago: March 3, 1999.

Urban Institute. *An Assessment of the Nation's First Block Grants*. Washington, DC, 1995.

U. S. Census Bureau. "Children and the Households They Live In." Census 2000 Special Reports. Washington, DC, 2004.

———. "Poverty." Washington, DC, 2000. Available at http://www.census.gov/hhes/www/poverty.html.

U. S. Department of Housing and Urban Development [HUD]. *Community Building in Public Housing: Ties that Bind People and Their Communities*. Washington, DC, 1997.

———. Community Development Block Grant [CDBG] Entitlement Communities: "Overview," "Program," and "Quick Facts." All accessed July 13, 2001, at http://www.hud.gov/offices/cpd/communitydevelopment/programs/entitlement/.

———. *HOPE VI: Community-Building Makes a Difference*. Washington, DC, February 2000.

———. "HOPE VI." Available at http://www.hud.gov/offices/pih/programs/ph/hope6/.

———. "Housing Choice Vouchers Fact Sheet." Washington, DC, n.d. Available at http://www.hud.gov/offices/pih/programs/hcv/about/fact_sheet.cfm.

———. "Is Where We Live More Important Than How?" *Research Works* 1 (August 2004).

———. *Moving to Opportunity for Fair Housing Demonstration Program: Current Status and Initial Findings*. Washington, DC, 1999.

———. *Moving to Opportunity for Fair Housing Demonstration Program: Interim Impacts Evaluation*. Washington, DC, 2003.

———. *New American Neighborhoods: Building Homeownership Zones to Revitalize Our Nation's Communities*. Washington, DC, 1996.

———. *Public Housing that Works: The Transformation of America's Public Housing*. Washington, DC, May, 1996.

———. *Rental Housing Assistance—The Crisis Continues: The 1997 Report to Congress on Worst Case Housing Needs*. Washington, DC, 1998.

———. "Section 8 Tenant-Based Housing Assistance: A Look Back After Thirty Years." Washington, DC, March, 2000.

———. *The Widening Gap: New Findings on Housing Affordability in America*. Washington, DC, 1999.

U. S. General Accounting Office. "HOPE VI Leveraging Has Increased but HUD Has Not Met Annual Reporting Requirement." Washington, DC, November, 2002.

U.S. Housing Act of 1937 (as amended), 42 U.S.C. §§ 1437 et seq.

U.S. Housing Act of 1949 (as amended), 42 U.S.C. §§ 1441 et seq.

Vale, Lawrence J. *From the Puritans to the Projects: Public Housing and Public Neighbors*. Cambridge, MA: Harvard University Press, 2000.

Venkatesh, Sudhir Alladi. *American Project: The Rise and Fall of a Modern Ghetto*. Cambridge, MA: Harvard University Press, 2000.

Verba, Sidney, Kay Lehman Schlozman, and Henry E. Brady. *Voice and Equality: Civic Voluntarism in American Politics*. Cambridge, MA: Harvard University Press, 1995.

Village of Schaumburg, IL. *Annual Action Plan, FY 2001: Community Development Block Grant*. Schaumburg, IL: Village of Schaumburg Planning Department, 2000.

———. *Consolidated Plan, 2000–2005*. Schaumburg, IL: Village of Schaumburg Planning Department, 1999.

———. 2000 Census Tables. DP-1 (General), 2 (Social), 3 (Economic), and 4 (Housing). Available at http://www.ci.schaumburg.il.us/vos.nsf/schaumburg/MFRK-5U4MLH.

———. Web site. "Introduction"; "History"; "Population"; "Housing"; "Economic Data"; "Government." Available at www.ci.schaumburg.il.us. Accessed June 26, 2001.

Von Hoffman, Alexander. "High Ambitions: The Past and Future of American Low-Income Housing Policy." *Housing Policy Debate* 7, no. 3 (1996): 423–446.

Von Hoffman, Alexander, and John Felkner. "The Historical Origins and Causes of Urban Decentralization in the United States." Cambridge, MA: Joint Center for Housing Studies, 2002.

Wacquant, Loïc J. D. "Three Pernicious Premises in the Study of the American Ghetto." *International Journal of Urban and Regional Research* 21, no. 2 (1997): 341–353.

Wallace v. Chicago Housing Authority, No. 03 C 0491 (N.D. Ill. June 2, 2005).

Warner, Michael. *The Letters of the Republic: Publication and the Public Sphere in Eighteenth-Century America*. Cambridge, MA: Harvard University Press, 1990.

Warner, Sam Bass, Jr. *The Private City: Philadelphia in Three Periods of Its Growth*, 2nd ed. Philadelphia: University of Pennsylvania Press, 1987. First published 1968.

Warren, Mark E. "The Self in Discursive Democracy." In *The Cambridge Companion to Habermas*, edited by Stephen K. White, 167–200. Cambridge: Cambridge University Press, 1995.

Webber, Melvin M. "Order in Diversity: Community Without Propinquity." In *Cities and Space*, edited by Lowdon Wingo, 25–54. Baltimore: Johns Hopkins University Press, 1963.

Weicher, John C. *Privatizing Subsidized Housing*. Washington, DC: American Enterprise Institute Press, 1997.

Wells, Susan. "Rogue Cops and Health Care: What Do We Want from Public Writing?" *College Composition and Communication* 47, no. 3 (1996): 325–341.

Whitaker, David T. *Cabrini Green in Words and Pictures*. Chicago: W3 Chicago, 2000.

White, Morton and Lucia White. *The Intellectual Versus the City from Thomas Jefferson to Frank Lloyd Wright*. Cambridge, MA: Harvard University Press, 1962.

Wilen, William P., and Wendy L. Stasell. "Gautreaux and Chicago's Public Housing Crisis: The Conflict Between Achieving Integration and Providing Decent Housing for Very Low-Income African Americans." *Clearinghouse Review: Journal of Poverty Law and Policy*. National Center on Poverty Law, July–August 2000.

Williamson, Thad, David Imbroscio, and Gar Alperovitz. *Making a Place for Community: Local Democracy in a Global Era*. New York: Routledge, 2002.

Wilson, William Julius. *The Truly Disadvantaged: The Inner City, the Underclass, and Public Policy*. Chicago: University of Chicago Press, 1987.

———. *When Work Disappears: The World of the New Urban Poor*. New York: Alfred A. Knopf, 1997.

Wirth, Louis. "Urbanism as a Way of Life." *American Journal of Sociology* 44 (1938): 1–24.

Wirth, Louis, and Eleanor H. Bernert, eds. *Local Community Fact Book of Chicago*. Chicago: University of Chicago Press (for the Chicago Community Inventory), 1949.

Wirth, Louis, and Margaret Furez, eds. *Local Community Fact Book*. Chicago: Chicago Recreation Commission, 1938.

Wright, Patricia, Yittayih Zelalem, Julie deGraaf, and Linda Roman. "The Plan to Voucher Out Public Housing: An Analysis of the Chicago Experience and a Case Study of the Proposal to Redevelop the Cabrini-Green Public Housing Area." Chicago: Nathalie P. Voorhees Center for Neighborhood and Community Improvement of the University of Illinois at Chicago, May 1997.

Wright, Richard. "Introduction." In Drake and Cayton, *Black Metropolis*, xvii–xxxiv.

———. *Native Son*. New York: Harper & Row, 1940.

Yack, Bernard. "Community and Conflict in Aristotle's Political Philosophy." *Review of Politics* 47, no. 1 (1985): 92–112.

Young, Iris Marion. *Inclusion and Democracy*. Oxford: Oxford University Press, 2000.

———. *Justice and the Politics of Difference*. Princeton, NJ: Princeton University Press, 1990.

Zorbaugh, Harvey Warren. *The Gold Coast and the Slum: A Sociological Study of Chicago's Near North Side*. Chicago: University of Chicago Press, 1976. First published 1929.

Zukowsky, John, ed. *Chicago Architecture and Design, 1923–1993: Reconfiguration of an American Metropolis*. Munich: Prestel-Verlag (with the Art Institute of Chicago), 1993.

Index

Made in the USA
San Bernardino, CA
21 August 2017